ISBN 978-1-331-53473-0
PIBN 10202409

1 MONTH OF
FREE
READING

at
www.ForgottenBooks.com

By purchasing this book you are eligible for one month membership to ForgottenBooks.com, giving you unlimited access to our entire collection of over 700,000 titles via our web site and mobile apps.

To claim your free month visit: www.forgottenbooks.com/free202409

LIFE AND TIMES

OF

WM. LYON MACKENZIE.

WITH AN ACCOUNT OF THE CANADIAN REBELLION
OF 1837, AND THE SUBSEQUENT FRONTIER
DISTURBANCES, CHIEFLY FROM UN-
PUBLISHED DOCUMENTS.

BY
CHARLES LINDSEY.

VOL. II.

TORONTO, C. W.:
P. R. RANDALL, No. 12 TORONTO STREET
1862.

LIFE AND TIMES

OF

WM. LYON MACKENZIE.

WITH AN ACCOUNT OF THE CANADIAN REBELLION
OF 1837, AND THE SUBSEQUENT FRONTIER
DISTURBANCES, CHIEFLY FROM UN-
PUBLISHED DOCUMENTS.

BY

CHARLES LINDSEY.

VOL. II.

TORONTO, C.W.:

P. R. RANDALL, No. 12 TORONTO STREET.

1862.

18765
4/12/91
6

CONTENTS.

8

CONTENTS.

LIFE

OF

WILLIAM LYON MACKENZIE.

CHAPTER I.

The Crisis approaching—Report of the Royal Commissioners, in Lower Canada
—The Effect on Upper Canada—Lord John Russell's Coercion Resolutions
for seizing the Public Chest of Lower Canada—They create a Hurricane of
Indignation in the Province—The Principle at Stake—Anti-coercion Meetings—Mackenzie's Reasons for thinking the Lower Canadians would succeed
in an Appeal to Arms—The Declaration of the Upper Canada Reformers—
Its private History—A Central Vigilance Committee formed in Toronto, of
which Mr. Mackenzie was Agent and Secretary—An Organization throughout the Country set on foot, in such a way that it could be used for Military purposes—It afterwards became the Instrument of Revolt—Mackenzie
attends a Series of Public Meetings as Agent of the Toronto Vigilance
Committee—The chief Actors in many of these Meetings become involved
in the Insurrection—Independence declared to be necessary, and Calls to
Arms are made—Disturbances at the Public Meetings—"Pikes and Rifles"
—Two Hundred Meetings held, and One Hundred and Fifty Vigilance
Committees formed—Some of the Leaders joined no Association.

THE crisis was now rapidly approaching. It was
to come first in Lower Canada, with which the fortunes of the Western Province were to become involved. The Royal Commissioners, appointed to inquire into the grievances complained of in Lower
Canada, had reported; and about the middle of April,
their reports—five in number—were made public.
The surrender of the casual and territorial revenue to
the Assembly, whose claim to control it had led to repeated and angry disputes, was recommended, on condition that the arrearages of salaries amounting to

£31,000 should be paid, and a civil list, amounting to about £20,000, should be granted, for the life of the King. The Legislative Council, it was recommended, should be erected into a court of impeachment for offending public servants. The demands for an elective Legislative Council and a responsible Executive were reported against. The decision of the Commissioners, on the subject of the Legislative Council, was in accordance with instructions they had received. In a dispatch, dated July 17th, 1835, Lord Glenelg informed the Commissioners that all discussion of one of the vital principles of the Provincial Government —a Crown-nominated Legislative Council was alluded to—was precluded by the strong predilections of the King, the solemn pledges repeatedly given for the maintenance of the existing system, and the prepossessions derived from constitutional analogy and usage. The decision thus communicated by way of instructions to the Commissioners was merely echoed by them. It affected Upper equally with Lower Canada; for Lord Glenelg, in his instructions to Sir F. B. Head, had stated as his reasons for not answering the part of the Grievance Report which referred to the constitution of the Legislative Council, that the instructions to the Commissioners contained views, on this point, which had received the deliberate sanction of the King.

The Imperial Government went beyond the recommendation of the Commissioners. Lord John Russell, on the 8th of March, obtained the assent of the House of Commons to resolutions which, among other things, authorized the seizing of the funds in the hands of the

Receiver General of Lower Canada, and applying them to purposes for which the Assembly would only grant them, on condition that certain reforms should be effected. They had voted the salaries of the judges; but they were to be paid only on condition that those functionaries should hold no other office under the Crown. In this way they had attacked what they considered an incompatible plurality of offices. The Council, refusing to concur with the House, made no report on the Supply Bill; and, therefore, in one sense, it might be alleged that the supplies failed in that House. The Assembly made certain of the supplies dependent upon a redress of grievances. On the 3d of October, 1836, the House had come to the resolution to adjourn their proceedings till His Majesty's Government should have commenced "the great work of justice and reform, especially by bringing the Legislative Assembly into harmony with the wishes and wants of the people." Lord John Russell contended that the demand for an Executive Council, similar to the Cabinet which existed in Great Britain, set up a claim for what was incompatible with the relations which ought to exist between the Colony and Mother Country. "These relations," he said, repeating the stereotyped official idea of those times, "required that His Majesty should be represented in the Colony not by Ministers, but by a Governor sent out by the King, and responsible to the Parliament of Great Britain." A Colonial Ministry, he contended, would impose on England all the inconveniences and none of the advantages of Colonies. If this system were adopted, and a British subject were wronged on the banks of the

52

St. Lawrence, His Majesty would have less right to interfere than if the injury had been committed on the banks of the Danube or the Bosphorus. As to the authority of the Imperial Legislature to remedy a defect in the cessation of supply, on the part of a Colonial Assembly, he apprehended that there could be no doubt. The same thing had been done only the year before with respect to Jamaica; and that was precedent sufficient. When a similar question was raised with regard to the Legislature of the Colony of New York, Dr. Franklin had admitted that the power, now contended for, resided in the Imperial House of Commons. With two such precedents, Lord John Russell deemed himself justified in resorting to a measure of confiscation, which led to rebellion.*

Mr. Hume had a better appreciation of the crisis. He looked upon the proceedings as involving a question of civil war. If the Canadians did not resist, they would deserve the slavish bonds which the resolutions of Lord John Russell would prepare for them; and he hoped that, if justice were denied to Canada, those who were oppressed would achieve the same victory that had crowned the efforts of the men who had established that American Republic, which had given a check to those monarchical principles which would otherwise have overwhelmed the liberties of Europe.

How little the House of Commons was conscious of the results that hung upon their decision, may be

---

* M. Louis J. Papineau, the leader of the insurrection in Lower Canada, stated in an account of the troubles which he published after he became a refugee, in Paris: "None of us had prepared, desired, or foreseen armed resistance," before these resolutions were passed.

gathered from the fact that, while Mr. Hume was speaking, the House was counted to see if there was a quorum. It was ascertained that there were over forty members present, and the debate went on to its fatal close. And in the House of Lords, the same apathy was shown. Not over one-tenth of the members, who frequently attend, came to listen to or take part in the debate; and except Lord Brougham, who entered on the journals his protest against such proceedings, not a single member opposed their passage. Mr. Gladstone saw nothing in the question raised but how the faithful servants of the Crown could be relieved from difficulty; and Mr. Labouchere echoed these observation with some flourishes of his own. Lord Stanley, who had been among the first to denounce the Legislative Council as the source of all the evils under which Upper Canada labored, and who had perhaps been the first to suggest to the Colonists a resort to the constitutional remedy of withholding the supplies, now denounced both these remedies, and declaimed about "the most odious and blood-thirsty tyranny of French republicanism."

The resolutions were carried, and the result which Mr. Hume had predicted, followed.* They were re-

---

* As these resolutions were the immediate cause of the insurrection in both the Canadas, they cannot well be omitted here:—

"1. That since the 31st day of October, in the year 1832, no provision has been made by the Legislature of the Province of Lower Canada for defraying the charges of the administration of justice, and for the support of the civil government within the said Province; and that there will, on the 10th day of April, now next ensuing, be required for defraying in full the charges aforesaid, to that day, the sum of £142,100 14s. 6d.

"2. That at a session of the Legislature of Lower Canada, holden at the City of Quebec, in the said Province, in the months of September and October,

ceived with a storm of indignation by the French Canadians. The local officials and their friends were

1836, the Governor of the said Province, in compliance with His Majesty's commands, recommended to the attention of the House of Assembly thereof the estimates for the current year, and also the accounts showing the arrears due in respect to the civil government, and signified to the said House His Majesty's confidence that they would accede to the application which he had been commanded to renew for payment of the arrears due on account of the public service, and for the funds necessary to carry on the civil government of the Province.

"3. That the said House of Assembly, on the 3d day of October, 1836, by an address to the Governor of the said Province, declined to vote a supply for the purposes aforesaid; and by the said address, after referring to a former address of the said House to the Governor of the said Province, declared that the said House persisted, among other things, in the demand of an elective Legislative Council, in demanding the repeal of a certain act passed by the Parliament of the United Kingdom in favor of the North American Land Company; and by the said address the said House of Assembly further adverted to the demand made by that House of the free exercise of its control over all the branches of the Executive Government; and by the said address the said House of Assembly further declared, it was incumbent on them, in the present conjuncture, to adjourn their deliberations until His Majesty's Government should, by its acts, especially by rendering the second branch of the Legislature conformable to the wishes and wants of the people, have commenced the great work of justice and reform, and created a confidence which alone could crown it with success.

"4. That in the existing state of Lower Canada, it is unadvisable to make the Legislative Council of that Province an elective body; but that it is expedient that measures be adopted for securing to that branch of the Legislature a greater degree of public confidence.

"5. That while it is expedient to improve the composition of the Executive Council in Lower Canada, it is unadvisable to subject it to the responsibility demanded by the House of Assembly of that Province.

"6. That the legal title of the North American Land Company to the land holden by the said Company by virtue of a grant from His Majesty, under the public seal of the said Province, and to the privileges conferred on the said Company by the act for that purpose made in the fourth year of His Majesty's reign, ought to be maintained inviolate.

"7. That it is expedient that so soon as provision shall have been made by law to be passed by the Legislature of the said Province of Lower Canada, for the discharge of lands therein from feudal dues and services, and for removing any doubts as to the incidents or the tenure of land in free and common soc-

jubilant at the imaginary success which had been achieved for them. The journals of the opposition were defiant. The seizure of the revenue was denounced as robbery. "Henceforth," said an English organ of the opposition, "there must be no peace in the Province—no quarter for the plunderers. Agitate! agitate!! agitate!!! Destroy the revenue; denounce the oppressors. Everything is lawful when the fundamental liberties are in danger. 'The guards

age in the said Provinces, a certain act made and passed in the sixth year of the reign of His late Majesty, King George the Fourth, commonly called 'The Canada Tenures Act,' and so much of another act passed in the third year of His said late Majesty's reign, commonly called 'The Canada Trade Act,' as relates to the tenures of land in the said Province, should be repealed, saving, nevertheless, to all persons, all rights in them vested under or by virtue of the said recited acts.

"8. That for defraying the arrears due on account of the established and customary charges of the administration of justice and of the civil government of the said Province, it is expedient that, after applying for that purpose such balance as shall, on the said 10th day of April, 1837, be in the hands of the Receiver General of the said Province, arising from His Majesty's hereditary, territorial, and casual revenue, the Governor of the said Province be empowered to issue from and out of any other part of His Majesty's revenue in the hands of the Receiver General of the said Province, such further sums as shall be necessary to effect the payment of the before mentioned sum of £142,100 14s. 6d.

"9. That it is expedient that His Majesty be authorized to place at the disposal of the Legislature of the said Province the net proceeds of His Majesty's hereditary, territorial, and casual revenue arising within the same, in case the said Legislature shall see fit to grant to His Majesty a civil list for defraying the necessary charges of the administration of justice, and for the maintenance and unavoidable expenses of certain of the principal officers of the civil government of the said Province.

"10. That great inconvenience has been sustained by His Majesty's subjects inhabiting the Provinces of Lower Canada and Upper Canada from the want of some adequate means for regulating and adjusting questions respecting the trade and commerce of the said Provinces, and divers other questions wherein the said Provinces have a common interest; and it is expedient that the Legislatures of the said Provinces respectively be authorized to make provision for the joint regulation and adjustment of such, their common interests."

die—they never surrender.' "* At public meetings the
Imperial resolutions were denounced as a breach of
faith and a violation of right.   Resolutions were come
to, to use as little as possible of imported articles
paying duty ;† and to raise a Papineau tribute in imi-
tation of O'Connell's Repeal Rent.

The Toronto Alliance Society, on the 17th of April,
expressed its sympathy with the Lower Canadians,
and condemned the coercion resolutions of the Imperial Government.

Success is the only thing that is generally held to
justify insurrection against a government; and though
it is impossible to lay down any general rule as to
the point at which submission to oppression ceases to
be a virtue, it is generally admitted that the initiation
of such a movement can only be excused by a reason-

---

* Montreal *Vindicator*, edited by Dr. O'Callaghan, M. P. P.† At a large
meeting, held at St. Scholastique, county of Two Mountains, M. Papineau
said:—"They [the British Ministry] are going to rob you of your money.
Your duty then is plain. Give them no money to steal! Keep it in your
pockets! [Loud cheers.] The British Ministry promised, fifty years ago,
when well drubbed, beaten, and humiliated by the Americans, to respect the
rights of the people. Now they think they are strong, and can trample under
foot those rights they solemnly promised formerly to respect. Let us examine what the Americans did under similar circumstances. Ten days before
they took up arms, they adopted the course which we are now about to recommend to you. They abstained from taxed articles which paid duties, and thus
deprived their enemies of money and power to oppress and tyrannize over
them. Even the women, handsome and patriotic as our own Canadian women, determined to assist their husbands, their fathers, and their brothers, in
resisting the horrible oppression which their tyrants were preparing for them.
I fervently hope, and in the name of mine and their suffering country, I call
on, I implore the women of Canada to follow the bright example set them, in
times like the present, by the patriotic women of America, and to assist me,
and us all, in destroying that revenue which our oppressors are forging into
chains for us and our children, and by all means in their power to discourage
the consumption of those articles which pay duties."

able prospect of success. If the question of the Lower Canada rebellion could be decided upon the merits of the principle at stake, we should be obliged to confess that what the Canadians fought for was just as sacred as that right of self-taxation for which Washington took up arms, and in defence of which the thirteen American Colonies threw off the yoke of England. If it is not permissible to tax a people without their consent—and the House of Commons had long before made a solemn declaration to this effect, in the case of the Colonies—on what principle could the proceeds of their taxes be seized upon by an authority which had deprived itself of the power to levy them?

On the 15th of June, Lord Gosford tried the effect of a proclamation, on the agitation which was convulsing society. He assured the people that the Imperial Parliament had neither violated nor was about to violate the just rights and privileges of His Majesty's Canadian subjects; he exhorted all concerned to discontinue writings of a seditious tendency and to avoid public meetings of a " dangerous or equivocal character." But the proclamation, which was torn to pieces by the *habitants* amid cries of " *A bas la proclamation*," produced no effect, if it were not to increase the fervor with which the coercion resolutions, as they were called, were denounced. The French Canadians rallied to the popular cries: " *Vive Papineau! Vive la liberté! Point du despotisme!*" In accordance with the Lower Canada practice, many of these meetings were held at the doors of the parish churches, after the conclusion of the religious service. M.

Papineau, the chief agitator, a man of commanding eloquence who was omnipotent with the French Canadian population, traversed the whole country from Montreal to Rimouski; holding meetings everywhere and exciting the people to the highest pitch of exasperation. While he was on the South shore of the St. Lawrence, Messrs. Lafontaine and Girouard were performing a similar mission on the other bank of the great river. Dr. Wolfred Nelson, too, bore his share in the work of popular agitation; having made a conspicuous figure at the first of the "anticoercion" meetings, which was held at St. Ours, in the County of Richelieu. Some of the meetings were attended by men with fire-arms in their hands.

In the beginning of July, Mr. Mackenzie discussed, in his newspaper, the question—" Will the Canadians declare their independence and shoulder their muskets?" After referring to meetings that had been held at L'Islet and Bellechasse, he proceeded, in the suggestive style, to say: " Two or three thousand Canadians, meeting within twenty-five miles of the fortress of Quebec, in defiance of the proclamation, with muskets on their shoulders and the Speaker of the House of Commons at their head, to pass resolutions declaratory of their abhorrence of British Colonial tyranny, and their determination to resist and throw it off, is a sign not easily misunderstood." He then proceeded to the question: " Can the Canadians conquer?" and gave several reasons for answering it in the affirmative. He, however, excepted the fortress of Quebec. He argued that they would conquer every thing but this; because they were united by the bond of a common language, a common religion, and a common origin. They had for twenty years steadily opposed the oligarchical system imposed upon them. Their leaders were bold and resolute, cool and calculating; full of fire and energy. As marksmen, they were more than a match for British soldiers. Their organization was better than Lord Gosford had any conception of. They had a large number of experienced officers among them, and were constantly receiving from France military men who had won laurels at the feet of Napoleon. The garrison of Quebec would rather desert than fight against their fellow subjects. Thousands of Englishmen, Scotchmen, and Irishmen, in the United States, would hasten to rally around the standard of the Canadians; especially if they were offered three hundred or four hundred acres of Clergy Reserves each. The Colonial Governors had no adequate means of resistance; and no House of Commons would sanction the spending of fifty or sixty millions to put down the rebellion.

Such were the opinions deliberately written and published by Mr. Mackenzie, on the 5th of July, 1837. The French Canadians appealed to the other British Provinces of America for co-operation, and looked to the United States for support. And this co-operation the leading Reformers of Upper Canada resolved to give.

On the 2d August, a " Declaration of the Reformers of Toronto to their Fellow Reformers in Upper Canada," was published in *The Constitution.** This document was virtually a declaration of independence, and

* See Appendix D.

it was afterwards called the "Declaration of the Independence," of Upper Canada, but there is reason to
doubt whether its purport was fully understood even
by all who signed it. Setting out with the declaration
that the time for the assertion of popular rights and
the redress of the multiplied wrongs of half a century,
patiently borne, had arrived, it entered into a long
recital of grievances, and ended with a pledge to
make common cause with Lower Canada, and a re-
solve to call a convention of delegates, at Toronto,
"to take into consideration the political condition of
Upper Canada, with authority to its members to appoint commissioners to meet others to be named on
behalf of Lower Canada and any other Colonies, armed
with suitable powers as a Congress to seek an effectual remedy for the grievance of the Colonists."*

This Declaration has a public and a secret history.
The public history is, that at a meeting of Reformers,
held at Mr. John Doel's Brewery, Toronto, on the
28th July, the troubles in Lower Canada were taken
into consideration. On motion of Mr. Mackenzie,
seconded by Dr. Morrison, a resolution was passed
tendering the thanks and expressing the admiration
of the Reformers of Upper Canada to Hon. L. J.
Papineau and his compatriots for their "devoted,
honorable, and patriotic opposition" to the coercive
measures of the Imperial Government. Other reso--
lutions were passed to make common cause with the
Lower Canadians, "whose successful coercion would
doubtless, in time, be visited upon us, and the redress
of whose grievances would be the best guarantee for
the redress of our own;" and, among other things,

* See Appendix D.

appointing a committee to draft and report to an adjourned meeting a declaration of the objects and principles which the Reformers aimed to carry out.*

The secret history is this. The document was a joint production in which O'Grady's and Dr. Rolph's pens were engaged. The draft was taken to a meeting, at Elliott's Tavern, on the corner of Yonge and Queen Streets, previous to its being taken before the adjourned meetings, at the Brewery, for adoption. Dr. Morrison, on producing the draft of the Declaration, laid it down as a sound canon that neither he nor any other member of the Legislature ought to be called upon to sign it. It was the privilege of persons outside the Legislature to raise questions of this nature, and the duty of the representatives to do their best to give effect to the wishes of the people in the sphere of action assigned to them. To this rule for the division of functions Mr. James Lesslie took exception. A document of grave import had been read to the meeting. It had been written by men who gave the most of their time to politics, and read to men who gave most of their attention to trade and commerce. The responsibility of signing such a document should not be thrown upon those who had not prepared it, and who knew least about its contents. The professional politicians ought to set the example, and then the others might follow. If the Declaration contained only an enumeration of facts, and if it were a proper document to be signed, the members of the

---

* The committee consisted of Messrs. James Harvey Price, O'Bierne, John Edward Tims, John Doel, John McIntosh, James Armstrong, T. J. O'Neill, and Mackenzie, with power to add to their number.

Legislature, such as Drs. Morrison and Rolph, ought
to set the example; and if they did so, he would follow.   Dr. Morrison found it necessary to append his
name to the Declaration, but as Dr. Rolph was not
there to pursue the same course, Mr. James Lesslie
refused to sign and he induced his brother William tɔ
erase his signature.   Next morning Dr. Rolph sent
for Mr. James Lesslie to inquire what had been done
at the meeting, and the latter replied by letter, repeating his objections to being put in the front rank
of a movement in which he ought to be a follower.
Dr. Morrison was not without reasons for his hesita-
tion and timidity, though it is too much to expect that
others will enter on a course fraught with danger, if
those who advise them to do so refuse to accompany
them; for on his trial for high treason, eight months
afterwards, this Declaration was attempted to be made
a ground of conviction.

At the meeting, held at the Brewery on the 31st of
July, at which the Declaration was adopted, a permanent Vigilance Committee was appointed.   It consisted of the members of the committee who had reported the draft of the Declaration; and Mr. Mackenzie complied with a request that he would become
agent and corresponding secretary.   The plan of proceeding was similar to that acted upon, in Lower
Canada, where the public meetings were held under
the direction of a central committee; and Mr. Mackenzie's duties as agent were to attend meetings, in
different parts of the country, taking, in Upper Canada, the *rôle* played by Mr. Papineau, in the sister
Province.   Meetings were at once arranged to take

place in Albion, Caledon, Chingacousy, Esquesing, Trafalgar, and Vaughan ; at Newmarket, Lloydtown, Churchville, and Cooksville.

The machinery of agitation, of which the motive power was in Toronto, was to have four several centres of action outside the city. At the meeting held in the Brewery, on the 28th of July, a plan submitted by Mr. Mackenzie, "for uniting, organizing, and registering the Reformers of Upper Canada, as a political Union," was adopted.* A net-work of societies

---

* The project was as follows:

"1. In order to avoid the mixture of persons unknown to each other, no Society is to consist of less than twelve or more than forty persons, and those to be resident as nearly as possible in the same neighborhood.

"2. Each of these Societies shall choose one of their number to be their secretary.

"3. The Secretaries of five of these Societies shall form a Committee, to be called the Township Committee.

"4. Ten of these Township Committees, of citizens residing in places the most convenient to each other, shall each select one of their number, and the persons so chosen shall form the County Committee.

"5. The District Committee shall consist of one member to be chosen from each County Committee within the limits of such district.

"6. Upper Canada shall be divided into four grand Divisions, as follows:

"The Western Division to consist of the counties of Kent, Essex, Middlesex, Oxford, Huron, and Norfolk.

"The Toronto Division to consist of Lincoln, Haldimand, Wentworth, Halton, York, Simcoe, and Durham.

"The Midland Division to consist of the counties of Northumberland, Hastings, Prince Edward, Frontenac, Lennox, and Addington.

"The Eastern Division to consist of the whole of the counties north-east of the Midland District.

"7. Within each of these Divisions there shall be a Committee of Division to be composed of two or three members elected from each of the District Committees within the same.

"8. The Executive shall consist of three persons, to be chosen from among the members of the several Committees of Division, and be invested with the necessary powers to promote the objects for which the Union is to be constituted."

When he first proposed this plan, Mr. Mackenzie explained and published.

was to be spread over the country; and care was to be taken to have them composed of persons known to one another. The objects of the organization were not declared in the programme of association; but the duty of supporting Lower Canada against a coercion which, if successful, it was feared would next be visited upon Upper Canada, was recognized.

When Sir Francis Bond Head resorted to the most unconstitutional means of influencing the elections of 1836, he carried despair into many a breast where hope had till then continued to abide. The coercion of Lower Canada by the Imperial Government and Legislature caused all such persons, in the Canadas, to look to a revolution as the only means of relief. Mr. Mackenzie was among those who came to this conclusion. But he only shared with a large class of the population a sentiment which was the inevitable produce of the existing state of things, and which affected masses of men, at the same moment, with a common and irresistible impulse. The Toronto Declaration of the 31st of July was the first step in the road to insurrection. It committed all who accepted it to share the fortunes of Lower Canada. The machinery of organization and agitation, which was created at the same time, became the instrument of revolt.

that " a plan, such as I have suggested, could be easily transferred without change of its structure to military purposes. The secretary of each subordinate Society of twelve might easily be transformed into a sergeant or corporal; the delegate of five Societies to a Township Committee, into a captain with sixty men under his command; and the delegate of ten Township Committees to a District Committee into a colonel at the head of a battalion of six hundred men."

The public meetings, which Mr. Mackenzie had undertaken to attend, now commenced. The first was held at Newmarket, " north of the Oak Ridges, and east of the line of King, and west of Guiliumbury," on the 3d of August. The agent of the Toronto Central Committee spoke an hour and a half; complaining, among other things, that the agents and petitions of the people had been unfairly treated, in London. A resolution was passed, approving of the Toronto Declaration, and appointing delegates to the Convention to be held in that city ;* most of whom afterwards became involved in the insurrection; one of whom was executed for high treason, and others became political refugees in the United States. The principal complaint made in the resolutions was, that the Constitution was " continually violated and trampled upon by the Executive, and countenanced by the Colonial Office and the English Parliament." To take these grievances and the general state of the Province into consideration was to be the business of the Convention. It was also resolved to abstain as far as possible from the consumption of duty-paying articles ; and to unite with the Lower Canadians, whose cause was declared to be the cause of Upper Canada, " in every practicable measure for the maintenance of civil and religious liberty." A political association and a permanent Vigilance Committee were formed. At the suggestion of Lount, cheers were given for Papi-

---

* Their names were Messrs. Samuel Lount, afterwards executed for high treason; Nelson Gorham, who became involved in the rebellion and was a long time a political refugee in the United States; Silas Fletcher, who also became a political refugee; Jeremiah Graham, and John McIntosh, M. P.P., who, though a party to the insurrection, was never arrested and scarcely suspected.

neau and the gallant people of the sister Province. Lieutenant Carthew, late of the British army, called on all persons opposed to Papineau to go to the right of the chairman; but he was followed by only two others.

Two days after, the second of the series of public meetings took place at Lloydtown. Messrs. Mackenzie, Lloyd, Lount, and Gibson, all of whom afterwards bore an active part in the rebellion, addressed the meeting. Mackenzie became head of the Provisional Government; Gibson was comptroller, and had besides a military position; Lloyd was the trusted messenger who carried to Mr. Papineau intelligence from his supporters in Upper Canada. No less than seventeen resolutions were passed. A resort to physical force was declared not to be contemplated. "Much," one of the resolutions affirmed, "may be done without blood." It was complained that "a bribed and pensioned band of official hirelings and expectants falsely assuming the character of the representatives of the people of Upper Canada, corrupted by offices, wealth, and honors bestowed upon their influential members by Sir F. B. Head, since they took their seats in the House of Assembly, have refused to allow a free trial to candidates ready to contest their seats—have refused to order new elections for members who have accepted places of gain under the government—have refused to institute a free and constitutional inquiry into corruptions practiced at the elections through Sir F. B. Head's patent deeds and otherwise; and although they were returned for the constitutional period which the death of the King has brought near to a close, they have violated the most solemn covenant of the British Constitution, by resolving that their pretended powers of legislation shall continue over us three years longer than they were appointed to act." Approval of the Toronto Declaration was expressed; and delegates to the proposed Convention were appointed.* The meeting protested against "the dastardly insinuations of those who profess fears that the Lower Canadians, in obtaining the just rights they have so long and so patiently supplicated, are actuated by the motive to establish the Catholic or any other denomination as a state Church in this Province."† [Separation from England was advocated, on the ground that the connection imposed upon the Province the evils of a state Church, an " unnatural aristocracy, party privilege, public debt, and general op-

* Dr. W. W. Baldwin and Messrs. Jesse Lloyd, James Grey, Mark Learmont, John Lawson, and Gerard Irwin.

† The authorities of the Roman Catholic Church in Lower Canada attempted to curb the revolutionary impulses of the people. At Montreal, the Bishop, before an assembly of over one hundred and forty priests or ecclesiastics, uttered the following words : " So solemn an occasion as the present had never presented itself; he saw nearly all his clergy met before him, and he was going to take advantage of the circumstance, to give to the pastors of parishes certain notices of the highest importance in the present circumstances of the country. The clergy were to use every effort to establish charity and union among their flocks ; they were to represent to their parishioners, that it is never permitted to revolt against lawful authority, nor to transgress the laws of the land ; that they are not to absolve in the confessional any indication of the opinion either that one may revolt against the government under which we have the happiness to live, or that it is permitted to break the laws of the country, particularly that which forbids smuggling ; and still less is it allowed to absolve those who may violate these laws." But the torrent of agitation was too powerful for the bishop immediately to control. On the Sunday after these resolutions reached them, the people of Laprairie and Vaudreuil met in separate places, and passed resolutions, disapproving, in strong terms, of all interference on the part of the clergy in politics. A priest in Two Mountains, who denounced the movement, had his barn burned by his parishioners.

pression." To avert much bloodshed on both sides, loss, and dishonor of a war between people of a common origin, the payment of a price for the freedom of the Province was suggested. If the question of independence was tested by means of the ballot, it was hinted that there could be no doubt as to the result. Elective institutions, extending even to the judiciary, were declared indispensable.

But the emblems, devices, and mottos, displayed at this meeting, were even more significant than the resolutions. On one flag was a large star, surrounded by six minor lustres; in the centre a Death's head, with the inscription: "LIBERTY OR DEATH." Another flag bore the word, "Liberty," in large letters, with figures of pikes, swords, muskets, and cannons, " by way of relief to the eye." Some bad verses, making a call to arms, were inscribed on a third flag.* It

---

* A full record of these doings seems to impose upon me the duty of publishing the following bad jingle:

> We* united were in days of yore,
> Again Quebec dares to the field
> Not that your noblest blood should pour
> Against the States domain to yield.
> With her she calls you to advance,
> On the broad path of truth and right.
> How answer ye the sons of France?
> " Up brave Canadians, to the fight."
> She points the way, she cheers you on,
> She bids you triumph for your right.
> " Dare ye not do what she is doing?"
> " Up brave Canadians, to the fight."
> And think ye Simcoe will not lend,
> In such a cause, her warrior tide?
> Nor Albion men their steep descend,†
> To share their peril at your side?

> * Upper and Lower Canada.
> † Albion is the name of a township near Toronto.

had been intended to erect a liberty pole, one hundred feet high; but the design was abandoned.

Mr. Mackenzie left Lloydtown accompanied by only a couple of friends. While stopping on his way, at the house of a farmer, named Godboldt, south of the Oak Ridges, he learned that the Orangemen would make an attempt to break up the Albion meeting. About fifty young farmers therefore mounted their horses, and escorted him to the village of Boltontown. It was the 7th of August. As soon as Mr. Coats had been called to the chair, the Orangemen declared their intention to put down the meeting, and to resort to force if necessary to accomplish their object. They, however, listened patiently to Mr. Mackenzie, till the reading of the Toronto Declaration was commenced; when they proceeded to violent interruption. Finding they were not numerous enough to prevent the adoption of that Manifesto, they grew more vociferous, rendering it impossible to continue the proceedings. They gave Mr. Mackenzie's escort five minutes to leave the place; threatening, if their mandate were not complied with, to bring out fire-arms which they professed to have all ready loaded, in one of the

Ireland will sound her harp and wave
Her pure green banner for your right,
Canadians never will be slaves!
" Up sons of Freedom to the fight!"
By LIBERTY's eternal name,
Our Country's proudest glory, Arm
Sweep from our shores oppression's shame,
Canadians! cleanse the locust swarm.
Degenerate Russell's desp'rate pleas,
Both Hume and Brougham have proved vain—
One short sharp hour your country frees,
Canadians! to the fight again!

houses. This threat was neither regarded on the one side, nor carried into effect on the other.

After the public meeting had been broken up, part . of the business it had on hand was transacted in Mr. Boulton's house. Delegates to the Convention were appointed, and a Vigilance Committee named. Resolutions were passed at all the other meetings, to use as little as possible of imported duty-paying articles, and expressing a hope that the bill to avoid an appeal to the people, on the death of the Sovereign, would, by the interposition of the Royal veto, be prevented from taking effect.

Some hours after, when several of those who had formed Mr. Mackenzie's escort to the place had gone, a collision between the two parties took place. Twenty-six Mackenzie men, mounted, were crossing the bridge over the Humber, when one of the opposite party seized the hindmost by the thigh, as if with the intention of forcing him into the river. Two others were attacked at the same time. All the twenty-six dismounted instantly, and fell upon their assailants with whatever was within their reach. Blood flowed freely; and some of the assailing party, as they lay on the ground, were made to confess that they had only got their deserts. Nobody was seriously injured. The victorious party now returned to the village; and placing themselves in the square gave three cheers for "Papineau, the deliverer, and his brave Canadians." The Orangemen returned to the attack; and there was another skirmish on the bridge, in which the twenty-six and their friends were again completely successful.

The meetings followed one another in rapid succession. The next was held in the township of Caledon, two days after that at Boltontown. Some of the resolutions passed at this meeting were drawn up with considerable skill, and one of them undertook to define the case in which an appeal to physical force would become a duty.* It was rather inferred from general

---

* A resolution moved by Mr. James Baird, and seconded by Mr. Owen Garrity, read thus:—"That it is the duty of the subjects of kings and governors to keep the peace, and submit to the existing laws; that it is equally the duty of kings and rulers to administer the government for the well-being and happiness of the community; and that when the existing laws and constitution of society become notoriously oppressive in form or administration, it is then, and at all times, the duty of free subjects, and for the benefit, safety, and happiness of all parties to call meetings, and ascertain, as far as can be done, the general opinion and estimate of all the good and evil which government dispense, as it is also the duty of a just government to protect its subjects in the peaceful exercise of such a precious and obvious right. If the redress of our wrongs can be otherwise obtained, the people of Upper Canada have not a just cause to use force. But the highest obligation of a citizen being to preserve the community, and every other political duty being derived from, and subordinate to it, every citizen is bound to defend his country against its enemies, both foreign and domestic. When a government is engaged in systematically oppressing a people, and destroying their securities against future oppression, it commits the same species of wrong to them which warrants an appeal to force against a foreign enemy. The history of England and of this continent is not wanting in examples, by which the rulers and the ruled may see that, although the people have been often willing to endure bad government with patience, there are legal and constitutional limits to that endurance. The glorious revolutions of 1688, on one continent, and of 1776, on another, may serve to remind those rulers who are obstinately persisting in withholding from their subjects adequate securities for good government, although obviously necessary for the permanence of that blessing, that they are placing themselves in a state of hostility against the governed; and that to prolong a state of irresponsibility and insecurity, such as existed in England during the reign of James II., and as now exists in Lower Canada, is a dangerous act of aggression against a people. A magistrate who degenerates into a systematic oppressor, and shuts the gates of justice on the public, thereby restores them to their original right of defending themselves, for he withholds the protection of the law, and so forfeits his claim to enforce their obedience by the authority of law."

principles than stated in so many words, that a state
of things existed in Lower, if not also in Upper Canada,
which would justify the people in resorting to arms
to relieve themselves from oppression. The legality
and the constitutionality of the import duties levied
on the authority of Imperial statutes, passed soon
after the conquest of Canada, were more than questioned. Taxation without representation was denounced as a tyranny not to be borne; "a badge of
slavery which our forefathers resisted, in the case of
Charles First's ship-money and the tea-tax at Boston."
The English law, which prevented Canadians from
purchasing tea, gunpowder, and other articles in the
cheapest market, was described as "pretended legislation." It was recommended that in case a refusal
to pay duties alleged to be illegally imposed led to
seizure, the question should be brought before the
courts for the opinion of a jury, and that the exercise
of unlawful authority should be steadily resisted.
The Toronto Declaration was approved; delegates to
the projected Convention appointed; and a Vigilance
Committee formed.

From Caledon to Chingacousy, the agent of the
Toronto Central Committee was escorted by about
twenty horsemen. Here a meeting was held in front
of the house of Mr. John Campbell, lot 24, in the
Second Concession, on the morning of the 10th August.
Trouble had been anticipated; and Mr. Francis Campbell, brother of John Campbell, on whose grounds the
meeting was held, went with the statutes under his
arm, ready to read the riot act, if necessary; and Mr.
John Scott, another magistrate, had gone there sur-

rounded by a number of Orangemen. Several of these and some of Mackenzie's supporters had fire-arms; others carried heavy clubs. The two parties were greatly exasperated against one another, and the Orangemen made use of threatening language. To prevent a collision, Mackenzie's party gave way. One John Wiggins, the master of an Orange Lodge, was appointed chairman; the other party not disputing with his supporters the majority, though it might have been matter of doubt on which side it was.

An adjournment to Mr. Campbell's house took place. What had become the usual routine of these meetings was gone through, and one of the resolutions mentioned independence as a state of existence that would have some advantages over that which the Province then enjoyed.

On the 12th August, Mr. Mackenzie was at Mr. John Stewart's, in the Scotch Block, Esquesing. Here at first his party were outnumbered, but after the opposition had retired, resolutions were passed declaring the boasted remedial measures of which the Lieutenant Governor had, on his arrival, declared himself the bearer, a deception; that the pretended constitution had been proved to be a mockery, and that the people were living under the worst description of despotism; that they were despised by the government to which, at great sacrifice, they had remained attached; while the people of the United States were in the enjoyment of the fullest extent of political liberty. "There is," wrote Mackenzie, in reference to this meeting, "discontent, vengeance, and rage in men's minds. No one can have an idea of the public feeling who has not taken the same means that I have to ascertain it."

The meeting held at Hull's tavern, Trafalgar, on the 14th August, was noteworthy chiefly for the excitement displayed. "I am glad," Mackenzie wrote, "they did not fight. Such excitement I never saw before. In every inn it is, 'Hurrah for papineau !'"

None of the speeches made by Mr. Mackenzie, at these meetings, were reported, or have been preserved. But the effect of his prodigious power, as a speaker, over a popular audience, must have been very great. The mission assigned to him by the Central Committee of Vigilance was not without its perils. It is not surprising that the Orangemen were exasperated at listening to speeches, resolutions, and declarations of a kind to which they were little accustomed, and which to them sounded like rank treason. Some of the resolutions bear internal evidence of having been drawn up by Mr. Mackenzie; and others might, I think, be affiliated to some of his political confreres in Toronto. We have already seen that some of the meetings were disturbed by Orangemen. But at Churchville, on the 15th August, their violence was carried to a greater extent than on any previous occasion. A contest for the chairmanship having been decided, by a large majority, in favor of Mr. Mackenzie's supporters, about fifty Orangemen, armed with clubs, climbed up the railing behind him. Mr. Edward Thompson, his opponent in the late election for the Second Riding of York, tried to induce them to desist; but they only answered the magistrate by threatening to throw him down unless he ceased to interfere. Of a number that surrounded Mr. Mackenzie, with clubs in their hands, one attempted to throw him down, but was prevented by Mr. Stewart of Esquesing. On this effort to rescue Mackenzie being made, the Orangemen fell furiously upon their unarmed opponents, with their bludgeons. Mackenzie was not injured. The Tory organs openly threatened that if he held any more meetings, he would be assassinated.* It was afterwards stated that a deliberate plot had been entered into, by the hostile party who attended the meeting, to take Mackenzie's life; and that one who was a party to it, had divulged the secret to a person who, at the proper time, would publicly reveal it. The story was, that two persons, dressed in fantastic habiliments, were to draw off attention by acting the part of Merry Andrews, while the assassin in the crowd was to shoot the intended victim. It was added, that a pistol was fired, and a gun flashed in the pan. But the evidence never came out; and the existence of the conspiracy remained unproved.

Mr. E. W. Thompson informed Mr. Mackenzie that if a meeting were held at Cooksville, next day, he should read the riot act and prevent its going on. But all this did not prevent Mr. Mackenzie from attending the remaining meetings except the Cooksville one, at which it had been announced that he would be present. From the Vaughan meeting he and Mr. Gibson were accompanied by a cavalcade of about a

---

* "Had not the attention of the ' boys,' " said the *Patriot*, " been called in an opposite direction by the cry that ' Mackenzie is coming this way,' it is much to be *feared* that he would not have escaped with his life; and as sure as he attempts to call another seditious meeting, in this part of the country, so surely will he lose the number of his mess."

hundred horsemen and some thirty carriages; and it appears to have been understood that, in future, the Orangemen, if they disturbed any more meetings, should be met by their own weapons.*

Between the beginning of August and the former part of December, when the outbreak occurred, two hundred meetings are said to have been held in the country, at nearly all of which the Toronto Declaration was read and sanctioned. One hundred and fifty Vigilance Committees, in connection with the Central Committee at Toronto, were formed. Disturbances at the meetings frequently occurred. The nature of the movement could hardly have been misunderstood by the most unreflecting spectator. But only some of the members of the branch societies were actually trusted with the secret of the intended revolt. Some of the active leaders joined no association; and although they apparently kept aloof from the movement, they were secretly among its most active promoters.

---

* Referring to the Vaughan meeting, a writer in *The Constitution*, August 23d, over the signature of " One who saw and heard," says: " We all separated with the understanding, that to produce good order there must be hickory sticks, 'pikes, and rifles,' at our future meetings, for Orange ruffians and Tory squires stand in need of such special constables as these; and with them are as meek as lambs. Go on, Canadians, forming your societies of from twelve to forty; or if it were only ten to begin with, you will soon add to your numbers. Meet seldom, but come prepared. To the Lower Canada meetings, every man brings his rifle for self-defence." The expression "pikes and rifles" was borrowed from a speech of the Hon. P. McGill, of Montreal, who, in recommending the Tories of that city to organize, said: " The organization, that it may combine both moral determination and physical force, must be military as well as political. There must be an army as well as a congress. There must be 'pikes and rifles' as well as men and tongues."

CHAPTER II.

A Commercial Crisis—Mackenzie promotes a Run on the Bank of Upper Canada—An Ingenious Mode of prolonging Specie Payments—An Extra Session of the Legislature—Mackenzie's Declamation on the Result of the Session—He attends more Public Meetings—Disturbances—Threats to assassinate Mackenzie—Revolutionary Literature—Shooting Matches—The Welland Canal Libel Suit—Mackenzie cast in Damages to the Amount of two shillings.

A COMMERCIAL crisis aided the public discontent. In May, the New York banks suspended specie payments; and those of Montreal followed. In Toronto, the Bank of Upper Canada was looked upon as the prop of the Government; and it was probably as much for political as commercial reasons that Mr. Mackenzie advised the farmers to go to the counter of the Bank and demand specie for their notes. At the same time, he had small confidence in the security which most of the banks then gave for the redemption of their issues; and it must be admitted that the previous conduct of the managers of the most important of these institutions, in refusing to answer reasonable questions, put to them before a committee of the House, was not calculated to inspire confidence. As a political weapon against the Government, an attempt to drain the banks of their specie by creating a panic could have no sort of justification, except in times of revolution. When Mr. Mackenzie produced a run upon the Bank of Upper Canada, a resort to armed insurrection was a contingency to which many were looking, with alternate hope and fear: hope that it might be avoided, fear that it would come.

The Bank of Upper Canada took an ingenious plan of fighting off the wolves that wished to carry away its gold and silver, leaving its own promises to pay in their place. The notes were paid in silver; and time was gained in the counting. The bank kept a number of its own friends at the counter, asking specie; and what was paid out to them during the day, was trundled back in a wheelbarrew, at night. A stratagem of this kind had the double advantage of economizing the specie, and, by prolonging the specie payment, tending to restore confidence.

If the Upper Canada banks had suspended specie payments, their charters would have been liable to forfeiture. Chiefly to prevent this result, Sir Francis Bond Head called an extraordinary session of the Legislature, on the 19th of June. In the course of the session, which lasted about a month, a bill of prospective indemnity for pursuing such a course was passed. In the meantime, the Commercial Bank, at Kingston, had suspended; and the Farmer's Bank, in Toronto, stopped soon afterwards. The Government loaned £100,000, by the issue of debentures, to the Bank of Upper Canada; £30,000 to the Gore Bank; and £40,000 to the Commercial Bank. But when the rebellion came, the suspension of specie payment followed.

The failure of Thomas Wilson & Co., Financial

Agents of the Province, in London, who were reported to have £140,000, the proceeds of an Upper Canada loan in their hands, a few weeks before, had increased distrust and inflamed the discontent.

At the close of the session, Mr. Mackenzie, in his journal, declaimed on the condition of public affairs with scathing bitterness. The style is characteristic of the man, when his soul was stirred to its inmost depths, and it gives such a good idea of his power of agitating masses of men, that I give an example:

"Canadians! Brother Colonists! Your mock Parliament has done its duty. For four long weeks have its members been marched and counter-marched by our Kentish drill-sergeant, aided by Corporals McNab and Robinson. Bills and badgerings have followed each other in quick succession; and the end of the farce is, that the banks and the Province have been handed over by a sham legislative enactment to Sir Francis, like a Jamaica or other bankrupt estate, to be made the most of, for the use of its foreign owners and creditors, or like a farm held for a term of years at a rack rent, to be impoverished in every possible shape by the holder before it be given up.

"Ye false Canadians! Tories! Pensioners! Placemen! Profligates! Orangemen! Churchmen! Spies! Informers! Brokers! Gamblers! Parasites, and knaves of every caste and description, allow me to congratulate you! Never was a vagabond race more prosperous. Never did successful villainy rejoice in brighter visions of the future than ye may indulge. Ye may plunder and rob with impunity—your feet are on the people's necks; they are transformed into tame, crouching slaves, ready to be trampled on. Erect your Juggernaut—the people are ready to be sacrificed under the wheels of the idol.

"The four pound loaf is at a Halifax shilling; the barrel of flour brings twelve dollars; woe and wailing, and pauperism and crime meet us at every corner of the streets. The settlers and their families on the Ottawa, in Simcoe, in the rear of the London District, and many new settlements, seldom taste a morsel of bread, and are glad to gnaw the bark off the trees, or sell their improvements for a morsel to keep away starvation.

"The settlers are leaving the country in thousands, for lands less favored by nature, but blessed with free institutions and just government.

"The merchants are going to ruin one after another —even sycophancy and degrading servility have failed to save them this time. They cry out, Why is it so?— I pity them not. Money, wealth, power, was their god, the Dagon of their idolatry. Let them cry aloud and spare not—perhaps even now he will help them.

"But why are want and misery come among us? Ah, ye rebels to Christianity, ye detest the truth, ye shut your ears against that which is right.

"Your country is taxed, priest ridden, sold to strangers, and ruined. What then? Ye share the plunder! Like the Lazzaroni of Italy, ye delight in cruelty and distress, and lamentation and woe.

"I know you. I have long watched your movements!"

Mr. Mackenzie continued to attend political meet-

ings in the country; and the exasperation of his enemies continued to increase. In Pickering, he met the
unfortunate Peter Matthews, who was among those
who were afterwards executed for high treason. At
Whitby, where he did not go, threats were made by
the opposite party to pull down the building in which
it had been announced a meeting would take place;
and the rendezvous was therefore changed to Mr.
Peter Perry's store. Nor was he at Malahide, where
there was a disturbance, where the riot act was read,
and the two parties came into collision in a general
fight. In Westminster, Middlesex, the friends of Mackenzie and the supporters of Papineau turned out in
such large numbers that the opposite party shrunk
from the attempt to carry out their scheme of
attack.

Threats, secret and open, were now made by the
Tory party to assassinate Mackenzie. An anonymous
letter, bearing the Hamilton post mark, was sent to
Mr. Charles Durand, Barrister of that place, informing him that Mackenzie would be assassinated. It
was signed "Brutus," as a guarantee of its sincerity.
The Tory press, more bold than anonymous letter
writers, was scarcely less explicit. Through this
channel, he was informed that "if he dared to show
himself in the London District, with the evil design
of poisoning the happiness of the contented settlers,
by agitation and strife, they would put it for ever out
of his power to repeat his crime."* And shortly
after, creditable witnesses swore that the source of the
danger lay much higher than the exasperated men

* *Toronto Patriot.*

who carried bludgeons to public meetings;* men who
bore the titles of honorable, and were thought to constitute excellent material out of which to make Executive Councillors, being charged with plotting Mr.
Mackenzie's destruction.   At the Mayor's Court, To-

* The following affidavits were published at the time:—

"Home District, ⎱   Before me, James Hervey Price, Esquire, a Commis-
  "To wit: ⎰ sioner for taking affidavits in Her Majesty's Court of
King's Bench, this day cometh William Howe, of the Township of York,
Coach Maker, who, being solemnly sworn on the Holy Evangelists of
Almighty God, voluntarily deposeth and saith, that about the hour of four
in the afternoon, yesterday, Monday, the 13th of November instant, as this
deponent was walking up the street leading from the public offices to the gate
of Sir Francis Head, in company with Mr. John Mantach, of this city, six or
seven persons came out at the Governor's door and out at his gate.   This deponent only knew two of them, the Honorable William Allan, and the Honorable John Elmsley.   They were talking about Mackenzie, and this deponent
distinctly heard the Honorable John Elmsley say to Mr. Allan, for he turned
to him while he spoke: "Mackenzie ought to have been shot at the time,
and the only thing to be done is to take him out and shoot him."   Mr. Allan
said something which this deponent could not hear distinctly, and the third
person, who was on Mr. Elmsley's right when they came out at the gate, went
betwixt the other two, and appeared to notify them that they were overheard,
on which they looked back and changed the conversation to a duel between
Mr. Allan McNab and some other person.   The other gentlemen, who had
been with them, went up straight towards King Street.   This deponent accompanied Mr. Mantach to Mr. Mackenzie's residence in York Street, and
offered to make affidavit to the above facts

                                     " (Signed)   WILLIAM HOWE."
   "Sworn, &c.

"Home District, ⎱   Before me, James Hervey Price, Esquire, a Commis-
  "To wit: ⎰ sioner for taking affidavits in the Court of King's Bench,
Home District, cometh John Mantach, of the City of Toronto, Book Binder,
late of the 79th regiment or Cameron Highlanders, formerly serving in
York garrison, who, being solemnly sworn on the Holy Evangelists of
Almighty God, freely and voluntarily deposeth and saith, that about the
hour of four in the afternoon, yesterday, Monday, the 13th of November
instant, as this deponent was walking up Graves Street, near His Excellency
the Lieutenant Governor's gate, in company with Mr. William Howe, Coach
Builder, Yonge Street, the Honorable Messrs. William Allan, Robert Bald-

ronto, Mr. Gurnett, who presided, denounced the habit that had begun to prevail of carrying deadly weapons; and called attention to several recent cases of stabbing with dirks.

The revolutionary literature of Ireland and America was ransacked, and made to yield its quota towards completing the public excitement. Mr. Mackenzie republished Paine's Common Sense, and from stereotype plates got out the first edition of the Bible ever printed in Canada. Trials of Irish patriots, who were fortunate enough to escape conviction, were reproduced. Patriotic poems, which had served in other causes, had the dust shaken from them, and were decked out in modern costume. Native bards imitated the examples which they found in other countries. The boldest words were first uttered in rhyme. Scarcely had the news of the coercion measure of Lord John Russell reached Canada, when these threatening

win Sullivan, and John Elmsley, Members of the Executive Council of Upper Canada, with several other gentlemen, came out at the said gate, from the Government House; and while the others, whose names this deponent doth not know, passed up the pathway, Messrs. Sullivan, Elmsley, and Allan, crossed over the street towards King Street, Elmsley in the middle, Allan on the left. Elmsley was saying to Allan, " Mackenzie should (or ought to) have been shot at that time, and the only thing to be done is to take him out and shoot him now." 'Sullivan perceived this deponent, whom he is personally acquainted with, and instantly got in the middle, between Allan and Elmsley, pinched their arms, and began to speak about McNab's gallant conduct respecting a duel. They walked on very fast, and parted from Elmsley at York Street, and this deponent thought it his duty to wait on Mr. Mackenzie and tell him what deponent had thus accidentally heard. Deponent's impression was that they were conspiring to use Lynch Law, and that the Mackenzie spoken of was the Editor of *The Constitution.*

"(Signed)   JOHN MANTACH.

" Sworn before me at Toronto, this 14th of November, 1837.

"J. H. PRICE, a Commissioner for taking Affidavits, &c."

utterances commenced. In Lower Canada, where the great majority of the French Canadians attended the "anti-coercion meetings," a large proportion of the British population were prepared to give their assistance to put down insurrection. To the question what would the Catholic Irish do, a response, dated Quebec, April 18, was published in a Montreal paper. The last verse asks as a favor that the Irish Catholics might be allowed to lead the van in the threatened contest :—

"Cheer on, cheer on, Canadian friends! Our foes we'd have you tell,
We rifles have in plenty, and we know their use right well—
For when the day of danger comes, we're with you to a man,
And all we ask, should strife commence, is to let us lead the Van."

Soon after we find figures of cannon significantly associated with the lyric effusions of Patriot pens. In the following, old Father Time is unfolding his long record from round a cannon :—

"Unfold, Father Time! thy long records unfold,
Of noble achievements accomplished of old,
When men, by the standard of Liberty led,
Undauntedly conquered or cheerfully bled ;
But know, 'midst the triumphs these moments reveal,
Their glories shall fade, and their lustre turn pale ;
Quebec rises up, and confirms the decree
That tears off our chains, and bids thousands be free."

From the "Lays of the West," fugitive pieces that struggled fatherless into existence, in the newpapers devoted to the work of inflaming the public mind to the requisite pitch, an example must conclude these extracts :—

"Arise, sons of Freedom! to glory arise!
Let Liberty's watchword resound to the skies ;
Raise, raise the proud pennon of Liberty high,
On, on! to its rescue, and conquer or die,

Nor dream that so glorious a pennant can fall,
Or that mankind's proud tyrants shall freedom appall,
No! forward, with faith and at honor's right hand,
Strike home for your freedom, your rights, and your land.
Remember your sires! O forget not their fame!
Nor stain ye the heirloom, their truth and their name;
Preserve the escutcheon as bright and as true,
As ere the great trust was confided to you.
Britannia, Hibernia, and Scotia unite,
Like sons of one father rush on to the fight;
As floods from the mountains together rush on.
'Your numbers as thousands, your destiny One.'"

The confessions of English statesmen that the thirteen Colonies of America were right in resisting taxation without representation, were turned to a profitable account. Mr. Atwood's apothegm that "the strength of the people is nothing without union, and union nothing without confidence and discipline," became a standing motto of the revolutionary party. And Mr. Hume's declaration, that if there had been no display of force there would have been no Reform Bill, was not without its effect in changing the Vigilance Committees into *nuclei* of military organizations. Shooting matches, first got up by Mr. Gibson, in which turkeys were the immediate victims, became fashionable. Drilling was practised with more or less secresy. An occasional *feu de joie*, on Yonge Street,* in honor of Papineau, with a hundred rifles, would be made the subject of boast in the press. Mr. Bidwell, who had refused to accept a nomination to the proposed Convention, and who kept at a safe distance from all these movements, could not refuse his legal advice that trials of skill among riflemen were perfectly lawful. The people were badly armed, and a

* A road, so called, running from Toronto, a distance of forty miles

brisk business in the manufacture of pikes began to
be carried on.   Some added bayonets to their rifles, on
the pretence that if they wounded a deer in hunting
and did not kill it, the supplementary weapon might
be found very useful; but of these there were very
few, and there was hardly a single bayonet in the outbreak north of Toronto.

The thread of the narrative of the initiatory steps
of the rebellion must be here interrupted, for the purpose of introducing an episode, in the shape of a libel
suit.*   While investigating the mysteries of the Wel-

* The passage charged as libellous is appended:—

"I have made some progress in auditing the proceedings of other years, and
beg to state, as the result of my observations, that the books of account are
improperly kept, and purposely with intent to defraud the public and the canal
proprietors; that many erasures have been made in the journal and ledgers to
the injury of the company and advantage of favorites, or the connections of
persons in office; that false entries have been made on the journal and ledgers
to a large amount; that there is an actual defalcation of great extent on the
part of the officers, now lately in charge.

"That the clerks have increased and decreased at their pleasure, and improperly altered and changed accounts of large amount, and made entries on the
books unauthorized by the minutes of the Canal Board, and often in direct
contradiction to the standing orders of that Board.

" The most of the entries on the books, since June, 1832, have been made by
an under clerk of intemperate habits, sometimes hired by the day for a short
time, and sometimes employed regularly—of late he has been paid by the year.
In my letter to the President, requesting that a Board should be summoned, I
stated 'that the confidential person who keeps the books under the Secretary's
superintendence is absent, and it is believed drunk, a state not unusual to him.'
Since I have been a Director, the Secretary of the Canal Company has sometimes been absent for a week at Niagara, the clerk absent at the bottle, the
workmen and others demanding payment of their accounts, and no one to
attend upon them.

" Patrick Grant Beaton, the clerk referred to in the letter requesting the
Special Board, as being deeply implicated in the affairs to which I called its
attention, is continued as the book-keeper in the office, with the concurrence
of the Directors, the same as if nothing unusual had occurred! When sober
he is a tolerable accountant, and I find that nearly all the entries on the jour-

land Canal iniquity, in 1834, Mr. Mackenzie published a statement of progress reflecting, among other things, upon the gross irregularities of a person of the name of Beaton, the clerk of the Canal Company. He was described as being of intemperate habits, accused of neglecting his duty, of making false entries in the books, and entries not authorized as far as the minutes of the Board showed, and of improperly charging accounts of large amount. It was admitted that, when not in his cups, he was a tolerable accountant, and Mr. Mackenzie stated that he had urged the Board not to allow the books again to come under Beaton's manipulation, till they should have been investigated by the Legislature.

The trial came off at Niagara, on the 12th October, 1837, before Mr. Justice Macaulay and a special jury.* In accordance with his usual practice, in such cases, Mr. Mackenzie undertook his own defence; his Soli-

---

nals and great ledgers for several years are by him, the others being in the handwriting of Mr. John Callaghan, a lock-keeper on the canal, and a Mr. Hiram Slate, Mr. Merritt's partner in the Port Colborne Mills, and lately a clerk to Garrison & Little, Contractors. I strongly urged the Directors not to let Beaton touch the books any more until the Legislature had investigated them—as to Mr. Clark he does not pretend to write in them—but they have given Beaton the most ample opportunity of continuing his dishonest practices, and of their motives for so doing the public must judge. The Assembly will have to take such books and papers as they can get, and in such a state of erasures and amendments as will suit the detected persons. The Directors allowing Beaton an opportunity to tamper with the books of account, after what has been certified by their own resolution, looks like as if they felt they were in the boat together."

* The names of the jurors were: Jeffrey B. Hall, Walpole; Austin Morse, Stamford; Malcolm Laing, Stamford; Jacob Servos, Gainsboro'; Wm. Fitch, Canboro'; Dr. Raymond, Niagara; George Lawrence, Niagara; William Hixson, Clinton; Nelson Boughner, Sherbrooke; Peter W. Tonbrock, Grantham; Allan Simmerman, Grimsby; J. W. Perkins, Walpole.

citor, Mr. Price, making occasional suggestions as to the examination of witnesses. Mr. R. E. Burns and Mr. Roland Macdonald, of St. Catherines, were counsel for the plaintiff, Beaton.

Mr. Charles Richardson, who had been concerned in the destruction of Mackenzie's printing office, at York, in 1826, had been rewarded with the office of Clerk of the Peace for the Niagara District. By him the jury list was furnished. So deficient was it that Mr. Mackenzie obliged the officers to add to it over a hundred additional names. He caused others to be struck off as bad; and yet one Austin Morse, disqualified by law, who was a violent political opponent of the defendant, somehow got on the jury. Nor was his name on the official list of jurors. "If," Mr. Mackenzie pertinently asked, "this name was not put into the ballot-box, how did it come out?"

Mr. Mackenzie, before the suit was commenced, admitted in writing to the plaintiff's attorney the authorship of the alleged libel, and confident of the truth of his statements he had challenged much higher game than Beaton to make his allegations subject of judicial investigation;* but the parties who had the con-

---

* In a letter to the editor of the *Upper Canada Courier*, by whom he had been attacked for his strictures on the canal management, he threw out this challenge:—

"If Mr. Merritt and his friends choose to go a step farther, and place all my numbers before a jury of the country, and assert that they are untrue and published from unjustifiable motives and for improper purposes, there also I will meet them; the whole bar of Upper Canada, Whig and Tory, is at their service; the Judges are not said to be prejudiced in my favor, nor the Sheriff, and as to the proofs of authorship and publication, I will deliver on demand copies of the several numbers, each endorsed by my own signature, to any person Mr. Merritt's attorney may name. For my own part, I have all along deter-.

trol of the canal, and were primarily responsible for the mismanagement, preferred to keep in the background and to put forward Beaton as the plaintiff. Mr. Mackenzie took care not to lose sight of this fact, and he determined in his address to the jury to take a latitude that would bring the conduct of Beaton's superiors under review. He asserted his right to make extracts from the three broadsheets, in one of which the alleged libel had appeared, with a view of explaining the motives he had in the publication. Mr. Justice Macaulay, with whom he had had the terrific literary duel which led to the destruction of his printing office eleven years before, interposed an objection. He did not think all the papers could be read. Mr. Mackenzie, referring to this circumstance, humorously replied: "The time has long gone past, but your lordship and myself will never forget it, when in an appeal to the public"—directed against the defendant— "your lordship cited the passage, 'The fool hath said in his heart there is no God;' adding that if the first half of the sentence were struck out, the Bible could be made to advocate infidelity." This gentle spurring of the memory of the judge, with the citation of an authority and a fact, caused his lordship to withdraw his objections. Mr. Mackenzie made a merciless analysis of the damaging evidence in the canal inquiry before the House of Assembly, placing the proved delinquencies of the managers in bold relief. The evi-

mined to employ no counsel in the courts in any matter whereof I consider myself correctly informed."

The plaintiff's attorney wrote to Mackenzie to send the papers, with a letter acknowledging the authorship and publication, and they were promptly forwarded.

dence proved Beaton's habits to be the reverse of
temperate, and the books of the Company bore upon
their pages ineffaceable evidence of the tampering to
which they had been subjected.   But the maxim then
universally accepted, in the British dominions, "the
greater the truth the greater the libel," was destined
to obtain a dubious triumph.   All night the jury were
shut up, unable to agree; but next day they found a
ground of unanimity in a verdict for the plaintiff,
with two shillings damages.

CHAPTER III.

The Rolls of Revolt—The intended Convention—Crisis in Lower Canada—Collision between the "Sons of Liberty" and the Doric Club, in Montreal—Arrests for Sedition and Treason at Quebec—M. Dufort arrives in Toronto with Messages from Papineau—Proposal of Mackenzie to seize four thousand Stand of Arms, to arrest Governor Head and his Councillors, to obtain possession of the Archives and Garrison, establish a Provisional Government, and call a Convention—The Government is aware of the Conspiracy, but instead of taking Measures to prevent its coming to a Head, encourage a Revolt.

By the commencement of November, one thousand five hundred names were returned to Mr. Mackenzie of persons enrolled, and ready to place themselves under arms—if arms could only be procured—at one hour's notice. In the Home District, in which Toronto was situated, the attendance on drill weekly was deemed a duty. The Gore District, further west, was not much behind its metropolitan neighbor. From one end of it to the other, political unions were in the course of formation. They selected their leaders and reported themselves to Mr. Mackenzie, the Agent and Secretary of the Central Vigilance Committee. The organizations in the country were now called Branch Reform Unions; and they were numbered according to the order of their formation: that of Lloydtown being No. 1. It does not appear that the Unions were bound to secrecy by the obligations of an oath.

There were two kinds of organization. In addition to the Vigilance Committees and Reform Unions, about seventy delegates had been elected to take part in a Convention, who were to send Representatives to a British American Congress. The meeting of an approaching Convention, which had been determined upon in the previous August, continued to be alluded to, after the rising had been determined upon. And if the movement had proved successful, the Convention would undoubtedly have been held. Some of the Unions were anxious that a day for the meeting of the Convention should be fixed. Seventy delegates had been appointed in the Home District alone. Mr. Mackenzie declared it inexpedient to take any immediate steps for the meeting of the Convention; and he publicly stated his opinion that "the suspension of the *Habeas Corpus* act, illegal arrests, martial law, and the seizure of Reformers, with their books and papers, were among the tender mercies to be looked for at the hands of the Sullivan Council."

In Lower Canada the crisis had arrived. The Legislative Session, convened in August, had produced no reconciliation between the Governor and the Assembly. The House told the Earl of Gosford that they had not been able to derive from " His Excellency's speech, or from any other source, any motive for departing even momentarily" from their determination to withhold the supplies until the grievances of the country were redressed. The Governor replied to the Address, charging the House with virtually abrogating the constitution by a continued abandonment of their functions; and as soon as the members

had left his presence, he issued a proclamation pro-
roguing the Legislature. The popular agitation continued. Monster meetings were called in different
parts of the country; at one of which, held at St.
Charles, on the river Richlieu, on the 23d of October,
five thousand persons are said to have been present.
The Roman Catholic Bishop of Montreal, M. Lartigue,
a relative of M. Papineau, who had before addressed
a large body of ecclesiastics at Montreal to discourage
insurrection, now, " impelled by no external influence,
but solely actuated by motives of conscience," issued
a pastoral enjoining the clergy and faithful to discountenance all schemes of insurrection. But the popular
frenzy was too great to be at once brought under control, even by the powerful influence of the Roman
Catholic Church. There is reason to believe, however,
that the influence of the Roman Catholic clergy
eventually did more than even the British troops to
crush the insurrection in Lower Canada.

A society called the Sons of Liberty, formed in
Montreal, and said to owe its paternity to Mr. Thos.
Storrow Brown, extended its branches throughout the
country.* On the 6th of November, a collision took
place between the " Sons of Liberty," headed by Mr.

---

* I have before me an unpublished letter in French, giving an account of
the commencement of the troubles, by one of the actors, by whom it was sent
to a friend in New Orleans. After relating the arrest of the parties connected
with *Le Libéral* at Quebec, he says : " Les chefs du parti populaire à Montréal
s'imaginant qu'ils auorient le même sort, et qu'ils ne serojent pas plus respectés
croirient prudents de se tenir à l'ecart pendant quelque temps. Brown, qui
écrit mieux qu'il se bat, avait comme tu sais, formé une société sous le nom des
fils de la liberté. Son projet reussisoit à merveille ; chaque jour ce corps
augmentoit en nombre, et deja de pareilles sociétés se formaient dans le cam-
pagnes."

T. S. Brown, and an organization called the Doric Club, at Montreal. One of the rules of the Sons of Liberty required them to meet on the first Monday of every month. This was their regular day of meeting. There was no secret about it. The magistrates issued a proclamation forbidding them to walk in procession. In the morning, placards appeared on the walls, calling on the members of the Doric Club to " crush the rebellion in the bud." True to the call, many of them prepared to come out and attack the Sons of Liberty, should the latter make their appearance. In a large yard, opposite the Presbyterian church in Great St. James Street, the latter organization met, and passed several resolutions, in an orderly manner. When they came out, the members of the Doric Club confronted them. Each party afterwards accused the other of making the attack. Before long, the Sons of Liberty were chasing their opponents on Great St. James Street, amid cries of " Call out the guard ! call out the guard !" Mr. Brown received some injuries. The Doric Club men were soon reinforced ; and while they claimed a victory in a subsequent fight, the Sons of Liberty alleged that they only fled before the military, in company with the Tories. The truth seems to be that each party obtained a victory in turn. The Sons of Liberty did not begin to assemble till two o'clock ; and at half past four, two companies of soldiers and some flying artillery were called out. The office of *The Vindicator*, a Liberal paper, which had for a long time been publishing seditious articles, was sacked by the Tory mob, and the types thrown into the street. The house of Mr. E. Jolen, in Dorchester Street, was entered; and the banner of the Sons of Liberty, with three guns—one of them said to be seven barrelled—and a sword were taken. Some of the windows of M. Papineau's house were broken; and the mob was with some difficulty restrained from destroying the building. Although some firearms were discharged on the first attack, nobody was killed.

On the 11th of November, Messrs Morin, Legare, Lachance, Chasseur, and Trudeau, editors, managers, and publishers of *Le Libéral*, were arrested for sedition at Quebec. This alarmed the popular leaders, who, for a time, made themselves less prominent. On the 16th of the same month, some further arrests were made; but this time they proceeded upon the graver charge of high treason.

While these occurrences were taking place in Lower Canada, a messenger bearing letters from M. Papineau, arrived in Toronto. To M. Dufort this mission had been entrusted.* The purport of the message was an appeal to the Upper Canada Liberals to support their Lower Canada brethren, when a resort to arms should be made. Mr. Mackenzie was convinced that the time to act had come. In the garrison at Toronto, there were only one soldier and three pieces of cannon; Sir F. B. Head having sent the troops to Lower Canada for the purpose, as he afterwards boasted, of entrapping Mackenzie and others into rebellion, by appearing to be wholly with-

* M. Dufort was on his way to Michigan, to get up an expedition to assist the Canadians, where, in connection with Judge Butler, a prominent member of the House of Representatives of that State, he formed a "council of war," embracing prominent and influential members of the House of Representatives, State's officers, and wealthy citizens.

out the means of resistance. Of the fifteen hundred men whose names had been returned on the insur‑rection rolls, only a very small proportion—perhaps not over one in five—had firearms of any description. There were lying in the City Hall four thousand muskets, which had been sent up from Kingston, and which were still unpacked. Mackenzie's plan was to seize these arms, together with the archives, the Lieu‑tenant Governor, and the Executive Council; and by this means to affect a revolution, *sans coup férir*, with‑out the loss of a single life. Chimerical as such a project would be, under ordinary circumstances, it must be remembered that the folly of Sir F. B. Head had left the Government at the mercy of any half hundred men who might have undertaken to carry such a project into effect.

Having made up his mind as to what ought to be done, Mr. Mackenzie one afternoon, early in Novem‑ber, called upon fourteen or fifteen persons with whom he had been acting in the organization of political societies throughout the country; and asked them to meet him that evening, at the house of Mr. Doel, on the north-east corner of Bay and Adeliade Streets.*

* Among the persons who assembled, on that night, to listen to a project of revolution, were: Dr. Morrison, a Lower Canadian by birth, who was prac‑ticing medicine in Toronto; Mr. John McIntosh, a Scotsman, who formerly owned and sailed a vessel on Lake Ontario, and who retired upon a moderate competence; Mr. John Doel, an Englishman, who by a brewery and the rise in the value of some real estate of which he was the owner, was well able to live on the interest of his money; Mr. Robert Mackay, a Scotsman, and grocer, in a good way of business; Mr. John Armstrong, a Scotsman and axe‑maker; Mr. Timothy Parsons, an Englishman, who kept a "dry goods" store; Mr. John Mills, a Scotsman by birth, and a hatter by trade; Mr. Thos. Armstrong, a Scotsman and carpenter, employing several men; Mr. John

They all attended. Dr. Morrison took the chair; and Mr. Mackenzie proceeded to give his views of what course it would be proper to pursue, in the crisis which had arisen. Fortunately his own account of this meeting has been preserved.

"I remarked, in substance, that we had, in a declaration adopted in July, and signed approvingly by many thousands, affirmed that our wrongs and those of the old thirteen colonies were substantially the same; that I knew of no complaint made by the heir of the House of Russell in 1685, against the Government of England overturned three years thereafter, that could not be sustained against that of Canada; that not only was redress from Britain hopeless, but that there was imminent danger that leading Reformers would be seized and sent to the dungeon; that the House of Assembly had been packed through fraud—the clergy hired and paid by the State—the endowment of a hierarchy begun in defiance of the Royal pledge—the public credit abused and the provincial funds squandered—offices created and distributed to pay partisans—emigration arrested—discontent rendered universal—and government converted into a detestable tyranny; while in Lower Canada chaos reigned, backed by the garrisoned troops; and British resolutions to leave no check in the hands of the people, upon any abuse whatever, had passed the House of Commons. Law was a mere pretext to plunder people systematically with impunity—and education,

Elliott, an Englishman and an attorney; and Mr. Wm. Lesslie, a bookseller and druggist, doing a good business. Mr. Elliott was never invited to attend another meeting.

the great remedy for the future, discouraged in Upper and unknown in Lower Canada—while defaulters, cheats, embezzlers of trust funds and of public revenue, were honored and encouraged, and peculators sheltered from the indignation of the people they had robbed. I stated, that when I saw how Ireland, the condition of which was fully understood in London, had been ruled, I had no hope for Canada, except in resistance, and affirmed that the time had come for a struggle, either for the rights of Englishmen in connection with England, or for independence. Canada, as governed, was an engine for the oppression of our countrymen at home.

"I spoke with great earnestness, and was only interrupted by some brief casual remarks.

"In adverting to the condition of society, I remarked, that Head was abhorred for the conduct of those he had upheld and cringed to; that in the city all classes desired a change—credit was prostrate, trade languishing—and asked if the proper change could be obtained in any possible way short of revolution?

"Still there was no answer.

"I stated that there were two ways of effecting a revolution: one of them by organizing the farmers, who were quite prepared for resistance, and bringing them into Toronto, to unite with the Toronto people; and the other, by immediate action.

"Dr. Morrison made some deprecatory or dissenting remark, but I continued.

"I said, that the troops had left; that those who had persuaded Head to place four thousand stand of

arms in the midst of an unarmed people in the City
Hall, seemed evidently not opposed to their being
used; that Fort Henry was open and empty, and a
steamer had only to sail down to the wharf and take
possession; that I had sent two trusty persons, separately, to the garrison, that day, and it was also 'to
let;' that the Lieutenant Governor had just come in
from his ride, and was now at home, guarded by one
sentinel; and that my judgment was that we should
instantly send for Dutcher's foundry-men and Armstrong's axe-makers, all of whom could be depended
on, and, with them, go promptly to the Government
House, seize Sir Francis, carry him to the City Hall,
a fortress in itself, seize the arms and ammunition
there, and the artillery, etc., in the old garrison; rouse
our innumerable friends in town and country, pro-
claim a Provisional Government, send off the steamer
of that evening to secure Fort Henry, and either induce Sir Francis to give the country an Executive
Council responsible to a new and fairly chosen Assembly to be forthwith elected, after packing off the
usurpers in the 'Bread and Butter Parliament,' such
new Assembly to be convened immediately; or if he
refused to comply, go at once for Independence, and
take the proper steps to obtain and secure it.

"I also communicated, in the course of my remarks,
important facts relative to Lower Canada, and the disposition of her leading men.

"Dr. Morrison manifested great astonishment and
impatience toward the close of my discourse, and at
length hastily rose and exclaimed that this was treason, if I was really serious, and that if I thought I

could entrap him into any such mad scheme, I would find that he was not my man. I tried to argue with him, but finding that he was resolute and determined, soon desisted.*

"That the proposition I made could have been easily and thoroughly carried into effect, I have never for a moment doubted; and I would have gone about it promptly, in preference to the course afterwards agreed upon, but for the indecision or hesitancy of those who longed for a change, but disliked risking anything on such issues. I made no request to any one about secrecy, believing that the gentlemen I had addressed were honestly desirous to aid in removing an intolerable burthen, but that much difference might exist as to the best means of doing so; and that the Government would be kept inactive, even if it knew all—its pretended friends, headed by a fool, pulling one way, and its enemies another."

About the 18th of November another plan of operation was decided upon. There were about a dozen persons present when the decision was come to. The organized bands, distributed over the country, were to collect together, and march upon Toronto by Yonge Street, the main northern entrance to the city, on Thursday, the 7th of December.† The management

---

* Dr. Morrison, I learn, from a reliable source, had no real objection to the scheme; but he distrusted some one in the room, and was afraid to commit himself. This he told to my informant; but who it was that was the object of his suspicion he did not state. The circumstance of his afterwards agreeing to a far more dangerous project for effecting the same object, is sufficient guarantee of the correctness of this information.

† In a public dispatch to Lord Glenelg, dated Toronto, December 19th, 1837, Sir F. Head affects to have known that the outbreak was to have taken place on the 19th; and in *The Emigrant*, he states that Mackenzie had fixed

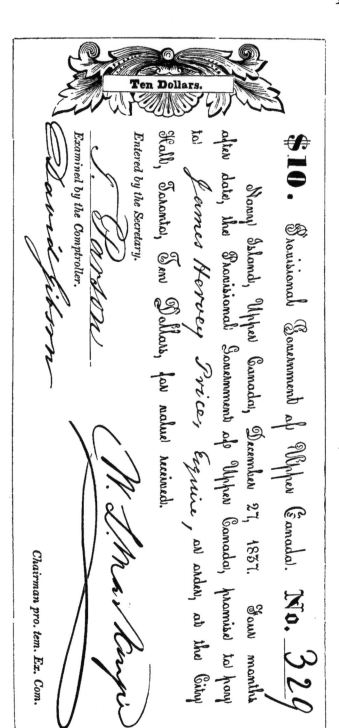

Ten Dollars.

$10. Provisional Government of Upper Canada. No. 329

Navy Island, Upper Canada, December 2nd, 1857. Four months after date, the Provisional Government of Upper Canada, promise to pay to James Hervey Price, Esquire, or order, at the City Hall, Toronto, Ten Dollars, for value received.

Entered by the Secretary.

J. Parsons

Examined by the Comptroller.

David Gibson

W. L. MacKenzie
Chairman pro. tem. Ex. Com.

of the enterprise was to be confided to Dr. Rolph, as
sole executive; and the details were to be worked out
by Mr. Mackenzie. The correspondence with Papineau and the other popular leaders in Lower Canada,
was to be conducted by the executive; and he was to
communicate intelligence of their intended movements to his associates. It was understood that the
day named for the rising should not be altered by
any less authority than that by which it had been
fixed. The insurgent forces were to be brought as
secretly as possible to Montgomery's hotel, on Yonge
Street, about four miles north of the city of Toronto,
between six and ten o'clock, at night, when they were
to march upon the city. A force of between four and
five thousand was expected. The four thousand
stand of arms in the City Hall were to be seized; the
Lieutenant Governor and his chief advisers were to
be captured and placed in safe custody; the garrison
was to be taken possession of. A convention, the
members of which had begun to be elected in the
previous August, was to be called; and a constitution,
which had already assumed shape and form, was to
be submitted for adoption.* In the meantime, Dr.

upon this day because a girl of the name of Julia Murdock was to be executed for poisoning her mistress, Mrs. James Henry, of Toronto; as a
number of men could be brought into the city under the guise of witnessing
the execution. The girl, he pretends, was to be rescued by "a number of
fine fellows," "from a horrid and ignominious death." The whole story,
however it got into the brain of Sir F. Head, is a pure fiction. "A number
of the best men in the Province," he tells us, "consented to be agitators in
such a cause" as the reprieving of the girl. However this may be, the files
of Mr. Mackenzie's paper show that he did nothing to increase the agitation.

* See Appendix E.

Rolph was to be administrator of the Provisional Government.* Such was the helpless condition of the Government, and so few were its willing supporters supposed to be, that all this was expected to be effected without the effusion of blood.

* It is the fate of persons who fail in an enterprise of this kind to have their motives misrepresented by their cotemporaries; and it is sometimes not till the prejudice of their time has passed away that justice is done to them. Sir F. Head frequently stated, in written documents, that the object of the insurgents was to rob the banks and set fire to the city; forgetting that they were mainly composed of the wealthiest farmers in the county of York, the very class whom he (when it suited him) called "yeomen" and "gentlemen." "There can be no doubt," he wrote on one occasion, "that could Dr. Rolph and Mackenzie have succeeded in robbing the banks, they would immediately have absconded to the United States." "Nothing," wrote Mr. Hincks, now Governor of British Guiana, in *The Toronto Examiner*, "in Sir F. Head's writings has given more disgust than this assertion." Of Dr Rolph, Mr. Hincks proceeded to say that "he was the most talented and highly educated man in the Province, and that there never was a man less likely to be influenced by pecuniary considerations." "With regard to Mackenzie," Mr. Hincks added, "it has been so much the fashion to accuse him of every crime which has disgraced humanity, that people really forget who and what he is. We can speak impartially of Mr. Mackenzie more particularly, because those who know us well, know that we have never approved of his political conduct. Let us not be misunderstood. We agreed with him on certain broad principles, more particularly Responsible Government, and when those principles were involved, we supported him, and shall never regret it. As a private individual we are bound in justice to state that Mr. Mackenzie was a man of strict integrity in his dealings, and we have frequently heard the same admitted by his violent political opponents. He was not a rich man, because he never sought after wealth. Had he done so his industry and perseverance must have insured it. We do not take up our pen to defend the political characters of either Dr. Rolph or Mr. Mackenzie; but when these false and malignant slanders are uttered, we shall always expose them. Are there ten people in Upper Canada who believe that the object of either Dr. Rolph or Mr. Mackenzie was to rob the banks and abscond to the United States?" This was written in 1838; and we venture to say that there is not to-day a single person in Upper Canada who, in good faith, would answer this question in the affirmative. In pecuniary matters, both Dr. Rolph and Mr. Mackenzie were men of the highest integrity; a fact to which their bitterest opponents would now readily testify.

Unless it were the day of the intended outbreak, none of the movements designed to end in armed insurrection and revolution were unknown to the Government. In the beginning of September, intelligence of the purpose to which the organizations in the county were being turned, was conveyed to the Lieutenant Governor.* Before the middle of November, a short time prior to the fixing of the day of rising, two Methodist ministers, Revs. Egerton Ryerson and John Lever, called upon Attorney General Hagerman one night at nine o'clock, and related what was going on in the townships of East and West Gwillimburg, Albion, Vaughan, and other places. One of them was fresh from these scenes of excitement, where he had been travelling in a pastoral capacity. They denounced to the Attorney General treasonable organizations, treasonable trainings, and treasonable designs upon Toronto. Mr. Hagerman was inclined to laugh in the faces of his informants. He did not believe, he said, there were fifty men in the Province who would agree to undertake a descent upon Toronto; he would like to see the attempt made. One of the preachers replied by declaring his belief that there were, in the Home District alone, more than five hundred persons who had already determined upon such an attack. The same representations had already

---

* Mr. Charles Fothergill stated, in a pamphlet which he published, that, "Early in September last [1837] the Governor was made acquainted with the nature, extent, and objects of these secret Committees in one of the most seditious quarters in the Home District by a magistrate of Pickering [Fothergill], who had taken measures to watch their every motion. But it was all without any useful effect. Sir Francis Bond Head was in such hands, that, if a prophet had risen from the dead, his admonitions would have been equally ineffectual."

been made to the Lieutenant Governor, in person; but as he paid no attention to them, this appeal was made from the Governor to the Minister. But it was in vain. The one was found to be as deaf and as obstinate as the other.

On the 31st October, Sir Francis Bond Head had refused the offer of a volunteer company to guard the Government House; preferring to wait, as he expressed it, till the lives or property of Her Majesty's subjects should require defence. To the very last, the Lieutenant Governor refused to resort to any measure of precaution against the threatened insurrection. On the 2nd December, a free-mason, who resided in Markham, informed Capt. Fitzgibbon that bags full of pike heads and pike handles had been collected; and that he had observed all the signs of a rapidly ripening revolt. Capt. Fitzgibbon sought out Judge Jones, to whom he repeated what he had heard. They went before the Executive Council together, where the statement was once more repeated. Mr. Justice Jones exclaimed: "You do not mean to say that these people are going to rebel!" Capt. Fitzgibbon replied that undoubtedly they were; when Mr. Jones, turning to the Lieutenant Governor, contemptuously exclaimed, "Pugh! pugh!" The length to which the Judge carried his obdurate scepticism may best be illustrated by the reception he gave Capt. Fitzgibbon on the night of the outbreak. "The over-zeal of that man," he complained, "is giving me a great deal of trouble" The insurgents were already at Montgomery's.

Nor is this all. Sir Francis Bond Head made it a matter of boasting that, "in spite of the remonstrances which, from almost every district in the Province," he received, he allowed Mr. Mackenzie "to make deliberate preparation for revolt;"* that he allowed him "to write what he chose, to say what he chose, to do what he chose;" that he offered no opposition to armed assemblages for the purpose of drill. Nor did he rest satisfied with doing nothing to check preparations, the nature of which he understood so well; he encouraged the outbreak.† For this purpose he sent all the troops from the Province;‡ and boasted that he had laid a trap to entice Mackenzie and others into revolt.§ Nothing could have been more culpable than this conduct of the Lieutenant Governor. To encourage men to the commission of an act, and then to punish its performance with death, as in the case of

* Vice Regal speech on the opening of the third session of the thirteenth Parliament of Upper Canada, December 28, 1837.

† " I considered that if an attack by the rebels was inevitable, *the more I encouraged them to consider me defenceless the better.*"—*Narrative*, p. 329.

‡ In his *Narrative*, Sir Francis Bond Head boastingly reports, " I purposely dismissed from the Province the whole of our troops," p. 337. But when this extraordinary conduct on the part of the Lieutenant Governor had been severely censured both in Parliament and by the Press, he denied that he had sent away the troops. " Many people," he says in *The Emigrant*, "have blamed, and I believe still blame, me for having, as they say, sent the troops out of the Province. I, however, did no such thing." He then proceeds to throw on Sir John Colborne the blame of an act, of which, before he had discovered that it was improper, he had eagerly claimed all the credit. " It was the duty of the Government," said Sir Robert Peel, in a speech in the House of Commons, January 16, 1838, "to have prepared such a military force in the colony as to have discouraged the exciters of the insurrection from pursuing the course they did." How great then must be the condemnation of the Lieutenant Governor!

§ The Earl of Durham, in his Report on British North America, January 31, 1839, says: " It certainly appeared too much as if the rebellion had been purposely invited by the Government, and the unfortunate men who took part in it deliberately drawn into a trap by those who subsequently inflicted so severe a punishment on them for their error."—pp. 59, 60

Samuel Lount and Peter Matthews, is more like murder with malice aforethought than any thing else to which it could possibly be compared.*

* Sir Francis Bond Head, however, was not responsible for the executions. He had left the Province before they took place; and many who were never admirers of his policy believe that he had too much magnanimity of character to have pursued a vindictive course in needlessly causing an effusion of blood. He released several prisoners, with arms in their hands, as soon as they were captured, though some of them, contrary to good faith, were arrested again.

DEATH OF COL. MOODIE.

ADRIAN=SHARP

CHAPTER IV.

Persons in the Secret of the intended Revolt—Commencement of the Rebellion in Lower Canada—The Battles of St. Denis and St. Charles—Mackenzie sets out to the Country to Organize the Revolt—An Appeal "to Arms".— Military Leaders Appointed—Mackenzie takes no Command—Change of the Day of Rising—Lount brings only eighty or ninety Tried Men to Montgomery's Hotel—A Guard placed on the Road leading to Toronto—Mackenzie cannot entice the Men to March on Toronto—He and three others set out to ascertain the State of the City—They take two Prisoners, one of whom shoots Anderson, one of his Guards—Mackenzie and Powell attempt to shoot at one another—Powell escapes and informs the Governor—How and by whom Col. Moodie was shot—Lount's men disheartened by the death of Anderson—The Rebel Commissariat without Provisions—Messengers sent to the City never return—Before morning Mackenzie again urges a March on the City—Next day (Tuesday, Dec. 5th) the Insurgent Force numbers Seven or Eight Hundred Men—Sir Francis Bond Head sends in a Flag of Truce to the Rebel Camp —Failure of the Negotiations—March for the City—Firing between the Loyalists and the Insurgents—Disorderly Retreat of the Latter—Burning of Dr. Horne's House—Escape of Dr. Rolph (Wednesday the 6th)—Western Mail intercepted—Division in the Rebel Camp on Thursday Morning—Council of War—A Party sent to burn the Don Bridge and intercept the Eastern Mails—Sir Francis Bond Head, having received Succor from a distance, determines on an Attack—The Battle of Yonge Street—Defeat of the Insurgents—Burning of Montgomery's Tavern and Gibson's House.

BY some means a knowledge of the intended rising reached several persons, from whom Mackenzie would have desired to keep it a secret. Dr. Morrison, who had so vehemently opposed the project of seizing the arms in the City Hall, and taking possession of the Government in the way it was first proposed was a

59

party to the arrangement finally agreed upon. He is believed to have disclosed the plan of insurrection to several persons. What was going on came to the ears of Dr. Baldwin.* The latter, it would seem, never mentioned it to his son, Robert; for that gentleman declared that he had no knowledge of it.† Mr. Bidwell had refused to become a member of the proposed convention, and he does not appear to have attended the meetings at which insurrection was organized. There seems to be no reason to believe, however, that he is entitled to plead ignorance of the movement. He was asked his opinion on the legality of the shooting matches; he was the bosom friend of Dr. Rolph, with whom he was in the habit of cordially co-operating; and it has been stated that, without working with the dozen persons in Toronto, who were actively engaged in the organization of the movement, he was secretly giving all the assistance he could.‡ He accepted expatriation at the

---

* Dr. Baldwin's Evidence before the Treason Commission, Toronto, December 13, 1837.

† His own statement, read January 2, 1838, was:—"With respect to the insurrection itself, I had no personal knowledge whatever of either the conspiracy itself, the intention to rise, or the attack on the city, or the persons said to be implicated in it; and since my return from England in February last I have been wholly unconnected with the parties or politics of the Province."—*Appendix to Assembly's Journals*, 1837–8, page 486.

‡ The following extract from a letter addressed to a person in Toronto is very explicit:—"When I was in Toronto, in the fall of 1837, I became acquainted with Mr. Bidwell. From him I learned the projected revolution, and general calculations to be entered into. To him, my brother-in-law, Judge Butler [a prominent member of the House of Representatives in Michigan] made several pledges in relation to my rendering assistance to the Provincial army, if a general concert was required." By the writer of this letter Mr. Dufort, who was in Toronto with letters from Mr. Papineau, was introduced to Mr. Bidwell

hands of Sir Francis Bond Head, when the revolt had failed.*

Two days before the insurgents occupied Montgomery's Hotel, Mr. Price advised a neighbor whose property was in an exposed position to make a conveyance of it, as something was likely to happen in the country.

There were a great many other persons who had also learned of the intended revolt, in the way it

to "consult on the proposed connection of the two Provinces." This statement was published some years ago by Mackenzie, in his *Flag of Truce*, without eliciting any denial from Mr. Dufort, whose attention was specially directed to it. On the 30th August, 1837, Mr. Bidwell wrote to Dr. O'Callaghan expressing his opinion that "all hope of justice from the authorities of England seems to be extinguished." At the same time, it is proper to observe that all the evidence produced against him by Sir Francis Bond Head, except the option to leave the Province or run the risk of having his letters opened, is worthless. It is true that his name was inscribed on the flag left by the rebels when they retreated from Montgomery's; but the Lieutenant Governor did not know that it was an old flag of 1831 with the last figure changed into a seven. Yet such is the fact.

* The day before the outbreak the Lieutenant Governor was sitting in a room in the Government House, the windows of which were blocked up with rough timber and loopholed. Mr. Bidwell sent in his card. When he was admitted to an interview he was apparently so alarmed as to be unable to speak. Sir Francis Bond Head, holding Mr. Bidwell's letters in his hand, pointed with them towards the window, saying: "Well, Mr. Bidwell, you see the state to which you have brought us!" "He made no reply," writes the ex-Lieutenant Governor, "and as it was impossible to help pitying the abject, fallen position in which he stood, I very calmly pointed out to him the impropriety of the course he had pursued, and then observing to him, what he knew well enough, that if I were to open his letters his life would probably be in my hands, I reminded him of the mercy as well as the power of the British Crown; and I ended by telling him that, as its humble representative, I would restore to him his letters unopened, if he would give me, in writing, a promise that he would leave the Queen's dominions forever. * * * He retired to the waiting-room, wrote out the promise I had dictated, and returning with it, I received it with one hand, and with the other, according to my promise, I delivered to him the whole of his letters unopened. The sentence which Mr. Bidwell passed upon himself he faithfully executed."—*The Emigrant.*

came to the knowledge of Dr. Baldwin; and theré were others in the background who were quietly forwarding their wishes for its success, as Mr. Bidwell appears to have been.

Previous to the day fixed for the outbreak in Upper Canada, the clash of arms had been heard in the Lower Province. On the 5th December, Lord Gosford proclaimed martial law, and offered rewards for the apprehension of the patriot leaders.* A detachment of twenty cavalry was sent from Montreal to St. Johns to arrest Dr. Davignon and Mr. Demaray, two prominent individuals, who had attended a great meeting of the six counties, at which seditious language was alleged to have been used. The prisoners were ironed, and then seated upon the bare boards of a wagon, confined in a most painful posture. Instead of being taken directly to Montreal by the railroad, it was resolved to take them, in the condition of felons, a distance of thirty-six miles, round Chambly and Longueuil, as if for the purpose of striking terror into the neighboring population. When the cavalcade had come near the borders of the St. Lawrence, it was met by a small party of Canadians who put the troops to flight and rescued the prisoners.

Dr. Nelson, who lived at St. Denis, and besides following his practice, carried on a brewery and distil-

* The following are the men and the figures:—"Four thousand dollars for Louis Joseph Papineau; two thousand dollars each, for Dr. Wolfred Nelson, Thos. Storrow Brown, Edmund Bailey O'Callaghan, Joseph T. Drolet, Jean J. Girouard, William H. Scott, Edward E. Rodier, Amury Girod, Jean O'Chenier; and four hundred dollars each for Pierre Paul Demaray, Joseph Francois Davignon, Julien Gagnon, Pierre Amiot, Louis Perrault, Dr. Alphonso Gauvin, Louis Gauthier, Rodolph Desrivieres."

lery, hearing of the movement for the arrest of himself and the other leaders, prepared for resistance.
From Lieutenant Weir, who was one of Col. Gore's
messengers, who appeared at St. Denis in plain
clothes, and was arrested when his mission became
known, the first intelligence of the number of troops
being sent on is said to have been learned. Five companies of troops, with one field piece, and a detachment
of Montreal Cavalry, under command of Col. Gore,
arrived at St. Denis, on the morning of the 23d of
November. The battle commenced about nine o'clock,
and lasted till nearly four in the afternoon; being
carried on with great bravery on both sides. From a
large stone store, four stories high, some of the men,
under the intrepid Dr. Nelson, kept up a galling fire
on the troops; till the latter, fatigued by a twelve
hours' march through deep mud before the battle commenced, their ammunition nearly exhausted, and
seeing that the patriots were being largely reinforced,
gave way. They left behind one cannon, some muskets, and five wounded. Captain Markham was carried away wounded by several shots. The loss of the
patriots was thirteen; that of the British troops much
larger.* In this encounter, Dr. Nelson was completely successful; but he did not find himself in a
position to sustain a prolonged contest.†

---

* Dr. Nelson, in an account which he has given of the affair, says:
"It could never be accurately ascertained what the loss of the besiegers was;
but it must have been considerable." One patriot account places it at fifty,
another at one hundred and twelve; but the latter figure must be an exaggeration.

† If reliance can be placed in the following extract from a manuscript letter
in my possession, written by one of the insurgents, the parish priest of St.'

Shortly after Col. Gore was ordered to return to St.
Denis; and on the 2nd of December, he marched from
Sorel with eight companies and three field pieces; but
the few remaining insurgents had abandoned the place
the night before his arrival. Dr. Nelson, as well as
Papineau, Brown, and others, escaped to the United
States. The property of Dr. Nelson was destroyed,
with the fortified house and defences.

At St. Charles, the insurgents, under Mr. T. S.
Brown, suffered a reverse. On the 25th of November,
five companies of the Royals, two companies of the
66th, with two pieces of artillery, and a small cavalry
force, under Col. Wetherall, marched on the town.
The whole force was between three hundred and four
hundred men. The house of M. Debartzch, built in
the substantial manner of an old French château, had
been taken possession of by the insurgents, and the
walls were pierced for the use of guns. Several acres
of ground were enclosed by barricades, in the form
of a parallelogram, between the Richlieu river and
the foot of a hill behind the house. This barricade
was formed by the trunks of trees banked up with
earth. The night before the battle, Brown sent a

Denis wielded the thunders of the Church with more effect than Col. Gore
had used his soldiers: "Wetherall qui voyait qu'il n'avait pas a faire à des
enfants, envoya chercher le curé de St. Denis et lui dit d'écrire aux habitans
de St. Denis que, s'ils ne se rendoient pas, il les vo[u]erait aux tormens de l'enfer,
et qu'il leur refuserait la sepulcre. * * * Le plan formait par le Col. Anglais
reussit à merveille, et sur cinq cents hommes que commandait Nelson le dimanche
au soir, il ne s'en trouve plus que cinquante lundi au matin qui ont pu resister
au menaces de leur curé." Col. Gore, in his dispatch of the 7th of February,
describing the result of his march upon St. Charles, says: "I was accompanied by Mons. Crenier, the parish priest, who gave me every information in
his power." At St. Hyacinthe the priest performed a like friendly office; in
fact, the priests did more than the troops to put down the rebellion.

number of the men from the camp to ascertain whether the troops were approaching; very few of them returned; and when the battle came on, he had only a handful of men, wretchedly armed, and in every way very ill prepared to encounter British troops. They had nothing but fowling pieces, and only about one hundred and fifty of these; many of them sadly out of repair. The real leaders to whom the people looked up were absent; and the insurgents had not much faith in "General" Brown's military skill. He had lost an eye in the affray of the 6th of November, at Montreal; and as the troops were approaching, he was thrown from his horse on the frozen ground and severely injured. When they arrived within range, he was outside the camp, having been to the village to beat up reinforcements there. When the firing was commenced by the troops, he did not return to the camp; and at the end of little more than an hour, he was on his way to St. Denis, and those within the stockade, at the commencement, who were not killed, were on the retreat or were taken prisoners. The barricades were stormed and carried; and every building within the enclosure was burnt, except the house of M. Debartzch. "The slaughter on the side of the rebels," writes Col. Wetherall, "was great." "I counted," he adds, "fifty-six bodies, and many more were killed in the building and the bodies burnt." He was much censured for what was deemed unnecessary slaughter.

This reverse was destined to have a discouraging effect upon the insurgents, in Upper Canada, where the work of final organization had commenced. Military leaders had to be chosen, and each assigned his post of duty. A tour of the neighboring country had to be made; and this duty fell to Mr. Mackenzie. On the evening of the 24th of November—less than twenty-four hours before the defeat at St. Charles—he left Dr. Rolph's house, on this mission. Just before starting, he mentioned to one or two persons who had not been parties to the plan of rising, what was going to take place; but he was very careful not to communi-cate the intelligence to any one on whose secrecy he felt he could not rely. Except in a single instance, no notices were sent beyond the limits of the Metro-politan county of York. A little after dark, the first night, Mr. Mackenzie, and a printer whom he had taken with him to strike off a revolutionary placard, arrived at a farmer's house about six miles from To-ronto, on the east side of Yonge Street. Some cases of type and a card press, with reams of variously colored paper, were taken for the use of the printer. Next morning an appeal to freemen to rise and strike for liberty was begun to be committed to type.* When it was ready for distribution, the printer set about its circulation. While engaged in distributing the papers, he stumbled upon a crowd of people at an auction, near Hog's Hollow, some six or seven miles north of the city, on Yonge Street. The Tories became in-censed at reading the revolutionary document; and as one of them, in his rage, was about to destroy the papers, the printer, who had never been told of the intended rising, threatened him with speedy retribu-tion from the patriots, if he did not desist; adding, to

* See Appendix F.

give force to his menace, that they were already on the road. The printer must have guessed at the object of the document he had printed; and having partaken somewhat too freely of liquor, appeared to have divulged a secret with which he had never been entrusted. Some fighting occurred between the two parties of whom the auction crowd proved to be composed. On his return to the house where he had left his types and press, the printer found the owner in a great state of alarm. The suspicious implements were hurried out of the house; and both types and press were thrown to the bottom of a well, whence the press was never recovered.

Meanwhile, Mr. Mackenzie visited Lloydtown, Stouffville, Newmarket, and other places in the North. His business was to make the necessary preparations for carrying out the plans agreed upon. Having no knowledge of military operations, he refused to assume a position of command for which he was by experience entirely unfitted. This determination he announced at Lloydtown, several days previous to the intended march upon Toronto. Samuel Lount and Anthony Anderson were then named to commands. Mr. Mackenzie deemed it essential to the success of the movement that it should be directed by persons of military skill and experience. He wrote to Van Egmond, who had been a colonel under Napoleon the Great, to be at Montgomery's Hotel, on the evening of the 7th, to lead the forces into the city,* and he

* Van Egmond was a native of Holland and, as a colonel in Napoleon's army, had seen much service. He also held an English colonelcy. He owned

. placed much reliance upon him and other veterans whose services he deemed it of the utmost importance to secure.

On the night of the 3d of December, Mr. Mackenzie, who had now been nine days in the country organizing the movement, arrived at the house of Mr. Gibson, some three miles from the city. He there learnt with dismay that, in his absence, Dr. Rolph had changed the day for making a descent upon Toronto, from Thursday to Monday.* Various reasons have been assigned for this change. There was a rumor that a warrant was out for the arrest of Mr. Mackenzie for high treason—which was true—and that cannon were being mounted in the park surrounding the Government House, which was false. The publication of certain militia orders is said to have been regarded as proof that the Government was on

---

thirteen thousand acres of land in the western part of the country; and entered the service of the rebels for patriotic rather than military motives.

* Silas Fletcher, who was a prominent actor in the rebellion, wrote to Mr. Mackenzie, from Fredonia, N. Y., July 29, 1840:—" On the Saturday afternoon previous to the outbreak back of Toronto, between three and five, I called to see Dr. Rolph at his house on King [Lot] Street, and asked him, as he was the Executive, whether any alteration was to be made or ordered by him as to the time of rising. He said that, as those who had the direction of the affair had, with his consent, fixed the day for Thursday, the 7th of December, at Montgomery's as a place of rendezvous, he would make no change or alteration whatever; you had left the city previously, to carry into effect a general agreement to rise on the 7th, on Thursday, and had informed me that you were on your way to Stouffville, to give and send round the circulars agreed on, so that all might come properly at the time settled upon. Dr. Rolph's exact words to me were; 'No, by no means! I shall expect every man to be active and vigilant, so as to be able to get up the expedition, and come in on the 7th and take the city.' On the same afternoon, (Saturday, the 2d,) I returned to Newmarket, and met with Thomas Lloyd and other friends on Sunday, who told me that Dr. Rolph had sent William Edmondstone, on

the alert.* The Lieutenant Governor, it was said, had a letter from the country disclosing all the plans of the patriots; and that the Council, concluding at last that there was real danger, had commenced a distribution of arms. The real truth was, as the verbal message sent to Lount stated, Dr. Rolph became alarmed, under the impression that the Government was giving out the arms at the City Hall, and arming men to fill the garrison and form companies to arrest the leaders of the expected revolt throughout, between then and the next Thursday; that they had already distributed one hundred stand of arms, and had become aware of the day fixed for the rising. These circumstances, the message added, rendered it necessary that Lount and his men should be in town on Monday night.† Regarding the change of day as a fatal error, Mackenzie despatched one of Gibson's servants with a message to Lount, who resided near Holland Landing, some thirty-five miles from Toronto, not to come till the Thursday, at first agreed upon. But it was too late. The messenger returned on Monday afternoon with the reply of Lount, that the

the same evening I had seen him, with orders to raise a sufficient number of men to come down and take the city within the next 48 hours—this is by the Monday night.

* There was something in this, as the following resolution passed at a meeting held at Pickering, on the 2nd of November, shows; but there is no reason to suppose that it influenced Dr. Rolph's decision:

"*Resolved*, That there being a report in circulation that the local militia are to be called out to Toronto, to guard the garrison, we are resolved not to turn out, except unanimously, and that we will all stand together to a man, and that, if we are compelled to fight, we will fight against the enemies of our country and not against its friends."

† Both Mr. Lount and Mrs. Lount told Mr. Mackenzie that this was the substance of the verbal message.

intended rising was publicly known all through the
North; that the men had been ordered to march, and
were already on the road. The rude pike formed the
weapons of the majority; a few had rifles; there were
no muskets.

Much annoyed at the unexpected change in the programme, Mackenzie, with the natural intrepidity of
his character, resolved to make the best of it. When
Lount arrived, in the evening, he brought only about
eighty or ninety men, exhausted with a march of between thirty and forty miles through deep mud, and
dispirited by the news of the reverse in Lower Canada. Though Dr. Rolph had met Mackenzie that
morning at Mr. Price's house, on Yonge Street, a
couple of miles or so from Toronto, they had no intelligence of the state of the town after ten o'clock.
Rolph had returned, and no messenger came to bring
Mackenzie and his friends any news of what was going
on in the city. Regarding it as all important that
communication with the city should be cut off, for the
purpose of preventing any intelligence being sent to
the Government, Mackenzie advised the placing of a
guard upon the road; and that the handful of jaded
men who had arrived, should summon all their powers
of endurance, and march on the city that night. No
one seconded his proposal. Lount, Lloyd, and Gibson
all protested against what they regarded as a rash
enterprise. They deemed it indispensable to wait till
the condition of the city could be ascertained, or till
they were sufficiently reinforced to reduce the hazard
of venture, in which all concerned carried their lives
in their hands, to reasonable limits.

'Thus the golden opportunity was lost. Delay was defeat. At this time the number of men under Lount, reinforced as they would have been in the city, would have been quite sufficient to effect the intended revolution; since the Government was literally asleep, and it was not embarrassed by a superfluity of true friends.

Failing in this proposal, Mr. Mackenzie next offered to make one of four who should go to the city, ascertain the state of matters there, whether an attack would be likely to be attended with success, spur their friends into activity, with a view to an attack the next evening, and bring Drs. Rolph and Morrison back with them. Captain Anderson, Shepard, and Smith, volunteered to join him. They started between eight and nine o'clock. Before they had proceeded far they met Mr. John Powell, with Mr. Archibald Macdonald mounted, acting as a sort of patrol. Mackenzie pulled up, and with a double-barrelled pistol in his hand, briefly informed them of the rising; and adding that, as it was necessary to prevent intelligence of it reaching the Government, they must surrender themselves prisoners, and in that character go to Montgomery's hotel, where they would be well treated. Any arms they might have upon their persons, they must surrender. They replied that they had none; and when he seemed sceptical as to the correctness of the reply, they repeated it. Mackenzie then said: "Well, gentlemen, as you are my townsmen and men of honor, I should be ashamed to show that I question your word by ordering you to be searched."

Placing the two prisoners in charge of Anderson and Shepard, he then continued his course, with his remaining comrade, towards the city. Before they had got far, Powell, who had returned, rode past them. While he was passing, Mackenzie demanded to know what was the object of his return, and told him, at his peril, not to proceed. Regardless of this warning, the Government messenger kept on. Mackenzie fired at him over his horse's head, but missed his mark. Powell now pulled up; and coming alongside Mackenzie placed the muzzle of a pistol close to his antagonist's breast. A flash in the pan saved the life of the insurgent chief.

Macdonald now also came up on his return. He seemed much frightened; and being unable to give any satisfactory explanation was sent back, a second time, by Mackenzie. In the meantime, Powell escaped. He dismounted, and finding himself pursued, hid behind a log for a while; and then by a devious course proceeded to Toronto. He at once proceeded to Government House, and aroused from his slumbers the Lieutenant Governor, who had gone to bed with a sick headache. His Excellency placed his family on board a steamer in the bay—the winter being unusually mild, there was no ice to impede navigation— in company with that of Chief Justice Robinson, ready to leave the city if the rebels should capture it. Mackenzie, having sent his last remaining companion back with Macdonald to Montgomery's hotel, now found himself alone. A warrant had for some time been out for his arrest, on a charge of high treason, and the Government, informed of the presence of the men at Montgomery's, was already astir. It would have been madness for him to proceed, companionless to the city, into the very jaws of the lion.

He turned his horse's head and set out for Montgomery's. Before he had proceeded far he found, lying upon the road, the dead body of Anderson, who had fallen a victim to Powell's treachery. Life was entirely extinct. Anderson and Shepard, as already stated, were escorting Powell and Macdonald as prisoners to the guard-room of the patriots at Montgomery's Hotel. Powell, who, on being captured, had twice protested that he was unarmed, slackened the pace of his horse sufficiently to get behind his victim, when he shot him with a pistol through the back of the neck. Death was instantaneous. Shepard's horse stumbled at the moment, and Powell was enabled to escape. As there was now only one guard to two prisoners, he could not have hoped to prevent their escape. Macdonald followed his associate.

On which side life had first been taken it would be difficult to determine; for, when Mackenzie got back to Montgomery's Hotel, he found that Col. Moodie, inflamed by liquor, had, in trying to force his way past the guard at the hotel, at whom he fired a pistol, been shot by a rifle. The guards who returned the fire missed their aim; when one of the men who was standing on the steps, in front of the hotel, levelled his rifle at Col. Moodie, of whom the light of the moon gave him a clear view, and fired the fatal shot. His name I have recently learned, from one to whom he related the circumstance, was Ryan. He sometimes went by the name of Wallace. After the retreat of the rebels he fled northward and took refuge in the woods, on the shores of Lake Huron, where, apart from any human being, he dragged out a wretched existence during the whole of the winter, gnawing roots and herbs. In the spring, when he had been reduced to a skeleton, he fell in with a vessel going to the States, and thus made good his escape. He never returned to Canada. Mackenzie's calumniators have sometimes stated that he shot Col. Moodie, though it was notorious that he was a mile distant at the time the event took place.* But as this calumny

---

* Captain Stewart, R. N., who accompanied Col. Moodie, gives the following account of the death of his companion:—"About 4 P. M., a large body of men came along Yonge Street. The magistrates in the neighborhood met at Col. Moodie's house. Col. Moodie wrote to His Excellency the Lieutenant Governor, and Mr. Drew volunteered to take the letter to Toronto. The magistrates separated to do the best they could. Shortly afterwards word was brought that Mr. Drew was taken prisoner by the rebels. Upon this Col. Moodie determined to go to Toronto himself, against the prayers of his wife and family. I (Capt. Stewart) insisted on going with him, as did also Captain Bridgeford. On the road we were joined by Mr. Prime Lawrence, Mr. G. Read, and Mr. Brooks. Col. Moodie suggested that we should arrange ourselves in close order, three abreast—Col. Moodie, myself, and the stranger in front. Col. Moodie said, 'If they (the rebels) have a guard, we must gallop through them, whatever be the result.' On nearing Montgomery's Tavern, we observed a guard across the road, armed with muskets, who desired us to stop or they would fire. We kept on steady right through them. I looked for our companions, and found only Col. Moodie by my side, who remarked, 'We are alone.' He put his hand on my arm and said, 'Never mind, push forward, all is right yet!' About one hundred and fifty men were then in front of Montgomery's door, and a voice called as we were passing, 'Guards, fire!' We passed Montgomery's, and about one hundred yards from it was found a strong guard posted in close order. We reached them, when pikes and bayonets were presented to our horses' breasts. Col. Moodie said, 'Who are you—who dare stop me on the Queen's highway?' The reply was, 'You will know that in time.' Col. Moodie then fired his pistol, and, at the same moment, three guns were discharged at us. Col. Moodie said, 'I am shot! I am a dead man!' Here Brooks says he desired them to charge. We were then taken into Montgomery's Tavern. Shortly afterwards Mackenzie came into the room and asked for me."

has long since ceased to be repeated. I do not add the statements of several eye-witnesses, in my possession, in refutation. Col. Moodie died in about a couple of hours after he was shot.

It has been usual to speak of Col. Moodie's death as a murder, as if every death occurring in an insurrection could by any possibility come within this category. The circumstances connected with the death of Anderson were more discreditable than those connected with the death of Col. Moodie: because in the first place there was treachery; in the latter there was not.

Lount's men were a good deal dispirited by the death of Anderson. And they had no particular reasons for being in good humor. Lingfoot, by whom Montgomery's hotel was kept, had no provisions to offer them; and none could be procured that night. The handful of countrymen, exhausted by their long march, with no man of military experience to excite their confidence, had to sup on bad whiskey, and recline upon the floor, where many from sheer fatigue fell sound asleep. The rest were still uneasy as to the state of things in the city. The bells had been set a ringing; and they were uncertain as to the rumors about the arrival of steamboats full of Orangemen and other loyalists. They had expected to learn the exact state and condition of the city from their friends there. Mackenzie with three companions, as we have seen, had failed to reach the city, where the wished-for in-

---

Col. Moodie's foolhardiness is admitted even by Sir Francis Bond Head. "He determined," says the ex-Lieutenant Governor, in *The Emigrant*, "that— coûte qui coûte—he would ride through them and give me information that they were marching on Toronto."

telligence might have been obtained. Other messengers were sent, but none returned. They were made prisoners.

It is probable that Dr. Morrison attempted to take to them the information they so much needed; for it is pretty certain that he passed the toll-gate on his way out.* The sight of Captain Bridgeford in all probability compelled him to go back.

By midnight, the numbers were increased; and before morning, Mackenzie, with his natural impetuosity of disposition, again proposed to march on the city; but he was again overruled. And indeed, the chance of success was already much diminished; because the Government had now had several hours for preparation. To Mr. Mackenzie's proposal it was objected that nothing was known of the state of the garrison. The city bells had sounded an ominous alarm. The forces expected from the west had not

---

* The fact, if such it be, was known to but very few; and even Mackenzie was ignorant of it, for a long time after. He was firmly of opinion that Dr. Morrison never crossed his threshold to go towards the rebel camp. There is a curious circumstance connected with the Doctor's Yonge Street walk that night with Captain Bridgeford, and the latter made no secret of the fact. When relating the circumstance one day to an acquaintance, he was asked how it was possible for him to distinguish Dr. Morrison from Dr. Rolph, in the dark; the two men were so nearly of the same size. A few nights afterwards Captain Bridgeford and his friend were sipping tea together; when a female, in the course of the conversation that ensued, asked Captain Bridgeford the same question about his power of identifying a person who was so like another; another person present remarked, by preconcert, that this had only been stated as an impression, not a positive fact. In this way Captain Bridgeford was confused; and a confession was extracted from him that he only spoke of an impression. That female repeated what Captain Bridgeford had said that night on the trial of the doctor for high treason. He did not owe his acquittal entirely to this circumstance, however; for an *alibi* was set up and was regarded as being proved.

arrived; and the Executive in the city, by whom the premature rising had been ordered, had sent no communication.

Next day, the relative force of the two parties was such that the patriots might, if properly armed, have obtained certain conquest. They had between seven and eight hundred men; but many of them were unarmed. The rest had rifles, fowling-pieces, and pikes. Many of those who were unarmed, returned almost as soon as they discovered there were no weapons for their use. Provisions, including fresh and salt beef from a loyalist butcher, who lived up Yonge Street, about two miles above Montgomery's, were obtained for the men; for Lingfoot, the keeper of the tavern, though a Tory, was not disinclined to turn an honest penny by serving the rebels.* Sir Francis B. Head claims to have had three hundred supporters in the morning and five hundred in the evening;† but the statement has been disputed and is open to doubt. His fears may be judged by his holding parley with armed insurgents. On Tuesday he sent a flag of truce to the rebel camp, with a message asking what it was they wanted. There is no reason to doubt that this was a stratagem to gain time.‡ Mackenzie re-

---

* On the Thursday morning, the day of the retreat, Mackenzie paid Lingfoot's bill for victualling the whole of the men; and as they could not make change, he gave him two dollars too much, remarking that it might go towards the next bill.

† *Narrative*, p. 331.

‡ *The Upper Canada Herald* argued that: "If an attack had been made on Tuesday, the city must have fallen. The flag of truce was sent on Tuesday forenoon, in order to gain time in that threatening emergency, and the fact that after having beaten to arms all night the Government could only muster

plied: "Independence and a convention to arrange details." He added that the Lieutenant Governor's message must be sent in writing, and feeling time to be precious he said it must be forthcoming in one hour.

Whom had Sir Francis Bond Head selected as the medium of communication between himself and the rebels? This question touches on one of the most painful subjects I have to deal with in this work. Mr. Robert Baldwin could hardly have been entirely ignorant of what every one who read the newspapers of the day must have been informed; but he had neither part nor lot in the revolt. But Mackenzie himself was not deeper in the rebellion than Dr. Rolph; and his acceptance of the post of mediator between the men he had encouraged into insurrection, and the Go-

---

a force of about three hundred out of ten thousand shows its deplorable weakness."

It is a melancholy fact, that even in his grave official dispatches, Sir F. Head could not narrate the occurrences of this insurrection with any thing like accuracy. In a dispatch to Lord Glenelg, dated Toronto, December 19th, he says: "On *Wednesday* morning we were sufficiently strong to have ventured an attack, but being sensible of the strength of our position, being also aware how much depended upon the contest in which we were engaged, and feeling the greatest possible reluctance at the idea of entering upon a civil war, I dispatched two gentlemen [one of whom he had shortly before advised the Colonial office not to treat with ordinary courtesy, as he was a 'republican' agent] to the rebel leaders, to tell them that, before any conflict should take place, I parentally called upon them, as their Governor, to avoid the effusion of human blood." The truth is, it was *Tuesday* and not Wednesday, when these gentlemen were despatched to the rebel camp; and the true reason was that the Lieutenant Governor feared an attack which he was not able to repel; for he admits, in the same dispatch, that on Tuesday morning he had only three hundred men. Fear, and not humanity was the real motive that induced him to treat with the rebels. That night, he confesses, in *The Emigrant*, "The sun set without our receiving succor or any intimation of its approach."

vernment against which they had been induced to rebel, is so extraordinary an act that it is almost impossible to account for it. The only possible explanation
lies in the difficulty of his position which arose from
his being asked to undertake this office.* Sheriff Jarvis, who had believed that an insurrection was approaching, long before any member of the Government could be induced to put the least faith in it, went
to Mr. J. H. Price—so the latter says—and appealed
to him, in the name of God, to give his assistance
"to stop the proceedings of those men who are going
to attack us." Mr. Price replied, with much reason,
that if he should go out it would be said that he went
to join the rebels. And he suggested: "Why not go
to Mr. Baldwin, Dr. Rolph, or Mr. Bidwell?" If
Rolph had persisted in refusing he would have lain
himself open to suspicion—as he did by a first refusal;
and if he had been arrested, the worst might have
happened. The Doctor's returning prudence may
have bid him go; and perhaps he thought he could
perform this mission without serious injury to his
friends in the field.† But the effect of his arrival

* Recorder Duggan, who was one of the two who first called upon Dr. Rolph
to ask him to accept this mission, tells me that the Doctor, in the first instance,
declined ; adding something to the effect that the constitution was suspended
and the powers of the Lieutenant Governor at an end. After they left the
house, Mr. Duggan remarked to Sheriff Jarvis, by whom he was accompanied,
that Dr. Rolph ought to be arrested ; as it was evident from his manner that
he was deep in the plot ; and that before twenty-four hours it would be easy
to find plenty of evidence against him. Mr. Jarvis said he should not like to
arrest him ; and the matter dropped.

† Samuel Lount, being examined before the Commission on Treason, Dec.
13, 1837, said : "When the flag of truce came up, Dr. Rolph addressed himself to me ; there were two other persons with it besides Dr. Rolph and Mr.
Baldwin. Dr. Rolph said he brought a message from his Excellency the Lieu-

with a flag of truce, about one o'clock, threw a damper
on the zeal of the men.   They fancied that when he

tenant Governor, to prevent the effusion of blood, or to that effect. At the
same time, *he gave me a wink to walk on one side*, when he requested me not to
heed the message, but to go on with our proceedings.   What he meant was
not to attend to the message.   Mackenzie observed to me that it was a verbal
message, and that it had better be submitted to writing.   I took the reply to
the Lieutenant Governor's message to be merely a put off.   * * *   I heard
all that was said by Dr. Rolph to Mr. Mackenzie, which is as above related."
Of this statement, Dr. Rolph, in 1852, induced the flag bearer, Hugh Carmichael, to sign a denial, in these terms: " During the going out and staying
on the ground, and returning to the city, as above stated, (all of which was
promptly done,) Dr. Rolph, Mr. Baldwin, and myself, being all on horseback,
kept in close phalanx, not a yard apart.   Neither of the persons mentioned
could have got off his horse, nor could he have winked to Mr. Lount and
walked aside and communicated with him, nor have said anything irrelevant
to the flag of truce, or against its good faith, as is untruly alleged, without my
knowledge."   There are yet three other witnesses besides Mackenzie; and as
it is not my business to accuse or excuse any body, but to get at the truth, their
testimony must be given.   Mr. Baldwin made a statement relating to the second visit to the rebels, when the answer of the Lieutenant Governor was
taken.   Carmichael alleges that till the flag of truce was at an end, Dr. Rolph
could not have done what was attributed to him by Lount, whose statement
was corroborated, in one way or another, by three or four persons.   Carmichael's statement, it will be seen, does not go to the extent of saying that, after
the Lieutenant Governor's reply was delivered and the flag of truce declared
at an end, Dr. Rolph did not tell Lount to take his men into the city.   It leaves
that question untouched.   Mr. Baldwin's evidence, taken in connection with
Carmichael's on this point, is very important.   " On the return of the Doctor
and myself, the second time," he says, " with the Lieutenant Governor's reply
that he would not give any thing in writing, we found the insurgents at the
first toll-gate, and turned aside to the west of Yonge Street, where we delivered
this answer; after which Dr. Rolph requested me to wait for him.   *I did wait
some time, during which he was out of my sight and hearing.*   I was then directed
to ride westerly; this occupied the time while I was riding at a common walk
from Yonge Street to the College Avenue, probably three-eighths of a mile.
The direction to ride westerly, as I then supposed, was for the purpose of the
flag being carried to the city by way of the College Avenue.   Shortly after
reaching the avenue, however, I was joined by Dr. Rolph, and we returned
together by way of Yonge Street.   I have no reason to know what communication took place between Dr. Rolph and the insurgents when he was
out of my sight and hearing."—*Appendix, Assembly's Journals*, 1837–8, p. 406.

appeared in the service of the Lieutenant Governor, the patriot cause must be desperate. Mackenzie did not venture to tell the real state of the case to more than five or six persons; for if it had been publicly announced, the fact might have reached town and occasioned the Doctor's arrest. The intelligence that Bidwell had been asked to accept the mission undertaken by Rolph created the false impression that they were both opposed to Mackenzie's movement. Lount, to whom he addressed himself, says Dr. Rolph secretly advised him to pay no attention to the message, but to proceed. Mackenzie told Lount this advice must be acted upon; and the order to proceed was given.

Lount was advised by Mackenzie to march his men into the city, without loss of time, and take up a position near Osgood Hall, on Queen Street. Mackenzie then rode westward to the larger body of insurgents, near Col. Baldwin's residence, and ordered an instant

Wm. Alves, who was present, says that on the second visit Dr. Rolph advised the rebels to go into the city. P. C. H. Brotherton, another of the insurgents, made oath to the same effect on the 12th December, before Vice Chancellor Jameson; stating that Dr. Rolph had told him, on the 8th, that "Mackenzie had acted unaccountably in not coming into the town; and that he expected him in half an hour after he returned with the flag." These statements are sufficiently conclusive as to the general fact; the only question that is not settled is whether it was on the first or second visit that Dr. Rolph told the insurgents to go into the city. Did he give this advice on the occasion of both visits? Mackenzie and Lount say the order to go into the city was given on the first visit. Against his positive evidence, Dr. Rolph produces his own denial and a statement from the flag bearer, who attempts to prove a negative from the alleged impossibility of the occurrence taking place. It must be explained that the statement signed by Carmichael was prepared in Quebec, where it was dated, and taken to Toronto for signature. Besides this, Carmichael has not been very consistent in his statements of the affair, having told a very different story at other times. The weight of the evidence is therefore entirely in favor of the correctness of Lount's statement.

march on the city. When they reached the upper end of the College Avenue, a second flag of truce arrived. The answer brought by Mr. Baldwin and Dr. Rolph was that the Lieutenant Governor refused to comply with the demands of the insurgents.

The truce being at an end, Dr. Rolph secretly advised the insurgents to wait till six o'clock, and then enter the city under cover of night. Reinforcements to the number of six hundred were expected in the city ; and they were to be ready to join the forces from the country, as soon as the latter arrived. Accordingly at a quarter to six, the whole of the insurgent forces were at the toll bar, on Yonge Street, about a mile from the principal street of the city, on which the Government House, west of the line of Yonge Street, was situated. Mackenzie harangued the men; attempting to inspire them with courage by representing that there would be no difficulty in taking the city. The Government, he said, was so friendless that it had only been able to muster a hundred and fifty defenders, including the college boys; and that the Lieutenant Governor's family had been put on a steamer ready to take flight. The actual force claimed by Sir F. B. Head, on Tuesday night, was "about five hundred."

The patriot forces were a half armed mob, without discipline, headed by civilians, and having no confidence in themselves or their military leaders. Lount's men, who were armed with rifles, were in front; the pikemen came next, and in the rear was a number of useless men having no other weapons than sticks and cudgels. Captain Duggan, of the volunteer artillery,

another officer, and the sheriff's horse fell into the
hands of the insurgents, when they were within about
half a mile of the city. At this point they were fired
upon by an advanced guard of loyalists, concealed
behind a fence, and whose numbers—of which the insurgents could have no correct idea—have been variously stated at from fifteen to thirty; and shots
were exchanged. After firing once, the loyalists, under
Sheriff Jarvis, started back at full speed towards the
city. The front rank of Lount's men, instead of stepping aside after firing to let those behind fire, fell
down on their faces. Those in the rear, fancying that
the front rank had been cut down by the muskets of
the small force who had taken a random shot at them,
being without arms, were panic stricken; and in a short
time nearly the whole force was on the retreat. Many
of the Lloydtown pikemen, raised the cry, "We shall
all be killed," threw down their rude weapons, and
fled in great precipitation. Mackenzie, who had been
near the front, and in more danger from the rifles
behind than the musketry of the loyalists, stepped to
the side of the road and ordered the men to cease
firing; being of opinion that one of the insurgents,
who had been shot, fell from a rifle bullet of an un-
skillful comrade. The impetuous and disorderly flight
had, in a short time, taken all but about a score above
the toll gate. The mortification of Mackenzie may be
imagined. Hoping to rally the men, he sent Alves
back to explain to them that the danger was imaginary; and putting spurs to his horse he followed at
a brisk pace immediately after, for the same purpose.
When they came to a halt, he implored them to re-

62

turn. The steamers, he said, had been sent off to bring the Orangemen from the other districts; that whatever defenders the Government had in the city were in a state of desperate alarm; that the success which could now be easily achieved, might on the morrow be out of their reach; for the moment the timidity of the patriots became known, the Government would gain new adherents; and that if they did not return, the opportunity for the deliverance of the country would be lost. In this strain, he addressed successive groups. He coaxed and threatened.* He would go in front with any dozen who would accompany him. Relying upon the succor they would meet in the city, he offered to go on, if only forty men would go with him. Two or three volunteers presented themselves; but the general answer was that, though they would go in daylight, they would not advance in the dark.

The majority lost no time in returning to their homes. And although some two hundred additional

---

* Mr. P. H. Watson, writing from personal knowledge, gives the following account of this affair, in a letter dated Rochester, N. Y., November 12, 1839: "When Mr. Mackenzie found (after the retreat on Tuesday night) that most of the men were unwilling to enter the city that night, and perceived the disastrous consequences that must inevitably result from delay, to encourage them and show that he himself was not lacking in the quality so essential to success, namely, physical courage, and with a want of which he had just been charging them (in very provoking and unmeasured terms of censure), he proposed to 'go forthwith into the city if twenty men would volunteer to follow him;' but he could not get out of the whole force even such a small number to go with him.

"Mr. Stiles, one of Lount's friends from the North, was so provoked at Mackenzie for making use of such strong language of censure, when he was haranguing them after the retreat, and vainly endeavoring to make them return, that he elevated his gun to shoot him (Mackenzie), and was only prevented from doing so by the interference of four or five of Mr. Mackenzie's friends who were standing by and observed him."

forces arrived during the night, the whole number, on the Wednesday, had dwindled down to about five hundred and fifty. One cause of the panic, on Tuesday night, arose from the alarming stories told by some persons who had joined them from Toronto, of the preparations in the city; how the Tories, protected by feather-beds and mattresses, would fire from the windows of the houses and make terrible slaughter of the patriots.

Dr. Horne's house, close to Yonge Street, was the rendezvous of spies. Miss De Grassi had gone thence past the rebel camp and returned with the information she gathered from observation. Horne himself had berated the Lieutenant Governor for treating with armed rebels; and insisted that they were not in sufficient force to give any reasonable ground of alarm. His house was therefore burnt by the rebels, as those of Montgomery and Gibson were subsequently by the loyalists.* In Horne's house a search was made for

---

* Montgomery was not a party to the conspiracy for effecting a revolution. He had no foreknowledge of the outbreak. Only a few days before he had vacated his tavern, which had been rented to Lingfoot, with whom he was boarding for a month, till he could move to a private house in the neighborhood. If he had been a party to the conspiracy, he was not the man to have left his house, which was to be the rebel rendezvous, at that critical moment, in the hands of a Tory, and without any provisions for the men.

It was sworn to on Montgomery's trial that he told the unarmed men to go get arms; but a person of the name of Reed, then dying in the hospital, whose evidence he was refused a commission to obtain, was prepared to swear that the order in question was given by another person. Much stress was laid on the fact, at the trial, that Montgomery had, at the request of the butcher's boy, put down on a piece of paper a memorandum of the quantity of meat furnished to Lingfoot; the boy being apprehensive that the chalk figures would rub out. But this is all he had to do with the rebellion in Canada.

"In burning that [Horne's] house, we followed the distinct and explicit

papers that might show what information was being asked by the Government or sent to it; and the fire was caused by the upsetting of the stove. Nothing whatever was taken out of the house. It is not permissible to judge of acts done during civil war—recognized by the Government sending flags of truce to the insurgents—as if they were committed in a time of peace. What would be dastardly arson, in the latter case, might be justifiable in the former.

That night Dr. Rolph sent a messenger to Montgomery's to inquire of Mackenzie the cause of the retreat. The answer was sent back in writing, and next morning, despairing, it would seem, of all hope of success, he set out for the United States, as a place of refuge. He was soon to be followed by a large number of others.

Wednesday opened gloomily upon the prospects of the insurgents. Rolph left for the States. Morrison remained in his house. Mackenzie called the men together and explained to them the reason for the strong censures he had used on the retreat the previous evening. If they had taken his advice and been ready to follow his example, Toronto would have been theirs. The enemy had, in the meantime, been largely reinforced. They were well officered; well armed, and had command of the steamers for bringing up further reinforcements. If the patriots were to succeed it was essential that they should have confidence in themselves. They were greatly in want of arms; the four thousand muskets and bayonets they had in-

orders of Dr. Rolph, our Executive, which were to do so before we set off for the city."—*Account of the Rebellion*, by Mackenzie, New York, 1838.

tended to seize were now ready to be turned against them.

Mackenzie, Lount, Alves, and several others set off on horseback to collect arms to intercept the western mail, which would convey intelligence which it was desirable should not be communicated to the friends of the Government, and to make prisoners of persons who might be carrying information for the Government to the disadvantage of the insurgents. The mail-stage, coming into Dundas Street, the principal western entrance into Toronto, was captured, and with the driver, mails, and several prisoners was taken to the rebel camp. Among the letters were some addressed by the President of the Executive Council to persons in the country, and containing information that the Government expected soon to be able to make an attack at Montgomery's. This exploit, which has sometimes been described as a vulgar mail robbery, was a natural incident of insurrection. It was a means of depriving the friends of the Government, against whom the rebels were in arms, of information that might have a great effect on the result of the contest. Admit the right of insurrection, and the detention of the mails follows as a matter of course. Mackenzie, not knowing that Rolph had fled, wrote to him to send the patriots timely notice of the intended attack; but of course he got no answer. The messenger never returned. A man on horseback told them that the Government intended to make the attack on Thursday, and the information proved correct.

Thursday found division in the patriot camp. Gibson objected to Mackenzie's plans, though they were

sanctioned by Col. Van Egmond, who, true to the original understanding, had just arrived. Gibson's objections led to a council of war. Those who objected to
Mr. Mackenzie's plan proposed no substitute. A new
election of officers took place. This caused great delay.
Gibson was unanimously elected Captain of one of the
companies, but he left his post the moment the enemy
appeared in sight.* In this respect he was neither
better nor worse than about one half of the patriot
force. The plan suggested by Van Egmond, and
adopted by Mackenzie, was to try to prevent an attack
on Montgomery's till night, in the hope that by that
time large reinforcements might arrive. And there
was some reason in this, as this was the day originally
fixed for the general rising, and a notification of the
alteration had been sent only to Lount's Division.
One man had a force of five hundred and fifty ready
to bring down, and many others who were on the way,
when they found it was all up with the patriots, to save
themselves, pretended they had come down to assist
the Government to quell the insurrection. A militia
colonel was to contribute a couple of fat oxen to the rebel cause. Another colonel had made the patriots a
present of a gun, a sword, and some ammunition.
Thousands whom prudence or fear kept aloof from
the movement wished it success. Under these circumstances, the only hope of the patriots seemed to lay in
preventing an attack till night. In order to accomplish this the city must be alarmed. Sixty men, forty
of them armed with rifles, were selected to go to the
Don Bridge, which formed the eastern connection with
the city, and destroy it. By setting this bridge and

* William Alves's Letter to Mr. Rudd, N. Y.

the adjoining house on fire it was thought the loyalist force might be drawn off in that direction and their plan of attack broken up. The party sent eastward was to intercept the Montreal mails. The rest of the men who had arms " were to take the direction of the city, and be ready to remove either to the right or the left, or to retreat to a strong position as prudence might dictate."

A party was sent eastward, as agreed upon; the bridge and house were fired and partly burnt; and the mails intercepted. But the delay of two hours occasioned by the council of war proved fatal. Three steamers had, in the meantime, been bringing reinforcements to the alarmed Governor.

Toronto contained twelve thousand inhabitants, and if the Government had not been odious to the great majority of the people, it ought to have been able to raise force enough to beat back four hundred rebels; for to this number the patriot army had been reduced. But neither Toronto nor the neighboring country furnished the requisite force, and Sir Francis Bond Head had awaited in trembling anxiety the arrival of forces from other parts of the Province.* Having, at length,

---

* On Tuesday, Sir Francis Bond Head says, "The sun set without our receiving any succor or any intimation of its approach."—*Emigrant*. This statement is entirely at variance with his public dispatch of the 19th December, in which he says: "By the following morning (Tuesday) we mustered about three hundred men, and in the course of the day our number increased to about five hundred." The story in *The Emigrant* about his being in a helpless condition is the true one. He confesses to have been overjoyed at receiving relief, on Tuesday night, from a distance: "I was sitting," says he, "by a tallow candle light in the large hall, surrounded by my comrades, when we sud-

determined on an attack, Sir Francis Bond Head assembled the "overwhelming forces" at his command,
under the direction of Col. Fitzgibbon, Adjutant General of the Militia. The main body was headed by
Col. McNab, the right wing being commanded by Col.
S. Jarvis, the left by Col. William Chisholm, assisted
by Mr. Justice McLean. Major Cafrae, of the militia
artillery, had charge of two guns.* The order to
march was given about twelve o'clock, and at one
the loyalist and the patriot forces were in sight of one
another. When the sentinels at Montgomery's announced that the loyalists were within sight, with music and artillery, the patriots were still discussing their
plans. Preparation was at once made to give them
battle. Mackenzie, at first doubting the intelligence,
rode forward till he became convinced by a full view
of the enemy. When he returned, he asked the small
band of patriots whether they were ready to encounter a force greatly superior in numbers to themselves,
well armed, and provided with artillery. They replied
in the affirmative, and he ordered the men into a piece
of thin woods, on the west side of the road, where they

denly heard, in the direction of the lake shore, a distant cheer. In a short
time, two or three people, rushing in at the door, told us that 'a steamer full of
the men of Gore had just arrived!' and almost at the same moment I had the
pleasure of receiving this intelligence from their own leader. I have said that
my mind had been *tranquilly awaiting the solution of the great problem;* but my
philosophy was fictitious, for I certainly have never in my life felt more deeply
affected than I was when, *seeing my most ardent hopes suddenly realized,* I offered
my hand to Sir Allan McNab." Where were the Toronto people?

   * Sir Francis Bond Head, dispatch to Lord Glenelg, December 19, 1837.
In *The Emigrant* he says: "On the morning of the 7th, we had such *an overwhelming force* that there remained not the slightest reason for delay," in making the attack.

found a slight protection from the fire of the enemy they had to encounter. A portion of the men took a position in an open field, on the east side of the road.

> "They have met—that small band, resolved to be free,
> As the fierce winds of Heaven that course over the sea—
> They have met, in bright hope, with no presage of fear,
> Though the bugle and drum of the foemen they hear;
> Some seize the dread rifle, some wield the tall pike,
> For God and their country—for Freedom they strike,
> No proud ensign of glory bespeaks their renown,
> Yet the scorn of defiance now darkens their frown.
> See the foemen advancing, and now sounds afar
> The clang and the shout of disastrous war.
> Yes! onward they come like the mountain's wild flood,
> And the lion's dark talons are dappled in blood." *

The men in the Western copse had to sustain nearly the whole fire of the artillery from Toronto; "And never," says Mr. Mackenzie, "did men fight more courageously. In the face of a heavy fire of grape and canister, with broadside following broadside of musketry in steady and rapid succession, they stood their ground firmly, and killed and wounded a large number of the enemy, but were at length compelled to retreat."

> O God of my country! they turn now to fly—
> Hark! the Eagle of Liberty screams in the sky!
> Where, where are the thousands that morn should have found
> In battle array on that dew-covered ground?
> The few that were there, now wildly have flown,
> Did fear stay the others?†   *   *   *

* I quote this from *Mackenzie's Gazette*, to give the spirit of the proceeding as far as it can be gathered from the expressions of the actors in it. A very wide poetic license is here taken; for assuredly the lion could be in no danger from the force brought into action by the insurgents.

† *Mackenzie's Gazette.*

"They, the rebels," says Sir Francis Bond Head, "were principally armed

63

Some are of the opinion that the fighting lasted an hour; but there are different opinions on this point. Mackenzie remained on the scene of action till the last moment; and till the mounted loyalists were just closing upon him.. "So unwilling was Mackenzie to leave the field of battle," says an eye witness, "and so hot the chase after him, that he distanced the enemy's horsemen only thirty or forty yards, by his superior knowledge of the country, and reached Col. Lount and our friends on the retreat, just in time to save his neck."* Immediately £1,000 reward was offered for his apprehension.† This day was the turning point

with rifles, and for a short time, favored by buildings, stood their ground." There were no buildings except a few scattered on the side of the road, through one of which the loyalists drove some shots.

* William Alves' letter to the Editor of the New York *Reformer:* Mr. Mackenzie's conduct, on this occasion, has been subject to much misrepresentation—chiefly the result of political malice. It is therefore better that I should give the statement of persons who were present, and who were in a position to know the facts. In an unpublished letter, addressed to Mr. Mackenzie, and dated Watertown, N. Y., August 13, 1838, I find the following statement:—"We are very sorry to learn from your kind letter, that any person should charge you with cowardice, in any part of your proceedings in Canada; and we are all ready to bear evidence of your courage and patriotism on the occasion of the first outbreak in that country." Signed, Edward Kennedy, John Stewart, jr., Thomas Tracy, Thomas Shepard, William Stockdale, Walter Chase, Michael Shepard, Gilbert T. Morden.

† He always kept a copy of this proclamation framed and hung up in a conspicuous part of his house:—

"Proclamation.

"By His Excellency, Sir Francis Bond Head, Baronet, Lieutenant Governor of Upper Canada, &c., &c. To the Queen's faithful subjects in Upper Canada,

"In a time of profound peace, while every one was quietly following his occupation, feeling secure under the protection of our laws, a band of Rebels, instigated by a few malignant and disloyal men, has had the wickedness and audacity to assemble with arms, and to attack and murder the Queen's subjects on

in his career. It witnessed the almost total wreck of long cherished hopes. The hope of peaceable reform had for some time been extinguished; that of successful revolution had been next indulged. Instead of finding himself the hero of a revolution, he only preserved his life by going into exile. Foiled in an enterprise in which he risked all, he lost all. Ruined in pro-

the highway, to burn and destroy their property, to rob the public mails, and to threaten to plunder the banks, and to fire the City of Toronto.

"Brave and loyal people of Upper Canada, we have long been suffering from the acts and endeavors of concealed traitors, but this is the first time that Rebellion has dared to show itself openly in the land, in the absence of invasion by any foreign enemy.

"Let every man do his duty now, and it will be the last time that we or our children shall see our lives or properties endangered, or the authority of our Gracious Queen insulted by such treacherous and ungrateful men. Militia men of Upper Canada, no country has ever shown a finer example of loyalty and spirit than you have given upon this sudden call of duty. Young and old of all ranks are flocking to the standard of their country. What has taken place will enable our Queen to know Her friends from Her enemies. A public enemy is never so dangerous as a concealed traitor. And now, my friends, let us complete well what is begun. Let us not return to our rest till treason and traitors are revealed to the light of day, and rendered harmless throughout the land.

"Be vigilant, patient, and active; leave punishment to the laws. Our first object is, to arrest and secure all those who have been guilty of rebellion, murder, and robbery. And to aid us in this, a reward is hereby offered of one thousand pounds, to any one who will apprehend, and deliver up to justice William Lyon Mackenzie; and five hundred pounds to any one who will apprehend and deliver up to justice David Gibson, or Samuel Lount, or Jesse Lloyd, or Silas Fletcher; and the same reward and a free pardon will be given to any of their accomplices who will render this public service, except he or they shall have committed, in his own person, the crime of murder or arson. And all, but the leaders above named, who have been seduced to join in this unnatural rebellion, are hereby called to return to their duty to their Sovereign, to obey the laws, and to live henceforward as good and faithful subjects; and they will find the Government of their Queen as indulgent as it is just.

"God save the Queen.

"THURSDAY, 4 o'clock, P. M., December 7.

"The party of rebels, under their chief leaders, is wholly dispersed, and

perty,* blighted in prospect, exiled and outlawed, with
a price upon his head, how complete was the wreck
of his fortune and his hopes!

The Lieutenant Governor thought it necessary, so
he has told the world, to "mark and record, by some
stern act of vengeance, the important victory" that
had been achieved over the insurgent forces.† In the
presence of the militia, he determined to burn Montgomery's hotel‡ and Gibson's dwelling house. In-

flying before the loyal militia. The only thing that remains to be done is, to
find them and arrest them."

* His ruin resulted from the failure of the insurrection. At the time of the
outbreak, his printing establishment was the largest and the best in Upper
Canada; and, although not rich, he was in good circumstances. In the previous year his account for public printing was $4,000. His book store con-
tained 20,000 volumes, and he had an extensive bindery. He had town lots
in Dundas, a farm lot in Garafraxa, and a claim to a proportion of the immense
Randall estate. A large amount was owing to him; and all he owed was
only about £750. Such of his moveable property as was not destroyed by violence or stolen was never satisfactorily accounted for; though part of it went
to pay some of his creditors, who got judgment against him under the fiction
of an absconding debtor.

† Emigrant.

‡ Sir F. Head has given the following account of this burning: "Volume
after volume of deep, black smoke, rolling and rising from the windows of
Montgomery's tavern now attracted my attention. This great and lofty
building, entirely constructed of timber and planks, was soon a mass of flames,
whose long red tongues sometimes darted horizontally, as if revengefully to
consume those who had created them, and then flared high above the roof.
As we sat on our horses the heat was intense ; and while the conflagration was
the subject of joy and triumph to the gallant spirits that immediately surrounded it, it was a lurid telegraph which intimated to many an anxious
and aching heart at Toronto the joyful intelligence that the yeomen and
farmers of Upper Canada had triumphed over their perfidious enemy, 'responsible government.'"—Emigrant. For this sneer at responsible government, there might have been some excuse at a time when opinion was divided
as to the merits of the system, as applied to a colony ; but when The Emigrant
was written, responsible government had tranquilized Canada and made it
prosperous and happy.

surgent prisoners alleged that Sir F. Head was urged to include the residence of Mr. J. H. Price in the programme of destruction, but that he refused to act upon the suggestion. But if he executed stern vengeance, he showed that he was not incapable of performing an act of clemency. He released several of the prisoners almost as soon as captured, bidding them go to their homes and return to their duties of allegiance. In some cases, however, the men, though released, were arrested again almost as soon as they arrived home, without having been guilty of any new act that would have warranted such a procedure.* After the defeat of the insurgents, and their retreat above Montgomery's, it would be difficult to justify these burnings on the plea of necessity; and indeed, the Lieutenant Governor, by whom they were ordered, does not appear to have felt the least embarrassment in describing them as an act of vengeance.

* The British Government afterwards pardoned some of these prisoners on the ground that the Proclamation contained a full amnesty of their offences.

CHAPTER V.

The Canadian Militia in 1837—Mackenzie's Account of his Escape from Montgomery's to the American Shore, with Notes by the Author.

THE militia who went to the succor of the Government was not generally a more warlike body of men than the insurgents under Lount. They were drawn from the same class—the agriculturists—and were similarly armed and equipped. A description of a party—as given to me by an eye-witness—who came down from the North, would answer, with a very slight variation, for the militia of any other part of the Province. A number of persons collected at Bradford, on the Monday or Tuesday, not one third of whom had arms of any kind; and many of those who were armed had nothing better than pitchforks, rusty swords, dilapidated guns, and newly manufactured pikes, with an occasional bayonet on the end of a pole. These persons, without the least authority of law, set about a disarming process; depriving every one who refused to join them, or whom they chose to suspect of disloyalty, of his arms. Powder was taken from stores, wherever found, without the least ceremony, and without payment. On Thursday, a final march from Bradford for Toronto was commenced; the number of men being nearly five hundred, including one hundred and fifty Indians, with painted faces and savage looks. At Holland Landing some pikes, which probably belonged to Lount, were secured. In their triumphant march, these grotesque-looking militiamen made a prisoner of every man who did not give such an account of himself as they deemed satisfactory. Each prisoner, as he was taken, was tied to a rope; and when Toronto was reached a string of fifty prisoners all fastened together were marched in. Fearing an ambush, these recruits did not venture to march through the Oak Ridges, in the night; and a smoke being seen led to the conclusion that Toronto was in flames. McCleod's tavern, beyond the Ridges, was taken possession of, as well as several other houses in the vicinity. In a neighboring store, all kinds of provisions and clothing that could be obtained were unceremoniously seized. At the tavern there was a regular scramble for food; and cake-baking and bacon-frying were going on upon a wholesale scale. Next morning, several who had no arms, and others who were frightened, returned to their homes. Each man wore a pink ribbon on his arm to distinguish him from the rebels. Many joined from compulsion; and a larger number, including some who had been at Montgomery's, suddenly turned loyalists when they found the fortunes of the insurrection had become desperate. When they marched into Toronto, they were about as motley a collection as it would be possible to conceive.

Such was the Canadian militia in 1837, at a time when Sir F. B. Head had sent all the regular troops out of the Province.

We left Mackenzie at the close of the defeat at Montgomery's; and he must now be allowed to tell the story of his escape in his own words.

"It evidently appearing that success for the insurgents was, at that time, impossible, the Colonel and many others gave way, and crossed the field to the parallel line of road west of Yonge Street," says Mackenzie. "I endeavored to get my cloak, which I had left at the hotel, through which Capt. Fitzgibbon's men were just then sending their six-pound shots with good effect, but too late. Strange to tell, that cloak was sent to me years afterwards, while in prison,* but by whom I know not.

"Perceiving that we were not yet pursued, I passed on to Yonge Street, beyond Lawyer Price's, and the first farmer I met, being a friend, readily gave me his horse—a trusty, sure-footed creature, which that day did me good service. Before I had ridden a mile the smoke rose in clouds behind me, and the flames of the extensive hotel and outbuildings arrested my attention, as also another cloud of smoke which I then supposed to be from the Don Bridge, in the city, which we had sent a party to destroy or take possession of. Colonel Fletcher, now of Chautauque county, N. B., handed me an overcoat, and told me he would make for the States, but not by the head of Lake Ontario.

"Although it was known that we had been worsted, no one interrupted us, save in friendship. Dr. ——, from above Newmarket, informed me that sixty armed friends were on their way, close by. I assured him it was too late to retrieve our loss in that way, and

* For a breach of the neutrality laws of the United States.

bade him to tell them to scatter. Some, however, went on, as volunteers for Sir Francis Bond Head; the rest returned to their homes.

"At the Golden Line, ten miles above the city, I overtook Col. Anthony Van Egmond, a Dutch officer, of many years' experience under Napoleon. He agreed with me that we should at once make for the Niagara frontier, but was taken, almost immediately after, by a party who had set out from Governor Head's camp, to gain the rewards then offered there.

" The Colonel was a man of large property, old, and known to be opposed to Head's party. Though not found in arms, he was placed in a cell, so cold that they had very soon to take him to the hospital—on his way to the grave.

" Finding myself closely pursued and repeatedly fired at, I left the high road with one friend (Mr. J. R.) and made for Shepard's Mills. The fleetest horsemen of the official party were so close upon us that I had only time to jump off my horse, and ask the miller (himself a Tory) whether a large body of men, then on the heights, were friends or foes, before our pursuers were climbing up the steep ascent almost beside me.

" When I overtook Col. Lount, he had, I think, about ninety men with him, who were partly armed. We took some refreshment at a friendly farmer's near by. Lount was for dispersing—I proposed that we should keep in a body, and make for the United States, via the head of Lake Ontario, as our opponents had the steamers; but only sixteen persons went with me. I had no other arms than a single-barrel pistol, taken from

64

Capt. Duggan during our Tuesday's scuffle, and we
were all on foot. Some of my companions had no
weapons at all.

"We made for Humber Bridge, through Vaughan,
but found it strongly guarded; went up the river a
long way, got some supper at the house of a farmer,
crossed the stream on a foot bridge, and by two next
morning reached the hospitable mansion of a worthy
settler on Dundas Street, utterly exhausted with cold
and fatigue.*

"Blankets were hung over the windows to avoid
suspicion, food and beds prepared, and while the Tories were carefully searching for us, we were sleeping
soundly. Next morning (Friday) those who had arms
buried them, and after sending to inquire whether a
friend a mile below had been dangerously wounded,
we agreed to separate and make for the frontier, two
and two together. A lad in his nineteenth or twentieth
year accompanied me,† and such was my confidence in
the honesty and friendship of the country folks, Pro-
testant and Catholic, European and American, that I
went undisguised and on foot, my only weapon at the
time being Duggan's pistol, and it not loaded. Address was now wanted more than brute force.

"We followed the Concession Parallel, and next to
the great Western Road saw and talked with numbers of people, but with none who wanted the Govern-

---

* There can no longer be any reason for withholding the fact, not here mentioned by Mr. Mackenzie, that the house of Mr. Absalom Wilcox, who had
several sons engaged in the revolt, one of whom was afterwards on Navy
Island.

† This was Allan Wilcox. I think he must have been a little older than
here stated, as he was then married.

ment reward. About three in the afternoon, we reached Comfort's Mills, near Streetsville; we were there told that Col. Chisholm and three hundred of the hottest Orangemen, and other most violent partisans, were divided into parties searching for us. Even from some of these there was no real danger. They were at heart friendly.

" Mr. Comfort was an American by birth, but a resident of Canada. I asked his wife for some bread and cheese, while a young Irishman in his employ was harnessing up his wagon for our use. She insisted on our staying to dinner, which we did. Mr. Comfort knew nothing of the intended revolt, and had taken no part in it, but he assured me that no fear of consequences should prevent him from being a friend in the hour of danger.* After conversing with a number of people there, not one of whom said an unkind word to us, my companion and I got into the wagon and the young Emeralder drove us down the Streetsville road, through the Credit Village (Springfield) in broad daylight, and along Dundas Street, bills being then duly posted for my apprehension, and I not yet out of the county which I had been seven times chosen by its freeholders to represent.† Yet, though known

* Comfort took out an old pocket-book, well filled with bank bills, laid it on the table, and told Mackenzie to take a supply, to which the latter replied: "I have plenty of that." This arose from his independent manner, for I doubt if he had much money on his person at the time.

† Comfort rode after them, at the distance of about half a mile, saying to Mrs. Comfort as he left his house, "Good-bye, wife, perhaps I may never see you again;" words which proved prophetic of her sad fate. Just after Mr. Mackenzie left Comfort, a man, named Falconer, who was distributing the proclamation offering a reward for the rebel leaders, went in. He mentioned that he knew Mackenzie.

to everybody, we proceeded a long way west before danger approached. At length, however, we were hotly pursued by a party of mounted troops; our driver became alarmed, and with reason, and I took the reins and pushed onward at full speed over a rough, hard-frozen road, without snow. Our pursuers, nevertheless, gained on us, and when near the Sixteen-Mile Creek we ascertained that my countryman, Col. Chalmers, had a party guarding the bridge. The creek swells up at times into a rapid river; it was now swollen by the November rains. What was to be done? Young W—— and I jumped from the wagon, made toward the forest, asked a laborer the road to Esquesing to put our pursuers off our track, and were soon in the thickest of the patch of woods near the deep ravine, in which flows the creek named and numbered arithmetically as the Sixteen.*

"The men in chase came up with our driver almost immediately after we left, took him prisoner, seized his team, gave the alarm to all the Tories and Orangemen in that part of Trafalgar, and in an hour or thereabouts, we were annoyed by the reports of rifles and the barking of dogs near by the place where we were hidden.

"Some who saw me at Comfort's Mills went and told the armed Tories of Streetsville, who instantly went to the worthy man's house, insulted and threat-

---

* When Comfort came up to about where Mackenzie left the wagon, he saw several men armed with guns, keeping sentry; and on his asking what it meant, they told him that Mackenzie and another person, who came that far in a wagon, had taken to the woods. The truth is, Mackenzie could easily have been taken, but he owed his freedom from capture to a friendly loyalist, whose name I do not feel at liberty to mention.

ened his intrepid and true-hearted wife,* proposed to make a bonfire of his premises, handcuffed and chained him, threw him into a wagon, and dragged him off to Toronto jail, and, as they said, to the gallows. He lay long in prison untried, and was only released to find his excellent wife (who had been in the family way) in her grave, the victim of that system of persecution and terror which often classes men in America, as in Europe, not according to their personal deserts, but

---

* Comfort had returned to within about two miles of his own house, when he was taken prisoner. A loyalist neighbor interested himself in Comfort's favor, and wrote to Hagerman in his behalf. The reply was unfavorable. Comfort's loyalist friend then asked, "Have you and Hagerman ever quarrelled?" Their reply was that there had been some difference between them years before. "Then," rejoined the friendly loyalist, "he remembers it against you; his answer is very unfavorable." Comfort's wagon and horses were taken and used by the captors all winter! He was first arrested by Col. Chisholm and Chalmers, and they appear to have sent him to Toronto without a guard, when he was stopped at the Credit Bridge by James McGrath, and again arrested. He showed Col. Chisholm's pass. McGrath swore Chisholm was the biggest rebel in the Province. Col. Star Jarvis examined the pass, and said they ought to respect it. But McGrath insisted on sending Comfort to Toronto under a guard, and prevailed. Comfort was sent to jail, where he remained three months.

While he was in prison, a party, under Harry Cole, with guns and bayonets rode briskly up to Comfort's house. The children were frightened. Mrs. Comfort hearing them scream, looked out, and when she saw the threatening demonstration she fainted and was carried to bed. Her fright arose from a notion that the armed men were killing the children. She had a succession of fits. When she came to herself, one of the men asked if she had any concealed arms, and desired her to give information for the conviction of her husband, assuring her, at the same time, that he was sure to be hanged. One brute cocked a pistol, and placing it at her breast, threatened to shoot her through, if she did not tell all she knew. This threw her into another fit. They then threw pails of cold water on her in bed. This revolting treatment led to premature confinement, resulting in her death, on the 16th of January, 1838. Great efforts were made to obtain leave for Comfort to attend the funeral, on the 21st, but Hagerman was immovable, and the poor man's prediction that he might never see his wife again was realized.

with reference to their politics, birth-place, faction, or religious profession.

"Our Irish driver had a kind heart. When I was exhibited by authority in the prison at Rochester, he came across to see me. He had been in the service of Judge Jones and others. I was ill of intermittent fever at the time, owing to close confinement and the swamp around me, and could only express the gratitude I felt for past acts of good will.

"Trafalgar was a hot-bed of Orangeism, and as I had always set my face against it, and British native-ism, I could hope for no friendship or favor, if here apprehended. There was but one chance for escape, however, surrounded as we were—for the young man had refused to leave me—and that was to stem the stream, and cross the swollen creek. We accordingly stripped ourselves naked, and with the surface ice beating against us, and holding our garments over our heads, in a bitter cold December night, buffeted the current, and were soon up to our necks. I hit my foot against a stone, let fall some of my clothes, (which my companion caught,) and cried aloud with pain. The cold in that stream caused me the most cruel and intense sensation of pain I ever endured, but we got through, though with a better chance for drowning, and the frozen sand on the bank seemed to warm our feet when we once more trod on it.

"In an hour and a half we were under the hospitable roof of one of the innumerable agricultural friends I could then count in the country. I had a supply of dry flannels, and food, and an hour's rest, and have often wished since, (not to embark again on the tempestuous ocean of politics,) but that I might have an opportunity to express my grateful feelings to those who proved my faithful friends in the hour when most required.

"I had risked much for Canadians, and served them long, and as faithfully as I could—and now, when a fugitive, I found them ready to risk life and property to aid me—far more ready to risk the dungeon, by harboring me, than to accept Sir Francis Head's thousand pounds. The sons and daughters of the Nelson farmer kept a silent watch outside, in the cold, while I and my companions slept.

"We crossed Dundas Street about 11 o'clock, P. M., and the Twelve-Mile Creek, I think, on a fallen tree, about midnight. By four, on Saturday morning, we had reached Wellington Square, by the middle road. The farmer's dogs began to bark loudly, the heavy tramp of a party of horsemen was heard behind us— we retired a little way into the woods—saw that the men were armed—entered the road again—and half an hour before twilight reached the door of an upright Magistrate, which an English boy at once opened to us. I sent up my name, was requested to walk up stairs, (in the dark,) and told that the house, barns, and every part of the premises, had been twice searched for me that morning, and that McNab's men, from Hamilton, were scouring the country in all directions, in hope of taking me. I asked if I had the least chance to pass downward by the way of Burlington Beach, but was answered that both roads were guarded, and that Dr. Rolph was, by that time, safe in Lewiston.

"Believing it safest, we went behind our friend's house to a thicket—he dressed himself, followed us, gave a shrill whistle, which was answered, and all three of us were greatly puzzled as to what safe course I could possibly take. As my companion was not known, and felt the chill of the water and fatigue, he was strongly advised to seek shelter in a certain house not far off. He did so, reached the frontier safely, and continued for four months thereafter very sick.

"At dawn of day it began to snow, and leaving foot-marks behind me, I concluded to go to a farm near by. Its owner thought I would be quite safe in his barn, but I thought not. A peas-rick, which the pigs had undermined all round, stood on a high knoll, and I chose it for a hiding-place. For ten or twelve days I had slept, when I could get any sleep, in my clothes, and my limbs had swelled so that I had to leave my boots and wear a pair of slippers; my feet were wet, I was very weary, and the cold and drift annoyed me much. Breakfast I had had none, and in due time, Colonel McDonell, the High Sheriff, and his posse, stood before me. House, barns, cellars, and garret were searched, and I the while quietly looking on. The Colonel was afterwards second in command to Sir Allan McNab, opposite Navy Island; and when I lived in William Street, some years ago,* he called on me, and we had a hearty laugh over his ineffectual exertions to catch a rebel in 1837.

"When the coast seemed clear, my terrified host, a wealthy Canadian,† came up the hill as if to feed his

* In 1844.   † Mr. G***.

pigs, brought me two bottles of hot water for my feet, a bottle of tea, and several slices of bread and butter; told me that the neighborhood was literally harassed with bodies of armed men in search of me, and advised that I should leave that place at dark, but where to go he could not tell me. He knew, however, my intimate acquaintance with the country for many miles round. Years thereafter he visited me when in Monroe County Prison, and much he wondered to see me there. I too, in those days, had taken but a surface view of the conduct of a cold-blooded reptile band, who pretended to love liberty, that they might thereby more effectually hoodwink and betray 'a working majority' of their trusting countrymen.

"After I had left his premises he was arrested; but had powerful friends, gave bail, and the matter ended there.

"When night had set in, I knocked at the next farmer's door—a small boy who lived, I think, with one of the brothers Chisholm, (strong Government men, collectors, colonels, &c.,) or who was their nephew or other relative, came to me. I sent in a private message by him, but the house had been searched so often for me that the indwellers dreaded consequences, and would not see me. The boy, however, volunteered to go with me, and we proceeded by a by-path to Mr. King's, who lived on the next farm to Col. John Chisholm's, which was then head-quarters for our Tory militia. The boy kept my secret; I had supper with Mr. King's family, rested for an hour, and then walked with him toward my early residence, Dundas village, at the head of Lake Ontario. We saw a small

65

party of armed men on the road, near the mills of an Englishman, but they did not perceive us. Mr. King is now dead, but the kind attention I met with under his hospitable roof I shall not forget. Why should such a people as I tried and proved in those days ever know hardship or suffer from foreign or domestic misrule?

"We went to the dwelling of an old friend, to whom I stated that I thought I would now make a more speedy, yet equally sure, progress on horseback. He risked at once, and that too most willingly, not only his horse, but also the knowledge it might convey that he had aided me. Mr. King returned home and I entered the village alone in the night, and was hailed by some person who speedily passed on. I wanted to take a friend with me, but durst not go to wake him up; there was a guard on duty at the hotel, and I had to cross the creek close by a house I had built in the public square; I then made for the mountain country above Hamilton, called at Lewis Horning's, but found a stranger there, passed on to the dwellings of some old Dutch friends, who told me that all the passes were guarded—Terryberry's, Albion Mills, every place.

"I got a fresh horse near Ancaster, from an old comrade*—a noble animal who did me excellent service—pursued my journey in a concession parallel to the Mountain Road above Hamilton, till I came near to a house well lighted up, and where a guard was

---

* Mr. Jacob Rymal. Mr. Mackenzie awoke him about midnight, explained his situation, and asked if he could let him have a horse. "The best I have," was the unhesitating reply.

evidently posted to question wayfarers—and, as it then seemed the safest course, pulled down the worm fence, and tried to find my way through the Binbrook and Glanford woods, a hard task in daylight, but far worse in the dark.

"For several weary hours did I toil through the primeval forest, leading my horse, and unable to get out or find a path. The barking of a dog brought me, when near daylight, to a solitary cottage, and its inhabitant, a negro, pointed out to me the Twenty-Mile Creek, where it was fordable. Before I had ridden a mile, I came to a small hamlet, which I had not known before—entered a house, and, to my surprise, was instantly called by name, which, for once, I really hesitated to own, not at all liking the manner of him who had addressed me, though I now know that all was well intended.

"Quite carelessly, to appearance, I remounted my horse and rode off very leisurely—but turned the first angle and then galloped on, turned again, and galloped still faster. At some ten miles distance, perhaps, a farm newly cleared, and situated in a by-place, seemed a safe haven. I entered the house, called for breakfast, and found in the owner a stout Hibernian farmer, an Orangeman from the North of Ireland, with a wife and five fine curly-headed children. The beam of a balance, marked 'Charles Waters, Maker,' had been hung up in a conspicuous place, and I soon ascertained that said Charles resided in Montreal, and that my entertainer was his brother.

"I took breakfast very much at my leisure, saw my horse watered, and fed with oats in the sheaf, and then

asked Mr. Waters to be so kind as to put me in the
way to the Mountain Road, opposite Stony Creek,
which he agreed to do, but evidently with the utmost
reluctance.

"After we had travelled about a quarter of a mile
in the woods, he turned round at a right angle, and
said that that was the way. 'Not to the road,' said I.
'No, but to Mr. McIntyre, the magistrate,' said he.
Here we came to a full stop. He was stout and burly;
I, small and slight made.

"I soon found that he had not even dreamed of me
as a rebel; his leading idea was, that I had a habit
of borrowing other men's horses without their express
leave—in other words, that I was a horse-thief. Horses
had been stolen; and he only did his duty by carrying
a doubtful case before the nearest justice, whom I inferred to be one of McNab's cronies, as he was a new
man of whom I had never before heard, though a freeholder of that district, and long and intimately acquainted with its affairs.

"This was a real puzzle. Should I tell Waters who
I was, it was ten to one but he would seize me for the
heavy reward, or out of mere party zeal or prejudice.
If I went before his neighbor, the new made justice,
he would doubtless know and detain me on a charge
of high treason. I asked Mr. Waters to explain.

"He said that I had come, in great haste, to his
house, on a December Sunday morning, though it was
on no public road, with my clothes torn, my face badly
scratched, and my horse all in a foam; that I had refused to say who I was, or where I came from, had
paid. him a dollar for a very humble breakfast, been

in no haste to leave, and was riding one of the finest horses in Canada, making at the same time for the frontier by the most unfrequented paths, and that many horses had been recently borrowed. My manner, he admitted, did not indicate anything wrong, but why did I studiously conceal my name and business? And if all was right with me, what had I to fear from a visit to the house of the nearest magistrate?

" On the Tuesday night, in the suburbs of Toronto, when a needless panic had seized both parties, Sheriff Jarvis left his horse in his haste—it was one of the best in Canada, a beautiful animal—and I rode him till Thursday, wearing the cap of J. Latimer, one of my young men, my hat being knocked off in a skirmish in which one or two of our men were shot. This bonnet-rouge, my torn homespun, sorry slippers, weary gait, and unshaven beard, were assuredly not much in keeping with the charger I was riding, and I had unfortunately given no reply whatever to several of his and his good wife's home questions.

" My chance to be tried and condemned in the hall where I had often sat in judgment upon others, and taken a share in the shapeless drudgery of Colonial legislation,* was now seemingly very good—but I did not quite despair.

" To escape from Waters in that dense forest was entirely hopeless—to blow out his brains, and he acting quite conscientiously, with his five pretty children at home awaiting his early return, I could have done it with ease, as far as opportunity went, for

* The Legislative Assembly had held its sittings in the Court House.

he evidently had no suspicion of that, and my pistol was now loaded and sure fire. Captain Powell, when my prisoner ten days before, and in no personal danger, had shot the brave Captain Anderson dead, and thus left eight children fatherless. No matter; I could not do it, come what might; so I held a parley with my detainer, talked to him about religion, the civil broils, Mackenzie, party spirit, and Dr. Strachan; and found to my great surprise and real delight that, though averse to the object of the revolt he spoke of myself in terms of good-will. Mr. McCabe, his next neighbor, had lived near me in 1823, at Queens-town, and had spoken so well of myself and family to him as to have interested him, though he had not met me before.

" 'I am an old magistrate,' said I, 'but at present in a situation of some difficulty. If I can satisfy you as to who I am, and why I am here, would you desire to gain the price of any man's blood?' He seemed to shudder at the very idea of such a thing. I then administered an oath to him, (and with more solemnity than I had ever done the like when acting judicially,) he holding up his right hand as we Irish and Scottish Presbyterians usually do.

" When he had ascertained my name, which I showed him on my watch and seals, in my pocket-book and on my linen, he expressed real sorrow on account of the dangerous situation in which I stood, pledged himself to keep silence for twenty-four hours, as I requested; directed me how to get into the main road, and feelingly urged me to accept his personal guidance to the frontier. Farmer Waters had none of the

Judas blood in his veins. His innate sense of right led him at once to the just conclusion to do to his fellow-creature, as he would be done by. I perceived, from his remarks, that he had previously associated with my name the idea of a much larger and stouter man than I am.

"When I was fairly out of danger he told the whole story to his neighbors—it was repeated and spread all over—he was soon seized and taken to Hamilton, and there thrown into prison, but afterward released.

"When I was passing the houses of two men, Kerr and Sidey, who were getting ready, I supposed, to go to church, I asked some question as to the road, again crossed the Twenty-Mile Creek, and at length re-entered the mountain path, a little below where a military guard was then stationed. While in sight of this guard, I moved on very slowly, as if going to meeting, but afterward used the rowels to some advantage in the way of propellers. Some persons whom I passed on the road I knew, and some I didn't. Many whom I met evidently knew me, and well was it for me that day that I had a good name. I could have been arrested fifty times before I reached Smithville, had the Governor's person and proclamation been generally respected. As it was, however, another unseen danger lurked close behind me.

"A very popular Methodist preacher, once a zealous friend, had taken a course of which I greatly disapproved, and I had blamed him.* Unkind words passed between us, through the press, he, like myself, having the control of a journal widely circulated. No

* Egerton Ryerson.

doubt many of his readers were affected thereby ; and to this, and not the love of lucre, I have ascribed the conduct of the two men whom I had interrogated as to the road. I have since learned that they warned an armed party, who immediately took horses and rode after me. I perceived them when a third of a mile off, after a part of Mr. Eastman's congregation had passed me, on their way home.

" I thought it safer to endeavor to put my huntsmen off the track, and on a false scent, than to keep on ahead of them ; so I turned short toward St. Catharines, when I got to Smithville, and seemed to have taken that road down hill at full speed. Instead of doing so, however, I turned a corner, put up my horse very quickly in the stable of a friendly Canadian, whose sire was a United Empire Loyalist, entered his hospitable abode, he being still at church, beheld my pursuers interrogate a woman who had seen me pass, and then ride furiously onward by the St. Catharines Road, and then went quietly to bed, and rested for some four hours, had a comfortable supper with the family, and what clothes I required. A trusty companion was also ready to mount his horse and accompany me the last forty miles, to Buffalo, should that attempt prove practicable.

" Samuel Chandler, a wagon-maker, resides in the Western States, but I do not now know where. He was forty-eight years of age when he volunteered, without fee or reward, to see me safe to Buffalo—had a wife and eleven children, and resided in Chippewa. He is a native of Enfield, Conn., had had no connection whatever with the civil broils in the Canadas ; but when told, in strict confidence, of the risk I ran, he preferred to hazard transportation, or loss of life, by aiding my escape, to accepting the freehold of eight thousand acres of land which would have been the reward of my betrayers.

"Other circumstances afterward excited his feelings, and he joined the party taken at the Short Hills, of whom Linus W. Miller, John Grant, John Vernon, himself and others, were tried before Judge Jones, at Niagara, sentenced to suffer death, but banished to Van Dieman's Land. Chandler soon escaped in a Yankee whaler, sailed round the world, and when he reached New York, on his return to his family, (after I had got out of Rochester prison,) I was in no condition to aid him, which I very unavailingly regretted. A more trusty, faithful, brotherly-minded man I have never met with; may Heaven reward Lord Durham's family for saving his life!

"It was about 8 o'clock on Sunday night, when Chandler and I left Smithville. We turned our horses' heads toward Buffalo, crossed the Twenty, ventured to take a comfortable supper with a friend, whose house was on our way, crossed the Welland Canal and the Chippewa River, steering clear of the officials in arms in these parts, and got safe into Crowland before daylight. We soon awoke Mr. C——,* left our horses in his pasture, and he immediately accompanied us, on our way to the Niagara River on foot.

"On inquiry, he found that all the boats on the

---

* I do not fill up the name of Mr. C * * * * *, not knowing whether he would desire to have it done or not.

river (except those at the ferries, which were well
guarded) had been seized and taken care of by the
officers of Government.   There was but one exception.
Captain M'Afee, of Bertie, who resided on the banks
of the Niagara, opposite the head of Grand Island,
was believed to have kept one of his boats locked up
beside his carriages.   I hesitated not a moment in
advising Mr. C—— to state the difficulty I was in to
him, in case he had a boat, for, although he had no
knowledge of, or belief and participation in, the outbreak, yet he was well known to be a strictly upright
man, benevolent, not covetous, a member of the
Methodist Episcopal Church, very religious, and in
all he said or did, very sincere.

"The brothers De Witt are censured, for giving up
to Charles II, (who had been himself a fugitive,) and
to a cruel death, three of his father's Judges; and the
poor and gallant Scotch Highlanders, whom a mam-
moth bribe of £30,000 could not tempt to betray the
heir to the Crown, when a wandering fugitive in the
native land of his royal ancestors, are held in honor.
The Irish peasants who refused to give up Lord Edward Fitzgerald to his country's oppressors, for gold,
the poor sailors who enabled Archibald Hamilton
Rowan to escape from Ireland and an untimely fate,
with the proclaimed reward on a handbill in their
boat, and the three bold Englishmen who saved the
life of the doomed Labedoyere, have the merited
applause of an admiring world.   Are these noble
citizens of Upper and Lower Canada, whom wealth
could not tempt to give up, nor danger deter from
aiding and saving, their fellow men, though many of

them were opposed to them in politics, and at a time of the strongest political excitement, are they less deserving of the meed of public approbation?

"Mr. Samuel M'Afee is now over sixty years of age, and, I think, he is of the New Hampshire family of that name, who played their part like men, in 1776. Our movement had proved a failure, and he knew it. He was wealthy—had a large family—and risked everything by assisting me; yet he did not hesitate, no, not even for a moment.

"As well as I can now remember, it was about nine on Monday morning when I reached his farm, which was one of the finest on the river—an excellent breakfast had been prepared for us, and I was much fatigued and also hungry. But there was a military patrol on the river, and before sitting down to a repast, I thought it safe to step out and see if the coast was clear. Well for me it was that I did so. Old Colonel Kerby, the Custom House officer opposite Black Rock, and his troop of mounted dragoons, in their green uniforms, and with their carbines ready, were so close upon us, riding up by the bank of the river, that had I not then observed their approach, they would have caught me at breakfast.

"Nine men out of ten, in such an emergency, would have hesitated to assist me; and to escape by land was, at that time, evidently impossible; Mr. M'Afee lost not a moment—his boat was hauled across the road and launched in the stream with all possible speed—and he and Chandler and I were scarcely afloat in it, and out a little way, below the bank, when the old Tory Colonel, and his green-coated troop of horse, with their waving plumes, were parading in front of Mr. M'Afee's dwelling.

" How we escaped here, is to me almost a miracle. I had resided long in the district, and was known by everybody. A boat was in the river, against official orders ; it was near the shore, and the carbines of the military, controlled by the collector, would have compelled us to return, or have killed us for disobedience.

" The colonel assuredly did not see us ; that was evident: he turned round at the moment to talk to Mrs. M. and her daughters, who were standing in the parterre in front of their house, full of anxiety on our account. But of his companions, not a few must have seen the whole movement, and yet we were allowed to steer for the head of Grand Island with all the expedition in our power, without interruption ; nor was there a whisper said about the matter for many months thereafter.

" In an hour we were safe on the American shore ; and that night I slept under the venerable Colonel Chapin's hospitable roof, with a volunteer guard."

CHAPTER VI.

Meetings of Sympathizers at Buffalo and Oswego—Thomas Jefferson Suther-
land claims to be the Author of the Project of occupying Navy Island—
Rensellaer Van Rensellaer becomes Commander-in-Chief of the Patriot
Army—Governor Head demands the Extradition of Mackenzie, and Go-
vernor Marcy refuses to surrender him—The first Twenty-six land on
Navy Island—A Provisional Government Established—Issues Procla-
mations—The Patriot Flag and Great Seal—How and of whom the Navy
Island Force was formed and how equipped—Habits of the Commander-in-
Chief—Bombardment—A Patriot Emissary sent through the Western Part
of Upper Canada returns with the Report that a Large Majority of the
People are waiting to join the "Liberators"—Four Hundred and Eighty-
two sworn Insurgents in the County of Hastings.

BEFORE the plans of the Upper Canada insurgents
were known, an influential meeting of the citizens of
Buffalo, a frontier city on Lake Erie, in the State of
New York, to express sympathy with the Canadian revolution, was held. At this meeting, which took place
on the 5th of December, an Executive committee of
thirteen, with Dr. E. Johnson at its head, was formed,
for the purpose of "calling future meetings in relation
to the affairs of the Canadas and to adopt such measures as might be called for by public opinion." This
committee afterwards played an important part in
forwarding the movements of the exiles and sympathizers. On the 6th of December, Mackenzie addressed a short letter, from the insurgent camp on
Yonge Street, to the Buffalo Press, explaining the at-

tempt at independence that was being made, and requesting such assistance as the citizens of the Republic might think proper to afford. Two days after, a
similar demonstration took place at Oswego. On the
11th of December, when Mackenzie had arrived on
the south side of the frontier line, the largest public
meeting ever seen in that city, was held in the theatre
at Buffalo to express sympathy with the Canadians.
" Our neighbors in the North," said Dr. Chapin,
" are at war, fighting for liberty. We have met to
express our sympathy and good wishes." After cau-
tioning the meeting to act prudently, he added, " I
have one word more to say; I have men now under
my protection, at my house, on whose life a price is
set, and whom I am bound to protect." " Who are
they?" was the prompt inquiry. " One of them is
William L. Mackenzie." At this announcement, the
chronicles of the day report, " the vast assembly
burst into a thunder of applause. We never saw
such a scene," the reporter adds; " never heard such
a shout of exultation."* When the outburst of enthusiasm had subsided, Dr. Chapin continued. " Fellow
citizens," he said, " Mackenzie's life is in our power—
he has thrown himself upon our protection—will you
protect him?" " We will," was the unanimous re-
spouse; to which was added a desire that he should
be brought forward. Dr. Chapin pleaded the sickness
and fatigue of his guest; but added, " To-morrow night
he shall address you. I am an old man; but at the
hazard of my life I will protect those who throw
themselves upon my hospitality. If any scoundrels, for

* Buffalo *Commercial Advertiser.*

the sake of the $4,000 reward that is offered for him, shall undertake to get him, they must first walk over my body. I want six strong, brave young men, as good sons as God has got among us, to go to my house to-night, for fear of any attempt on the part of the loyalists." "A hundred are ready," was the response. "No," rejoined the venerable Doctor, "I want only six. Who'll go?" "I—I—I" was heard all over the theatre. The first who sprung upon the stage were accepted. Mr. Stow, being called upon to address the meeting, demanded: "Shall we refuse the Canadians what was granted by a corrupt court of France to Franklin, when he went upon the same errand?" By giving their sympathy and assistance, the people of the United States, he argued, would only be doing what England did in the wars of the Peninsula, the taking of Copenhagen, and the attack on the Turkish fleet at Navarino. The meeting broke up with cheers for Mackenzie, Papineau, and Rolph.

Next night, true to the promise made by Dr. Chapin on his behalf, Mackenzie appeared at the Buffalo theatre, where he addressed a large and enthusiastic audience. He explained the causes of the revolt, and argued that Canada was suffering all those evils which caused the thirteen Colonies, now become the United States, to throw off their allegiance to England; a country of which the Government at home was good, but uniformly bad abroad.

Before the meeting closed, Mr. Thomas Jefferson Sutherland stated his intention of going to Canada, as a volunteer, to assist the Canadians to obtain their independence; and he asked if any others present were willing to join him.   At his request, a person in the meeting asked the people present to contribute arms and munitions of war for the benefit of the people of Canada, and to take them to the Eagle tavern.   In accordance with this suggestion, contributions of arms were made.   Sutherland claims the conception of the plan of occupying Navy Island with a military force; and on the 19th of December, 1839, he made oath that he set about carrying this project into effect without the privity or co-operation of Mackenzie.*   He added that Mackenzie only joined the Navy Island expedition out of motives of personal safety. Mr. Mackenzie had not been long in Buffalo before he was introduced to Mr. Rensellaer Van Rensellaer, by some of the principal people of the place.   They represented him as a cadet of West Point; and as having gained experience under Bolivar, in South America; both of which representations proved incor-

---

* I find in a manuscript book of "Navy Island Memoranda," the following document, without date, to which ninety-seven names are appended; that of Sutherland being first: "We, the young men residents of the City of Buffalo, whose names are hereunto subscribed, pledge to each other our mutual support and co-operation, for the commendable purpose of aiding and assisting our Canadian brethren in their present struggle for liberty and those principles which have given to the world that asylum which we have the honor of calling our home, and which pronounces to mankind the sacred dogma of equality."

On the 21st of December, Marshal Garron wrote from Rochester to N. P. Benton, District Attorney: "I arrived here last night at ten o'clock; sent for General Gould and some others of this place.   There is much excitement here; forty soldiers marching the streets of Rochester to-day under drum and fife; two pieces of cannon went off this morning, and three-fourths of the people here, I learn, are encouraging and promoting the thing, and seven-eighths of the people at Buffalo, and all along the lines are taking strong interest in the cause of the patriots; many furnishing arms, and large quantities of provisions contributed and forwarded to them, and volunteers continually going on."

rcct. He was a son of General Van Rensellaer of Albany, and belonged to the influential family of that name, in the State of New York.* Another person to whom Mr. Mackenzie was introduced was Mr. Sutherland, of Buffalo, who was described as a military man of experience. Sutherland soon showed that he was totally wanting in discretion, by publicly recruiting for volunteers for Canada, issuing a public call for a military meeting, and marching through the streets to the sound of martial music. Mackenzie, seeing the folly of the procedure, begged Sutherland to desist; but it was to no purpose.

At that time, it was thought that Dr. Duncombe was at the head of a large force in the Western District of Upper Canada; and Mackenzie wished the friends of the Canadian insurgents to go over to Fort Erie, on the

---

* He was for some time employed as a clerk in the Post-office, at Albany, under his father. He married a daughter of Maj. S. S. Forman, of that city. After his connection with the Canadian patriots, and his imprisonment for a breach of the United States Neutrality Laws, arising out of that connection, he settled at Albany. Of a proud and ambitious temper, his disappointments cast a melancholy gloom over his existence. He became pecuniarily embarrassed, and the loss of one of his children, to whom he was devotedly attached, caused him to take the dreadful resolution of putting an end to his existence. On the 1st of January, 1850, his wife and her father complied with an invitation to visit at the house of a friend. He remained at home, complaining of being unwell, but promised that if he improved he would follow. In the course of the afternoon, he ordered a man-servant to fill a portable furnace with charcoal and place it in the library. This was done. After a while more charcoal was ordered and taken. The servant went a third time of his own accord to take a fresh supply, when he found his master stretched pale and lifeless upon the sofa. Van Rensellaer was of a literary turn of mind, and in his latter years spent much of his time among books, occasionally contributing articles to agricultural periodicals. The Albany newspapers, in chronicling his melancholy death, described him as "highly respected in the circle of his acquaintance, and in his intercourse with the community, quiet and unobtrusive."

Canada side, and there organize a force that should
join that of Duncombe, or act separately, if that should
appear to be the best course.   But he was overruled;
and it was determined that the refugees and their
friends should take up a position on Navy Island.
This island, awarded to England by the Treaty of
Ghent, is situated in the Niagara River, a short distance
above the world-renowned cataract.   A swift current
sweeps past the island on either side, on its way to
the vast abyss below; but its navigation is practicable
for steamers or row boats.   Van Rensellaer had been
urged by Sutherland to take command of the Patriot
forces; Sutherland, being previously unknown to Van
Rensellaer, had brought a letter of introduction from
Mr. Taylor, a previous Speaker of one branch of the
Legislature of New York.   He was told that he would
derive his authority from Dr. Rolph and Mackenzie;
and he was to be invested with the entire military
command.   Van Rensellaer's own account of the reasons that induced him to accept this position,* represents him as wishing the success of the cause of republicanism, and desirous to imitate the example of Sam
Houston, in Texas.   " Dr. Rolph," says Van Rensel-

---

* He was impressed with the idea "that Canada was only prevented from
throwing off the yoke of foreign despots; and notwithstanding the unfortunate
issue of the ill-concerted battle of Toronto, that a vast majority of the people
were in favor of a political revolution; that if one successful battle was fought
and a good stand maintained for a time, they would concentrate their forces,
and do their own fighting afterwards.   With the hope of being instrumental
in hastening a crisis so desirable to all the republican world my wish as a
Northerner to see the chivalrous example of the South in the case of Texas
emulated here—my innate detestation of tyranny and oppression, however
manifested—finally relying upon numberless promises of being sustained, and
trusting in the smiles of heaven, I accepted the offer."

laer, "went so far as to propose, himself, and to insist that I should have the power to arrest any member of the Executive Council, provided it became necessary to do so, in order to prevent his interference in my department. Mr. Mackenzie," he adds, "after a slight show of opposition, was obliged to acquiesce."

In the meantime, it became known that Lieutenant Governor Head was about to make a requisition upon Governor Marcy, of the State of New York, for the extradition of Mr. Mackenzie as a fugitive from justice, for alleged crimes growing as incidents out of the insurrection. Dr. Bethune was selected as the bearer of the dispatch in which this demand was made. Governor Marcy declined to comply with the application, on the ground that the offences charged, being incidents of the revolt, were merged in the larger imputed crime of treason, a political offence excepted by the laws of the State of New York from those for which fugitives could be surrendered. Attorney General Beardsley, at the request of Governor Marcy, drew up an elaborate opinion, in which the inadmissibility of the demand was shown. But, before the demand was presented to Governor Marcy, Mr. Mackenzie had passed from the limits of the State of New York; and as he was on British territory, the proper course would have been for Sir Francis Bond Head to send to Navy Island and take him. The real object of this demand was to obtain possession of a political refugee, under the pretence that he was guilty of other offences, and execute him for high treason, with which he was charged. Without seeing the documents in which the demand was made, and trusting to public rumor

that one of the charges related to the death of Colonel
Moodie, Mr. Mackenzie declared his readiness to
meet that charge and submit to a trial. " I distinctly
offered," he says, " by letter addressed to Mr. Secretary Stanley, to go over at once to Toronto, and stand
my trial on any charge that had been made by Governor Head, or that might be made by any other person, relative to the part I took in the death of Col. Moodie, no matter who might be the judge or jurors."

On the thirteenth of December, Van Rensellaer and
Mackenzie landed on Navy Island. They called at
Whitehaven, on Grand Island, ten miles from the
City of Buffalo, on the way. There they expected to
find assembled the volunteers, by whom they were to be
accompanied, and of whose numbers, enthusiasm, and
equipment so much had been said. These volunteers
had been represented as two hundred and fifty strong,
and as having two pieces of artillery and some four
hundred and fifty stand of arms, besides provisions
and munitions in abundance. The surprise both of
Mackenzie and Van Rensellaer must have been great
when they found only twenty-four volunteers waiting
to accompany them. " I was not prepared," says Van
Rensellaer, " for such a surprising falling off. Mr.
Mackenzie, on noticing it, sank inert and spirit-broken
upon the frame of a cannon, where he passively reclined until aroused by a false alarm."* But even
this crushing disappointment was not to put an end

---

* The published letter of Van Rensellaer, dated March 30, 1838, from which
I here quote, was written in a spirit of hostility to Mr. Mackenzie, to whom
the writer, in a letter now in my possession, dated Albany, February 24,
1840, admits that he was unjust.

to the enterprise. It was expected that the promises of assistance so liberally made would be realized; and, says Van Rensellaer, "trusting in the good faith of our friends and in Providence, the word was given, 'Push off.'"

A provisional government, of which Mr. Mackenzie was President, was organized on the island. A proclamation, dated Navy Island, December 13, 1837, was issued by Mr. Mackenzie, stating the objects which the attempted revolution was designed to secure, and promising three hundred acres of public lands to every volunteer who joined the Patriot standard.* A few days after, another proclamation was issued, adding $100 in silver, payable by the 1st of May, 1838, to the proffered bounty.† The fulfilment of the promises held out in these proclamations must, however, be dependent upon the success of the cause in which the volunteers were to fight. By way of burlesquing the rewards offered by Sir Francis Bond Head for Mackenzie and others, the first proclamation offered the sum of £500 for the Lieutenant Governor of Upper Canada. The offering of this reward was the main cause that induced Sir Francis, on his return to England, to forego his intention of passing through the

---

* See Appendix G.

† "PROCLAMATION.—Three hundred acres of the most valuable lands in Canada will be given to each Volunteer who may join the Patriot Forces now encamped on Navy Island, U. C. Also, $100 in silver, payable on or before the 1st of May next.

"By order of the Committee of the Provincial Government.

"W. L. MACKENZIE,

"*Chairman Pro. Tem.*

"Navy Island, Tuesday, Dec. 19, 1837."

States. At his request, Sir John Harvey, Lieutenant Governor of Nova Scotia, secured him a passage in a vessel sailing from Halifax.

The Patriot flag, with its twin stars, intended to represent the two Canadas, was hoisted; and as a government, even though it be provisional, is nothing without a great seal; this requisite was also obtained. Besides the twin stars, the great seal showed a new moon breaking through the surrounding darkness, with the words *Liberty—Equality.* The Provisional Government issued promises to pay in sums of one and ten dollars each. They are said to have been freely taken on the American side;* but what amount was issued I cannot ascertain. Dr. Rolph was appointed, on the 28th of December, " to receive all the moneys which may be subscribed within the United States on behalf of the Canadian patriots struggling to obtain the independence of their country ;" but he declined to act in that capacity.

The men were quartered in huts made of boards; and the head-quarters of the Provisional Government and the General-in-Chief differed from the rest only in being of greater dimensions.

How the handful of men who first took possession of Navy Island came to be swelled to between five hundred and six hundred, must now, for the first time, be explained. All the correspondence on Navy Island was conducted by Mr. Mackenzie; and the numerous

---

* The best proof of the truth of this assertion is to be found in an official report of one of the Patriot Generals to Mackenzie, dated January 26, 1838, relating an offer of the owner of the brig *Virginia,* to sell her for $8,500, and take his pay in bonds.

letters addressed both to him and Van Rensellaer, none of which have ever been published, are now in my possession. Let it not be supposed that the Provisional Government was free from the trouble of dealing with applications for situations. Surgeons offer their services to attend the wounded; engineers seek employment in their line of business; military veterans offer to train citizens into soldiers. Several persons who have held positions as officers in the militia of the different States, and some who have been in the army of the United States, tender their services on condition that they obtain equivalent positions in the Patriot army. The motives of persons offering their services were various. Most of them appear to have been impressed with the idea that it would be a fine thing to join an army intended to give liberty to an oppressed people. Some betray their hatred of England; others, their fear that the fact of that country possessing a large part of this continent, is a source of danger to the United States. Some want employment; others seek adventure. A large number of those who went to the island, or whose services were offered, were provided with letters of introduction guaranteeing their respectability. To come to details, by way of example: A society sends word it has money to give to the cause; and could, if the law permitted, send one hundred men. An old man offers four hundred acres of land in Canada for the soldiers. "Are you sufficiently supplied with cannon?" one person writes, "and if not, let me know whether it be very important that you should be supplied with them." A man who lost $3,000 worth of property in Canada, by what he describes as the fraud of enemies, wants to know whether he would get it back, if he assisted the Patriots and they were successful. A person writes to inform Van Rensellaer that there are, at Batavia, two thirty-six pounders, one eighteen pounder, two thousand stand of arms, one hundred cannon balls, five hundred musket cartridges, and various other materials. Another sends a lot of cartridge boxes, by way of Schlosser. The state of the roads prevents one person desirous of volunteering from going and taking a six pound brass cannon with him. One letter tells of a meeting at which a resolution was come to to join the Patriots, in case of war between England and the United States. A dejected correspondent relates how the interference of one man prevented fifteen volunteers from starting. At a meeting held to denounce the destruction of the Caroline, which I shall soon have occasion to describe, ten volunteers started for the island. A number of persons forward provisions; and they are careful to remark that their object is not to aid in a war against England, but that the duties of humanity forbid them to see their fellow men exposed to the possibility of want. One old cannon is sent and another is promised, with the remark, " If you want cannon, we are ready to cast them for you."

An ex-member of the Legislature of New York, with two certified captains, go with a letter of introduction, to confer with Van Rensellaer as to what measures the sentries—of an arsenal I presume—might take to furnish warlike supplies, without infringing the law. A Rochester editor gives a letter of introduction to " an efficient friend of the Patriot cause."

Several Germans, residing in Philadelphia, political refugees from their own country and members of patriotic associations in Europe, "intimately connected with the Liberals and Republicans of France, Switzerland, Germany, and England," send word that they are desirous to "hasten to the standard of liberty, rather from their burning love of the immortal cause than with any expectation of reward." They are represented as men of education and great influence; one, who was a major in the Prussian army, had gained distinction; and they could bring assistance from Europe. Daniel McCleod, late major in the Grenville Militia, who was making a tour along the frontier, in company with Silas Fletcher, to beat up volunteers and arms, reports that they will dispatch several Canadians to the island next day—the letter is dated Watertown, January 2d, 1838—with two field pieces and other arms. He reports that "arms in abundance can be had for the asking." In the same letter, the notorious Bill Johnson—Admiral Johnson I believe he was called—who afterwards took up a position among the Thousand Islands of the St. Lawrence, is described as a man in whom it is perfectly safe to confide. Fletcher gives him a separate certificate, describing him as a gentleman of intelligence, equal to fifty ordinary men. He is recommended for a commission, because "he can greatly annoy the Kingstonians;" and besides "his influence" is described as being so great "that he can raise, in this quarter, two hundred bold volunteers as ever drew a trigger." From Sackett's Harbor, Fletcher writes: "The inhabitants led us into town by a procession, colors flying,

68

guns roaring, and shouts of 'God prosper the Patriots!'" A letter with seven signatures suggests, that if the proclamation of the Patriots "can be so amended that the aggrieved can have their just due, in case of success, you can have the assistance of many wealthy and able citizens, who were driven from their lands and property in Canada, during the last war." From another source go funds, blankets, guns, and men. An old man writes: "I have followed the greatest cavalry officer in the world, Murat, from the deserts of Africa to the cold plains of Russia. I have fought at Lodi and Hohenlinden, at Moscow and Waterloo." After asking a commission in the cavalry force for a well trained lad of nineteen, he adds: "I am now old and poor; but if you will grant my request, I will send you my son, the last descendant of a noble line of warlike commanders of France." A man who has been "preaching the gospel," in the neighborhood of Toronto, sends the Patriots word of what is doing on there. Another Canadian declares his belief that all is over, unless there be a war between Canada and the States. A vigilant friend warns the Navy Islanders that the Tories have sent a negro cook to poison all the Patriots; and Sutherland, being in Buffalo, hears the same story and repeats it. A sympathizer, in offering to raise a cavalry squadron, desires to know how soon a regiment will be required, and if equipments can be furnished by the Patriots. The Patriots are warned that the United States Marshal is going to interfere with them. Van Rensellaer is warned that the United States Government is about to demand and insist upon receiving back the arms

said to belong to it; and he is asked whether, if it
should come to a question of having to surrender
either to Great Britain or his own Government, it
would not be better to have to deal with a generous
foe than a false friend. A friend sends the system of
tactics drawn up by order of the United States Secretary of War for the discipline of citizen soldiers. A
West Point graduate contributes instructions for the
defence of the island. A company of riflemen, under
a leader who served in the last frontier war, offer their
services. An American militia officer, who has command of a regiment, is ready to raise one for the Patriot service. An Upper Canadian writes that he
can raise forty volunteers. The Patriots are notified
of the approaching arrival of three loads of armed
men and fourteen kegs of powder. A present of
grape shot is announced. The next boat is to convey
two or three pieces more artillery. From another
quarter are to be presented two hundred muskets,
besides other arms and stores. It is announced that
provisions are being sent; and that the country people are doing wonders. "An empty hand, a stout
heart, and fair knowledge of military tactics," are proffered. Donations of blankets, boots, shoes, and
stockings are sent from one quarter; from another
go blankets alone. A baker sends one hundred and
seventeen loaves of bread "for the good of the cause."
On the 30th of December, arrangements were made
for getting eight tons of grape and nine pound shot
made. A discreet man, if such a one could be found,
could raise three hundred volunteers in Albany. Two
loads of beef, pork, and bread, are sent, "with some

gentlemen well equipped for fight." The son of a
Lieutenant-Colonel in the United States army, who
has been two years at a military academy and is a
pretty good master of military tactics, could bring a
number of young men with him. One hundred
muskets, word is sent, may be expected in forty-
eight hours. A late Lieutenant in the United States
army, who was in the war of 1812, desires to be appointed Brigadier General of the patriot force. A
letter from Batavia, N. Y., says: "We have sent off
from our village four loads [of volunteers], and at the
moment I am writing, another load is on the point
of starting." This correspondent was about getting up
a county meeting; at which he expected something
"substantial" would be done for the Patriots. In
making a donation of a cannon, a sympathizer ex-
plains how he got it. "I have been keeper of the
State arsenal of this place for more than thirteen years.
When I took charge, I found that gun in the village,
but not in the arsenal. I have therefore, in my annual
returns to the commissary department, never reported
said gun." This guardian of the State arsenal had
mentioned his intended destination of the stray gun,
at a public house; and "some of the citizens felt and
expressed a warm anxiety in favor of the project, and
now talk of mounting and completely equipping it for
service, by voluntary subscription."

In this way was the force on Navy Island augmented from the original number of twenty-six to
about six hundred. From the 15th to the 31st of
December, the majority of those present were British
subjects. After that date, the American element was

probably in the ascendant.* The arms and provisions were chiefly obtained from the States. The rolls of names have been preserved, with a partial diary of occurrences.

Van Rensellaer's conduct, while on the island, has been the subject of much obloquy. While his bravery is admitted, he has been especially accused of almost habitual intemperance; and though he denied the charge, in letters it has fallen to me to peruse, Gibson, Graham, and others, who were on the island with him, have left on record their opinion that his intemperance ruined the prospects of the Patriots. One who was a witness of his habits, assures me that Van Rensellaer made a pretty equitable division of his time between drinking brandy, of which he always had a bottle under his head at night, and writing love-letters. His own account, contained in an unpublished letter, gives him more serious employments.† He admits to have been occasionally under strong mental excitement, and particularizes two occasions: when the Patriots fired

---

* Van Rensellaer, in a published letter dated March 29th, 1838, stated that the Canadians always continued in a majority on the island; but I am not sure that his authority is reliable on this point.

† He describes himself as spending the day in "plodding four weary miles through mud and water, round our little republic, to dispose of the recruits and superintend the erection of defences. On my return, nearly prostrate with fatigue, haggard and careworn, when seated in my quarters to partake of a much needed meal, perhaps a call to receive a boat load of visitors, or an alarm which was always occurring at first, attended to in person, would compel me to leave it untouched. So at night, when reclined in full dress to snatch my 'day's' slumber, the same causes would often oblige me to forego even that; and for the first fortnight I never had more than an hour's sleep at a time, frequently not more than two hours out of twenty-four. Nor did I undress myself once during the whole period of my stay. * * * I was ever ready to incur any danger and willing to submit to any hardship or privation, in order to inspire my men with confidence, and to insure their comfort and welfare."

their first gun, and again, "when Capt. Elmsley, with his boat's crew, at early dawn, made his way in safety round the island, under fire of our guns. He came off, I am told," adds Van Rensellaer, addressing Mackenzie, on the information of the spy Genouing, "to seize you on your intended passage to the American shore."* Having the entire military power in his hands, Van Rensellaer chose to keep his plans to himself, and his refusal to act or explain his intentions finally exhausted the patience of his men. The latter were anxious to cross to the main land.

---

* Genouing, an American by birth, was employed as a spy by the Federal authorities, and it was admitted by District Attorney Rodgers that he rendered important service to the Government. He acted under the orders of General Worth. But so odious was his calling regarded by the American people that wherever he presented himself he was set upon by a mob; and for safety he was once locked up a fortnight in a private room of the District Attorney. After some time he fled to Toronto, the American authorities being unable to protect him; but whether he remained there or went back to some part of the States where he was not known, I am not aware. The royalists had a number of spies in their service, one of whom offered to sell their secrets to the Patriots; but he would tell nothing unless he were paid. His name was Jones, an Englishman by birth, and a dentist by profession. He was a sort of sub-spy, employed by one Matthew Hayes, who had been a sergeant in the Fifteenth Regiment. He went to Navy Island on the 21st December, learnt what he could, repeated what he knew to his employers, and became a witness against some prisoners who were afterwards taken. While on the island, he was suspected and detained by Mackenzie, when he employed Jones to carry letters to the royalist forces. Early in January, he offered to sell the secrets of his employers. He pretended to know the point of intended attack, and said the simplicity of the plan was a guarantee of its success. He could, he said, instruct the Patriots how to throw up works in an hour that would frustrate the project. He also added, that if a thousand Patriots were to cross to the main land, half the royalist army would desert and join their standard. Among the host of other spies who visited the island were persons named Farnsworth, Smith, Wrigley, and Thorne. From these persons the royalists must have been thoroughly acquainted with the condition and force of the island.

The defences made on the island consisted of trees thrown along the lower banks, and extending into the water, where there was reason to anticipate that a landing would be attempted. A road was cut in the woods round the island, near the margin, that men and cannon might be moved to any point where required. A loyalist force, at first under Col. Cameron, and afterwards under Col. McNab, appeared on the Chippewa side, and a bombardment commenced. The island was scarcely out of musket range of the main land, where the British forces were stationed; and one man, on the main land, was killed from the island by a musket or a rifle. But for all this, the fire of the loyalist cannon and mortars, kept up day after day, was almost entirely harmless; only one man on the island being killed by it. The extent of the mischief done by the Patriots was greater, because they were not baffled by woods, on the main land, where the enemy was encountered. But the effect of the fire of the twenty-four cannon in possession of the Patriots was very small. Many of the houses on the Chippewa shore were pierced with stray balls; but the number of persons killed was insignificant. The men got impatient under the ineffectual efforts they were making; and Van Rensellaer was repeatedly urged to lead them to the enemy who neglected to come to them. In reply to these importunities, he would answer that when his plans were complete he would announce them; that in the meantime it was for the men to hold themselves ready to execute his orders. At one time he consented that the forces should cross to the main land; and Capt. Gorham went to Buffalo to try

to get a steamboat for that purpose, but the vigilance
of the United States authorities prevented his succeeding.   Van Rensellaer stated in a letter to Mackenzie, dated Buffalo, January 21, 1838, that when
they were about securing the steamboat New England,
Gen. Scott outbid the Buffalo Committee by $500, and
carried off the prize.

What gave courage to the patriots was the belief that
the moment they crossed over to the main land, they
would be joined by large numbers of the population
anxious to revolutionize the Government.   Chandler,
who assisted Mackenzie in his escape, was sent over
to distribute proclamations and ascertain the feeling
of the country.   He returned to the island with the
report that a large majority of the population was ripe
for revolt, and only awaiting assistance to fly to arms.
Such loose information as this is liable to mislead;
but there were parts of the country from which Mackenzie had much more precise information.   From
the county of Hastings he had lists of four hundred
and eighty-two persons who had " pledged themselves
upon oath to embark their lives, their honor, and
their fortunes in the cause of liberty."*   Hastings
was far from being one of the most disloyal counties
in Upper Canada; and when it furnished nearly five
hundred sworn rebels, some idea may be formed of the
extent to which the revolutionary feeling had infected
the population.   With such information as this in his
hands, a man of Mr. Mackenzie's impetuous tempera-

---

* These words are from the secret communication. The four hundred and
eighty-two were distributed as follows: Bellville, 41; Thurlow, 93; Sidney,
165; Rawdon, 86; Tyendenago, 37; Huntingdon, Madac, and Hungerford, 60.

ment was not likely to be at ease under the inaction to which Van Rensellaer, as Commander-in-Chief, doomed the men under his control. But it is not difficult to conceive why Van Rensellaer hesitated to move in the face of a vastly superior force, in the midst of a Canadian winter, where a single night's piercing frost might prove fatal to an army on the move.

69

CHAPTER VII.

Destruction of the Steamboat Caroline by the Loyalists—Proceedings of the United States and the State Authorities in regard to Neutrality—Colonel McNab knighted—Swords presented to him and Captain Drew by the Upper Canada House of Assembly—Was the Destruction of the Caroline necessary or advisable?—Trial of Alexander McLeod for the murder of Amos Durfee—England apologizes for the Destruction of the Caroline—The Steamer Sir Robert Peel burnt in retaliation—Mrs. Mackenzie on Navy Island—Mackenzie goes to Buffalo, is arrested for a Breach of the United States' Neutrality Laws, and enters into Recognizances—The Steamboat Barcelona takes the Patriots from the Island.

UP to the 29th of December, the volunteers on Navy Island had increased slowly, and they did not yet number quite two hundred. About an hour after midnight, an event occurred which for some time threatened to produce war between England and the United States. "We observed," says Mr. Mackenzie, "about one o'clock, A. M., a fire burning on the American side of the river, in the direction of the small tavern and old storehouse, commonly called Schlosser. Its volume gradually enlarged, and many were our conjectures concerning it. At length the mass of flame was distinctly perceived to move upon the waters, and approach the rapids and the middle of the river above the falls. Swiftly and beautifully it glided along, yet more rapid in its onward course

Navy Island, the Headquarters of the Insurgents, as seen by the light of the burning Caroline.

as it neared the fathomless gulf, into which it vanished in a moment, amid the surrounding darkness. This was the ill-fated steamboat Caroline."

Col. McNab, in ordering the vessel to be cut out, acted under the misapprehension that she had been purchased by what he called the "pirates" and rebels* on Navy Island. The ownership of the vessel is not a matter of much importance, since she was running for the accommodation of the patriots. But she was being run as a private speculation by her owner, Mr. William Wells. Col. McNab, in the course of the 29th, sent two officers to watch the movements of the Caroline.† They reported that they had seen her land a cannon and several men armed and equipped as soldiers; and that she had dropped anchor on the east side of Navy Island. He therefore determined

---

* Rebels they certainly were, but by no possible latitude of language could they be called pirates. Sir Francis Bond Head readily adopted the loose and inaccurate designation, and even Mr. Fox, the British Minister at Washington, applied it to the American portion of the force. Piracy is described by writers on international law, as "robbery or a forcible depredation on the high seas, without lawful authority, and done *animo furandi*, and in the spirit and intention of universal hostility." This description was totally inapplicable to a body of men whose sole object was to revolutionize the Government of Upper Canada, and set up another in its stead.

† Alexander McLeod, being at Buffalo, on Christmas eve, heard that the *Caroline* was going to run between Schlosser and Navy Island; and he went and informed Colonel McNab of the fact. On the morning of the 28th, he, Captain Graham, and some others went round the island in a boat, but did not see her. About two in the afternoon, they saw her crossing from Schlosser to Navy Island. Though Sir Allan McNab refused, in his evidence in McLeod's trial for the murder of Durfee, in the Caroline fray, to give the names of the persons from whom he received his information about the vessel, there can be no doubt that McLeod was one of them.

to destroy her that night.*   Captain Drew,† R. N., was instructed to collect a force of volunteers to burn, sink, or destroy the vessel.‡   The requisite number of volunteers were obtained, and at the moment of their embarkation, many of them were kept in ignorance of the service they were required to perform. All Captain Drew condescended to tell them, in asking them to take part in the enterprise, was " that he wanted a few fellows with cutlasses, who would follow him to the devil."§

The expedition comprised seven boats,|| with an average of about nine men each, armed with pistols, cutlasses, and boarding pikes.   This force of some sixty persons pushed off from the mouth of the Chippewa River about eleven o'clock.   The jolly boats

---

* Sir Allan McNab's evidence in McLeod's trial.   John Sheridan Hogan used to complain that the credit of the project for destroying the Caroline, due to him, was usurped by another.   Whatever truth there may be in this story, it will afterwards appear that Hogan entered into a conspiracy for bringing about a war between England and the United States, on account of the destruction of this vessel.

† On the 20th of December, Col. McNab, entrusted with the command of the loyal forces on the frontier, appointed Captain Drew to take charge of the Naval Department, and to organize a force of armed vessels and boats as a flotilla to protect the landing, and transport one thousand men to Navy Island They were never sent.

‡ Captain Drew's letter to Colonel McNab, December 30, 1837.

§ Sir Francis Bond Head's dispatch to Lord Glenelg, Toronto, February 9, 1838.   Most of the commanders of the boats selected their own men.   Colonel McNab asked some besides Capt. Drew; and though some, if not all of these were in the secret, Col. McNab did not give his final orders, which were verbal, till a few minutes before the boats started.

|| Captain Drew says there were only five boats, but in this he is contradicted by a dozen Canadian witnesses on the McLeod trial, all of whom state from personal knowledge—being engaged in the expedition—that seven boats started, and five reached their destination.   One grounded on Buckhorn sland, and another was provided with inefficient rowers.

were respectively commanded by Captain Drew, Lieu-
tenants M'Cormack, John Elmsley, and Christopher
Bier, all of the Royal Navy; Mr. John Gordon, captain of the steamboat Britannia, running on Lake
Ontario; Mr. Thomas Hector, of Kingston, and Lieutenant Battersby of London, Canada West. When
they had got opposite Navy Island, Captain Drew
ordered the men to rest on their oars, when he said
to them: "The steamboat is our object; follow me."*
Captain Drew, in his report of the transaction, leaves
it to be inferred that he expected to find the steamer
at Navy Island; but whether there were good grounds
for such an expectation or not is of no consequence,
since his orders were to destroy the steamboat wherever he could find her.† But they soon discovered
that she was at the wharf at Schlosser, on the United
States side of the Niagara River.‡ The boats went
silently towards the fated vessel, and do not appear
to have been discovered till within a few yards of

* Lieutenant Bier and Mr. Cleverly's evidence in the McLeod trial. Sir
F. Head (dispatch to Lord Goderich, February 9th, 1838) says Drew communicated to the men the object of the expedition as soon as they had pushed off;
but it is not likely they would rest on their oars in that rapid current till they
got in shelter of Navy Island.

† Sir Allan McNab's evidence in McLeod's trial. Lord Ashburton was
hardly warranted in stating, in his letter to Mr. Webster, July 28, 1842, that
"the expedition was sent to capture the Caroline where she was expected to be
found on the British ground of Navy Island, and that it was only owing to
the orders of the rebel leader being disobeyed that she was not so found."
The orders of the rebel leader were not disobeyed.

‡ Captain Drew in his report to Col. McNab, December 30th, 1837, states that
a vessel was "moored between an island and the main shore." It is called
Horne's Island, and is about thirty rods from the main land—Evidence of
James King on McLeod's trial. But several witnesses who accompanied him,
stated under oath, when their evidence was taken by commission in McLeod's
trial, that she was fastened to the wharf at Schlosser.

her.* The hands belonging to the steamer had gone to Niagara Falls that night, and Mr. Wells had allowed strangers—two of whom were sailors—to occupy their berths till their return.. They came back at twelve; but the strangers do not appear to have left before the attacking party arrived. The crew of the steamer, which was only of forty-six tons measurement, consisted of two men and a black boy. The watch on deck was prevented by the shade of the buildings from seeing the boats till they were near; and at first he supposed the crews to be Indians. The sentry on the gangway hailed the approaching boats, and in a hurried manner called out, "Boat ahoy! who comes there?"† A man in the leading boat replied, "Friends."‡ The sentinel then, turning to alarm the slumbering crew of the doomed vessel, shouted, "Turn up, boys, the enemy are coming!"§ In reply to the sentinel's demand for the countersign, Captain Drew said: "I'll give it to you when we get on board."‖ At this time, Captain Drew was close to the vessel; and the sentinel, fully comprehending that an assault was to be made on the vessel, is said to have fired; but whether with a pistol, a musket, or a rifle, it is impossible to determine from the conflicting evidence. He denies having fired at all, or being armed. The steamer's crew being surprised asleep, and having scarcely any other arms on board

---

* Captain Drew says they were not discovered till within twenty yards; Sir F. B. Head says fifteen.

† Sir F. B. Head's dispatch, February 9th, 1838.

‡ Daniel J. Stewart, on McLeod's trial.

§ Evidence of Mr. John Harris, of London, C. W., in McLeod's trial.

‖ Sir F. B. Head's dispatch, February 9th, 1838.

besides the piece discharged by the sentinel, hardly any resistance was offered. In a couple of minutes the vessel was in possession of the assailing party; and in the fray that took place on deck five or six persons were killed.* There was much hallooing, cursing, clashing of swords, and firing of pistols. Persons on board the boat when she was boarded state that some one ordered the gangway to be guarded; adding, with an oath, "Show the rebels no quarter." It is in evidence that forty or fifty shots were fired. The men on board were almost utterly defenceless, the attacking party met hardly any resistance when they got on board. At this time the light in the companion way was put out to prevent the assailants distinguishing those below. One person, desperately wounded, was taken ashore by orders of Captain Drew.† Captain Drew cut down one man in the fray, disabled another, "and with the flat of his sword, driving three before him, occasionally hastening them with the point, he made them step from the vessel to the wharf."‡ One shot was fired from the American shore on the assailing party. By the orders of Captain Drew, Lieutenant Elmsley and some of the men went on the American shore, and cut the vessel from her moorings, previous to setting fire to her, to prevent the destruction of other property by the spreading of the flames. The lamp was placed in a large basket, used for carrying Indian corn, and the

* Captain Drew's report. One of them was killed by Lieutenant McCormick. "His death was caused," says McCormick, in the evidence in McLeod's trial, "by a blow from me immediately after he had wounded me."

† Sir F. B. Head's dispatch, February 9th, 1838.

‡ Evidence of Mr. Smart Light, of North Oxford, in McLeod's trial.

cross-bars of the windows torn off and placed above the lamp, which set them on fire.* The vessel was then towed out, by the boats, from the wharf, till she was under the influence of the current. She was cut loose by Mr. Edward Zealand, of Hamilton.† If the strength of the current had not been too great,‡ it seems probable that an effort would have been made to take the Caroline across the river to the Canadian shore; for both Colonel McNab and Captain Drew give that as a reason for setting her on fire and sending her over the mighty cataract, above which she was found moored. When she had been towed out about fifteen or twenty rods, the victorious expedition gave three cheers and abandoned her to the force of the current.

When Mr. Wells, the owner of the boat, had managed to escape to the shore, he fancied he was pursued, but soon met instead of the assailants two of his men. "You are hurt," he said to King. "Yes, they have almost cut me to pieces," was the reply. The body of Amos Durfee lay between the inside railroad and the old warehouse. He had been shot in the back of the head, and his brains were scattered around. The pistol must have nearly touched him when it was fired, for his cap was singed with the powder. The ball had gone quite through the head.

Under all the circumstances, the right of the British authorities to destroy the Caroline, even by the inva-

* Evidence of James H. King on McLeod's trial.

† Edward Zealand's evidence in McLeod's trial.

‡ The force of the current was stated on McLeod's trial to be about five and a half knots an hour on the American side, and six knots on the Canadian side of Navy Island. Whatever it may be, its force must have been pretty well known before the expedition set out.

sion of American territory, cannot be successfully disputed.* The refugees had been seduced by American citizens into abusing the right of asylum; and they found among these citizens a large number who had joined their standard, and engaged in a war against a nation with whom their own Government was at peace.† The executive government was not armed

* Vattel lays down the principle applicable to the case: "Il est certain que si mon voisin donnait retrait à mes ennemis lorsqu'ils auraient du pire et se trouveraient trop faible pour m'échapper, leur laissant le temps de se refaire, et d'épier l'occasion de tenter une nouvelle irruption sur mes terres, cette conduite, si préjudiciable à ma sureté et mes interêts serait incompatible avec la neutralité. Lors donc que mes ennemis battus se retirent chez lui, si la charité ne lui permet pas de refuser passage et sûreté, il doit les faire passer outre le plus tôt possible, et ne point souffrir qu'ils se tiennent au aguets pour m'attaquer de nouveau; autrement il me met en droit de les aller chercher dans ses terres. C'est ce qui arrive aux nations qui ne sont pas en état de faire respecter leur territoire; le théâtre de la guerre s'y établit bientôt; on y marche, on y campe, on s'y bat, comme dans une pays ouvert à tout venants." The Americans had themselves in 1818 asserted and acted upon the principle laid down by Vattel. The Seminole Indians, who inhabited Florida, then a Spanish possession, were in the habit of making incursions upon the neighboring territory of the United States. On the 18th May, the United States forces, under Gen. Jackson, pursued the savage enemy, and in doing so took possession of Pensacola, and Barrancas Fort, in West Florida, though they were at peace with Spain. President Monroe, in his second annual message to Congress, Nov. 17, 1818, said: "The right of self-defence never ceases. It is among the most sacred and alike necessary to nations and individuals; and whether the attack be made by Spain herself or those who abuse her power, its obligation is not the less strong. * * * In pursuing these savages to an imaginary line in the woods, it would have been the height of folly to have suffered that line to protect them. Had that been done, the war would never cease. Even if the territory had been exclusively that of Spain, and her power complete over it, we had a right, by the law of nations, to follow the enemy on it, and to subdue him there." The Senate, however, did not approve of all that was done in this case by the United States forces.

† On this subject Henry Clay said, in the American Senate, on the 5th January, 1838; "If any citizens of these United States choose to renounce their citizenship and enter into the concerns of foreign states, he (Mr. C.) would not dispute their right to do so; but, so long as they remain citizens of this

with legal powers necessary to restrain its own citizens.* But it had not been entirely inactive. On the day of the Yonge St. retreat, and two days after the meeting of sympathizers was held at Buffalo, District Attorney Benton for Northern New York was officially instructed to watch and prosecute all violators of the neutrality laws. At the same time, Mr. Forsyth, Secretary of State, by direction of the President, called the attention of Governor Marcy, of the State of New York, to the contest, and asked his prompt interference to arrest the parties concerned, if any interference of a hostile nature should be made in the state of New York against a foreign power in amity with the United States. Similar letters were, on the same day,

country, they ought not to be allowed to take part in a foreign war with which this country has no concern." And Mr. Webster, in an official letter to Mr. Fox, dated April 24, 1841, gives it as the settled opinion and practice of the Federal Government that neutral states are bound to be strictly neutral; and that it is a manifest and gross impropriety for individuals to engage in the civil conflicts of other states, and thus to be at war while their government is at peace. War and peace are high national relations which can properly be established or changed only by nations themselves."

* Mr. Poinsett, Secretary of War, in instructing General Scott, January 5, 1838, to proceed to the Canadian frontier, to endeavor to preserve the neutrality of American citizens, said:—"The Executive possesses no legal authority to employ the military force to restrain persons within our jurisdiction, and who ought to be under our control, from violating the laws by making incursions into the territory of neighboring and friendly nations, with hostile intent." And on the same day, President Van Buren, by Special Message, called the attention of Congress to this defect in the national legislation; and recommended such a revision of the laws as would "vest in the Executive full power to prevent injuries being inflicted upon neighboring nations by the unauthorized and unlawful acts of citizens of the United States, or of other persons who may be within our jurisdiction and subject to our control." On the 10th of March, 1838, an act was passed for the purpose of more effectually restraining military enterprises, from the United States into the British Provinces.

addressed to the Governors of Michigan and Vermont, within the borders of which latter states some of the Lower Canada insurgents, after the defeat at St. Charles, had taken up their quarters. They had collected at Swanton, Highgate, and other places; and on the 6th December had, with three pieces of cannon, and small arms and ammunition, obtained from citizens of the United States, made a descent upon Canada, been repulsed, and retreated to Vermont. The governors of these states were directed to prosecute without discrimination all persons who had committed a breach of the laws enacted for the preservation of the neutral relations of the United States. Governor Jenison, of Vermont, issued a proclamation enjoining neutrality on its citizens. In New York, Mr. Marcy took the same course. But the destruction of the Caroline added to the sympathy for the cause of revolution, in Canada, an almost uncontrollable indignation at the invasion of American territory, which all classes of Americans joined in representing as unwarranted by the law of nations and not justified by the circumstances of the case. The President informed Congress that a demand for reparation would be made; public meetings were held to denounce what was considered as a wanton outrage; the press aided in inflaming the public excitement,* and it was said that, when General Burt had collected from 1,500

---

* Of the poetic effusions, the following example is from the Rochester *Democrat :—*

"DESTRUCTION OF THE CAROLINE.

"Oh, what were the dreams, as they sunk to rest,
   Of that devoted band,

to 2,000 militiamen to guard the frontier of New York.
State, it was with the greatest difficulty they could be

Who lay, as a babe on its mother's breast,
  On the shores of their native land ?
Breathed they of fire, or of streaming blood,
  Or the thundering Cataract's whelming flood ?

"Strong manhood's Godlike form was there,
  With his bold and open brow,
And age, with his wearied look of care,
  And his floating locks of snow;
And the agile form of the stripling boy,
  With his throbbing pulse of hope and joy.

"They dreamed of the happy hours of home—
  Of a blessed mother's prayer—
Of the cherished wife in that sacred dome—
  Of the lisping prattlers there ;
And the stripling dreamed of his young love's smile,
  When he left her, bound for the ' fatal isle.'

"Oh, what was that dim, ominous sound,
  That struck on the sleeper's ear,
Yet roused him not from his rest profound,
  'Till the unsheathed blade was near ?—
And it seemed as the air and rocks were riven,
  By the slogan of death and the wild shriek given.

"Ah! vain was the strife of the struggling few,
  With a well-armed murderous band ;
For the gallant bark, with her blood drenched crew,
  Is floating from the strand,
And the young boy's *quarter cry* it bore
  To the purple wave, with his own heart's gore.

"On—wildly onward—sped the craft,
  As she swiftly neared the verge ;
And the demon guards of the black gulf laughed,
  And chanted a hellish dirge ;
And the booming waters roared anew,
  A wail for the dead and dying crew.

restrained from going over to Navy Island to join the insurgents and sympathizers collected there. The feeling that an unjustifiable outrage had been committed by British subjects on American territory continued to inflame the population and to influence opinion in Congress.*

"As over the shelving rocks she broke,
  And plunged in her turbulent grave,
The slumbering Genius of Freedom woke,
  Baptised in Niagara's wave,
And sounded her warning tocsin far,
  From Atlantic's shore to the polar star."

"The young boy's quarter cry" mentioned in the fifth verse, has reference to a monstrous rumor which obtained extensive credence, that Captain Drew had, with his own sword, run a boy through. Some of the witnesses on McLeod's trial stated that they never saw the boy again ; but the newspapers of the day mentioned where he had been seen after his escape.

* On the 13th of February, 1841, Mr. Pickens brought in a report from the Committee of the United States House of Representatives, on Foreign Affairs, on the burning of the Caroline and the imprisonment of McLeod ; in which the following language was used :

"It is believed that, even in war, a neutral power has the right to trade in contraband articles, subject, of course, to seizure and confiscation, if taken within the jurisdiction of either of the contending parties. What is contraband of war is not always certain. Treaty stipulations frequently include some articles, and exclude others recognised in the law of nations. Trading in contraband articles is no excuse for invading the territory and soil of a neutral and independent power, whose private citizens may choose to run the hazards of such a trade. In this instance, there were two foreign powers engaged in war ; but all concerned in the outbreak or excitement within the British jurisdiction, claimed to be British subjects, in resistance of the authorities of Canada, a province of the British empire. Even admitting, then, that the Caroline was engaged in contraband trade, yet it was with citizens who claimed to be subjects of the same empire with those who were styled the legitimate officers of the Province. Abstractly speaking, how was a private citizen to decide who were right and who wrong in these local disputes ? And which portion of citizens of the same province must our citizens refuse to have any communication with ? But the boat was merely used for one day as a ferry boat ; and on the night of the day she commenced running, she was

I have an unpublished letter of District Attorney Rogers to Van Rensellaer, written on the day before the Caroline was destroyed, in which it was stated:—"The public authorities upon this frontier cannot and will not remain inactive in case our soil is made the theatre of operations for either of the belligerent armies. It is the duty as well as the policy of this Government to maintain a strict neutrality with Great Britain, and no means will be spared on the part of the public authorities to sustain and enforce the laws enacted for that object." The letter concluded by expressing a hope that if Van Rensellaer had any intention of landing his forces on Grand Island, it would be abandoned.*

However justifiable the destruction of the Caroline may have been in the eye of international law, it was

---

seized while moored at the wharf in Schlosser, and burnt. Several men were assassinated; certainly one, who fell dead upon the dock. Now the insinuation of the British Minister, [Fox,] that Schlosser was 'nominally' within the territory of the United States, may well be retorted, as we can with equal truth say that Navy Island was 'nominally' within the 'territory' of the British Government; for at the period to which we allude, the people collected there had as effectually defied the Canada authorities as any portion of our people had disregarded ours. Yet British authority thought proper to pass by Navy Island, then in its 'nominal' territory, and in the plenitude of its power, to cast the ægis of British jurisdiction over American soil. This was truly extending over us that kind guardianship which they had not the ability at that time to extend to a portion of their own territory, and which recommends itself to us, full as much from its assumption as from its love of right or law."

And Mr. Stevenson, the American Minister, in London, took the ground that the forces on Navy Island, commanded by an American citizen, were engaged in a civil war; and that as respects belligerent and neutral rights, civil wars are not distinguishable from other wars.

* Grand Island is an American island, situated a little higher up the Niagara River than Navy Island.

an act of great rashness. A militia colonel, without the least authority from his superiors, orders the invasion of the territory of a nation with whom his government is at peace; and when that nation was using efforts, not very successful it must be confessed, to maintain neutrality in a contest in which they were no way concerned. The British Government assumed the responsibility of the act; and with a degree of haste that was justly censured at the time, conferred the honor of knighthood on Col. McNab before the reclamation of the American Government had been disposed of. The Upper Canada House of Assembly tendered its thanks to the men engaged in the destruction of the Caroline, and granted swords to Colonel McNab and Captain Drew.

If the right to destroy the Caroline was clear, the necessity and expediency of exercising it are open to doubt. Nine days before the event, when there was only a handful of men on the island, Col. McNab had ordered Captain Drew to "organize such a force of armed vessels and boats for a flotilla," as would protect the landing and transport of a thousand men from the Chippewa shore to Navy Island; and Sir Francis Bond Head states that, after a fortnight's occupation of the island, by the patriots, there were plenty of boats lying idle on the shore, and "everything was in readiness to enable an overwhelming force to land, and with the point of the bayonet clear the island."* The militia are described as having been eager for the

---

* *The Emigrant.* On the 9th of January, Sir John Colborne, writing to Lord F. Somerset, from Montreal, said: "Not less than five thousand men are assembled under Col. McNab," on the Niagara frontier.

attack; and several wagons full of athletic negroes are said to have craved the honor of leading the forlorn hope in the anticipated attack.*   It would seem from these statements that there was no urgent necessity for destroying the steamer at the American shore, since the Patriots could have been dispersed by other means. It is not necessary to inquire into the correctness of this statement; it is sufficient that it was made on the authority of the Lieutenant Governor of the day. There were on the island, at that time, less than two hundred men; but they were inspired with such a desperate determination that far from having provided any boats for their escape, they had taken the pins out of the screws of the scows and burnt the oars, resolved, if attacked, to conquer their assailants or die in the attempt.

> "If 'sons of liberty' can keep
> No resting place but this,
> Then here we'll stand—or wildly leap
> Into the dark abyss." †

The Caroline had only been cut out of the ice on the 28th, and she was destroyed on the night of the only day on which she had run between Schlosser and the island.   The Washington authorities, in these ante-telegraph days, could not have been aware that she was carrying articles contraband of war; though rumor might have wafted them some intelligence of her intended movements, and their officers, as well as those of the State of New York, on the frontier, might

---

* Sir Francis Bond Head's *Emigrant.*

† From a poem entitled, "Liberty and Navy Island," dated January 29, 1837.

have known of what was going on. Sir Francis Bond Head, however, far from complaining of the exertions made by Governor Marcy to preserve the neutrality of citizens of New York, declared his appreciation of them, and had proposed to meet him in Buffalo on the very day on the night of which the Caroline was destroyed. If, as I think, these facts prove, that the destruction of the vessel at the United States bank of the river was not a necessity, it was in the last degree inexpedient.

President Van Buren seems to have been sincerely anxious to avoid a war with England; and it required all his address to prevent the Caroline massacre from interrupting the friendly relations of the two countries. The demand upon England for "reparation and atonement" was two years and a half undisposed of. In the meantime, Alexander McLeod was arrested on a charge of having murdered Amos Durfee, whose body was left on American territory, at Schlosser, as already described. While the whole question was still open, the British Government demanded his "immediate release." The demand was refused;* and

---

* In communicating to Mr. Fox, British Minister at Washington, that refusal, Mr. Secretary Forsyth said: "The transaction out of which the question arises, presents the case of a most unjustifiable invasion, in the time of peace, of a portion of the territory of the United States, by a band of armed men from the adjacent territory of Canada, the forcible capture by them within our own waters, and the subsequent destruction of a steamboat, the property of a citizen of the United States, and the murder of one or more American citizens. If arrested at the time, the offenders might unquestionably have been brought to justice by the judicial authorities of the State within whose acknowledged ter ritory these crimes were committed; and their subsequent voluntary entrance within that territory places them in the same situation. The President is not aware of any principle of international law, or indeed of reason or justice, which entitles such offenders to impunity before the legal tribunals, when

McLeod was put upon his trial,* in the Circuit Court
of the State of New York, at Utica, in October, 1841.
It commenced on the fourth, and lasted eight days.
Whether McLeod was guilty or innocent—the jury
declared him not guilty—it must be admitted that

coming voluntarily within their independent and undoubted jurisdiction, because they acted in obedience to their superior authorities, or because their acts
have become the subject of diplomatic discussion between the two Governments. These methods of redress, the legal prosecution of the offenders, and
the application of their Government for satisfaction, are independent of each
other, and may be separately and simultaneously pursued. The avowal or
justification of the outrage by the British authorities, might be a ground of complaint with the Government of the United States, distinct from the violation
of the territory and laws of the State of New York. The application of the
Government of the Union to that of Great Britain, for the redress of an authorized outrage of the peace, dignity, and rights of the United States, cannot deprive the State of New York of her undoubted right of vindicating, through
the exercise of her judicial power, the property and lives of her citizens."

In the report of Mr. Pickens, already quoted, it was argued that the Federal
Government had no power to give up McLeod. "Jurisdiction," it was said,
"in State tribunals over criminal cases, and trial by a jury of the venue, are
essential points in American jurisprudence; and it is a total misapprehension
of the nature of our system to suppose that there is any right in the Federal
Executive to arrest the verdict of the one or thwart the jurisdiction of the
other. If such a power existed, and were exercised, it would overthrow, and
upon a vital point, the separate sovereignty and independence of these States."
Mr. Secretary Forsyth also took the ground that the Federal Government had
no power to interfere in the matter; and that the decision must rest solely
with the State of New York.

* Alexander McLeod was a Scotchman by birth; and was born at the Feus
of Carnoustie, about half way between Dundee and Arbroath. His father was
from Inverness. Alexander enlisted as a soldier when young; and about the
year 1825, emigrated with his parents and the rest of the family to Upper
Canada, He and his sister Margaret first kept a store in Kingston. He afterwards moved to Toronto, where he carried on the business of a grocer. In politics, he was at this time strongly opposed to the Family Compact. A few years
before the rebellion, he was appointed Deputy Sheriff of the District of Niagara;
and about the same time joined the Orange Society. As Deputy Sheriff, it
fell to him to execute an order for the extradition of Jesse Happy *alias* Solomon
Moseley, a fugitive slave from Kentucky, who, in effecting his escape, had

many a man has been hanged upon much weaker evidence than that which was produced against him.. Three witnesses swore that they saw him get into one of the boats engaged in the expedition; one, that he' saw him get out on the return of the boats; two, that they had heard him admit being present;. three, that he had killed one man. One of them swore that he admitted. that he had killed Durfee. On the part of the defence, an *alibi* was set up : the witnesses. brought forward to establish it, being Margaret. Morrison, of Bellevue Cottage, near Stanford, mother of a girl who lived with McLeod, but whether they lived as man and wife she could not say; and one other of the girl's relatives. William Press, a tavern-keeper, at Niagara, swore that he took McLeod, a little before dark, in a wagon, from Chippewa to Morrison's house. Besides over a dozen persons who took part in the expedition, and who must have been McLeod's accomplices if he were guilty, swore that he was not there,

---

carried off one of his master's horses. An attempt was made to rescue the fugitive, in which one Herbert Holmes was killed by the officials, and others wounded. Mr. Mackenzie relates an incident in proof of his courageous disposition. When the latter was Mayor of Toronto, McLeod went from Niagara to that city and took the disease. "I put him into the Cholera Hospital," says Mr. Mackenzie, "where I personally saw his case; he was well attended to, recovered, and returned home; but I did not see that the fear of death alarmed him. in the least." In Mackenzie's trial for the Welland Canal libel, McLeod did all he could to correct the fraudulent list of special jurors said to have been made out by Charles Richardson, Clerk of the Peace. It is said, and Mr. Mackenzie believed the report, that McLeod positively refused to hang Moreau, one of the Canadian Patriots convicted of high treason. While Deputy Sheriff, he became deeply involved in debt; and on the death of Sheriff Hamilton, February 19, 1839, he was balked in his expectation of succeeding to the office. He was about forty years of age at the time.of the Caroline outrage, and is still living near Toronto.

or that they did not see him and were not aware of his presence.*

The verdict of "not guilty" probably prevented a war between England and the United States. The English view of the matter was that the destruction of the Caroline was a public act, performed by persons obeying the orders of their superior authorities; and that no one engaged in it could be held individually accountable. The authorities of the States were probably not very anxious for a conviction; but they had to appease public indignation by the ceremonial of a trial.

The folly of the destruction of the Caroline, under the circumstances described, is best proved by the necessity which England was under of finally apologizing for the act. Lord Ashburton, while engaged in the settlement of the north-east boundary question, addressed to Mr. Webster, under date, Washington, July 28, 1842, an apology for the invasion of American territory. "I am instructed," his lordship said, "to assure you that Her Majesty's government consider this [the violation of American territory] a most serious fact, and that far from thinking that an event of this kind should be lightly risked, they would unfeignedly deprecate its existence; looking back to what passed at this distance of time, what is, perhaps, most to be regretted is that some explanation and apology

* Sir Allan McNab; Mr. John Harris, of London, C. W.; Edward Zealand, Hamilton, C. W.; W. S. Light, North Oxford; Robert Armour, Cobourg; John Gordon, Captain of the Steamer Britannia; Christopher Beer, of Chippewa; H. R. O'Rielly, of Hamilton; Shepherd McCormick of London, C. W.; Frederick Cleverly, London, C. W.; Thomas Hector, of Toronto; Neil McGregor, of Chippewa; J. P. Battersby, of Ancaster.

for this occurrence was not immediately made." This apology was accepted in the conciliatory spirit which marked Lord Ashburton's letter, and the President consented to "make this subject, as a complaint of violation of territory, the topic of no further discussion between the two governments."

The British steamboat, Sir Robert Peel, was burnt in retaliation, on the 29th of May, 1838, while taking in wood at Well's Island, three miles from French Creek.

Mrs. Mackenzie was the only female who spent any length of time on Navy Island. She arrived there a few hours before the destruction of the Caroline, and remained nearly a fortnight with her husband, making flannel cartridge-bags, and inspiring with courage, by her entire freedom from fear, all with whom she conversed. At the end of about a fortnight, ill-health obliged her to leave. Mr. Mackenzie accompanied her to the house of Captain Appleby, Buffalo, and while on his way he was arrested, in the railway car, by the United States Marshal for a breach of the neutrality laws. He entered into recognizance in $5000 for his appearance, and returned to the island the next morning, where he remained till Gen. Van Rensellaer announced his intention to evacuate it, with the force under his command, on the 13th of January. There was much excitement when he was arrested. A Mr. Burton, who was suspected of having informed against him, was greeted with hisses and groans, and handed round to be gazed upon by the crowd as a monstrosity. Three gentlemen immediately stepped forward and entered into recognizances for the amount required.

The Buffalo Committee of thirteen seems to have had more power than the Provisional Government, for the question of evacuating the island was decided by it. At this time, Mr. Mackenzie seems to have had very little influence with Van Rensellaer, who was vested with the entire military command. It is matter of surprise that the island, which was intended as a *point d' appui* from which to take a liberating army into Western Canada, was permitted to be occupied by insurgents, and American citizens who sympathised with them, for a period of over a month without being assaulted by the vastly superior force on the main land, who were spending their time in an inglorious and inactive campaign.

On the evacuation of the island, another difficulty with the States' authorities was very near occurring. Captain Drew ordered two schooners to be placed in the middle of the stream, between Navy Island and the American shore, to watch the steamboat Barcelona, said to be taking the islanders across, to bring her to in case she attempted to pass, and if she should succeed in passing to follow her until she was captured, or at least till it was seen on what part of the shore she landed. But whether from a misapprehension of Captain Drew's orders—which were changed two or three times in one day, has been disputed—fortunately no collision occurred.

CHAPTER VIII.

WHEN the patriots took possession of Navy Island,
they expected soon to be able to cross over to the

main land and join Dr. Duncombe's forces in the West.
The doctor, who had been in constant correspondence
with the Lower Canada patriots, had under his command between three and four hundred men; but a
large number of them were without arms.   They
were assembled at Brantford, whither Colonel McNab,
with a detachment of about three hundred and sixty
men, repaired.   On his approach, Dr. Duncombe retreated to a place called Scotland.   Colonel McNab
was reinforced at Brantford by one hundred and fifty
volunteers and one hundred Indians, under command
of Captain Kerr.   When a plan of attacking the insurgents simultaneously at three points had been
agreed upon, and was to have been executed next
morning, Dr. Duncombe retreated.   He told the men
that Mackenzie had been defeated near Toronto, and
they had better disperse.   In the meantime, Colonel
McNab, learning of the anticipated retreat, dispatched
messengers to Simcoe, Woodstock, and London, requesting all the volunteers that could be mustered to
march down and intercept the rebels.   On the 14th
of December, while at Scotland, his force was increased
by about one thousand additional volunteers.   Hundreds more had been expected to join Duncombe,
from the neighborhood of St. Thomas and other places
in the west.   Here Colonel McNab seized all Duncombe's papers, as well as those of Eliakim Malcolm,
and took several prisoners, whom he sent under an
escort to Hamilton.   In spite of the retreat of Duncombe, and the dispersion of his men, Colonel McNab
sent to the Lieutenant Governor a strong recommendation to sanction the raising of volunteer companies of

PORTRAIT OF McLEOD.

one hundred and fifty men each. While at Scotland, deputations of insurgents visited him offering to surrender their arms, take the oath of allegiance, and, if necessary, form part of his force. In other places large numbers of undetected rebels, when they found the tide turning against them, joined the loyal forces; so that the number of volunteers was no proof of the popularity of the government. At a place called Sodom, township of Norwich, many of Duncombe's men surrendered themselves to Colonel McNab, who, with a degree of humanity that reflects credit upon him, after receiving what arms they had, permitted them to return to their homes, on condition that they should again surrender themselves, should His Excellency not extend the Royal clemency to them. Some of the ringleaders were sent to London, under an escort, for trial, where Joshua Guilam Doan, for whose apprehension a reward had been offered, was executed, on the 6th of February, 1839.

On the 19th of December, 1837, Colonel McNab mentions a report that considerable disaffection prevailed in the western district, particularly in the neighborhood of Sandwich. But the insurrection was put down in the western part of the Province without a shot being fired.

In the "Navy Island memoranda," I find the original order of Van Rensellaer to General Sutherland to set out to Detroit to make preparations for making a descent upon Canada.* But when he reached the

---

* "HEADQUARTERS, NAVY ISLAND,
December 28, 1837.

"Brigadier General Sutherland will repair with all dispatch to Detroit and its vicinity, and promote every arrangement for making a descent upon. Canada, in favor of the Patriots, as he in his judgment may deem most advis-

Western frontier, he was destined to encounter a rival, in the person of Henry S. Handy, of Illinois. In Michigan, what was called the Patriot army of the North West had been organized, and Henry S. Handy, of Illinois, had been appointed Commander-in-chief. His command extended over the whole of Western Canada. The other officers were James M. Wilson, Major General; E. J. Roberts, Brigadier General of the first Brigade; Dr. Theller, Brigadier General, to command the first Brigade of French and Irish troops to be raised in Canada. A number of colonels were also appointed and sworn in. The staff was then made out and the organization commenced. The council of war proceeded to collect men and materials of war.* Theatres and public houses were made depots for arms. When things had gone on smoothly for some time, the friendly Governor of Michigan, about the 1st of January, quietly intimated to Handy and General Roberts, that he should be obliged to disperse the Patriot forces, and that they must move to some other place. The council then placed the troops and munitions under the control of General Handy, by whom a contract was made for the steamboat McComb, and the schooner Anne was

able, after consulting with the Canadian and American friends of the cause in that quarter.

"R. V. R., &c., &c., &c.

* I take this relation from General Handy's elaborate manuscript reports. The council of war here referred to must have been that formed in Michigan by the exertions of M. Dufort; and in deference to the wishes Mr. Bidwell expressed in Toronto in the previous November, some of the leading men of Michigan had given all the aid in their power to this scheme of co-operation with the Patriots.

also obtained for the purpose of effecting their removal to the point of intended operations. On the night of the 5th of January, the arms, munitions, and provisions, were put on board the schooner, and she was taken down the river a short distance and moored. Her sails were on another vessel; and without the tow of a steamboat she was helpless. It was intended to place the troops on the steamer McComb, and then use her to tow the schooner; but before this could be done, the Brady Guards with a few United States regulars, under General Brady, seized the steamer and placed a guard over her. A contract was then made for the steamer Brady to take her place; but she also was seized. General Handy then ordered General Wilson to take the troops in squads, during the night, to Gibraltar, on American Island at the mouth of the Detroit River opposite Fort Malden, to man the yawl-boats with six oarsmen each and thus tow the schooner down the river. When they arrived at River Rouge a sail was obtained for the schooner, and she started under command of Colonel Davis for Gibraltar. On the way she encountered the steamer United States, with sixty men on board; but on seeing the three pieces of ordnance on the deck of the Anne, the steamer made off for the Canada shore. Colonel Davis was probably alarmed by the sight of this steamer; for, instead of continuing down the river, he returned after going ten miles below Detroit. General Handy, learning this disobedience of his orders, sent instructions to General Roberts to take the command. On the 6th of January, Handy sent an order to Colonel Davis of Mount Clements, to move his two companies of riflemen from the mouth of the Clinton River to Peach Island, six miles above Detroit, where next morning the general was to join him with recruits. That day, General Handy received an intimation from the Governor of Michigan that he and the Brady Guards would probably be at Gibraltar on the 18th, from which point he should be obliged to disperse the troops. Gen. Handy then sent an order to Brigadier General Roberts to put all the arms and munitions on board the schooner Anne, and to put the troops on board the sloops, scows, yawl-boats, and canoes, in the morning before the Governor would arrive; to land the troops on Bois Blanc Island, and to moor the schooner Anne in the small bay, near the head of the island and directly opposite the fort; to discharge from the schooner every thing except three cannon, and thirty men under Colonel Davis to man them. A temporary fortification was to be thrown up; on the evening of the 8th the schooner was to be made ready for action, and on the morning of the 9th the tri-colored flag was to be raised and the surrender of the fort demanded. In case of refusal a brisk cannonade was to be opened; the troops, with a heavy piece of ordnance, landed, and the fort carried by storm. At the same time, General Handy, with Colonel Davis' troops, was to take possession of the public stores at Sandwich and Windsor, and march thence to Malden and take command.

On the morning of the 7th, General Handy started from Mount Clements to meet Col. Davis; and in the afternoon of the next day, an express from General Roberts reached him, with the intelligence that General Sutherland had arrived from Cleveland with about two hundred troops ; and that, in virtue of the instructions he had received from General Van Rensellaer, he claimed the command. General Handy had no idea of being balked in his ambition to lead the troops; and he found that it was necessary for him to hasten, with all possible speed, to Gibraltar, where General Theller, in violation of the orders and appointment he had received from the Council of War, had taken up the cudgels against General Roberts, and done all in his power to place General Sutherland at the head of the command. The Ohio troops had no knowledge of the organization of the North Western army, and thinking the order of General Van Rensellaer ought to be respected, a serious difficulty as to who should have the command arose. A compromise was proposed : "That if," says General Handy, " Sutherland would implicitly obey the orders of the Commander-in-chief sent to General Roberts, the command should be given to him until by express I could reach the island." To this proposition General Roberts assented; and the command of the schooner was given by General Sutherland to General Theller. But the expectation of landing on Bois Blanc Island was disappointed. " Either by adverse winds or through disobedience of orders," says General Handy, " the landing was made on Sugar Island." General Theller sailed the schooner round the foot of Bois Blanc, and when passing the fort she was hailed by the sentinel, who, receiving no answer, fired into her. General Theller, so Handy was informed, when opposite Amherstburg, fired a nine pounder into the town, instead of aiming at the fort, contrary to all usages of war, as he had not even demanded the sur- render of the place.   After this exploit General Thel- ler returned and moored the schooner near the camp on Sugar Island, for the night.   General Roberts of the Patriot army denounced the firing upon the town, without a demand for surrender being pre- viously made, as a piratical act; and he recommended General Handy to arrest Generals Sutherland and Theller for disobedience of orders.

On the 9th, General Sutherland called for sixty vo- lunteers, for whom arms were ready, to proceed with him to Bois Blanc Island.   Boats and craft were got ready to make a landing.   General Sutherland then ordered Colonels Dodge, Davis, and Brophy, with eighteen others, on board the schooner Anne, which then sailed round to the foot of the island, and moored in a small basin near the head of the island, opposite Fort Malden.   General Sutherland, with his sixty volunteers, landed on the island near the light-house, where he hoisted the tri-colored flag and issued his proclamation to the citizens of Upper Canada.

---

* "PROCLAMATION TO THE PATRIOTIC CITIZENS OF UPPER CANADA.—You are called upon by the voice of your bleeding country to join the Patriot forces, and free your land from tyranny.   Hordes of worthless parasites of the Bri- tish Crown are quartered upon you to devour your substance—to outrage your rights—to let loose upon your defenceless wives and daughters a brutal soldiery.

"Rally, then, around the standard of Liberty, and victory and a glorious future of independence will be yours.

"THOMAS J. SUTHERLAND, *Brigadier General,*
"Commanding Second Division Patriot Army, U. C.

"HEADQUARTERS, SECOND DIVISION, ⎫
    Bois Blanc, U. C., Jan., 9, 1838." ⎭

The schooner Anne, only about half rigged, having but one small sail, was drifted towards the main shore, where she was beached in three feet of water.* A brisk fire—so Handy reports—was now opened upon her by the royalist troops on shore. General Sutherland ordered the yawl-boat to row him to the foot of the island, where he discovered that the schooner had been boarded by the British troops. Returning to his men, he, without landing, ordered them to retreat immediately to Sugar Island. The men entreated him to permit them to go with their boats to the rescue of the schooner, but he positively refused to grant their request; and, with apparent alarm, cried out, " Away to Sugar Island! Fly, fly, fly, all is lost!"† He then hurried to the main body of the troops on Sugar Island, whence the destruction of the schooner could be seen. Though it is not certain, General Theller is believed to have followed the instructions of General Sutherland in taking the schooner where he did. " I have no doubt," says General Handy, in his report, " that General Theller has the Patriot cause at heart, but for want of cool discretion, and perhaps that skill which a man of his rank should have, he may have

---

* Colonel Bradley states there was only one sailor on board, and that he was shot at the helm, after which the vessel became unmanageable. The schooner Anne appears, from a statement of General Handy, to have been given to the Patriots by Captain Gillet, who assisted them in other ways.

† Colonel Bradley afterwards denounced Sutherland as a coward, and said that if a landing had been effected Amherstburg would easily have been taken. It was also stated that three hundred or four hundred Canadians would have joined him as soon as he had landed. These added to those under Sutherland's command would, it was contended, have been more than a match for any resisting force they would have met. By this means a triumphant entrance into the western part of Canada had been expected.

committed an error; but as to General Sutherland, his course of conduct, after that period—his entire recklessness, gross violation of good faith, together with the fact (as reported to me) of his being closeted in a room in Detroit with Colonel Prince, for some hours, and his immediate departure from Gibraltar, there leaving his side-arms, and starting for Point au Pelé on foot, travelling on the Canadian side, meeting Colonel Prince and there suffering Colonel Prince to take himself and his aid with his single arm—gives me good ground to believe that he was both a traitor and a coward."

The Governor of Michigan seems to have used a great deal of gentleness in the performance of his duty of dispersing the patriots and sympathizers. On the morning of the 8th, he, with the Brady Guards and a number of United States troops, fell in with General Handy at Gibraltar. In an interview, which lasted only a few minutes, the Governor requested Handy to seek other quarters, as he had come down to disperse the Patriots, none of whom were then at that point.

On the afternoon of the 9th, General Handy, acting on the suggestion of General Roberts, dispatched two persons in a canoe to arrest Generals Sutherland and Theller on Sugar Island, for having committed a piratical act, in violation of orders; but, in consequence of the roughness of the river, they had to land on Grosse Isle. The messengers were Colonel Chamberlain and Colonel Wilkins.* The latter was the

---

* While sentencing Colonel Vreeland, in the summer of 1838, for taking part with the Patriots, Judge Wilkins said :—

"The Constitution and Laws of your country give ample freedom of opinion

judge before whom General Theller was tried for a breach of those neutrality laws in which the accused had the judge for an accomplice! Handy dispatched Mr. Lawton, his secretary, to Detroit with General Roberts's report of what had occurred; but the secretary was so much alarmed that he burnt the report instead of getting it printed. In consequence of the rumors that got afloat, the American public lost all confidence in Generals Handy and Roberts.

About noon on the 10th, the steamboat Erie arrived at Gibraltar with Handy's Adjutant General, Paymaster, Commissary, and Quartermaster, with some stores. General Roberts, Colonel Mackenzie, Major Fryer, and some others, started in company with General Handy for Sugar Island. General Sutherland, on being introduced to General Handy, proffered him the command, which the latter refused to accept. He gave as reasons for this refusal that the troops had no sufficient supplies of arms, ammunition, blankets, or camp equipage; that the United States authorities were making great efforts to put down the Patriots; that the confidence of the public had been lost by the failure of the first attempt to strike a blow in the West for the liberation of Canada, that, until the orders he

and of speech to every citizen. We all can sympathize with the suffering friends of liberty every where, and there is and can be no restraint imposed upon the utterance of our opinions. But beyond this, until our common country constitutionally calls us to the field, we can do and ought to do nothing in our own jurisdiction. The flag of freedom may be planted in the Canadas, and we all may pray for its triumph over what we conceive to be oppression and tyranny; nay, we might join it there; all this can be done with impunity, but the law prohibits us from organizing a hostile expedition in our own country, with the intent of invading the possessions of peaceful powers."

73

had given had been disobeyed—though the truth was, Sutherland was just as much the commander-in-chief as he was—there was not a piece of ordnance west of Toronto in possession of the British troops, but that the arms and ammunition which had fallen into the hands of the loyalists, when they captured the schooner Anne, would be sufficient for a winter's campaign for a thousand men.* General Sutherland then proposed to leave it to the troops to decide which of the two should be their commander; and after both he and Handy had addressed them, the seven hundred men, with two exceptions, voted for Handy.

General Handy then ordered General Roberts to place a guard on the steamer, till he could learn the situation of the arms and ammunition; his intention being, if he could raise sufficient for one hundred and fifty men, to make an immediate descent on Fort Malden. On examination he found that there were not over sixty firearms on the island fit for use. The steamboat then returned to Detroit with General Sutherland. This discarded general—if we accept Handy's account of the affair—was very far from keeping the obligation into which he entered when he appealed to the troops to elect their general. Sutherland at once called a meeting, in Detroit, for the purpose of procuring volunteers. He got into difficulty. For pub-

---

* Colonel Radcliffe, of the Canadian militia, tells a different story:—"He found on board," he says, "twenty-one persons; one killed, eight wounded, twelve prisoners, three pieces of cannon, not very useful, about two hundred stand of arms, buff cross-belts, and ammunition, but of this a small supply." The Canadian militia, in boarding the vessel, waded up to their arms. Captain Ironside was one of those who boarded the schooner; her flag was taken by him.

lishing his proclamation,*. in the United States, he was arrested and held to bail. General Handy remained several days on the island drilling the troops, and in expectation of the arrival of arms, ammunition, and provisions, from Detroit. But no supplies arrived, and the accumulation of ice had cut off all the ordinary means of communication for weeks. The ice was now descending the river in large quantities; and unless the men made their escape, they were very likely soon to find themselves without provisions and unable to get away. In this condition of things, General Handy called on the friendly Governor of Michigan for succor. He sent an express to him, desiring him to go to Sugar Island with a steamboat, in company with no other person than General Brown, for the purpose of dispersing his—General Handy's— forces. The Governor consented; and next evening he and General Brown met Handy at Gibraltar, whence they proceeded in the steamer Erie to Sugar

* "PROCLAMATION TO THE DELUDED SUPPORTERS OF BRITISH TYRANNY IN UPPER CANADA.—You are required to lay down your arms, and return quietly to your homes. The Patriot army of Upper Canada desire not bloodshed. We fight only for liberty, and personal and public safety.

"Your persons and property shall be protected, all your private rights preserved to you, your homes secured, your possessions untouched, on condition that you yield up your weapons and return to your accustomed occupations.

"You are now enjoying a moiety of liberty vouchsafed to you from motives of caprice or interest on the part of your rulers. We will secure to you all the blessings of freedom by a permanent and honorable tenure.

"Avoid then the horrors of war. Enrage not soldiers already exasperated by oppression. Save yourselves from confiscation. Cease resistance, and all will be well with you.

"THOMAS J. SUTHERLAND, *Brigadier General,*
"Commanding Second Division, Patriotic Army, U. C.
"HEADQUARTERS, SECOND DIVISION, }
Bois Blanc, U. C. Jan. 10, 1838." }

Island. General Roberts, who had the troops in a line
on the bank, amidst their camp fires, received them with
a salute.   The Governor and General Brown visited
General Handy's quarters; after which the arms and
ammunition were taken on board, and the troops escorted the Governor and General Brown to the river
bank.   One boat with the troops landed at Gibraltar
about one o'clock in the morning.   The Governor
took from General Roberts a receipt for the arms;
after which the boat left with the Governor and General Brown for Detroit.

But the idea of renewing an attack on Fort Malden
was not given up.   The men were taken to some shan-
ties, that had been used by canal laborers, about four
miles from Gibraltar, where they were drilled without
arms for some ten days.   General Handy was waiting
in expectation of succor arriving; but the vigilance of
the United States Marshal and the troops under General Brady stood in the way of the execution of any
arrangement for that purpose.   The Governor, " for
reasons which," says Handy, " we will not require,"
called out six hundred of the militia to enforce the
neutrality of the United States.   Three hundred of
them had the City Hall of Detroit for their headquarters.   An extraordinary plot, in which the militia
was implicated, was formed.   On the night they received their arms they stacked them in the outer porch
of the City Hall, for the purpose of having them taken
for the use of Handy's men, who were to become volunteers and have their services paid for by the State
while they got ready to make an attack on Fort Malden!   But the rival general, Sutherland, ignorant of

this extraordinary arrangement, arrived in Detroit from Pontiac, on the second night of the occupation by the militia of the City Hall, seized the arms and secreted them. But they were retaken next day. "This course of conduct," says Handy, "highly exasperated the Governor"—who was favorable to the Patriot movements—and the citizens; and from that time General Brady refused to trust the militia with arms. "Thus," says Handy, in his manuscript report from which this statement is taken, "was the third and last arrangement to carry out the campaign broken up either by treachery or ignorance."

. The United States Marshal got out sixty writs for the arrest of Handy's officers; and that functionary called on Generals Roberts and Handy, and informed them that, if they would disperse the men, the writs would be returned unserved. Next day the men were assembled at Gibraltar; when General Handy informed them that all prospects of carrying out the campaign were at an end, and they unanimously resolved to disband. But at the same time, they "took a solemn obligation" to hold themselves ready for the Patriot service; and that they would again assemble whenever Handy should require them to do so.

General Handy admits, in an unpublished letter, that "the Executive and-many worthy officers of the State [of Michigan] and United States have been more or less concerned in our exertions to sustain the Canadian standard; and he predicts that they will assuredly hereafter do more. This letter is without date, but the accompanying documents prove it to have been written near the end of May,

1839. These facts have a significance which time
has done nothing to impair. I have it from more
than one source, though I cannot vouch for the accuracy of the statement, that, if Toronto had fallen,
some of the principal men in the United States army
would have resigned their commissions, and entered
the Patriot service.

Colonel Vreeland and General McLeod* arrived on
the Western frontier, soon after the time of the evacuation of Navy Island, with a brigade to join the army
of the North-west. Vreeland reported himself Commander of the brigade; but he was in fact, Handy
says, Colonel of ordnance and Inspector of commissariat.† Between him and McLeod there was no good
feeling. The latter denounced him in his official reports to Van Rensellaer as a " Judas" and a " traitor."
Under a promise from Vreeland that he would supply
them with arms, including seven or eight pieces of
artillery, and plenty of ammunition, a Patriot force
crossed over, on a cold night in February, to Fighting
Island, when they found themselves without other
means of defence than forty-three firelocks which they
had taken with them, and some of which were useless.
The truth is, however, that General Scott had seized
the arms on the night previous. On the 25th of Fe-

---

* Donald McLeod was born at Fort Augustus, Invernesshire, Scotland. His
father was a common soldier, and he himself became a sergeant in the British
army. After his discharge he taught school at Brockville, Upper Canada.
On the breaking out of the rebellion, he became a refugee in the United States,
and attracted thither a good many Canadians. While there he was very active in the service of the Patriots. After it was all over, he got office in Canada, from Dr. Rolph, and, I think, now enjoys some sort of retiring allowance.

† I find from the original minutes a meeting at which he was appointed, held
at Canneaut, January 29, 1838, that Vreeland was Brigade Inspector.

bruary they encountered a force of British Regulars, stated by McLeod to have been five hundred in number. Five of the Patriots were wounded, and McLeod gives it as a rumor that the British troops lost five killed and fifteen wounded.

The refugees were frequently in danger from secret enemies or private assassins. On the 21st of January, 1838, Van Rensellaer wrote from Buffalo to Mackenzie, who was in Rochester, to warn him that there were desperadoes in the former city whose object was to assassinate him.

Soon after they left Navy Island, Mackenzie and Van Rensellaer found it impossible to continue work together. In the month of February, an expedition was planned for the purpose of making a descent upon Kingston. Van Rensellaer claims to have planned it, and though this seems to be true, there is reason to believe that before this time he had agreed not to interfere further with the affairs of Canada.* However this may be, he and Mackenzie were playing at cross purposes, and the latter came to the resolution to have nothing to do with the expedition, if it was to be directed by Van Rensellaer. " I cannot," said Mackenzie, in a letter to a friend, " sail in a boat to be piloted as. he thinks fit." While Van Rensellaer sought the control of the expedition got up at French Creek to make a descent upon Kingston, Mackenzie was most anxious that he should not have it. On Mackenzie's part

---

* On the 10th of February, 1838, Captain Graham wrote to Mackenzie that Van Rensellaer had passed through Rochester on the previous night with the intention of "getting up another Navy Island explosion on the St. Lawrence," and this seems to be the first Mackenzie heard of it.

this desire arose from the utter unfitness of Van Rensellaer, as proved by his conduct on Navy Island, for such a command. Mackenzie was no military man, and desired no command for himself, but when he found that it was to be vested in Van Rensellaer he resigned all connection with the movement.

It had been arranged, by correspondence carried on by Mackenzie, that a rising should take place in Canada, when the expedition crossed. Fort Henry was garrisoned by civilians; a person in the fort had agreed to spike the guns, on the approach of the Patriots, and at a concerted signal to throw open the gates for their admittance. The intended assault became known in Kingston, and sixteen hundred men were placed under arms with a view of defending the place. At Ganonoque two companies of Regulars had been stationed, in addition to the local force. Near the end of February, Van Rensellaer crossed from French Creek, a village situated on the American side of the St. Lawrence, a short distance below Kingston, to Hickory Island, about two miles from Ganonoque, with a force that has been variously stated at from fifteen to twenty-five hundred men. Van Rensellaer, while here, kept ·his bed, in such a state of intoxication that he could ·not give an intelligent answer to any question put to him. The men, disgusted or alarmed, began to move off in squads, and when all chance of success had been lost, a council of war was held, and it was determined to retreat. The morning after the island was evacuated, Van Rensellaer reports that the loyalists were upon it two hundred strong.

Van Rensellaer published a letter, dated Albany,

March 29, 1838, in which he blames Mr. Mackenzie for having interfered with his plans, by way, it would seem, of accounting for his own failure. That letter contained accusations against Mr. Mackenzie which Van Rensellaer himself afterwards admitted to be unjust. In an unpublished letter addressed to Mr. McMahon, and dated Albany, February 24, 1840, he says: "Since I have had time for reflection, for arriving at correct information, and for weighing dispassionately circumstances which led me to an unjust conclusion, while penning my statement, although I am yet of opinion that he has committed errors— and who has not?—I am bound as a man of honor to admit that all my charges, whether expressed or implied, against his moral integrity or honesty of purpose, are, as far as my present knowledge and information extend, incorrect." After which confession he exclaims, " I am mightily relieved."

Soon after this, Gen. McLeod dispatched Col. Seward with about four hundred men to Point au Pelé Island, some forty miles south east of Amherstburg. On the 4th of March, McLeod was on the point of joining them, when he received a dispatch from Col. Bradley, informing him that they had been defeated, with a loss of fifteen or twenty missing, and retreated to the American shore. " The loss of the enemy," says McLeod, in an unpublished letter, " is fifty or sixty, and a great number wounded." The loyalist troops were supported by cavalry and artillery, and one of the Patriot colonels attributes their retreat principally to want of artillery. The British troops were under Colonel Maitland, and consisted of five companies of Regu-

74

lars, with about two hundred militia and Indians. Nine prisoners were taken by the British, among whom was General Sutherland. He was not taken on the island, and his trial was afterwards declared illegal by the British Government and his release ordered. He was, however, kept in prison for a long time.

From this western frontier a combination of great force, extending over the two Canadas, was soon to be made, and but for the occurrence of an accident, it is impossible to say what the result might not have been.

CHAPTER IX.

Mr. Mackenzie's Movements—He Commences the Publication of *Mackenzie's Gazette,* in New York—Is joined by his Family—Canadian Relief Association—Treason Legislation—Execution of Lount and Matthews—Prisoners escape from Fort Henry—Monster Conspiracy for Revolutionizing Canada, and how it was Frustrated—General Handy Superseded by General Bierce—The Short Hills Expedition.

WHILE the abortive expeditions of Bois Blanc and Point au Pelé were in progress, Mr. Mackenzie was sounding the public feeling in other places. He visited some of the Patriot leaders of Lower Canada, at Plattsburg, soon after leaving Navy Island, and went to New York, Philadelphia, and other places.

When the question of evacuating Navy Island was before the Buffalo committee of thirteen,* Mr. Mackenzie had become impressed with what he conceived to be the necessity of establishing a public journal to express the views of the Patriots in Canada, and their friends in the United States. The project was finally carried out by himself. On the 17th of April, the prospectus of *Mackenzie's Gazette* was published, and the first number of the paper made its appearance, on the 12th of May, in New York, and was continued till the close of 1840. During the greater part

* On this committee were Dr. Johnson, a former Mayor of Buffalo, Mr. Seymour, Master in Chancery, Mr. Macy, Mr. Wilkinson, and other local celebrities.

of this time, the paper was published in Rochester, a frontier city on the Genesee River. To establish a newspaper, under the circumstances, appealing chiefly to the public interest on a single question, must have been up-hill work. On the 17th July, 1838, the publisher complained, that of the subscribers to the *Gazette*, about one-fifth had paid "from one dollar to three each," and the remaining four-fifths had paid nothing. We do not, however, find many subsequent complaints of this nature, and the commercial success of the venture was probably quite as good as could have been expected.

In May, Mr. Mackenzie was joined by his family, in New York; all of whom, except Mrs. Mackenzie, had till now remained in Canada. There had necessarily been but little intercommunication between them, and that had taken place indirectly and for the most part through friends passing between Canada and the States.

In March, steps were taken to organize the Canadian refugees. At a meeting of some of these persons, held at Lockport, State of New York, on the 19th of March, 1838, a committee was formed to ascertain the numbers, location, and condition of the Canadian refugees in the States, and to draw up articles of association by "means of which their sufferings may be mitigated and a redress of their grievances obtained," and—such was the latitude given— "to adopt such other measures as, in their discretion, may best conduce to their welfare."* This organiza-

* The committee consisted of Dr. A. McKenzie, Messrs. George H. Clark, Samuel Chandler, Michael Marcellus Mills, Dr. J. T. Willson, Silas Fletcher,

tion was called the "Canadian Refugee Relief Association." It was resolved to send agents of the association through the country, and the formation of branch unions was part of the plan. Dr. McKenzie, formerly of Hamilton, was President of the Association, and all correspondence was ordered to be directed to him at Lockport. The subject of this biography was not present at the meeting, for I find the circular of the association addressed to him by Dr. McKenzie. It appears, from a letter written by Dr. McKenzie, on the fly-sheet of this circular, that General McLeod was one who was to be entrusted with the work of general organization. He had just come from the West, was "not discouraged," and was on the point of starting for the River St. Lawrence under instructions of the general committee. Dr. McKenzie sighed for the advice of William L. Mackenzie, and deplored the "ignorance or want of action," which he was obliged to witness in reference to the affairs of Canada. This association proceeded to the execution of schemes in which W. L. Mackenzie took no part, and in which he was in no way concerned, either by advising or otherwise. It will hereafter be seen that several of the members of this committee were personally engaged in the ill-advised Short Hills expedition; and, at least, one of them appears to have been concerned in the destruction of the Sir Robert Peel, in which twelve are said to have been engaged.

In the session of the Canadian Legislature for 1837-8, several bills were introduced relating to per-

Dr. Charles Duncombe, William L. Mackenzie, General D. McLeod, William H. Doyle, James Marshalls, Jacob Rymal, and Nelson Gorham.

sons charged with high treason and treasonable practices. By an Act passed on the 12th of January,
judges were forbidden to bail persons under such
charges, without an order from the Lieutenant Governor, and providing that no writ of *Habeas Corpus*
granted in their behalf should be made returnable in
less than thirty days ; and all applications for such
writs were required to be reported to the Lieutenant
Governor. Another Act was passed providing that
if any subjects of Her Majesty should, in company
with subjects or citizens of foreign states, carry on
warlike expeditions within the Province they should
be liable to be tried and punished by court-martial ;
and that citizens or subjects of foreign countries so
offending should be tried either before the civil tribunals or courts-martial. A third Act was passed providing that trials for these crimes might be held by
commission out of / the District in which they were
committed. It was not till the next session, held in
the course of the year 1838, that provision was made
for the more speedy attainder of persons indicted for
high treason. In January, 1840, the House of Assembly, at the instance of Mr. Edward Thompson, the
successor of Mr. Mackenzie in the representation of
East York, addressed the Lieutenant Governor to
cause immediate steps to be taken to confiscate the
property of persons who had been convicted of treason since December, 1837. But penalties of forfeiture, were, I believe, never enforced in respect to the
property of persons attainted of treason.

In the spring of 1838, executions for high treason
commenced in Canada. On the 12th of April, 1838,

Samuel Lount and Peter Matthews, the first of the victims, were executed at Toronto. Lord Glenelg, hearing that there was a disposition, on the part of the local officials in Canada, to treat with undue severity persons who had been concerned in the revolt, remonstrated against such a course being pursued.* But Sir George Arthur, who, like his predecessor in the Lieutenant Governorship of Upper Canada, had fallen in with the views of the Family Compact and imbibed some of their violent political passions, failed to carry out his instructions to use his influence to prevent the adoption of extreme measures. The Executive Council determined to interpose their harsh decision to prevent the possibility of the Royal

* In a despatch dated Downing Street, March 14, 1838, addressed to Sir George Arthur, Lieutenant Governor of Upper Canada, in these terms:

"Sir, representations have reached this department from various quarters that during the present session of the Legislature of Upper Canada, measures of unusual severity and of extensive application have been proposed against those who may have been in any way implicated in the late insurrection in the Province. As these representations have not reached me in any official form, I am inclined to hope that they may prove exaggerated; but I shall await with anxiety your report of the proceedings of the Legislature during their present Session.

"Her Majesty's Government are fully alive to the difficult position in which, at such a period of alarm and confusion, the Legislature and the Government of Upper Canada are placed. But as I trust that the causes of apprehension so lately existing are now, through the loyalty of the great body of the population, almost entirely at an end, I earnestly hope that they will be as distinguished by moderation after success, as they have been by gallantry in the time of danger. Nothing, I fear, would be more likely to impair the moral effects of the late events than unnecessary severity; I trust, therefore, that while every measure will be adopted essential to the security of the Province, *your influence will be successfully exerted in moderating the zeal of those, if such there be, who might be disposed to proceed to extreme measures,* and in allaying the irritation which, however natural, cannot but be attended with danger to the public peace."

clemency saving Lount and Matthews from a death upon the gallows. " Petitions," Sir George Arthur admits, " signed by not less than eight thousand persons, have been presented in their favor within the last three or four days." Lount had been a political opponent of the brother of Chief Justice Robinson, by whom the prisoners were tried. There was, indeed, no question about their guilt; but the Chief Justice afterwards performed the ungracious office of assuring the Executive Council that " he saw no ground upon which he felt that he could properly recommend a pardon or respite." Attorney General Hagerman closed his ears to the cry of mercy, and only regretted that the gallows had not more victims. The general impression to-day is that the execution of these men was a judicial murder. Sir Francis Bond Head had led them into the trap—had encouraged the rebellion when it was his duty to have taken measures to suppress it in its incipient stages—and there can be but one name for the execution of men whom the Executive had enticed into the commission of the crime for which they were made to suffer death. There is reason to believe that Lount could have purchased his life by putting the Government in possession of evidence that might have tended to place others in the position he occupied; but he resolutely refused to accept it on such terms; and, instead of blaming others for his fate, continued to the last to express fervent wishes for the cause in which he offered up his life.*

* His widow, Elizabeth Lount, in a letter addressed to Mr. Mackenzie, under date, Utica, Macomb Co., Michigan, December 8th, 1838, says:

"DEAR FRIEND.—I have been perusing a piece in one of your papers taken

Much has been said about the salutary effects of the strangulation of these men, as an example to others. The facts which I shall adduce, and which have never before been published, will show that the number of men who afterwards organized in Canada, with a view to revolt, was much greater than before. Instead of striking awe into men's minds, the effect was sometimes to produce a feeling of revenge. I find a remarkable example of this in the case of one of Lount's friends, who, after he had been at the Short Hills expedition, distinctly states : "I have been doing all in my power ever since to avenge the blood of Lount and support the cause he died for."

When Lount and Matthews were executed, a number of other political prisoners, under sentence of death at Toronto, could witness, from the jail windows, a fate which they expected soon to be theirs. Shortly

from the *Christian Guardian*, * * stating that my husband had spoken very · much against you, which assertion I and my family know to be false ; and I am persuaded you were acquainted with Mr. Lount years enough to think otherwise. He ever taught his family to respect Mr. Mackenzie as one of the most honest and honorable men he ever met with. I was with him during the three last days of his life. Instead of berating his friends, he prayed for their success, as well as his country's freedom, and believed Canada could not long remain in the power of such merciless wretches as have murdered its inhabitants for their love of liberty. But he forgave his enemies and prayed they might repent of their wickedness, although he considered himself unjustly put to death by them, and wished me never to ask life of his enemies. But my anxiety would not allow me to leave the least undone that was in my power to do towards saving his life, therefore I appeared before Sir George Arthur in behalf of my husband, as has been stated. His answer was, 'If your husband is as well prepared to die as is represented, perhaps he will never again be as well prepared, if reprieved now, and I do not think he can be prepared to die without bringing other guilty men to justice, as the Council thinks he knows of many whom, I think, if he would make known, mercy would be shown to him, and I wish you would return direct to the jail and tell him this from me.' He made me several other answers which are not stated here." ·

75

after, their sentences were commuted to transportation for life ; and they, with others who were banished without trial, were sent to Fort Henry, Kingston, for safe keeping,till they could be sent off to Van Dieman's Land.   From Fort Henry they managed to effect their escape;* and John Montgomery and several others, after great suffering, succeeded in reaching the United States.†

About the 1st June, many persons who had been connected with the rebellion, crossed the frontier line, at the West, and took refuge in Michigan.   And now commenced an organization for revolutionizing Canada, comprising a much larger number of Canadians than has ever been suspected.

The centre of the organization was in Michigan, and Gen. Handy was among the most active in its promotion. Lodges were formed, every member of which took an oath to be subject to the Commander-in-chief, Gen. Handy, and not to obey any order except from him to General Roberts.‡   Handy signed blank commissions,

---

* The names of those who escaped were: Edward Kennedy, Wilson Read, Thos. Tracy, Thos. Shepard, John Marr, John Stewart, Stephen Bird Brophy, Michael Shepard, Walter Case, John Anderson, John Montgomery, Gilbert Fields Morden.

† For an account of this escape, never before published in detail, see Appendix H.

‡ Whether the oath was changed before the affair of Sandwich, next winter, when Gen. Bierce had supplanted Handy in the command, or not, I cannot say ; but Col. Prince afterwards read the following oath at the Sandwich assizes.   Mr. Mackenzie says he never heard of this oath ; it was read in Court by Colonel Prince and published :

"You do solemnly swear, in the presence of the Almighty God, that you will bear allegiance and fidelity to the SONS OF LIBERTY engaged in the PATRIOT service and in the cause of CANADIAN INDEPENDENCE—that you will obey the orders of your superior officers in whatever department you may

and sent some trusty individuals through the Provinces to form revolutionary societies, and enroll all in whom he thought he could confide. In every square mile of settled country a person was appointed to grant commissions in the secret army of revolt. Handy's commissions were given to the captains; and the associations were left to elect their own colonels. Couriers and spies, one hundred in number, were constantly kept in motion through the Provinces, taking intelligence daily to Handy. Each of them had a beat of ten miles, at either end of which he communicated with others; and this distance he regularly made both ways every day. Two hundred companies, of one hundred men each, were enrolled; making an aggregate force of 20,000 men in the Canadas, ready to rise whenever called upon; and through the system of couriers in operation, they could have been called into action with the least possible delay. The 4th of July, 1838, was fixed upon for striking the first blow. The Patriot standard was to be raised at Windsor, a Canadian village opposite Detroit; and when this was

serve—that you will never communicate or in any way divulge the existence or plans of said association. You also swear that you will devote your time, your person, your interest in promoting said cause, so far as may be consistent with your other duties—that you will never sell, barter, or in any way alter any badge that may be bestowed upon you for the purpose of designating your rank in said association. You also swear that you will not disclose or in any way communicate to any person the contents or purport of this Oath, and that you will not converse with any person in reference to this Oath, except in Convention, or with the man who first presents it to you."

(Signed,)	James Brewer,	Henry De Forest,
	Jno. Alexanderson,	Major Ward,
	James Chafey,	A. D. Burdennis,
	H. H. Dennis,	George S. Reid.

accomplished, the couriers were to be prepared to transmit the intelligence, with all possible speed, and a general rising was to take place. The first thing to be done was to seize all available public arms, ammunition, and provisions, and then the fortification of some prominent point designated was to be commenced.

If an accident had not occurred to prevent the execution of this plan, it is difficult to say what would have been the result. Before Windsor was occupied, it was necessary for Handy to be possessed of a good supply of arms. The State Arsenal of Michigan was his reliance. Some of the sentinels were men who had, years before, served under Handy, and others had been in the Patriot service the year before. They had proffered him their confidence; they unbolted the windows, and thus prepared the way for the robbery of the arsenal which it was their duty to protect. The keys of the magazine, at Detroit, were placed in the hands of Gen. Roberts, by another trusty keeper. Gen. Roberts obtained two scows of about twenty tons each, and took them up within a few rods of the arsenal. About thirty men were then sent into the building to remove 15,000 stand of arms, fifteen cannon, and ammunition.

And now took place the occurrence which defeated all Handy's plans. In cases of combined insurrection and invasions, there will be individuals who, with no motive but plunder, will try what they can snatch from the general confusion. A ruffian of this stamp, named Baker, came across the path of Gen. Handy. He got up an expedition on the Black River, and induced forty men to join him by falsely representing that he was authorized by Gen. Handy to cross to the Canada shore with the men as freebooters. They seized some flour, and being discovered and followed to the Michigan shore, the affair created a commotion that set Gen. Brady of the United States army—who appears to have used his best exertions to put down all these expeditions—on the alert. A new guard was set on the arsenal; and on the day before Windsor was to have been captured, preparatory to a general rising in Canada, the conspiracy had collapsed from the want of arms.

Generals Handy and Roberts sent a delegation to Cleveland to see what could be done after this new failure. Gen. Putnam, whom Handy had appointed to command the brigade of London Guards, after the standard of the Patriots should have been raised and sustained in Canada, was consulted. He and others had reasons, whatever they may have been, for supplanting Handy by Gen. Bierce. Gen. Handy seems to have been poorly repaid by his associates for all his exertions and sacrifices. He appears to have been thoroughly unselfish, so far as pecuniary considerations go; having at one time conducted extensive hydraulic operations with the hope of making from $200,000 to $300,000, for no other purpose than that of being able to devote it to the revolutionary cause in which he had engaged.*

Mr. Mackenzie appears to have had no connection whatever with this movement, of which, in spite of the

* This account is taken from General Handy's official, and of course unpublished, reports.

change of Commander-in-chief, the attack upon Windsor, in December following, must be regarded as the final result. In 1839, Mr. Mackenzie made affidavit that, when he heard of these intended expeditions at Short Hills, and against Prescott and Windsor, through the public press, he wrote to Lockport, earnestly urging those whom he thought likely to have influence with the refugees—the Refugee Association Committee, no doubt—to abandon all such attempts as injurious to the cause of good government in Canada. He was still favorable to the independence of the Canadas; but he was not convinced that the means proposed were calculated to secure the object. He came to this conclusion, it would seem, in February, when he refused to "sail in the same boat" with Van Rensellaer, to be piloted as the latter might think fit. Besides, he was under bonds to take his trial for a breach of the neutrality laws of the United States, with the provisions of which he was not acquainted, when, at the instance of persons in Buffalo, he joined the Navy Island expedition.

Of the Short Hills affair, which took place in June, 1838, he first learned from the frontier newspapers. Those who took part in it, I find, claim to have had five hundred and twenty-six men, well armed and equipped; but it is quite certain that there was not over one-fifth of this number who fell in with the lancers at Overholt's Tavern. The rest, if there were any such number as is alleged, must have been Canadians. A few men crossed the Niagara River, in small bodies, taking with them what arms they could. These they deposited at an appointed place, which was reached by a march of some fifteen miles in the woods, and went back for more. These arms must have been intended for Canadians. In this way, eight days were spent before the parties were discovered. Being fired upon by a body of lancers from Overholt's Tavern, they finally set fire to it; taking prisoners all that survived, but shortly afterwards releasing them. The invaders soon after dispersed, going in different directions; but thirty-one of them were taken prisoners,* and it is believed very few escaped.

* "Among them were James Moreau, an American, who was then Colonel; Benjamin Wait, a native of Upper Canada, then Major; Samuel Chandler, an American by birth, who had been many years a resident of Upper Canada, and who acted as commissary; Jacob Beamer, who was concerned in the insurrection in the London District, under Dr. Duncombe; Alexander McLeod and John McNulty, both of whom were of the Montgomery Tavern insurgents; and a Dr. Wilson, who seems to have been an active and influential partisan among them."—*Solicitor General Draper's Narrative of the Short Hills Affair.* Moreau was hanged at Niagara for his participation in this affair.

CHAPTER X.

Mr. Mackenzie Declares his Intentions to become an American Citizen—
Hunters' Lodges—Secret Convention in Cleveland, at which a Provisional
Government for Upper Canada is formed, and a Republican Bank, with a
Moonshine Capital of Seven-and-a-half Millions of Dollars established—
Federal Spies on the Frontier Movements—Sir George Arthur's Spies—
The American Government declares its inability to prevent marauding Ex-
peditions on the Frontier—The Prescott or Windmill Point Expedition—
The Leaders of that Expedition try to throw the blame of the Failure on
one another—Mr. Mackenzie had no connection with it—Ferocious Disposi-
tion of the Militia.

NOT till the autumn of 1838, did Mr. Mackenzie
take the initiatory step provided by the federal constitution for becoming a citizen of the United States.*

* "CITY OF NEW YORK, ss.

" Be it remembered that William Lyon Mackenzie, late of the United Kingdom of Great Britain and Ireland, appeared in the Marine Court of the City
of New York, held in the City Hall of the said City, on the fifth day of September, in the year of our Lord, one thousand eight hundred and thirty-eight,
(the said Court being a Court of Record, having Common Law Jurisdiction,
and a Clerk and Seal,) and declared on oath, in open Court, that it was bona
fide his intention to become a citizen of the United States, and to renounce
forever all allegiance and fidelity to any foreign Prince, Potentate, State, or
Sovereignty whatsoever, and particularly to the Queen of the United Kingdom of Great Britain and Ireland.

"In testimony whereof, the Seal of the said Marine Court of the City of
New York is hereunto affixed, this fifth day of September, in the year of
our Lord, one thousand eight hundred and thirty-eight, and of our Independence the sixty-third.

"JOHN BARBENE, *Clerk.*"

View of the Battle of Windmill Point, below Prescott, Upper Canada, (from the Ogdensburg side of the St. Lawrence) November 13, 1838.

But he never felt entirely at home in the States, and almost always continued to sigh for an opportunity of returning to his beloved Canada. His private letters contain frequent references to the subject.

It is difficult to determine whether the organization set on foot by Handy was identical with what was known as Hunters' Lodges. But I am inclined to think that it was not. The oath which he speaks of as having been taken by his followers is quite different from that usually ascribed to the Hunters.* Hunters' Societies are generally supposed to have originated in the State of Vermont, in May, 1838. I have been able to track some of their proceedings, and to unravel some of their conspiracies.

A convention of the Hunters' Lodges of Ohio and Michigan was held at Cleveland, from the 16th to the 22d September, 1838. There were seventy delegates present. Mr. Mackenzie was not cognizant of the intended meeting, and the result of its deliberations were not officially communicated to him. He was not a member of the society, and by its rules none but the initiated could be admitted to its secrets. But

---

* The following I find in the publications of the time, given as the Hunter's oath :—"I swear to do my utmost to promote Republican Institutions and ideas throughout the world—to cherish them, to defend them ; and especially to devote myself to the propagation, protection, and defence of these institutions in North America. I pledge my life, my property, and my sacred honor to the Association ; I bind myself to its interests, and I promise, until death, that I will attack, combat, and help to destroy, by all means that my superior may think proper, every power, or authority, of Royal origin, upon this continent ; and especially never to rest till all tyrants of Britain cease to have any dominion or footing whatever in North America. I further solemnly swear to obey the orders delivered to me by my superior, and never to disclose any such order, or orders, except to a brother 'Hunter' of the same degree. So help me God."

a Master of a Lodge did communicate to him surrep-
titiously a general idea of what was done.   A Republican government for Upper Canada was formed with
a President, Vice-President, and Secretary of State, of
Treasury, and of War.   A Commander-in-Chief, Com-
missary-General, Adjutant General, two Brigadier Generals, and a long list of Majors and subalterns were
named.   A Republican Bank was formed, and a day,
not stated in the letter from which I derive this information, was fixed for commencing the invasion of
Canada.   "There never," says Mr. Mackenzie's informant, "was such an organization before; and if we
do not succeed it will be by reason of some traitor."
But some others gave a much less flattering account
of the Cleveland proceedings.   Dr. Duncombe was
among the actors in this convention.   Against what
point the organization was intended to operate Mr.
Mackenzie was not informed, even in the irregular
way in which this information was conveyed to him.

These Lodges had different centres, and there does
not appear to have been, at all times, perfect harmony
between the various central committees.   The ambition of individuals to exercise a controlling influence
seems to have led to an occasional playing at cross-
purposes.   All the Lodges in Ohio and Michigan were
required to report to the central committee, at Cleveland.   There appears to have been some serious
charges brought against the Cleveland committee,
arising perhaps out of the management of the Bank
scheme.   "If the Cleveland committee," I find it suggested by the Master of a Lodge required to report to
that centre, "has forfeited the confidence of the friends

of our cause by peculation or other gross mismanagement, then we must organize *de novo*."

From "a circular address to the different Lodges upon the subject of a Joint Stock Banking Company," I learn the details of the whole Bank scheme. The name was to be "the Republican Bank of Canada," and the officers and directors were first elected on the 16th of September, 1838, for the period of one year. There are reasons for giving Dr. Duncombe credit for the paternity of the scheme. I find the circular among Mr. Mackenzie's papers, under the head of Duncombe, and that he was, among his numerous accomplishments, a currency doctor, is proved by his subsequently writing a book on banking. The circular sets out with the enunciation of certain principles relating to government and currency; one of which is that "gold and silver should be the only legal money of a country;" but then it is added that necessity may be made a plea for breaking through this rule, in which case, it is laid down, the paper should be issued by a "Republican Bank controlled by the people." Then follows the offer of the stock of a Republican Bank, and those who subscribe to the stocks are fairly warned that they need expect to receive back their money with interest only in case "the cause triumphs;" otherwise they must be content with the reflection that they have given so much to establish "liberty, equality, and fraternity," in Canada. The bank was to make loans for the Patriot service before individuals could expect discounts. The capital of the Bank was to be $7,500,000, divided into $150,000 shares of $50 each to commence with; but it was afterwards to be increased so as to give every individual on the continent the chance of becoming the lucky possessor of a share, and after the $7,500,000 had been disposed of, no one would be allowed the privilege of taking more than one share. As some compensation for this abridgment of liberty, no limit was placed upon subscriptions to the original stock. " The vignette of the bills," we read, " are to be the heads of the late Martyrs to the cause of liberty in Canada; the head of Matthews on the left end of the bill; the head of Lount on the centre of the bill, with the words in a semi-circle over it, " the murdered;" and the head of Moreau on the right end of the bill, with the names of these heroes under their heads, with a motto, " Death or Victory;" on the margin of the bills will be the words " Liberty, Equality, Fraternity." The circular ends with the prayer: " God prosper the cause of Liberty, Equal Rights, and Brotherly Love;" another proof, I should say, of Duncombe's authorship. It was stated in evidence, on the trial of the Windsor prisoners captured in December, 1838, that the greater part of the stock was actually sold; but this is not credible. And I find from a letter written by a person who was in all the secrets, dated Cleveland, November 1, 1838, that up to that period only $300 had been secured, although the convention had by resolution, bound themselves to raise $10,000 in a fortnight. Of this bank Mr. J. Grant, jr., appears to have been President, and Messrs. B. Bagley and S. Moulson, Vice-Presidents.* A Canadian refugee;

* One account states that a Cleveland merchant of the name of Smith was President, and that it was under his management that the stock was sold; but

writing from Cleveland, said the conventionists were "all Americans, men of poor fortunes." "Whether they will account for the moneys received," he adds suspectingly, "time will tell." The Patriots—Canadian refugees I presume to be meant in this case—were appointed only to minor offices in the organization; and on the 1st of November, their Commander-in-chief—Bierce is no doubt intended—had taken "no effective measures to raise and embody men." The person whose letter I am quoting, himself no less than a General, says: "I am here poor and penniless. I applied to Dr. Smith, a few days ago, for some assistance from the funds collected, but to no purpose; they have got the management in their own hands, and will act as they think proper."

At this time the Federal Government had spies on the frontier endeavoring to unravel the conspiracy going on for the invasion of Canada. A stranger to Mr. Mackenzie writes to him from Washington, to assure him, on "undoubted authority," that the United States authorities are on the alert. "There are two United States officers on the frontier," he says, "one called John W. Turner and the other Captain N. Johnson, who are, as I understand, expressly deputed by the collector of Oswego, to keep an eye on any movements of men, arms, or munitions of war. Capt. Johnson is now ostensibly on the Erie and Ontario steamboat agency, and he can be identified on boats in that capacity. He has already possessed himself of the sign of communication of the Patriots, and thinks

the names I have given are appended (copied) to the copy of the circular prospectus in my possession.

he has a key which will give him access to important information. He now enjoys the confidence of the Patriots; look out for him. Duncombe, McLeod, Johnson, and others are watched." The writer was probably in one of the departments at Washington. He appears to have had access to the reports of these spies; for he is enabled to tell Mr. Mackenzie that "the organization on the frontier is immense." At the Cleveland Convention the two spies, Johnson and Turner, were present.

Sir George Arthur too had his spies on the frontier. Hayes continued to supply him with whatever he could learn of these movements. The information these persons obtained, whatever credence it might be entitled to, created great alarm at Toronto. They told him that, at the end of October, there were at least forty thousand persons in the invasion plot, on the frontier States, which was "carried on by means of masonic lodges, secretly established in almost every town along the frontier, the members of which communicate with each other by private signs, and are divided into several grades of initiation."* Hunters' Lodges are no doubt intended.

But when Sir George Arthur had learned something of the plot, the expedition of Windmill Point was on the eve of taking place, and it had been carried into effect two days before Mr. Secretary Forsyth could reply to Sir George's complaint, conveyed to the

---

* The Cleveland conspirators were of opinion that the spy who gave this information to Sir George Arthur, had given Mr. Bagley as his authority; but still Bagley does not seem to have been suspected by his fellow conspirators.

President through Mr. Fox. The Federal Government, as we have seen, had previously learned, from its own spies, some particulars of these movements. But it pleaded its inability to arrest them. "The utter impracticability," said Mr. Forsyth, "of placing a frontier extending nearly one thousand miles, in a military attitude, sufficiently imposing and effective to prevent such enterprises, is evident." But, it was added, regular military armaments and the movement of armed bands to any considerable extent from the American side of the line, would be successfully repressed; and the Federal Government promised to use all the means at its disposal to put down all other hostile preparations.

Between the 1st and 10th of November, the Hunters' Lodges were concentrating their forces for an attack on Prescott.* On Sunday morning, the 11th, two schooners, in tow of the steamer United States, left Millen's Bay between Sackett's Harbor and Duck Creek. The steamer United States left Millen's for Prescott, having on board men, arms, and munitions of war. The men who came down in the steamer were transferred to the schooners in the evening; one of which was in command of Van Shultz, a brave Pole,†

---

* The places at which there were Lodges, according to statements made by prisoners taken at Prescott, were: Oswego, Salina, Liverpool, Syracuse, Auburn, Great Bend on the Black River, Palema, Dexter, Evan's Mills, Watertown, Brownville, Lerayville, Sackett's Harbor, Cape Vincent, Chaumont, Millen's Bay, Alexandria, Orleans, Flat Rock, Ogdensburg, Rossie Village.

† Van Shultz Nils Sezoltevki, a native of Poland, was at this time only thirty-one years of age. He had been residing near Salina, N. Y.; he was introduced to some of the Patriots by Mr. Stone, a merchant of that place. In October, 1838, he was in New York, where he signed commissions in

and the other in charge of the notorious Bill Johnson. While on their way down the river, the management of the expedition was discussed by Colonel Van Shultz, Captain Buckley, Colonel Woodruff, and others. Van Shultz proposed to land, immediately on their arrival, on the Prescott wharf, all the men in the expedition, about six hundred in number; then, after leaving a sufficient force to guard the boats, to divide them into three bodies, with the principal of which he should march through the village, while Colonel Woodruff should lead one wing round on one side and another person the other, on the other side. The three bodies were then to meet between the village and the fort, in case any resistance were offered from that point.* But the fort was only then in course of construction, and there was not a man in it.† Van Shultz proposed to keep the schooners in the river below the fort for the purpose of preserving a communication with Ogdensburg, and transporting provisions, ammunition, and reinforcements of volunteers. With the fort, the village, and river at his command, the artillery he had with him with what more he expected to find in the fort, he fancied he should be able to prevent the British boats descending till the numbers of the invaders and the inhabitants by whom they would be joined would become irresistible. He was opposed to first landing on the American side, at Ogdensburg, fearing that the number who would refuse to go back

cipher, as commander of the Patriotic Army. He obtained some Polish and German recruits, whose expenses he paid.

* A *Narrative of the Expedition to Prescott*, by Sebastian John Meyer, who took part in it.

† *General Bierge's Account of the Prescott Expedition.*

to the vessels would be greater than that of the additional volunteers who would be obtained.

The principal officers of the expedition opposed the plans of Van Shultz; yet, in skill and bravery, they were all very far his inferiors. They did land at Ogdensburg; when General Bierge, who was to have commanded the expedition, fell sick with a suddenness that created a suspicion of cowardice, which he was never able to remove. The men lost courage on seeing their leader show the white feather; and instead of crossing one thousand strong, as they had been taught to believe, Van Shultz took over about one hundred and seventy men in one of the schooners, about nine o'clock, on the morning of the 12th. Bill Johnson managed to run the other schooner upon the bar, with many arms and much ammunition on board. She never crossed to the succor of Van Shultz.* The steamer United States was prevented from passing down below the town by the British steamer Experiment. The schooner which had been aground started in tow of the Paul Pry for the Canada shore, and when fairly in the Canada waters—the magistrates of Ogdensburg had sent Lieutenant Fowell a request, to which he acceded, not to fire in American waters— the Experiment opened upon her with grape and canister. The Paul Pry now left the schooner to her fate, and hastened to take shelter at Ogdensburg Lieutenant Fowell now ran the Experiment within ten yards of the schooner; and was about taking her in tow, when he found himself in shoal water, and the United States coming rapidly down upon him. The

* Sebastian John Meyer's *Narrative.*

Experiment found it necessary to move towards the town, when a brisk fire took place between her and the other two vessels. The schooner got into Ogdensburg, and the United States, having received some shot in her hull, and one of her engines being struck by an eighteen pound ball, followed soon after.*

On hearing of the expedition, Captain Sandom, commanding the Royal Navy in Upper Canada, set out from Kingston in pursuit, with a detachment of forty men and a party of marines, in the steamer Victoria, accompanied by the Cobourg. He arrived at two o'clock, on the morning of the 13th; and the men having been landed, they, with a party of militia, under Colonels Young, Frazer, and Gowan, proceeded in two columns to attack the invaders, who were strongly posted behind stone walls, on rising ground. After an engagement of an hour's duration, the invaders were driven into a large circular stone mill, of which the walls were of immense thickness, and a stone house adjacent.† Capt. Sandom with an armed steamer took up a position on the river below the mill; but the fire of his guns made no impression on the thick walls. The men in the mill and the stone house kept up a galling fire, both true and steady; and as no impression was being made on the buildings, it was deemed best to withdraw the greater part of the loyalist forces, at three o'clock in the afternoon, leaving strong pickets to prevent the escape of the invaders, till heavy artillery could be obtained from Kingston.

* Lieutenant Fowell to Captain Sandom.
† Col. Young's Report.

Meanwhile Colonel Van Shultz, not receiving the expected reinforcements from the leaders of the expedition who remained in Ogdensburg, and not being joined by any of the inhabitants, was reminded by the one hundred and seventy men under his command of the hopelessness of their position. They begged him to lead them back to the States. But there was not a single boat at their disposal, and the British steamer Experiment kept a vigilant look-out on the river. During the night, Van Shultz dispatched a man across the river on a plank, to implore that boats might be sent. On Tuesday evening, he received for reply that a schooner would be sent over to take them away. They carried their wounded down to the river bank, and waited with anxiety for the promised vessel; but she came not.* The Paul Pry did cross during the night of Thursday, and, not being able to go very near the shore, sent two small boats to the windmill. Mr. Preston King, afterwards a member of Congress, declared that Col. Worth of the United States Army, suggested that an attempt should be made to rescue the Patriots from the windmill, and that for this purpose he would permit the Paul Pry, then in the custody of the United States Marshal, to be used.† Though the American shore had been lined with thousands of spectators during the day, only from twenty-five to twenty-six persons accompanied Mr. King in the Paul Pry; and though the visit led to a council of war being held in the windmill, no practical result followed. Some small

* Letter of Van Shultz, dated December 1, 1838.

† Published letter of Preston King to Mr. Gilbert, dated Ogdensburg, October 6, 1840.

boats, expected to follow, never went. Colonel Worth refused to allow the Paul Pry to go back a second time; and thus the attempt to rescue Van Shultz and his devoted band was at an end.

On the 16th, at noon, Colonel Dundas returned to Prescott from Kingston with four companies of the Eighty-third regiment, and two eighteen pounders and a howitzer. The guns were placed in position with all possible dispatch, on rising ground, about four hundred yards from the house and the mill occupied by the invaders. Nearly every shot perforated the massive mill. When this last battle commenced, Colonel Van Shultz says he had only one hundred and eight men left. He was surrounded by a force which he estimated at two thousand. At the same time, Captain Sandom took up a position on the river below the mill with two gunboats and a steamer; but the fire of his eighteen pounders, less effective, failed to produce a breach in the thick walls of the mill. About dark, Colonel Dundas moved closer to the buildings; while the militia acted on both flanks, supported by a company of the 93d, to prevent the escape of the enemy. Under cover of night, the division of Van Shultz's men, who were in the stone house, took refuge in the brushwood on the bank of the river, where, with their commander, they were taken prisoners. Van Shultz had undertaken the defence of the house with ten men, because he could get no one else to do it. A flag of truce was displayed from the mill, whence the firing had ceased; and Colonel Dundas accepted an unconditional surrender.

There were probably not less than one hundred and fifty lost, in killed and wounded, on both sides, though the official reports are somewhat contradictory on this point.*

One hundred and fifty-seven prisoners were taken, of whom eleven were executed, including the gallant and heroic, but misguided and betrayed leader, Col. Van Shultz. They were fastened to a rope, with Van Shultz at the head, and in this way marched to Fort Henry.

The various leaders in this ill-starred expedition tried to throw the responsibility of the disaster upon one another, no one being willing to accept it. Bill Johnson, who induced many to take part in it, went over to the windmill in a small boat on Monday night, and took away some of his friends, telling them

---

* Colonel Plomer Young, in his report of the 14th of November, giving an account of the first battle, "computes" the killed and wounded of all ranks at forty-five. Colonel Van Shultz, who states the original number of his men at one hundred and seventy, says, that on the commencement of the last battle he had only one hundred and eight men left; thus confessing to a loss of sixty-two men up to that time. But this must be an error, as is proved by the number of prisoners captured. Besides, Bill Johnson, who took away four of Van Shultz's men, alleges that he sent him fifty others. If this statement were true, which I doubt, Van Shultz must have lost about one hundred men up to the time of the last battle. Van Shultz complains that he did not receive the expected reinforcements, but this can hardly be taken to mean that he did not receive any at all. In the battle of the 16th he reports that he lost only one man, and Adjutant General Foster gives the entire British loss at forty-five killed and wounded. If this be correct, Colonel Young's computation of the loss in the first battle must have been very wide of the mark. An eye-witness assures me that on the morning after the last battle, when the windmill had been evacuated, he counted one hundred dead bodies. This would include the whole loss of the invaders in killed, for although an hour's cessation of hostilities was given on the Friday before the steamers took up their position near the mill, for burying the dead, the invaders were unable to bury theirs for want of shovels.

that he was certain the expedition must fail; and, after that, had the baseness to induce a number of Americans to go over and join Van Shultz and his devoted band.* When Van Shultz had been sentenced by a court-martial to be executed, he execrated "the miserable cowardice of General Bierce and Bill Johnson."† "I only wish," he said, "those cowardly rascals, General Bierce and Bill Johnson, might be punished, who brought us into this prison, and I would die content."‡ He relied upon them for reinforcements, but Bierce feigned sickness, and Bill Johnson pretended that, after he had given up two hundred and seventy stand of arms in his possession, he was deprived of his commission by his superiors, and left without the power to act. Eatis, another leader, remained inactive at Ogdensburg. General Bierce retaliated on Van Shultz, by alleging that the act of crossing to the Canada side was unauthorized; that he himself had been at Ogdensburg four days before, when he became convinced that if the place were not not taken by surprise it could not be taken at all; that a large number of persons in and near Prescott would join the standard of the invaders, if the town and fort were taken; but that otherwise no assistance could be expected from the inhabitants, who would be obliged to rally to the call of Colonel Young to defend the town. Van Shultz

---

* This admission was afterwards made by Johnson to Mr. Mackenzie, at Albany.

† Letter from Van Shultz to Mr. J. R. Parker, Oswego, dated Fort Henry, December 1, 1838.

‡ Letter published in the Watertown *Jeffersonian*, December 1, 1838.

Bierce adds, acted rashly and in ignorance of all these facts.*

Van Shultz, when under sentence of death, which was sternly carried into effect, caused his thanks to be publicly made known to the officers and men of the Eighty-third Regiment, for the kind treatment he had received from them. He declared that the prisoners owed their lives to them; that it was owing solely to their protection, after they surrendered, that the militia did not kill the greater number of them. Unhappily this ferocious disposition on the part of the militia is attested on the highest authority. In commending the conduct of Colonel Dundas, Sir George Arthur said: "To his determined resolution, indeed, it is to be ascribed that the militia of the country gave any quarter to the brigands; nothing, I believe, but the presence of the regular troops having saved any of them from being cut to pieces."

Van Shultz was in New York a short time before the expedition against Prescott, but he neither consulted or in any way communicated with Mr. Mackenzie, who was then living there. "I knew nothing of the expedition," Mr. Mackenzie publicly promulgated in his *Gazette* of the 14th of November, 1840, "never saw or wrote a line to Van Shultz, was four hundred miles distant, and had nothing to do with the matter whatever; nor did any of the sufferers, when on trial, or going to the gallows, or to banishment, once name me."† And he afterwards made the same remark

---

* Bierce's *Account of the Prescott Expedition.*

† This statement is fully borne out by official documents. See *Correspondence Relating to the Affairs of Canada,* Part II. : published by the House of Com-

with regard to the Windsor expedition, with which he had no connection whatever.

A simultaneous attack upon different points seems to have been at one time intended, and several of those who took part in the Prescott expedition were led to believe that it would take place. Montreal and Quebec they expected would at the same time be assaulted, and they were told that three weeks would be sufficient to achieve the independence of Canada. Each man engaged in the expedition was to receive twenty dollars bounty, ten dollars a month while on service, and one hundred and sixty acres of land, when the new government was established.*

mons, 1840. From pages 56 to 76, inclusive, the space is taken up with an alphabetical list of the prisoners taken at Windmill Point, with a column containing the names of "persons living in the United States, accused by the prisoners of advising or taking part" in the expedition. The only prominent Canadians mentioned in this connection were Drs. Rolph and Duncombe. The latter was an American by birth, and his connection with the expedition goes to show that it was no stranger to the Cleveland conspiracy. But whatever connection Dr. Rolph may have had with this expedition, either by advising or assisting, there is reason to believe that he had very little to do with the frontier movements on the American side.

* Mr. W. H. Draper's Report to Lieutenant Governor Arthur, January 21, 1839.

CHAPTER XI.

President Van Buren's Neutrality Proclamation—Its Reception by the Re-
fugees—Real Motives of the Federal Government with regard to Canada—
Traditional Policy of Leading Statesmen of the States on the Subject—Sir
George Arthur renews the Reward of £1000 for the Apprehension of Mr.
Mackenzie—Judge Jones urges that Mr. Mackenzie ought to be given up by
the Americans—Mr. Mackenzie addresses large Public Meetings at New
York, Philadelphia, Washington, and Baltimore, in favor of the Destitute
Canadian Refugees—The Windsor Expedition—Col. Prince orders Prison-
ers to be Shot in cold blood.

A FEW days after the Prescott expedition, President Van Buren issued a proclamation calling upon
the citizens of the United States to give neither countenance nor encouragement to persons who, by a breach
of neutrality, had forfeited all claim to the protection
of their own country; but to use every effort in their
power to arrest for trial and punishment every of-
fender against the laws, "providing for the performance of their obligations by the United States."
From this moment, many of the Canadian refugees
in the States, and others who sympathized with them,
denounced Mr. Van Buren in the strongest terms of
censure they could command. "His officials assure
me," Mackenzie, who had been in Washington, wrote
to Dr. O'Callaghan, " that he is every thing Fox wishes
him to be ;" and there can be no doubt that the refugees generally believed that he was doing all he

could to preserve the neutrality of the United States. And I see no reason to doubt that he did his duty, in that respect, to the best of his ability.

I have, however, been enabled to penetrate beneath the surface of fair appearances to the real motives of the American Government with regard to Canada. In February, 1838, an interview took place between a General of the United States Army and a leading Canadian Patriot, in which the General said: "I am desirous, for your own good, for that of the refugees generally, and for that of the Canadians in Canada, to make you acquainted with the views of our Government and of myself relative to the difficulties existing in Canada. It is the wish of us all and of the people of the United States, nine out of ten, that you should effect your emancipation; but we do not see the slightest shadow of hope for you *at present*. If the outbreak had occurred one year sooner, or was to [occur] one year later than now, there would be no doubt of your success, which is our cordial wish; but as there is [now] no hope for your success, and as an attempt followed by failure would surely end in a dreadful loss of life, and expose the resident people of Canada to harsher treatment than they might otherwise experience, we are, out of humanity, determined to suppress any movement on your part. It would take a force of 6,000 men, well armed, to enter Canada, and they should take with them a large supply of arms, etc., for the people, and also to commence, for contingencies, with £200,000, to be followed by £2,000,000 more. This supply the Patriots cannot now procure, and without it they cannot succeed. If you had only arms you might do; [here he derives the necessity of such a large amount of cash;*] if you could get a small loan, with that you could purchase, if necessary, 50,000 stand of arms in the States; there would be no difficulty in conveying them into Canada in less than three months; but you cannot get the money or the arms; so you must give up your hope for the present. If you are about any preparation for invasion, pray discontinue, and prevail on your friends to abandon your project." At the interview in which the American General thus expressed himself, there was a bank president present; a circumstance which, says the Canadian Patriot, "prevented both the General and myself saying *all* that each wished; and although I met him once since, he has been so beset by his friends and our enemies, that I have not ventured to sound him on some delicate points. He plainly told me, at both interviews, that it was necessary for the United States to go to war; that such an occurrence would be of the greatest advantage to them." The General is now in the Federal Army, and the Canadian Patriot, who had the interview with him, is still living: circumstances which induce me to withhold their names.

Nor must it be supposed that the views expressed by the United States General regarding Canada were confined to military men. A civilian, who has since been a member of the Federal Government, wrote to Mr. Mackenzie, under date Washington, March 30, 1841: "Of one thing you may rest assured, that no

---

* These words are in the letter from which I transcribe this account of the American General's speech.

man in America more ardently desires the cessation of British power on this continent than I do, or more anxiously watches for an opportunity to promote that great and noble object, which is alike important to the peace and well-being of the United States and the freedom and progress of the oppressed people of the colonies." At this time, there were few people on the face of the earth freer than these very colonists; the full control of all their local affairs having been unreservedly granted to them. Even Mr. Calhoun, strange as it may seem, remarked to Mr. Mackenzie that the United States wanted more free territory. His idea may have been that it would be required as a balance to an equivalent portion of slave territory to be acquired in Cuba and elsewhere.

Another leading Patriot who visited the Federal capital a few days after the issue of Mr. Van Buren's neutrality proclamation, wrote to Mr. Mackenzie, under date Washington, December 20, 1838 :—" The President and most of his intimate friends hide their partiality for, or fear of, England, under the philanthropic love they have for peace, under the philosophic faith they have that justice and argument must be all powerful, in this moral and enlightened age, and will force England to discontinue its tyranny. Their hearts and their prayers are with us, and that's all. I told them to leave the duty of prayers to the chaplains of their houses; that they had other duties to perform." And again: "On all sides," he is speaking of the leading politicians of both parties, "they are agreed that it is possible that the warfare on the borders may end in collision between the governments, if the pride of England urge it to declare war; that they ought not themselves to begin it, because the natural and rapid increase of population on the lakes, in Michigan and Wisconsin, must inevitably, within a few years, give them the Canadas with lighter sacrifices than at present, when they are greatly weakened by the greater inequality that exists between the two parties than had ever been the case in this country" before. All the leading politicians at Washington urged the sending of agents to England and France by the Canadian Patriots; and M. Papineau's subsequent visit to France seems to have been in some such capacity.

This has been something like a traditional policy on the part of American statesmen. An unpublished autograph letter, written by ex-President Madison to the then President Monroe, in my possession, goes to prove this. The letter is dated Montpelier, November 28, 1818. After some reference to the impressment question, Mr. Madison says: "The remaining danger to a permanent harmony would then lie in the possession of Canada [by England]; which, as G. B. ought to know, whenever rich enough to be profitable will be strong enough to be independent. Were it otherwise, Canada can be of no use to her when at war with us; and when at peace will be of equal value, whether as a British colony or an American state. Whether the one or the other, the consumption of British manufactures and export of useful materials will be much the same. The latter would be guarded even against a tax upon them by an article in our Constitution. But, notwithstanding the persuasive nature of these considerations, there is little probability

of their overcoming the national pride which is flattered by extended dominion, and still less perhaps
ministerial policy, always adverse to narrow the field
of patronage. As far as such a transfer would affect
the relative power of the two nations, the most
unfriendly jealousy could find no objection to the
measure; for it would evidently take more weakness
from Great Britain than it would add strength to the
United States. In truth, the only reason we can have
to desire Canada ought to weigh as much with Great
Britain as with us. In her hands, it must ever be a
source of collision which she ought to be equally
anxious to remove, and a snare to the poor Indians,
towards whom her humanity ought to be equally
excited. Interested individuals have dwelt much on
its importance to Great Britain, as a channel for
evading and crippling our commercial laws. But it
may well be expected that other views of her true
interest will prevail in her councils, if she permits
experience to enlighten them."*

The recent prediction of Mr. Secretary Seward that
these British-American Provinces will make excellent
States of the Federal Union, and the still more recent
official avowal of President Lincoln that the great
work of the last half century has been to destroy
European power in America, preclude the belief that
the secret wishes and ultimate policy of the leading
men of the United States have changed. There had
been, years before the war between the North and the

---

* For the opinions of Washington, Jay, Adams, Franklin, on the importance of Canada forming part of the United States, see Mackenzie's Trial at Canandaigua: pp. 248—9—50—1.

South broke out, leading politicians in the Northern States, in favor of breaking up the Federal Union with a view of the non-slaveholding States forming a connection with British America. For obvious reasons, I withhold their names.

Two days after the surrender of Van Shultz, Sir George Arthur issued a proclamation renewing the reward of £1,000 for the apprehension of Mr. Mackenzie. The pretext for this procedure was the pretence that he had been seen, on the 17th of November, in the neighborhood of Toronto. On that very day he was in Philadelphia, where he addressed a meeting of five thousand persons. About a month after, he was warned that an attempt would be made to kidnap him, and take him over to Canada. Judge Jones, an old political opponent, wrote to a brother judge, in the State of New York, complaining that the political refugee was not given up to the vengeance of his enemies; though he must have known that there is nothing on which England more prides herself than that she is enabled to offer an asylum to all classes of political refugees, and that about the last thing she would consent to do would be to surrender one of them for punishment.

As Kossuth did afterwards, in the case of Hungary, Mr. Mackenzie held a series of public meetings in some of the principal cities of the States, in favor of Canadian independence. The first was held at Vauxhall Garden, New York, on the 15th of November. While disclaiming all intention of interfering with the domestic arrangements of other nations, or violating the neutrality laws of the United States, the meeting expressed its abhorrence of the executions which had taken place in Canada, for political offences; called on the Federal Government to insist on full and complete satisfaction for the Caroline outrage, and recalled to grateful recollection the services rendered in the American revolution by Lafayette, Montgomery, De Kalb, Kosciusko, Steuben, and other foreigners. A committee was formed to collect funds for the relief of the "suffering republicans of Canada," who had been driven into exile. In Lower Canada, Dr. Nelson had, a few days before, made a new appeal to arms,* and

---

* On the night of the 3d of November, the *habitants* between the Yamaska and Richelieu Rivers flew to arms, and leaving their villages, assembled at St. Ours, St. Charles, and St. Michael. The *habitants* of Beauharnois are represented as having risen *en masse*, and made a great many prisoners. About four thousand concentrated at Napierville, under command of the intrepid Dr. Nelson, Côté, and Gagnon, between the 3d and the 6th. Sir J. Colborne dispatched the *corps* under Major General Sir James McDonald and Major General Clitheroe to march to Napierville to attack them. The troops did not arrive till the morning of the 10th, and the insurgents had left the night previous. A small body of them were attacked by the militia while on the march from the La Colle to Rouse's Point. They were overpowered, lost three hundred stand of arms and one field-piece, and were driven across the frontier. On the 9th a party of insurgents, under Dr. Nelson, came into collision with a body of volunteers who had taken possession of a church at Odell Town, in which they suffered great loss. Major Carmichael, with a detachment of the Seventy-first Regiment and two battalions of Glengary Militia marched to Beauharnois on the 10th. The insurgents were driven back, and four or five men of the Seventy-first Regiment were killed and wounded. See Sir John Colborne's *Dispatch to Lord Glenelg*, November 11, 1838. On this occasion the militia is said to have committed great atrocities. The following statement is from an unpublished letter among Mr. Mackenzie's papers:—

" L'ACADIE, April 2, 1839.

"A probable estimate of property destroyed by the *volunteers* and troops at the command of Sir John Colborne in the county of L'Acadie, during the month of November, 1833:—74 houses and 22 barns burnt, $49,760; 6 houses interior destroyed and 335 houses pillaged, $26,800; total, $76,560; 243 children and 131 women turned into the street naked in the month of November."

issued a Declaration of Independence on behalf of a Provisional Government for that Province, followed by a proclamation, offering security and protection to all who should lay down their arms and cease to oppose the new authority that claimed to be in existence before the old one had expired. Notice was taken of this circumstance by the meeting, which tendered its sympathy to Lower Canada.

Mr. Mackenzie was not, at this time, in the secrets of the Lower Canada Patriots any more than in those of the pretended government of Upper Canada which had been set up at Cleveland. Dr. Robert Nelson had been in New York a short time before, and, calling on Mr. Mackenzie, proposed to tell him the plans of the Lower Canada Patriots, when Mr. Mackenzie stopped him, by saying: "Tell me nothing, more or less; as I am to take no part, I have no means to aid, and I want to know nothing either as to what has been done or may be intended." On the 12th of June previous, he had been indicted, at Albany, for a breach of the neutrality laws of the United States, for the part he had taken in the Navy Island expedition, and while

---

The atrocities committed by the militia beggar description. Colonel Angus McDonell, commanding the Fourth Regiment of Glengary Militia wrote his uncle, Bishop Macdonell, November 19, 1838: "We proceeded down towards Beauharnois by a forced march, burning and laying waste the country as we went along; and I must say it was a most distressing and heart-rending scene to see this fine settlement so completely destroyed, the houses burnt and laid in ashes, and I understood the whole country to St. Charles experienced the same; the wailing and lamentation of the women and children, on beholding their houses in flames and their property destroyed; their husbands, fathers, brothers, sons, dragged along prisoners, and such of them as did not appear were supposed to be at the rebel camp." The details of some of these atrocities it is impossible to put into print.

79

the trial was hanging over him, he had an additional reason for being anxious to keep clear of all similar movements.

At Philadelphia Mr. Mackenzie addressed the vast assemblage for an hour and a half. "There was a general cry of 'Go on,'" a local journal reported, "whenever he evinced a disposition to bring his speech to a close." He was further described as "a plain business-like speaker, using no rhetorical flourishes, and keeping in a rather homely strain as close to the point as possible, which, combined with his earnestness and fluency, enabled him to fix the attention of his hearers much longer than is usual in a popular assembly."* A committee similar to that of New York was appointed. In an address to the citizens which this committee issued, they disclaimed the idea of asking for arms or recruits; they only asked for sympathy and the means of alleviating the sufferings of the refugees. But it does not appear that any collections were made. In a letter addressed to Mr. Mackenzie, dated Washington, December 20th, 1838, the writer says: "You have seen splendid assemblies in Albany and New York; large committees appointed to make large collections. Not a man of them has moved; not a farthing has been obtained. The directions from Washington have in a moment staid and cooled the warmest enthusiasm." One of the leading refugees appealed to Congress to succor his distressed compatriots; but the written constitution was pleaded as a bar to their doing so. Mr. Mackenzie then went to Washington, and there held a meeting very much to

* *Pennsylvanian,* Nov. 19.

the annoyance of Mr. Van Buren. Two of the Washington papers refused to publish an advertisement announcing the intended meeting ; the other two published it. Some of the Heads of the Departments sent circulars to their clerks, ordering them not to attend. About a thousand persons were present at the meeting, the failure of which had been predicted, even by some who favored it. The last of these meetings, held at Baltimore on the 22d of November, was well attended.

We have seen that Bierce superseded General Handy in the command of the "Army of the North-West." He was a lawyer, living at Akron, Portage County, Ohio ; where, about that time, he was United States Attorney. He was appointed by the Cleveland Committee of Hunters. Handy's plan of first raising the standard of revolt at Windsor, and then causing a simultaneous rising of the organized corps in Canada to take place, was abandoned under the new management. Prescott was probably thought to be a better point of operations for the purpose of obtaining a footing in the Province, from its more central position on the frontier, and the readiness with which the windmill could be converted into a fort. But when Van Shultz had failed at Prescott, Mr. Bierce was to revive the project of Handy at Windsor. For this purpose men were collected at various points on the frontier, to the number of nearly four hundred. Monroe County, Michigan, supplied about one hundred refugees and Patriots ; Buffalo, something over sixty ; Rochester, seventeen.* The Rochester and Buffalo men took

* Heman A. Keep, one of the Windsor expedition.

steamer at the latter city, and received a reinforce-
ment at Munroe. From this place they walked to
Swan River, the central rendezvous of the party. At
this point they remained forty-eight hours, their numbers then being three hundred and sixty-two. On the
morning of the third day, they marched to the Junction, four miles from Detroit, equipped themselves
and made ready to cross into Canada, where they
seem to have expected that they were about to commence a winter campaign. General Bierce and most
of the Patriots are said to have been well supplied
with money—the proceeds it may be of the Cleveland
banking scheme—and Commissary Bronson, of Buffalo,
had a good supply both of money and provisions. The
men had been led to expect that a steamer would be
in readiness to take them over from the Junction;
but no steamer was there. A fatality attended all
these movements, from the battle of Yonge Street till
now: there was always some great want; some fatal
blunder was committed; some gross neglect of duty
occurred; some act of indiscretion, or cowardice, or
some fatal delay marred the whole plan. Such are
the results of civilians undertaking to conduct warlike operations. By night the men had marched to
Detroit; a steamer was ready to take them across; but
General Bierce, whom they had never seen, was not
ready. They were ordered to march back into the
woods; and having obeyed, they returned next night
to the outskirts of the city, prepared to cross. General Bierce sent his aid to say that the steamer was
not ready; though the men had the evidence of their
own senses that it had steamed up twenty hours be-

fore. They were irritated and soon became suspicious. Was Bierce bribed by the agents of the British in Detroit? Or did he hold back from cowardice? Such were the questions they asked themselves. Two full companies left in disgust. The delay was ruinous to the expedition. A knowledge of the encampment was spread abroad; and couriers were sent through the Western District to bring up men from the defence of Windsor, Sandwich, and Fort Malden.* On the night of the fifth day, when the numbers had been much reduced by desertions, General Bierce was ready to cross, the steamer was ready, and a crossing was made.† Bierce is said to have shown a strong disinclination to cross; and to have been finally compelled to do so by the reproaches of the officers and men under his command.

In going down to the steamer Champlain, on the evening of the 3d of December, the invaders marched openly through the streets of Detroit, and were allowed to pass within sight of the sentinels stationed at the public arsenal, without interruption. On the following morning, when the attack was made upon Windsor, a large concourse of persons, of which the number has been estimated as high as 5,000, stationed themselves on the wharves, steamboats, and other vessels, cheering the invaders on; and when the tri-colored Patriot flag displayed its twin stars and the word "Liberty" in the breeze, on Canadian ground, the air was rent with

---

* Heman A. Keep.

† Some of the prisoners stated the number who crossed at three hundred and fifty; but this was probably an exaggeration. Keep stated it at only one hundred and sixty-four.

shouts of applause from the assembled multitude on the American shore.* The small band of daring invaders were marched in two divisions: the first being commanded by Cols. Putnam and Harvell; General Bierce bringing up the rear, and having a special regard to his own personal safety. On landing, he had briefly addressed the men, and issued a proclamation to "the citizens of Canada."† On approaching a house

---

* Report of Henry Sherwood, Judge Advocate, on the case of the Windsor prisoners, January 26, 1837.   Heman A. Keep.

† The address was in these terms:—

"SOLDIERS! the time has arrived that calls for action—the blood of our slaughtered countrymen cries aloud for revenge. The spirits of Lount, and Matthews, and Moreau, are yet unavenged. The murdered heroes of Prescott lie in an unhallowed grave in the land of tyranny. The manes of the ill-fated Caroline's crew can only be appeased by the blood of the murderers.

" Arouse, then, soldiers of Canada! Let us avenge their wrongs! Let us march to victory or death; and ever, as we meet the tyrant foe, let our war cry be: 'REMEMBER PRESCOTT.' "

Here is the proclamation, signed by William Lount, who was taking this means of avenging the execution of his father:—

"CITIZENS OF CANADA! We have received the Standard of Liberty on our shores. It is not an ensign of oppression, but of protection. We have returned to our native land, not as enemies, but as friends. Charges, false as the hearts of our oppressors, have been made against us; and you have been told that we are pirates, robbers, banditti, and brigands. You have been told that we came to plunder and destroy ; and that the reward for which we are contending was indiscriminate robbery. False is the charge—alike false and deceptive. We come to restore to our beloved country, that liberty so long enjoyed, and so tyrannically wrested from us. This is our only object—this is the end of our desires, and of our ambition. When this is accomplished, gladly will we return to the cultivation of our beloved fields, and the enjoyments of the domestic fireside.

" No one who remains at home shall be molested in his avocations—those, only, found in arms, or aiding our oppressors, will be treated as enemies; those aiding us in restoring liberty to Canada, will be hailed as friends to us, to Canada, to humanity.

" Let every one, then, who has not the spirit to engage in the cause of liberty, remain at home, and pursue his usual avocations in peace.

used as barracks for the militia, shots were exchanged
between the occupants and the invaders; and a Capt.
Lewis, from the London District, who was with the
latter, was killed. The invaders set the building on
fire, and two militia-men are said to have been burnt
to death. The sentinel was shot. A negro who refused to join the assailants was killed; and Staff-sur-
geon Hume, who went up to them under the supposi-
tion, it is said, that they were Canadian Militia, lost
his life, and his body was barbarously mutilated after
death. The steamer Thames, embedded in the ice,
shared the fate of the barracks. As the flames from
the building and vessel curled up in the gray of the
breaking morn, three cheers were given from the
Detroit shore, and answered by the invaders. While
the barracks were being taken, Bierce remained in the
rear.

After this, the party proceeded towards the centre
of the town, to the cries of " Remember Prescott," and
" Remember the Caroline," where the principal division was met by a militia force under Col. Prince
and Captain Spark, and driven into the woods, where
they were not immediately pursued. The rear-guard
remained at a distance with a number of prisoners.
Col. Broderick, with detachments of royal artillery
and the Thirty-fourth Regiment and a nine pounder,
arrived from Amherstburg. Bierce resolved to retreat,

"But above all, let those who ask for honor, and glory, and their country's
good, espouse the cause of the Patriots of Canada.

"Head Quarters, Patriot Army, Windsor, Nov. 30.

"By order of the Commander-in-Chief,

"WM. LOUNT, *Military Secretary.*"

and leave the larger body of the men who had taken refuge in the woods. Signals were made to the steamer Erie, which had a detachment of United States troops on board, to come to their rescue, but she declined. The retreating party were reduced to the necessity of picking up canoes, or whatever they could find, in which to escape. One of the boats was fired upon by the cannon while crossing, and one man was killed. The United States steamer Erie, in attempting to cut off the escape of these persons, fired several ineffectual shots.

In this raid, twenty-five of the invaders lost their lives, and forty-six more were taken prisoners. Of the twenty-five, four were taken prisoners and shot, in cool blood, without the form of a trial, by order of Col. Prince. This act was condemned by Lord Brougham and others in terms of great severity; and there can be no doubt that, whatever excuses may be made for it, Colonel Prince committed a terrible mistake. If the opinion of the Attorney General of Upper Canada was of any value, in such a case, Col. Prince might have pleaded it as authority. In the month of March previous, the magistrates of Sandwich, with Col. Prince at their head, had complained to the Lieutenant Governor that the American prisoners, taken in the schooner Anne, and at Point au Pelé, were not punished; and the case being referred to Attorney General Hagerman, that functionary reported that "they might have been put to death by their captors, at the moment they were taken, as outlaws, who had forfeited all claim to the protection of the laws of every civilized nation." It is sufficient to say that the general verdict of mankind has not held Colonel Prince excused for the slaughter of these men without even the form of a trial.

80

CHAPTER XII.

Mr. Mackenzie removes to Rochester—Disorganized state of the Refugees—
Canadian Political Prisoners in England—General Handy reappears upon
the Scene—He sends McLeod to the West to get up an Organization—
McLeod's Reports—Proposals to bring Indians into the Patriot service—
Materials of war—Associations of Canadian Refugees formed at Rochester,
Auburn, and Cincinnati.

So long as Mr. Mackenzie remained at New York, he was between four and five hundred miles from the nearest centres of frontier operations. During the last three quarters of the year 1838, he had been occupied in the publication of a newspaper; and was now about to yield to the solicitations of his friends to remove to Rochester, where it was thought its influence would be more directly felt. In the early part of January, 1830, he visited that city, and resolved to remove there with his family and Printing Office.

After visiting Rochester, he gave an account of the condition of the refugees in a private letter, which I have received, with many others, from the person to whom it was addressed. "Their organization and union," he said, "apart from that of the associations who aid them, is nothing. They have little influence, nor will it increase until a better system is adopted." He thought Canada could easily be revolutionized, "if men would go right about it." "I shall try," he said, under date Rochester, Jan. 10, 1839, "to get up such an organization here and on the other side, and to make such use of that already in operation, as will probably somewhat change the aspect of Canadian affairs. The material is before us if we choose to make use of it."

Early in February, Mr. Mackenzie moved from New York to Rochester, with his family, in express carriages. The last number of the *Gazette* issued in New York bore date January 26, and the next number made its appearance in Rochester, on the 23d of February.

About New Year, 1839, twelve Canadian prisoners, three of whom had been convicted of political offences and the other nine, transported by Sir George Arthur, without form of trial, arrived in England, on their way to Van Dieman's Land. All of them were under sentence of transportation for life. The transportation of the nine unconvicted prisoners had been ordered under authority of an act of the Legislature of Upper Canada, empowering the Lieutenant Governor to grant a pardon to all persons charged with treason, who should, previous to their arraignment, confess their guilt. He could attach to the pardon whatever condition he thought fit.

While in the custody of the jailer at Liverpool, a writ of *Habeas Corpus* was issued, and the prisoners were brought before the Courts of Queen's Bench and Exchequer, Westminster, and their discharge moved for. Their case excited much interest in England; and the most absurd opinions were expressed regarding them. "One person would ask," a journal of the day reported, "'How are they dressed?' and become utterly astonished, not to say disappointed, when he

found that they wore ordinary hats, coats, and breeches."
It was decided that they were legally held in custody,
and that the jailer of Liverpool was justified in assisting the captain of the vessel in which they had been
brought to England.

Petitions were presented to the Crown impugning
the legality of the sentences, and praying that they
might not be carried into effect. The Courts of
Queen's Bench and Exchequer had only decided one
of the three questions which the cases involved. They
had not decided whether the compulsory removal
of the prisoners from England, or their compulsory
detention in Van Dieman's Land, would be legal. In
some of the cases, the Imperial Government was of
opinion that Sir Francis Bond Head's proclamation
of December 7, 1837, amounted to an amnesty of their
offences. And it was inferred by those who attended
the discussions before the courts, "that the judges entertained a very grave doubt whether the Government
could lawfully proceed further against the prisoners,"
unless they could be brought to trial for treason in
England.* "A trial," the Marquis of Normanby
confessed, "must have resulted in their acquittal," because, among other reasons, such a prosecution would
have been justly regarded with the utmost disfavor
by the court and jury.

The group of prisoners, as given in the wood-cut,
was taken for a London periodical while judgment was
being delivered upon Mr. Hill's application for a rule
nisi, for an attachment against the Liverpool jailer.

---

* Dispatch from the Marquis of Normanby to Sir George Arthur, Downing
Street, July 23, 1839. See Appendix I for names of persons imprisoned for
their participation in the revolt, in U. C.

At the extreme left of the group is Paul Bedford, a Canadian farmer, who resided in the London District. The second, Lenies Miller, was an American law-student, living at Rochester, at the time of the outbreak. William Reynolds was the third, an American from Philadelphia. The next was Finlay Malcolm, whose uncle of the same name had previously been a representative of the London District, in the Upper Canada Legislature. After him comes John G. Parker, who had been a storekeeper in Hamilton. Randal Wixon, the sixth in the group, was a schoolmaster and a Baptist minister. He had charge of *The Colonial Advocate*, it will be remembered, while Mr. Mackenzie was in England. Leonard Watson, the next, was living near Montgomery's at the time of the outbreak there. The eighth was Ira Anderson, at whose tavern political meetings had frequently been held. Then comes William Alves, a carpenter, who was working at Montgomery's hotel, at the time of the rebellion. James Brown, the tenth in the group, was a Canadian farmer from the London District. Robert Walker, the next, was a native of Scotland, a blacksmith by trade, and had emigrated to Canada some years before. James Grant, whose position is at the extreme right of the group, was a native of Upper Canada.

At this period General Handy, whom Bierce had superseded, some months before, in the command of the Army of the North-west, again appears upon the scene. He reappears in his old character, why or by what means does not appear. On the 1st of January, 1839, he directed General McLeod, in whom he had great confidence, to proceed to the West to get up a military organization, and report his proceedings.* McLeod returned " 3,250 efficient men ready for service when called for." The summary of his report, which I find in manuscript, is without date; but as McLeod was in Chicago, in execution of his mission, on the 14th of March, it was probably not before April or May when he made his return. At Coldwater, Missouri, were fifteen hundred Indians and five hundred volunteers, to be commanded by General J. B. Stewart, formerly of the United States Army; at Chicago five hundred and sixty Catholic Irish, to be commanded by A. Smith. Considering the size of Chicago, in 1839, it must have been a central point for the collection of these men, for they could not have been resident there. On the Desplain River were two hundred and fifty men, but whether they were Indians or whites is not stated. They must, I should think, have been Indians. They were to be commanded by Colonel W. R. Miller. At Kankakee, one hundred and forty French Canadians were ready to take the field under Francis Brodieau. On the line

---

* I find a manuscript copy of the order, which is in these terms:—

"HEADQUARTERS, Windsor, U. C.,
January 1, 1839.

"GENERAL DONALD McLEOD—Sir: You will forthwith proceed to the West, as far as your judgment may dictate, and in your discretion you will organize and arrange in military order, and commission all such individuals as you may deem worthy, and give them such directions as in your judgment may seem expedient, and direct, if you receive no further orders, all the affairs connected with the Patriot cause according to the best of your judgment, until you are enabled to make your returns.

"I am, sir, with much respect, yours, &c.,

"H. S. HANDY,
"Commanding General, N. W. A. P."

of the Illinois and Fox Rivers were three hundred Canadians, Dutch, and Irish, who were to be commanded by Major Luddington.

From men General McLeod proceeds to material of war. About arms no difficulty was anticipated. Besides the men reported by McLeod, Handy mentioned a great many more whom he could raise. "Of the several tribes of Indians," he said, "in the States of Mississippi, Illinois, Missouri, and Wisconsin Territory, and west of the Mississippi River, I have a general knowledge, and for reasons hereafter to be explained, I have a social and friendly alliance with them." If he could raise sufficient means to clothe and pay them, he could get as many as he would be willing to receive. He then turns to Canada. "From the enrollment of the returns from the Upper Province during the last summer," I quote the exact words of the document, "which amounts to 38,000, I can safely calculate on 4,000 efficient and determined men." Indians, I presume, are meant here, as in the other cases; but I doubt very much whether the Canadian Indians could have been induced to fight against the government. Donations of lead sufficient for a campaign had been promised, and from twenty to forty three and four pounders were to be cast, near Detroit, for the use of Light Artillery. A gentleman in Detroit had nearly brought to perfection a cannon that would be able to fire from fifty to sixty times a minute. In spite of the Bank scheme, of which nothing is said by Handy, the greatest difficulty was confessed to be the want of money. "If I should succeed," he says, "in obtaining my anticipated means, "I can purchase from a factory thirty thousand stand of muskets, by paying one-fourth in advance and the remainder on credit." Handy and McLeod had, a few nights before, had a conference with a number of Indian chiefs, at Detroit, by whom they were assured that the services of their warriors could be relied upon, if the means of paying them could be found. As nothing came of these preliminaries of an extensive organization, it is probable that the movement collapsed for want of money.

On the 12th of March, Mr. Mackenzie issued a confidential circular, calling a special Convention "to be composed of Canadians, or persons connected with Canada, who are favorable to the attainment of its political independence, and the entire separation of its government from the political power of Great Britain," to be held at Rochester. About fifty persons attended this Convention, which met at six o'clock on the evening of the 21st, and concluded its sittings next day. An Association of Canadian Refugees was formed, of which Mr. Montgomery was appointed President, Mr. Mackenzie, Secretary, and Samuel Moulson, of Rochester, Treasurer. A confidential circular, dated "Office of the Canadian Association, Rochester, March 22, 1839," was issued, in which questions were proposed and suggestions made. While the independence of Canada was the ultimate object aimed at, another object was to prevent all isolated or premature attempts, such as had recently failed at Ogdensburg and Windsor, from being made.* The

* The objects stated in the circular are subjoined:—

"*Resolved*, That a society be now constituted from among inhabitants of Ca-

notion of attempting to secure the independence of Canada, by means of invading parties from the States,

nada, who have left that country within the last two years, or who are refugees from thence, or emigrants from political causes, or who, having been born British subjects, are desirous of aiding the Canadians in the achievement of independence of British political power, and that said society be called 'the Canadian Association.'

"And we declare that the objects for which this Association is established, are—

"1. To aid in obtaining for the people of the North American Colonies the unrestricted power to choose their form of government, by means of conventions of delegates of their appointment, whose acts should afterwards obtain their concurrence ; and to assist by all lawful means in removing from this northern continent the cruel yoke of the British government.

"2. To prevent as far as possible hasty and ill-planned expeditions or attacks upon parts of the Canadas, designed or begun by, or in the name of, Canadian refugees, or persons in Canada.

"3. To discountenance publicly and privately all burnings of private property in Canada, and all attempts on the life of any person untried and unconvicted of crime, however deserving of condemnation and death by the Canadians.

"4. To discountenance all attempts to invade the Canadas from these States, so long as the Government and Legislature of the Union shall consider this nation bound by treaties to abstain from such invasions.

"5. To act in concert with any benevolent and patriotic society or societies within this State or any of the United States, formed or to be formed to aid the Canadian people by all lawful means in obtaining relief from the British yoke, or who may be associated for the purpose of relieving those who have been forced in their hour of distress to seek refuge in this free country from the heavy hand of British tyranny.

"6. To convey to some central place, for the benefit of the laboring classes among the refugees, all the information that can be obtained as to the best situation for their obtaining temporary employment.

"7.   *   *   *   *   *   *   *

"8. And lastly, to profit by the example of those who have recently exercised power in Canada, to imprison, murder, hang, rob, and banish worthy and estimable reformers, and kind and generous friends and neighbors, by exerting our whole individual and united influence, when Canada shall become free, to prevent the like cruel treatment of the Orangemen and loyalists. Our earnest desire is to see Canada free and happy, not to indulge in ourselves, or encourage in others, a revengeful and bitter spirit against our known or supposed enemies, after their power to oppress our country shall have been taken

was discarded. But the idea of Americans succoring the Canadians, in case they should themselves strike for independence was unquestionably included in the plan. This was shown by one of the questions asked in the circular :

" In case the people of Canada shall give indications that they are determined to struggle, as the fathers of this republic struggled, against British oppression," the question ran, " by planting the standard of freedom on their own soil, and rallying round it, what help are they to expect from your society or neighborhood, in men and arms? Be pleased at the earliest possible day to send us a table with the following particulars :

" Names of volunteers in the township of ——— who would be ready, in case five thousand men joined them on this side, to go into Canada, armed as the soldiers of freedom, as soon as the Canadians should have planted the standard on their own soil, rallied round it, and sought their assistance.

" In the table state what arms each man has; what means he has of transporting himself to a place of rendezvous; and mark with a star the names of any who have served in the armies of this Union, England, or any other power, stating the rank held in the same."

A similar Convention, under the name of an " Agricultural Meeting," had been held at Auburn, in Ja-

away, but to bring into operation the Christian rule, to do unto others as we would wish them to do towards us, were they in our situation or circumstances and we in theirs."

The blank at the mystical number "seven" leaves room for the play of the imagination, and is suggestive of a project of Canadian independence.

nuary, at which Mr. Mackenzie was present and took a leading part. A special Executive Committee had been formed at that Convention, and the information sought in the circular issued from Rochester was to be laid before both the Auburn Executive Committee and the Rochester secret Special Committee. The Association was bound by no oath or affirmation, nor were its members under penalty to perform any obligation whatever.

These associations appear to have differed from that of the Cleveland in very essential particulars. The Rochester Association was composed of Canadian Refugees; the Cleveland Association was composed almost entirely of Americans. The former laid it down as a rule that the independence of the Canadas must first be asserted by the resident Canadians, and then, but not till then, extraneous assistance might be afforded them. Mr. Mackenzie claimed for the Rochester Association that it prevented small marauding expeditions being got up. At the same time, its members were preparing to second the efforts of the Canadians, should the standard of revolt be again raised within the Provinces. Certain it is that no expeditions were fitted out against Canada after this time, although there were extensive organizations in the border States, of which the object was to assist in bringing about the independence of Canada. There was formed an auxiliary Association of Canadian Refugees in Cincinnati, in which there were no Americans. Dr. Duncombe was connected with it. But the plan of uniting the Canadian refugees, instead of allowing Americans to form schemes for the "liberation" of

Canada, appears to have originated with Mr. Mackenzie, in January, 1839.

The circular of the Rochester Association does not appear to have elicited many replies, though there were refugees scattered all over the Union, from Maine to Florida. A few reply that they are under obligations to report to Lockport or elsewhere. A letter from Florida volunteers the statement that "in the South, all about the Gulf of Mexico, are hardy maritime people, bred from childhood to fishing, slaving, privateering, wrecking, and piracy, ready, if they can get commissions from any government, to cruise against the rich trade of England." These materials would be available, as privateers, the letter adds, if "we can only establish a fixed government [in Canada] for three weeks." On the 18th of May, the receipts of the society amounted to seventy-seven dollars, and it had not yet appointed any traveling agents.

In the month of May, General Handy wrote to Mr. Mackenzie, recommending, if the Rochester Association should second the project, "that a call be made for a general representation from the Provinces, and that a General Congress be formed, with the President, etc., of Canadians solely." His object was to have a united representation from both Provinces, that they should stand together in their united strength, under one banner, "as did the thirteen United States during the Revolution." The project, however, came to nothing.

CHAPTER XIII.

Trial of Mr. Mackenzie for setting on foot and providing Means in the United
States for carrying on a Warlike Expedition against Canada—He memorial-
izes the Judges to let him be put on his Trial—His Address to the Jury—
Conviction—Is Sentenced to Eighteen Months' Imprisonment and to pay a
fine of Ten Dollars for doing what the United States Marshal officially stated
Nine-tenths of the People of Buffalo had done—From the Jail Door to his
Upper Room—A Portrait of Ephraim Gilbert, the Jailer—Mr. Mackenzie's
Treatment in Prison—He is Shot at through the Jail Window—Sickness and
Despondency—Death of his Aged Mother—He gets out of Jail by a Strat-
agem to visit her Death-bed—Sees the Funeral from his Jail Window—
Efforts for the Mitigation of his Punishment—He is ordered the Use of the
Jail Yard after nearly Eleven Months' Close Confinement—Hundreds of
Thousands petition for his Release—His Pardon.

WHEN Mr. Mackenzie was indicted, at Albany, in
June, 1838, Mr. Badgley, by his instruction, informed
the court that he would be ready for trial next day.
He kept his word, and attended before the court ; but
Mr. District Attorney Benton was not ready. The
court required him to be present again in October. In
September, Mr. Benton assured him the trial would
come on. Mr. Mackenzie again attended at Albany ;
when the District Attorney had found reasons, in a
statute of Congress—could he previously have been
ignorant of it?—for trying the case at Canandaigua,
Ontario County. About a month before the June session of the Circuit Court, Mr. Benton informed Mr.
Mackenzie that the case might come on on the very first

day of the session. The defendant attended at Canandaigua; and, his patience being exhausted, he, on the second day after the court opened, addressed a memorial to the judges expressing a desire to be allowed to be put upon trial on the charge preferred against him; he had never shrunk from a trial, and had no wish that it should be waived. He complained that the District Attorney had refused him a list of the witnesses on whose evidence the Grand Jury, at Albany, had found the indictment, and thought they ought to appear before the Petit Jury.

This memorial was presented on the 19th of June, 1839, and the trial commenced before the United States Circuit Court, on the next morning. It lasted two days. The recognizances, into which Mr. Mackenzie had entered, having expired some time before, and not having been renewed, his appearance before the court was a voluntary act. The judges were Messrs. Smith Thompson, of the United States Supreme Court, and Alfred Conklin, Circuit judge of the Northern Division of New York. The prosecution was conducted by Mr. N. S. Benton, United States District Attorney. Mr. Mackenzie, as had been his custom in cases of libel, undertook his own defence. No jurors were challenged.* The jury appears, however, to have been irregularly struck. The sheriff, a

---

* The Jurors who tried the case were all from Ontario, one of the counties forming the District, viz:

Dr. Otis Fuller, Naples, Foreman; Alfred Nichols, Naples; William Carter, E. Bloomfield; Andrew Rowley, Victor; Ezra Newton, Hopewell; Jacob Salpaugh, Manchester; D. Benton Pitts, Richmond; Seth Gates, Phelps: Moses Black, Seneca; James P. Stanton, Gorham; Valentine Stoddard, Canadice; Booth P. Fairchild, Canandaigua.

county judge, and the county clerk were required by the law of New York to be present at the drawing of juries; and several weeks' public notice of the day of drawing was required to be given. These conditions were not complied with in this case. A deputy of Marshal Garrow, who had been on a species of detective frontier service, drew the jury in the presence of the county clerk. Nor was the requisite notice given.

The indictment under a law of 1794, and another of 1818, never before put into execution,* charged the defendant with setting on foot a military enterprise, at Buffalo, to be carried on against Upper Canada, a part of the Queen's dominions, at a time when the United States were at peace with Her Majesty; with having provided the means for the prosecution of the expedition; and with having done all this within the dominion and territory, and against the peace, of the United States. It was stated in evidence, though afterwards denied by persons present, and in opposition to all the printed reports of the meetings at the time, that Mr. Mackenzie, at a meeting in the Buffalo theatre, in the winter of 1837, called upon the people of the States to imitate the example France had set them in their own case, of aiding a revolution in another country; that, at Black Rock, he had stated, in reference to four or five wagon loads of muskets on

---

* In the case of Texas there had, in 1835, been open enlistments; and Mr. Price, who held the office of District Attorney for Southern New York, then gave it as his opinion that the law of 1818 did not make it penal to combine or confederate to promote expeditions against Texas, a part of Mexico with the government of which the United States were at peace. Money was borrowed in Wall Street, and stocks issued on the security of lands to be conquered

their way to Navy Island, that they would be of great, use to the Patriots ;* and that on two several occasions, while the forces were on Navy Island, he was there;, that a proclamation—a copy of which was exhibited —the incomplete proof sheets of which were sent to defendant to read, was printed at Buffalo and sent to Navy Island.   After the evidence for the prosecution was concluded, Mr. Mackenzie addressed the jury for, six hours.   "His speech," says a Rochester paper,†. "was really a powerful effort. He enchained the audience, and at its conclusion, if a vote had been taken· for his conviction or liberation, he would have had a strong vote in his favor."

The averments in the indictment were certainly not, all fully made out.   The calling on the Americans for assistance was not setting on foot an expedition ; and it was certainly not shown that Mr. Mackenzie furnished the means.   He had lost everything he pos- sessed by the outbreak in Canada ; and after leaving Navy Island he had to pledge his gold watch to raise money to take him and Mrs. Mackenzie to Rochester, But the jury overlooked these refinements, and went upon the broad fact of his undoubted connection with the Navy Island expedition.   He defended himself at great length and with much ability ; often going, it may be, in the range of his arguments, beyond the limits usually taken by counsel in such cases.   He

---

* These arms had been taken from the Court House at Buffalo; regarding which transaction, Mr. Mackenzie said in his address to the Jury: "I can and do solemnly declare before God and man, and I absolve all men from secrecy in the matter, that I knew nothing of the intention of any person to take these arms."

† The *Daily Democrat.*

showed what the French did for the Americans, in their revolution; what the Dutch did for the English; what the United States had done for, and in, Texas; and how they had fitted out an expedition to Greece, in violation of their treaty obligations with Turkey. "I think it hard," he said, "to be singled out and dragged here at this time; but as I require an asylum in your country, I am bound, and I do sincerely wish, to pay the utmost respect to your laws. Indeed it is admiration of your free institutions which, strange as it may seem, has brought me here to-day." He pointed out the anomaly of allowing their own citizens to escape, while he and one other foreigner were pounced upon. "The processes," he remarked, "were innumerable, the fees beyond precedent; the convictions may be—George Washington Case and William Lyon Mackenzie, aliens; but of Romans not one!"* "We are poor, exiles, refugees, wanderers in your land, little cared for, or indeed despised; and is not this misery enough? Must we be placed as felons and criminals before your people, and singled out for the cell, the victims of British interest, British influence, and British gold? Surely you will never say it! Such a verdict would consign me to a prison, and leave my children without bread; but to you it would be perpetual infamy. The civilized world would cry shame upon the base hypocrisy of such truculent policy." He seems to have felt that the freedom with which he dwelt on the partiality and inconsistency of the

* Bierce, who had led the Windsor expedition, was not molested, nor had other Americans who took a leading part in the Prescott expedition been brought to trial by the Federal Government, though their guilt was notorious.

American Government, might not help his case; but that consideration did not restrain him. "I have been told," he remarked to the jury, "to say pleasant things to you, to use honied words, and avoid any topic that might touch the national pride or wound the national vanity; but as I did not stoop to flatter power in the few on the other side of the great lakes, it is not likely that I shall cringe to it here, as apparently vested in the many." He told them, very plainly, what had been their traditional policy, in regard to Canada.

"Why," he asked, "should there be deception used? You want Canada. I know it. I never yet talked seriously to an American who did not admit a desire to see European government removed from the North. Your verdict against me would blind nobody to your real views. Look back. In 1774 your Congress bade Canada revolt, and in 1775 Washington sent messengers to Nova Scotia for the like purpose. The same year he wrote to R. H. Lee, (see Washington's writings, pp. 173 and 174,) 'Would it not be politic to invite the Canadians to send members to Congress?' The committee of your Congress, at same time, wrote Gen. Schuyler, 'Congress desires you to exert your utmost endeavor to accede to a union with these colonies, and that they form from their parishes a provincial convention, and send delegates to this Congress.' Again, (p. 70,) General Washington writes Arnold and his officers, " to consider themselves as marching, not through the country of an enemy, but of our friends and brethren, for such the inhabitants of Canada have proved themselves to be in this unhappy contest.' And again, (vol. 5, p. 389,) General Washington writes Landon Carter, 'The accounts you had received of the accession of Canada to the Union were premature. It is a measure much to be wished, and I believe would not be displeasing to the people; but, while Carleton remains among them, with three or four thousand regular troops, they dare not avow their sentiments, if they really are favorable, without a strong support. Your ideas of its importance to our political union coincide exactly with mine. If that country is not with us, from its proximity to the Eastern States, its intercourse and connection with numerous tribes of western Indians, its communion with them by water, and other local advantages, it will be at least a troublesome if not a dangerous neighbor to us; and ought, at all events, to be in the same interest and politics as the other States.' Why was this union not then consummated? Because they were treated as now. They assisted Gen. Montgomery with men, carriages, and provisions on all occasions. When he was before Quebec many parishes offered him their aid as volunteers, and were refused—the peasantry were ill-used and plundered of their property—and their religion made a mockery of—neither was a force sent to protect them. (Sparke's Washington, 3, p. 361, 2.) The generous Lafayette, too, writes John Jay, from Paris, 1787: 'I was nine years ago honored with the choice of Congress, to command an army into Canada, and never have I ceased to enjoy the prospect of its enfranchisement.' (Sparke's Diplom. Cor. 10, p. 64.) He had not changed his opinions in 1818, nor when here in 1824, as I know from his conversation with

myself.   Had he lived to this day he would have been
ashamed of and grieved at this prosecution, and so
will many more of the best friends of free institutions.
John Jay, to whom he wrote, was so impressed with
the importance of the Canadas that he included them
as a part of the States in his arrangements for the
treaty of 1783.   John Adams was for continuing the
war with England after 1782, rather than not have
the Canadas free.   He writes Samuel Adams: 'As
long as Great Britain shall have Canada, Nova Scotia,
and the Floridas, so long will Great Britain be the
enemy of the United States, let her disguise it as
much as she will.' (Sparke's 10, p. 257.)   And, (p.
316,) 'If peace should unhappily be made, leaving
Canada, Nova Scotia, or the Floridas, or any of them,
in her hands, jealousies and controversies will be perpetually arising.'   And Benjamin Franklin was fully
impressed with the deep importance of possessing the
northern colonies.   Congress, too, in the first constitution, unanimously offered free entrance to the delegates of Canada to Congress without even the formal-
ity of a vote of States.   On the 8th of May, 1778,
Congress addressed your country, and told the people
to 'expect not peace while any corner in America is
in the possession of your foes.   You must drive them
away from this land of promise, a land flowing with
milk and honey.   Your brethren at the extremities
of the continent already implore your friendship and
protection.   It is your duty to grant their request.
They hunger and thirst after liberty.   Be it yours to
dispense to them the heavenly gift.   And what is
there to prevent it?'   In 1812, the one thing wanted

was Canada, and 'the means were provided' in the person of General Hull, whom you afterwards sentenced to be shot. Do the 18,000 soldiers, the flower of the English army, the pleasantries occurring daily on 3,000 miles of frontier, the territory connecting England with the Indians on your rear, the Maine boundary, and the St. Lawrence navigation, afford evidence that Canada has ceased to be to you an object of deep solicitude? And if not, what will the world say of the motives which dictated this prosecution ?"*

The court admitted that the " mere meeting together of individuals, or the raising of money or the collection of arms," referred to by the defendant, " to send to Texas, was no violation of the law ;" because these acts did not constitute the fitting out of an expedition. And Judge Thompson was careful to tell American citizens exactly how far they could go without overstepping the limits of the law. They could give their sympathy a practical shape by personally carrying to the oppressed money and supplies.† He added that,

---

* When the question of annexing Canada to the United States was raised, within the Province, in 1849, Mr. Mackenzie counted about a thousand United States newspapers, North and South, that gave a favorable response ; while, if I recollect rightly, he told me he did not find one seriously opposed to the project.

† The same opinion had before been judicially given in the case of Texas. In 1835, the matter being brought before the Grand Jury of the Circuit Court of New York, they asked the opinion of the judge on the effect of the law of April 20th, 1818, and the reply was: " This section [612] applies only to military expeditions and enterprises to be carried on from the United States against any foreign power with which we are at peace. No person shall begin or set on foot or provide the means for any military expedition or enterprise, to be carried on from thence; that is, from the United States or the territory within their jurisdiction. Donations in money or any thing else to the inhabitants of Texas, to enable them to engage in a civil war with the sovereignty of Mexico, is in no sense beginning or setting on foot, or providing the means

in the case of Canada, he had no doubt, the " oppressions detailed by the defendant really existed or do exist, and that all the zeal he has displayed has been the zeal of a patriot." But the greater part of the judge's charge bore strongly against the defendant. He told the jury they must accept the law from him; and he told them to assume a great many things which had not been matter of proof, but which were to be accepted as facts, such as that Canada was a Province of England, and that Queen Victoria had succeeded to the rights of William IV.

At two o'clock the jury retired; at half past four they sent for a copy of the statutes of Congress, and at five they came into court with a verdict of "guilty." The defendant gave eighteen reasons why the sentence to be passed upon him should be merely nominal. The court had power to imprison for three years and levy a fine of $3,000; but Judge Thompson took into consideration that this was the first trial under a law passed in 1794, that the defendant had evidently been ignorant of its provision, that the case involved no moral turpitude, and that the defendant had acted with a zeal which actuates men who, however mistaken, think they are right. The sentence was that he should be confined in the county jail of Monroe, for eighteen months, and pay a fine of ten dollars.

The irregularity in drafting the jury having been now discovered, Mr. Mackenzie brought it before the notice of the court, but Judge Conklin said it had

for a military expedition from the United States or their territory. The answer therefore to the question put by the Grand Jury is, that the facts do not amount to any offence under the 6th section of the act referred to."

been done under an order of the court. The exile, convicted of a breach of neutrality, in which Marshal Garrow had declared three-fourths of the people of Buffalo had been concerned, was ordered and conducted to jail by Deputy Marshal Macfarlane, and placed under close confinement. He was, however, permitted to go to his house, on the way. His wife's sister, Mrs. John McIntosh, and her husband, had come from Toronto to see him, for the first time since the rebellion at Toronto. When he went to the jail, accompanied by Mr. McIntosh, he expected that he would be allowed to return home for the night; but when he was once within the walls of the dungeon its doors were closed upon him.

The room assigned to Mr. Mackenzie was in the third story. To reach it you pass into a wide passage from the main entrance, on the ground floor through the office and a second door; thence through a door on the right leading to a flight of straight iron-shod stairs, with an iron railing on one side and a wall on the other; then, from this landing, by a ladder, through a trap door fastened by bar and lock, into a large room extending over one entire side of the prison. In this room, where criminals whose lives have been forfeited by their crimes are strangled, were dangling ropes and other hideous apparatus of death. You pass by an ascent of a few steps through a side door into a corridor, at the upper end of which, on the left side, was the room set apart for William Lyon Mackenzie. As you pass up the corridor you cannot fail to see, through the lattice-barred door, on the right, the crowd of abandoned women, who divide their time between that apartment and the streets of Rochester. This was the only way in which the political prisoner could be reached by his family, or friends; and they were exposed, while on their passage through the jail, to the coarse jests of brutal men, and the ostentatious brutalities of still more brutal women.

Ephraim Gilbert, the jailer, had fallen into the exact niche which Nature designed him to fill. He was of low stature, and looked as if he had seen about fifty-five wilting summers and as many very hard winters. He had an exaggerated hook nose, fleshless, fallen-in cheeks, over which Nature seemed to have grudged him skin enough to spread. His sunken eyes, round and peering, combined with a long habit of watching, gave him a tiger-like appearance. His nails, long and filthy, resembled the claws of an animal perpetually digging in the dirt. His whole aspect was of that sinister cast which caused one to shrink from a contact with him. You felt, in regarding him, that, if cast into the sea, he would have more power to pollute it, than it would have to purify him.

For the first three months of his confinement, Mr. Mackenzie was shut up in a single room, with an iron door, which he was never once allowed to pass.

> "Within a cell—a barred and lonely cell—
> He musing stands. Upon his limbs no chain
> To wake him from his trance-like spell
> And clanking, writhe his heart in deeper pain.

> "What was his crime? His country's love!
> For her he fain had freedom gained;
> This was th' offence. For well he strove—
> And failing—freedom's star too would.

" He sought a home among the bravely free,
   He called for aid—for arms to crush the foe—
   And asked if freedom's sons would tamely see
   Their brothers sink beneath the victor's blow.

" For this he finds a cell !—a prisoner lone !
   For this immured ! he's torn from freedom's light !
   And still he hopes—still speaks in trumpet tone
   Against the ills which his own country blight."*

When the room in which he was placed had to
undergo extensive repairs—being new floored and
plastered, and getting a new door—he was allowed a
little more freedom ; but the moment the plaster was
dry, he was again subjected to the same close confinement. Except his own family scarcely any friend was
permitted to see him ; though he was kept on constant
exhibition by the jailer, crowds of strangers being
allowed to feast their eyes upon a live rebel leader.
Having a perhaps somewhat morbid fear that he might
be poisoned if he accepted food at the hands of the
jailer, his meals were regularly taken from his own
house; and sometimes his children were refused admission to him. Besides, if he had accepted the jail
fare, all he would have got would have been a preparation of Indian corn called " mush," and molasses and
sour bread ; and only two meals a day at that. On
Sundays no one was ever allowed to visit him. During
the first three months, he gave the jailers $36 for per-
mitting his friends to visit him ; but when he had no
more to give, they began to refuse admission to visitors they did not know ; and if admitted they were sent
away immediately after three o'clock P. M. Twice,

* These with three additional verses, dated Lockport, September 24th, 1839,
were published October 5th, 1839, under the signature of " Hamish."

83

when he was sick, his physicians were refused admittance. Built on low marshy ground, the jail is surrounded with stagnant water during the greater part of the year; and as Mr. Mackenzie was particularly susceptible of miasmatic influence, he suffered severely from the debilitating effects of marsh fever, and was a good deal dispirited. Medical certificates that the close confinement had a very injurious effect on his health having been laid before the Board of Supervisors, they, without having any power in the matter, suggested that he should be permitted a little more exercise within the walls of the building. "The charges upon which Mr. Mackenzie was convicted," they said, "are not looked upon by the community as very venial nor in any way compromising his moral character, and therefore would frown down indignantly upon any extraordinary enforcement of official authority." But the jailer and the sheriff did not allow him as much freedom as the supervisors had suggested. From June to December, he was never once permitted to breath the free air. Unless Mrs. Mackenzie or some of his little children remained with him, he never saw a human being after dark; and when they wanted to go away, they would often have to remain an hour, knocking at the door, before any one would appear to let them out; and they, not unfrequently, suffered detention of greater or less duration—sometimes extending to an hour—at some of the stages from the outer door of the prison to his room. At the same time, there was laxity enough in some parts of the Monroe prison discipline. Criminals were allowed to leave the jail, to visit their families, to frequent

256

2   3   4   5   6   7   10 11 12

Canadian State Prisoners in England (from an illustration in the London Sun.)

taverns, and roam about the town. Names and particulars were given in proof of this laxity of discipline.

On the 12th of October, 1839, the imprisoned fugitive had a narrow escape for his life. A little before
noon, as he was standing at one of the windows, looking out to see whether a friend, Mr. Kennedy, was
coming, a slug shot coming through one of the panes
whizzed past him and penetrated the plaster on the
opposite side of the room. He opened the window
and asked the jailer's boy, who was outside, if he saw
any one in the direction whence the shot must have
come. The boy said he had not. "Who fired the
shot," said Mr. Mackenzie, in a private letter, "I shall
probably never know;" but, with the expectation of lon-
gevity, which he always entertained, he added that the
escape afforded "another chance for old age, with the
pains and penalties attached to it." The jailer, on inquiry, learned that a tall, stout man, with a gun in his
hand and a dog by his side—having the appearance
of a sportsman—had been seen beyond the mill-race,
whence the shot must have come, about the time of
the occurrence. A buckshot was found to have penetrated one of the adjoining windows, and several others
struck the wall. At the time of the occurrence, the
stone-breakers, who were usually in the jail-yard, were
at dinner, and Mr. Mackenzie had only just approached
the window. The blasting of rocks was going on in
the vicinity, so that the discharge of a gun would not
be likely to attract much attention. In Buffalo, in
1838, he had been warned that assassins were on his
track, and a young man, about his size, a brother of

General Scott's secretary, had been assassinated under circumstances which gave rise to the suspicion that he had been mistaken for Mr. Mackenzie.

By this time the effects of the close confinement in the room of a jail, surrounded by miasma, had broken the luckless prisoner's health. He could not take the food which his children regularly carried to him, and medicine seemed to give no relief. His means were exhausted, and the approach of a gloomy winter inclined him to despair. He had depending on him a mother, ninety years of age, a wife in delicate health, and six helpless children. He became impressed with the idea that he could not survive fourteen months more of such confinement. The wet weather, which was setting in, rendered the visits of his family more difficult. Memorials, numerously signed, sent to the Executive for his release, remained unanswered. He had applied, through a friend, to be permitted the limits of the city, on giving security not to go beyond them, and been refused. He now, October 23, 1839, memorialized the President himself. He offered to give up the publication of his paper for the remaining fourteen months of his term, to go to any part of any State, whether north of Albany or south to New Orleans, or, as an alternative to continued imprisonment, even to accept transportation to Texas. "Better it were," he said, to President Van Buren, "at once to give me up to the power of England than thus destroy my constitution and deprive my helpless infants of protection." On the day that this memorial was written, the Secretary of State, Mr. Forsyth, instructed Marshal Garrow to see that no unnecessary severity was inflicted on the prisoner, but the propositions in the memorial received no attention from the President. From the first the Secretary of State had approached the matter with the greatest reluctance, and would have avoided it altogether if he could.

When Mr. Mackenzie memorialized the President, he had become alarmed, from the accounts given him by Mrs. Mackenzie, for the health of one of his children. He was not permitted to go to see her. "My dear little girl," he said, "grew worse and worse; she was wasted to a skeleton; but I, who had watched over her in a former illness, and procured the best physiciaus and surgeons Toronto could afford, durst not even visit her. I had followed four of her sisters and a brother to the churchyard, but I might not look upon her. Messrs. Poinsett, Van Buren, and Forsyth, with Judges Conklin and Thompson, Marshal Garrow, and Sheriff Perrin, would not even bestow that privilege. One fine day she was carried, with the physician's consent, to the prison, and her mother and I watched her for forty-eight hours, but the jailer vexed us so that she had to be taken home again where she was soon in the utmost danger, and when her poor little sister comes to tell me how she is at dusk in the evening, the jailer will tell her to wait in the public place in the jail, perhaps for an hour or more, till supper comes, as he can't be put to the trouble of opening my cage twice."

By the middle of November, the memorials for the release of the political prisoner had been signed by between fifty and sixty thousand persons. The exertions made had procured him a larger space to walk in; medicine had, at last, produced a salutary effect, and he was better in health. He was allowed to walk in the hall into which his room opened, and to take exercise six hours in the day, in the attic, which extended over the entire building.

In December, an event occurred which had a serious effect upon the captive exile's health and spirits. His aged mother, to whom he was devotedly attached, sickened and died. When, after making all the efforts he could to be allowed to go see her on her death-bed, he had come to the conclusion that he would not be permitted to do so, he addressed to her a farewell letter, full of the affection he had always borne towards her.* But when all efforts to obtain the desired

---

* It is without date, and is as follows:—

"MY DEAR MOTHER:—I entertain feelings of the deepest and most lasting gratitude to you for your kindness to me in youth, for your tender care over me, for the education you gave me, and for the many manifestations of sincere and undoubted affection you have shown towards me. The doctor tells me you are dying, and it is very hard that the cruel government people will not let me take a last farewell at your bed-side, but they will not do it. I, therefore, write these lines, which some friend will read to you, I hope, and bring me your answer, and any word you have to send me. Our last meeting here in the jail was a long and happy one. I did not think that it would be the last, but I fear the hard hearted Americans will grant no relief. The will of that Power to whom you have so fervently prayed for many a year be done. We must submit. If all the wealth of the world were mine, and it would carry me to your bedside, I would give it freely. But wealth I have none, and of justice there is but little here. I think we will before long get out of this difficulty; that I will be at liberty; that the family will again be comfortable; and sorrow fills my heart when I am told that you will not have your aged eyes comforted by the sight. When [I was] in London, you sent me several texts to comfort me. One of them, the Ninety-first Psalm, from first verse down to the ninth, will surely now be your great strength. If aught that I could do would spare you a little longer, how glad would I be to do it, for I cherish for you the warmest and most abiding affection; but if your hour is come, alas! I can do nothing. I will write again to-morrow."

interview appeared to have failed—when the entrea-
ties of Mrs. Mackenzie and the exertions of a number
of prominent citizens of Rochester had proved fruit-
less—Mr. John Montgomery hit upon an expedient by
which it was accomplished. He was keeping a hotel,
and one of his boarders was in his debt. It was arranged that the boarder should be sued and Mr. Mackenzie brought out as a witness, under a writ of *Habeas Corpus ad respondendum.* Mr. Montgomery induced the State Attorney to give permission to hold
the court in Mr. Mackenzie's house. At first, the
sheriff flatly refused to obey the writ, but on consulting Judge Gardner he concluded that it was better to
comply, and he and Ephraim, the jailer, accompanied
Mr. Mackenzie to his house. The magistrate was not
very punctual in arriving; he was very kind and very
cold when he did arrive, and was some time before he
got sufficiently warmed to open his court; and when
it did open witnesses who had nothing particular to
say were examined at considerable length. By this
stratagem, Mr. Mackenzie's last interview with his
aged and dying mother was protracted five or six
hours. It was an affecting scene. The mother was
leaving an only son, overwhelmed with calamities:
failing health—for the ague had again returned upon
him—increasing poverty; a helpless family dependent upon him; and a prison for his home. The jailer
and the sheriff were waiting, in a room adjoining that
into which the door of the bed-room opened, and the
interview must come to a close. Summoning, for the
last time, all her fortitude, the dying mother pro-
nounced the last farewell, bidding her son trust in

God and fear not. "I asked her," he wrote a few days after, "if she had that comfort for the future which she expected in former years, and found that she was as happy in the prospect of a blessed eternity, as the most steadfast martyr of ancient days." The expectation of seeing him had kept her up for some days, and though she conversed freely while he was present, she never spoke after he had gone back to his dreary prison. Mr. Clark, the magistrate, who was father of "Grace Greenwood," wept like a child at what he had witnessed, on his return home.

From the windows of his dungeon, the political prisoner could see pass the funeral of his mother, which he was not permitted to attend. His agony was intense. While his mother was known to be dying, and at the time of her funeral, a friend remained with him in the prison. He never, till released, recovered from the effects of this blow occasioned by his mother's death.

Mr. Secretary Forsyth's instructions to Marshal Garrow had not the desired effect of producing any considerable mitigation of the severity to which the prisoner had been subjected. On the 14th of January, 1840, he memorialized Mr. Seward, Governor of the State of New York, on the subject. But the laws of the State gave that functionary no power to act in a matter which concerned the United States alone. "Nevertheless," said Governor Seward, in his reply of the 27th of the same month, "I acknowledge most freely that your offence being of a political character, I think it is to be regarded in a very different light from crimes involving moral turpitude, and that a distinction ought to be made as far as possible between the treatment of persons convicted of political offences and those of the other class;" and he wrote to the Sheriff of Monroe County expressing this opinion and the desire that the prisoner's position might be made as comfortable as possible. Besides he did not fail to make it understood that, in his opinion, almost every thing depended, in such a case, upon "the kindness, humanity, and discretion of the sheriff and jailer."

This correspondence having been brought under the notice of the President, Mr. Forsyth was instructed, on the 20th February, 1840, to express to Marshal Garrow the willingness of the Chief Magistrate of the Republic "that Mr. Mackenzie should have the benefit of any indulgence, consistent with a just execution of the law, which is extended to persons undergoing punishment for analogous offences committed under the laws of the State." But these instructions produced no effect, and further complaints being made, the President found it necessary to rap the underlings on the knuckles for their inhumanity and disobedience of orders. Mr. Marshal Garrow gave himself not the least trouble on the subject. He neither visited the prison nor notified the sheriff or jailer of the instructions he had received. In the meantime, memorials for the release of the political prisoner, signed by immense numbers of persons, continued to reach the President; and Dr. Webster, of Geneva College, and Dr. Smiles, of Rochester, certified that the close confinement "has an injurious effect on his highly susceptible nervous system;" and that out-door exercise was absolutely necessary to sustain his general health.

It was under these circumstances, that the President's instructions to Marshal Garrow were repeated with something like a reprimand to that official for his remissness. "The directions you received from this department," said Mr. Secretary Forsyth, under date Washington, April 14, 1840, "were given in a spirit entirely favorable to the application of Mr. Mackenzie, and conformable to the views which the Governor of New York, and the friends who have been in correspondence with Mr. Mackenzie on the subject, have expressed in their letters to him." " It was sufficiently known," he adds, at this department, "that no cases entirely similar to that of Mr. Mackenzie, which grew out of an act of Federal legislation, could arise under the laws of the State of New York. The words ' analogous (not similar) offences' were therefore used, and intended to point to offences of a political character." "It was therefore to the manner of executing sentences incurred under the laws of the State for offences of that character that your instructions directed you to conform; and they were supposed to be sufficiently definite to convey that idea."

In what way it was customary to treat such prisoners, Mr. J. C. Spensor, in a letter which had found its way to the Department of State, described. Mr. Mackenzie's offence, Mr. Spensor showed, differed "from all offences under State laws in being political in its character, and in no respect involving the violation of private rights. It is in fact less heinous," he added, "than the misdemeanors recognized by our (the State) laws. The treatment of prisoners of that grade has always been more mild and lenient than that of felons. The secure detention of their persons has been supposed to be the principal object of the law. They have accordingly been confined in the same kind of apartment usually assigned to imprisoued debtors; have been allowed the free exercise of the jail yard, and to take exercise in any part of the building. Their food has usually been supplied by themselves or their friends, and they have not been confined to the prison diet. In fine, every indulgence consistent with their safe keeping has, so far as my knowledge extends, been granted to them." The President, through Mr. Forsyth, instructed Marshal Garrow to make Mr. Spensor's statements his rule of action in Mr. Mackenzie's case.

Mr. Garrow took his time to attend to this second order. Eight days after Mr. Forsyth's letter had been written, he had paid no attention to it. On the 22nd April, the political prisoner thus described how the dreary months of confinement had been spent: "This is the eleventh month of my confinement. For about three months I never crossed the threshold of one solitary prison room for a day. For the last three months I have not been allowed to go down stairs, even inside, but am kept continually in the upper story of the building. The door of my apartment opens within five feet of the door of the female dungeon; and the women's cells are close by. The howling and yelling of twelve or eighteen unhappy creatures at all hours, night and day, I shall never forget. I am locked up, as usual, like the felons in Newgate." On the 25th April, the Sheriff ordered the jailer to allow

Mr. Mackenzie the use of the jail yard.* The rigor of his punishment was now abated, and Mr. Mackenzie was allowed to take exercise as prescribed in the Sheriff's order.

One day, observing a stranded log in the mill race, on one side of the grounds, he pushed it with a stick to set it free ; and when it gave way, the force of the motion by which it was dislodged carried him down into the water. He was seen to go in; and instantly the rumor flew through the city that William Lyon Mackenzie had attempted to commit suicide. He had on a dressing gown which helped to buoy him up; and he got out without assistance, though not without difficulty.

The prisoner's birthday was duly celebrated by a number of friends, who dined with him in jail, on the 24th of March. Some of them, contrary to rule, smuggled in wine in their pockets; and towards the close the veritable Ephraim Gilbert was sent for. His health

---

* The document is a literary curiosity :

ROCHESTER, 25th April, 1840.

Ephraim Gilbert,

DEAR SIR.—You will Let William L Mackenzie have Exercise in the Yard or on the publick ground of the Jail Dureing such parts of the day time as you May deem nessary for the benefit of his health, and he is in no cas or under any pretence whatever to go beyound the Limmits or bounds of the public ground Connected with the Said Jail and he is not to be permitted to have any Conversation with the Prisoners which air at work in and about the said Yard or ground (a thing which I presume he will not have the *Least desire to do*) and you will also give him all other indulgences which you may think will be beneficial to his health, and with his safe keeping and that of all Prisoners confind in Said Jail, and in giving thos indulgences I am in hopes and, I think you may expect that Mr. Mackenzie will giv as little unnessary trouble as posable under the circumstances and the Construction of the Prison.

Youers Respectfully,

Darius Perrin, Sherrif of Monroe County.

was duly drunk, very much to his annoyance; but Gilbert could not well refuse to drink himself, and with a little pressure he melted so far as to take a forbidden glass. I find too a note dated January 1st, 1840, accompanying some "bottles of generous wine," sent the prisoner by a friend; not the least acceptable of the many communications he received, it may be presumed.*

The memorials to the President for the prisoner's release now had hundreds of thousands of signatures attached to them. Congress had also been petitioned on the subject. It is amusing to read the letters he received on the question of his pardon. One could not present a petition to Congress, because it would be an interference with the power of the President. Another had no objection to support a petition; but it would not do for him to bring forward a matter belonging to the members for Northern New York. One department of the government could not interfere, lest it should encroach on another and separate branch of the government. Some had peculiar notions about

---

* From Philadelphia, a friend wrote him:

"In the minority of James the Sixth, the Scottish Parliament was held (or fenced, in the language of that time) in the Tolbooth of Edinburgh, as a place of strength. In my time a portrait of that King hung in the great hall of that prison, and under, in gilt letters, the following verses as near as I can recollect:

    "'A prison is a place of care,
    A place where none can thrive,
    A touch-stone true to try a friend,
    A grave to bury one alive;
    Sometimes a place of right,
    Sometimes a place of wrong,
    Sometimes a place of rogues and thieves
    And honest men among.'"

the pardoning power; and a fellow refugee acted the part of the comforter by boldly declaring his opinion that, as a matter of principle, the President was bound to refuse to grant a pardon. "The President's position in this matter," a friend wrote from Washington, "is very peculiar, and such as you could hardly be expected to appreciate in all its bearings. In addition to the other obvious considerations that tie up his hands in the matter, there is the high constitutional indelicacy, if not impropriety, of the Executive stepping behind the Judiciary and supplanting its functions." Another friend assured him that the President had, at Saratoga, declared to different persons that he should not comply with the petitions for a pardon, unless desired by the British Government to release the prisoner. Did that government present such a request? Or did the petitions become too numerous for Mr. Van Buren to resist? The latter seems to be the true explanation; for Mr. Mackenzie was afterwards informed, at Washington, that the President, adverse to a release to the last, felt himself unable to resist the demand of three hundred thousand petitioners. About the 12th of April, Mr. Forsyth told a friend that Mr. Mackenzie would soon be pardoned, but that it was necessary to keep the matter secret for a few days; and on Sunday evening the 10th of May, 1840, he was permitted to bid adieu to the horrors of what he called the American Bastile.

CHAPTER XIV.

Bad Effects of Mackenzie's Imprisonment on his Business—The Southern States and Canada—Visit to Washington—The Democrats Friendly to the Canadian Patriots—Matured Opinion of Society in the States—Mackenzie's Last Gazette—Schemes for getting him into the Clutches of the Canadian Government—A Kidnapping Enterprise—Systematic Arrangement of his Papers—Asks to be Admitted to Practice at the Bar—Poverty—" The Volunteer"—The Gold Medal Melted—Mackenzie Opposed to New Frontier Movements—John S. Hogan and Dr. A. K. McKenzie enter into a Conspiracy to bring about a War between England and the United States — Mackenzie's (W. L.) House takes Fire—He regrets the attempt at Revolution in Canada—Removes to New York—Again denounces Frontier Movements—Is appointed Actuary of the New York Mechanics Institute—Commences " Sons of the Emerald Isle"—Resigns Situation of Actuary—Is nominated to an Inspectorship in the New York Custom House—Publishes a few Numbers of another Newspaper—Takes a large House on the strength of his Expectations—Receives an Appointment in the Archives of the New York Custom House—His Lives of Hoyt and Butler—" Life and Times of Martin Van Buren"—Private Opinion of the Effect of Annexing Canada to the States—Becomes Connected with the New York Tribune—Removes to Albany, and attends the Convention for Revising the State Constitution —Receives a generous offer from Mr. Bruce, and declines it—A Partial Amnesty excludes Mackenzie—Death of one of his daughters—Regrets the Rebellion—General Amnesty—Visits Canada—Rencounter with Col. Prince —Is burnt in Effigy in Kingston and Toronto—Riot—Removes with his Family to Canada—Is elected to the Legislative Assembly—In the House— His Hopeful Disposition—Traits of Character—The " Mackenzie Homestead"—Pecuniary Embarrassments—Sickness and Death.

THOUGH Mr. Mackenzie had exerted himself with all the energy his enfeebled strength would permit— though he had continued to conduct his newspaper and had compiled the *Caroline Almanac* which contained matter enough, compressed in small type, to have made a volume of respectable dimensions—his business failed to thrive while he was imprisoned. Till the death of his mother, the family never suffered want; but after that event, the gaunt spectre sometimes threatened to enter the door. But, in this respect, there was still worse in store for them.

"The more I see of the South," Mr. Mackenzie wrote privately ten days after his release; "the more I see it is our great enemy. It is southern slaveholding influence that keeps Cuba dependent, distracts Mexico, and enslaves Texas. That influence has crushed thus far the American feeling for Canada." These views were confirmed on a more intimate acquaintance with the facts.

Shortly after his release from prison, Mr. Mackenzie revisited Washington and Philadelphia. At Washington, he had private interviews with a number of senators and leading men from all parts of the Union. "I heard much and saw much," he wrote privately from Albany, on the 6th of July, on his way back, "and am sure that we of the North have nothing to hope from the party in power. Van Buren is with the South, the English importer and the capitalist, who rule this nation for their own advantage. There is much and well founded discontent among northern members —even of those who go with the party in power—and some of them were so plain as to wish trouble on the frontier—though I place no names here—while others hinted that the North might push matters to the length of a disunion from the slave-driving South." He still hoped for the independence of Canada, to which he was not permitted to return, and where rewards for his apprehension, schemes for his extradition, and plans to kidnap him were still kept alive; and as the result of his visit to Washington he felt, " on the whole, greatly encouraged." His health was much improved, and he was delighted with a day's visit to the Catskill Mountains.

But, every thing considered, Mr. Mackenzie regarded the Democratic party as most friendly to Canada; and on the 27th of August, he privately expressed that opinion to a friend. " They would, even if no war grew out of the Maine boundary question," he said, " be friendly to us—" advocates of Canadian independence—" and help us, while Webster and Clay, with the whole British party at their back, and old Black Cockade in the Presidential chair, would go all lengths with the English Ministry to crush us."

But the greater the exile's practical knowledge of the working of American institutions, the less was the admiration he had felt for them, when viewed from a distance. " Over three years' residence in the United States," he said in the last number of his *Gazette*, on the 23d of December, 1840, " and a closer observation of the condition of society here, have lessened my regrets at the results of the opposition raised to England in Canada, in 1837–8. I have beheld the American people give their dearest and most valued rights into the keeping of the worst enemies of free institutions; I have seen monopoly and slavery triumph at their popular elections, and witnessed with pain ' the bitter fruits of that speculative spirit of enterprise to which,'

85

as President Van Buren says in his late excellent
Message, his 'countrymen are so liable, and upon
which the lessons of experience are so unavailing;'
and although the leaders of parties here may not say
so to their followers, yet the conviction grows daily
stronger in my mind that your brethren of this Union
are rapidly hastening towards a state of society, in
which President, Senate, and House of Representatives will fulfil the duties of King, Lords, and Commons, and the power of the community pass from the
Democracy of numbers into the hands of an Aristocracy, not of noble ancestry and ancient lineage, but of
monied monopolists, land-jobbers, and heartless politicians."

Soon after, the publication of the *Gazette* was closed,
the press and types were sold; and the family sub-
sisted on the proceeds, so long as they lasted. The
injury inflicted on the publication by the absence of
Mr. Mackenzie's personal superintendence, while in
prison, was never overcome; and the paper ceased to
be profitable before it ceased to exist.

The Canadian authorities resorted to every possible
expedient to get Mr. Mackenzie in their power, for
the purpose of strangling him. Rewards for his apprehension were held out as a premium to kidnappers; and his personal and political enemies clubbed
their dollars into blood money to make the temptation strong enough for some vile man-catcher to undertake the detestable speculation. In the winter of
1838, a Canadian judge wrote to an American judge,
suggesting the " exchange" of Mackenzie for a num-

ber of Prescott and Windsor prisoners.* The offer
embraced a hundred for one; and while the men to be
given up were guilty of invading Canada, Mr. Mackenzie, for whom it was proposed to exchange them,
had had no connection whatever with the expeditions.
Coming from an old political enemy like Judge Jones,
the offer had all the appearance of a revengeful thirst
for the blood of a fallen foe. And it surely did not
become Judge Jones to drag the ermine through the dirty
waters of insurrectionary strife. The attempt to obtain possession of a political refugee, who had sought
an asylum in another country, will forever remain a
blot upon his memory.

There can be no question that the suggestion made
by Judge Jones had the authority of the Colonial Executive; because a similar proposition was afterwards
put forth, in the name of the Executive Council. In
a report to Sir George Arthur, dated Feb. 4, 1839,
the Executive Council, presided over by Mr. Sullivan,
said: "Were it positively understood that such men
as Johnson, Birge, Bierce [Bierce], and Mackenzie
would be seized and delivered up, as having violated
the refuge afforded them, there would be no objection
to the release of hundreds of obscure criminals; because we might be assured that if certain punishment
awaited their leaders, notwithstanding their escape
across the border, [at least half of them were Americans and never lived in Canada,] the whole conspiracy
would fall to the ground for want of leaders." So far
as it relates to Mr. Mackenzie, this is precisely the
same as if Louis Napoleon were to expect England to

* Judge Jones to Judge Fine, of Ogdensburg.

give up French political refugees, who had escaped to that country. With American citizens who had invaded Canada, in time of peace, the case was different; the duty of the Federal Government was not to hand over these leaders, but to enforce against them its own laws for the maintenance of neutrality. If this had been done, the prosecution of Mr. Mackenzie would have ceased to wear a partial aspect.

Sir George Arthur approved of the project for exchanging prisoners for refugees; and the authorities of the State of New York were sounded on the subject. Mr. W. H. Griffin, Post-office Surveyor, went upon this odious mission. Not finding Mr. Seward at Albany, he conversed with Mr. J. A. Spensor on the subject. Mr. Spensor told him that the principal obstacle to the proposed arrangement was the public indignation its execution would excite; and he suggested that, under the circumstances, it would be better to kidnap the refugees, adding an assurance that, if this were done, the State authorities—Mr. Seward and the rest—would not be disposed to regard the act as a breach of amity.*

Why should such a hint not be improved? Had Canada no bloodhounds ready to snatch Sir George Arthur's four thousand dollars by kidnapping Mackenzie? It seemed not; for a private subscription of two thousand dollars more, set on foot by one of the exile's old political opponents, had to be added. And now surely here is temptation enough in the shape of blood money, to turn mercenary men into kidnappers!

* Letter from Mr. Griffin to the Hon. R. N. Tucker, dated Gananoqué, U. C., May 14, 1839.

On the 14th November, 1840, Mr. Mackenzie received from several respectable citizens of Rochester warning that an attempt would be made in a day or two to seize him, drag him on board the steamer Gore, and carry him off to Canada.*   Among them was Mr. Talman, who called three times at Mr. Mackenzie's house that day without finding him.   The last time, he left word that Mr. Mackenzie should, by no means, leave his house after dark that night.   But this warn-ing was not heeded: not arriving till after night, he went to see Mr. Talman.   The substance of the infor-mation, received from various sources, was the same. A guard was placed upon his house.

The matter being brought before the attention of the authorities, was made a subject of judicial investigation before Mr. Wheeler, on the 20th of Nov., 1840.   Seve-ral witnesses were examined; the principal of whom, Mr. Wells, stated the result of a conversation he had had with Mr. James Cameron, son-in-law of the late Mr. Drean, of Toronto, and brother-in-law of Mayor Powell, of that place, and sometime clerk in the Bank of British America, at the Rochester House seven years before.   Mr. Cameron commenced the conversation

---

* Some warned him verbally, and one, Mr. Wells, one of the publishers of the Rochester *Daily Whig*, in writing. He said: "Wm. L. Mackenzie— Sir:—I take the liberty of informing you that a plan is in contemplation to carry you to Toronto. It is this: The steamboat Gore [Capt. Thomas Dick] will be in this port in a day or two. She is to be at the wharf at the mouth of the river, with steam up, &c., to surprise and muffle your face, and put you in a carriage which will be in waiting, and take you to the boat. A British officer is in this place, and has disclosed the circumstances to me. Although we have had some personal difference, I cannot consent to have you kidnapped. Be on your guard.

"Nov. 14, 1840.   W. A. Wells "

by introducing the subject of the Canadian troubles, and asked Mr. Wells whether he had not had some difficulty with Mr. Mackenzie that had created an unfriendly feeling between them. Receiving a reply in the affirmative, Cameron, thinking he might safely trust a person who was on such terms with the object of the kidnappers' desire, then unfolded to him the scheme. Mr. Mackenzie was to be decoyed to the lower part of the city, by an invitation from one whom he regarded as a friend; he was then to be seized by two powerful men, a handkerchief tied round his mouth, and dragged into a carriage, with a pistol pointing at his face under a threat that his brains would be blown out if he made a noise. In this state he was to be taken on board the steamer Gore, at Frankfort—the mouth of the Genesee River—which was to be ready waiting with steam up. In her next trip she was to bring over another person, a Scottish military officer, who was to assist in the kidnapping. All this was to be done with the consent of the persons in charge of the steamer. Cameron mentioned that, in addition to the reward offered by the Canadian government for the apprehension of Mackenzie, he expected to get a Colonial appointment. Cameron's counsel did not cross-examine the witnesses, but took a technical exception to the form of the warrant. The evidence was deemed sufficient to justify the magistrate in binding Cameron over to answer the charge, but the case was quashed when it came before the grand jury.

Cameron afterwards pretended that he had hoaxed Wells in the conversation at the Rochester House;

but there is little reason to accept so shallow a pretence. According to his account he was somewhat "oblivious" of what had occurred at the interview with Wells; and men in their cups are very much in the habit of blurting out truth which at other times they would conceal. The idea of kidnapping Mackenzie was not a new one. A long train of preliminaries pointed to precisely such an enterprise as that in which Cameron told Wells he was engaged. Besides, the steamer left the upper wharf that night at an unusual hour, and without ringing her bell. At the mouth of the river, seven miles below the head of the Genesee navigation, where he was to have been put on board, she waited till near midnight. These are circumstances of suspicion, too strong to be neutralized by the action of the grand jury on the case.

In the winter of 1840-1, Mr. Mackenzie commenced that systematic arrangement of his papers to which he always afterwards adhered, and which has been sufficiently described in the introduction to this work.

About a month before the last number of his *Gazette* was issued, Mr. Mackenzie memorialized the Judges of the Court of Common Pleas, in the county of Monroe, to be allowed to be admitted to practice at the bar. Fifteen barristers, in a separate memorial, backed up the application. The applicant was willing to submit to the usual examination prescribed for barristers, but a few days after the memorial had been taken into consideration, Judge Dayton wrote to inform him that it had been unanimously refused by the court. The refusal appears to have proceeded upon the ground of his being an alien. But this did not prevent him, a few months later, about March, 1841, from notifying the public that William Lyon Mackenzie's Law Office was to be found in an upper room in St. Paul Street. It was a last effort of despair, and came to nothing.

The clouds of adversity gathered thick and gloomily over the exile's head. Bereft of his property by an insurrection, in which he had borne a leading part; he had known what it was to commence the world anew among strangers. A long imprisonment had ruined the precarious profession of a journalist, who appealed to the public sympathies only upon a single subject. He found himself without occupation, and with only very limited and uncertain means of subsistence. At this period, it would frequently happen that, for twenty-four hours on a stretch, the family had not a morsel of food, and neither light nor fire. Yet no father could be more assiduous in his endeavors to provide for his family. After a day and night's enforced fast-ing, he would go shivering forth in the morning's cold, hoping to collect a small sum due to him, or, failing in that, to borrow from a friend the means to purchase bread for his famishing children. Many a time, when all else failed, did his ever faithful friend, John Mont-gomery, divide with him his last sixpence, or his last meal. The younger children never ceased to cry for food, while those more advanced in years suffered in silence. What could the father do? Whither turn for succor? He tried another newspaper—*The Volun-teer*—of which the first copy appeared on the 17th of April, 1841, and the last on the 10th of May, 1842. During that period only nineteen numbers were issued.

They were printed when the means to print them could be obtained. This attempt to revive a general interest in the Canada question failed, and without that interest a paper devoted to it could not live.

In the summer of 1841, the massive gold medal, the gift of the electors of York, was melted into an ingot. In May, 1838, a loan of one hundred and ten dollars had been obtained upon it, in New York, and on the 23d of June, 1841, Mr. Mackenzie was notified that the ingot had realized $146 13, after deducting the expense of melting and assaying. The amount of the loan with interest was $129 60, and the balance coming to him was $16 53. The intelligence of the melting of the medal reached him on the very day when silver spoons had been given to the landlord to make up the amount of a quarter's house rent! The day to redeem never came. During the winter of 1841–2, the exile and his family drank the cup of poverty to the dregs. One night, when the younger children were crying for food, he went to the cupboard to see whether there was nothing to be found there. All he got was a book, of which, by the light of the feeble embers that formed the only light and the only fire, he discovered that the title was "The Dark Ages," at which he could not refrain from indulging in a hearty laugh, after which the family went supperless and breakfastless to bed.

During this winter Mr. Mackenzie expressed, in decided terms, in private letters to friends, his strong disapproval of all projected movements against Canada. Writing to his eldest son, on Christmas day, he said: "We have stories here about boats to be captured—

eagles—Gen. —— hordes from Kentucky—balls cast-
ing at Akron, and what not. I'm glad I'm free of it
all ; it will end in picking some folks' pockets—it may
end Windsor or Prescott fashion, but can do no great
good." It appears from the letters of other refugees to
him that he had been long inactive.' In August, 1840,
one of them reproached him : " You will not propose
any plan yourself, nor adopt those that are formed"
by others.

In the beginning of the year 1842, Lord Ashburton's intended visit to the United States was a subject
of conversation. On its success depended the settlement of some very delicate questions. From the
North-east boundary difficulty and the destruction of
the Caroline, many had anticipated—some hoped,
some feared—war. The chances of an international
quarrel were likely soon to pass away. While they
lasted, John Sherdan Hogan and Dr. A. K. McKenzie
entered into a conspiracy to improve them. Hogan
was to be arrested as a party to the Caroline outrage;
and, after his committal, he was to give a history of
the whole affair, in an address to the public, admit
himself to have been a participator, and throw himself on the protection of the British Government.
This scheme was developed in a letter written by Dr.
Mackenzie to Wm. Lyon Mackenzie, and dated Lockport, February 15, 1842. It was carried by Hogan
himself to Rochester. W. L. Mackenzie replied that
he would be no party to the scheme; that an attempt
to execute it would be dangerous, as Hogan would
probably be maltreated by the mob. But Hogan appears to have got alarmed at a scheme which was not

without danger to him. He wrote to Dr. Mackenzie that he was going to get married in the following June; and that if it were supposed that he had anything to do with the Caroline affair, his prospects would be entirely ruined. He therefore appealed to Dr. McKenzie, as a proof of his friendship, to send him a pair of good pistols, which he promised to return when he got to Canada. He was arrested, in spite of this protest; but he was discharged after the case had undergone a judicial investigation.

Mr. Mackenzie's pecuniary circumstances experienced no improvement; and to make things worse, his house took fire in March, and a portion of his furniture was burnt. The family suffered much from sickness, the result of pinching want. "The more I see of this country," he wrote privately to his son, under date March 15, 1842, "the more do I regret the attempt at revolution at Toronto and St. Charles."

And now, despairing of any measure of success in Rochester, where he had spent three and a half weary years, the repentant outlaw turned his regards once more towards New York. On the 10th June, 1842, he left with his family for the latter city in the canal line boat Henry Allan, and with two dollars and fifty cents in his pocket. For the thirty-nine dollars passage money he obtained credit from Mr. John Allan, from whom he received the kindest treatment; and the night before starting he obtained a loan of twelve dollars from Mr. Henry Allan. Without this, though he had borrowed ten dollars from Mr. John Fisk, he would have been unable to move. "I feel," he wrote to his son, "it very hard to be thus forced from place to place, at my time of life; but poverty and age are a conjunction in my lot, and it's no use to fret." He states very plainly the cause of his removal: "After an utterly ineffectual attempt to live here with my family," he says, "I'm starved out." In the same letter he denounces, in strong terms, the movement on the frontier for a new raid upon Canada. "Some new scheme of plundering the gulls in the wind!" he says. "An attack upon (!!!), and much more, never to be done, by way of raising the wind. I presume —— could give you the history of it if he chose. He has been at Lewiston, but I have not heard from him. Of course it is base humbug; but —— and all such have ever found gulls. It may injure the Van Dieman's Land prisoners."

After his arrival at New York, the unfortunate refugee spent most of his time in collecting some of his old debts and devising ways and means to live, till an influential political friend—Mr. Ewbank, I believe— obtained for him the situation of Actuary of the New York Mechanics' Institute. He refused situations in two or three newspaper offices, because he would not occupy a subordinate position on the press; and this disposition to be every thing or nothing was no bad illustration of his character. In his new office, Professor Gale, of Columbia College, had been his predecessor. He could have gone into business; but declined to do so, because the chances of success were not promising. "I could have got credit," he wrote to his son James; "but a store here, commenced in times like these, on other men's means, with high house and store rents and great scarcity of money among the people, would have proved a source of embarrassment." He was pleased with his new office. "The prospect brightens," he said, "and I may enjoy a little ease in my old days;" a hope which was never realized. His emoluments were chiefly derived from fees; and these were paid with so little punctuality or honesty, that his new employment proved but a slight mitigation of his distress. Among the fragmentary "Reminiscences" he has left, I find the following note, under date September 8th, 1842. "My daughter Janet's birthday; aged thirteen. When I came home in the evening, we had no bread—took a cup of tea without it; and Helen, to comfort us, said it was no better on the evening of my own birthday, the 12th of March, 1842." At the close of the year, however, he considered himself "very comfortably settled." "I was much behind, when I got into the office," he wrote privately, December 24th, "but during the year for which I am engaged, I have no doubt that I shall place myself and family once more in comfortable circumstances, the more gratifying as we have suffered much poverty and long continued privation." Such was his pride in his children, his ideas of duty, and his appreciation of the advantages of education, that he continued to keep them at good schools.

While in this situation, Mr. Mackenzie commenced a work entitled "*The Sons of the Emerald Isle, or Lives of One Thousand Remarkable Irishmen.*" On the 3d of February, 1844, he made application for a copyright, and entered into a written agreement with Burgess, Stringer & Co., of New York, to become the publishers. In July, 1843, he speaks of having nearly five hundred

of the biographical sketches ready; but only two numbers—there were to have been eight or ten in all,
averaging fifty pages each—were published. The subjects selected were Irish patriots or their descendants;
and the concise sketches contain a multitude of facts
and much matter of novel character. He had access
to sixteen thousand old American newspapers, extending over a period of forty years, from which he was
enabled to study the character of the men and the
measures of that time. He wrote to his son James,
after the first two numbers were out, that the work
would be immensely profitable; but want of means
seems to have prevented his continuing it.

At the end of the year, he gave up his office in the
Mechanics' Institute, retiring with an unanimous approval of his conduct. Owing to the remissness of the
members in paying, it turned out a poor place; and in
January, 1844, he declares that he has had as hard
times in New York as he ever had in Rochester. Having been introduced to the son of President Tyler, Mr.
Mackenzie was offered an Inspectorship of Customs,
at New York, at $1,100 a year; but when the nomina-
tion was sent to Washington, it was rejected by the
Secretary of the Treasury, because the nominee was a
British outlaw and had attacked the late President. He
had issued three numbers of a new paper, called the *New
York Examiner*, but he gave it up on his nomination to
this office. Tyler wrote him that he might have any
other office in his gift of equivalent value. Always
anxious to cloak his poverty under a genteel exterior, he
now, on the strength of the expectations thus raised,
moved to a large house in William Street, at a rent of

$450 a year. The same feeling urged him to the greatest sacrifices to keep his family genteely dressed; and if they starved they made a presentable appearance. How little did the outside world know of the sufferings of those tastefully dressed delicate children! How cheerless that large house, with its big rooms and marble mantles to the very casement! The son of the President visits the outlaw in mid-winter. As the only fire is in the cooking stove, he must be entertained in a fine large room, furnished in a style a little above the common shabby genteel. The room where the solitary fire is, serves for study, nursery, and kitchen; and there so much space in that large house! In that room, the author of *The Sons of the Emerald Isle* is sketching his portraits amid impediments of culinary occupations and crying babies. A servant is kept; and with singular devotion that true hearted Irish girl is content to starve with the rest. If any thing is going, she will get more than her share; but if there is nothing, she is never heard to complain. Late rising, as a means of extracting from the blankets —almost the solitary remnants of the Canada wreck— a warmth which want of fuel prevents being generated in a more regular way, is indulged in. When the promised situation comes, it is in the shape of a temporary clerkship, in the archives office of the New York Custom House, with a salary of only $700 a year. Out of this it was impossible to pay $450 rent; and in the beginning of July, it became necessary to move to Williamsburg, across the East River, to a house renting at $250 a year.

While engaged in the Custom House, it became Mr.

Mackenzie's duty to read a correspondence between Messrs. Jesse Hoyt and Benjamin Franklin Butler, of a very extraordinary character. Hoyt had been collector of customs at New York, and in that capacity had embezzled $250,000. Mr. Mackenzie, thinking that, in his haste to secure the money, Hoyt had forgotten that he had left certain private letters in the public archives, induced Mr. Henry Ogden to call upon him and ask him to take them away. Hoyt replied that he had already taken all he wanted. By permission of the collector Mr. Mackenzie copied the letters; and he had official authority to do what he pleased with them. He sent copies of several of these letters to President Polk; and the result of their perusal was to prevent the appointment of Coddington to the collectorship of New York. Mr. Mackenzie then, on the 1st of June, resigned his office; and in 1845 published *The Lives and Opinions of Benjamin Franklin Butler, United States District Attorney for the Southern District of New York, and Jesse Hoyt, Counsellor at Law, formerly Collector of Customs for the Port of New York;* a compact octavo volume of one hundred and fifty-two pages. In a very short time, fifty thousand copies were sold; when an injunction was obtained from the court of Chancery, to restrain the further publication of the work. The copies went up to double the previous price. The injunction was granted at the instance of Mr. Hoyt, and on a complaint that three of his letters were comprised in the publication. While the publishers made a very large profit on the book, the author, to avoid all ground for the imputation of improper motives in the publication, refused to take any remuneration for his labor ; though he lived on borrowed money for several months while he was preparing the work for press. He took out a copyright and assigned it without consideration to the publishers. Chancellor Walworth, on appeal, dissolved the injunction granted by the Vice Chancellor, after the lapse of two and a half years; deciding that the author had a right of property in the book, and that a Court of Equity had no power to restrain its publication. Unsuccessful attempts were, at different times, made before grand juries to indict the author for the use he made of these letters, but without avail. No new edition of the work was given to an eager public by the publishers, Cook and Co., of Boston.

In 1846, Mr. Mackenzie published *The Life and Times of Martin Van Buren*, a closely printed octavo volume of three hundred and eight pages. It is enriched by contributions from the bundle of letters left by Mr. Hoyt in the New York Custom House; though a large portion of the materials are drawn from other sources. Of this work he sold the copyright to Mr. Wm. Taylor of New York for $1,000, of which $400 was paid at the time of the agreement, and the remainder when the copy was completed. The sale of copyright is dated Nov. 25, 1845, and the book was to be completed by about the 15th of January following. This work dealt Van Buren his political death blow. He never rose again. While in prison, at Rochester, the author was severe in his comments on Van Buren's administration; but after his release all this was forgotten, and at different places he made speeches, in public, in favor of the administration. Before the next Presidential election, he wrote privately to a friend: " If Van Buren fails being elected, God help us exiles! we shall have a poor time of it." It was the discovery of the damning evidence, in the Hoyt and Butler papers, that caused Mr. Mackenzie to alter his opinion of Van Buren and to change his course towards him.

During eight years, Mr. Mackenzie's political opinions had undergone a great change. When the Oregon difficulty threatened war, " I fervently pray," he said in a private letter to his son, January 9, 1846, " that we may escape it, its burthens, its massacres, its enormities, and its devastations. That England and America should fight about a desert wilderness, or empty country beyond the Rocky Mountains, would only be wicked and barbarous. It is true the fight might be for Oregon as a pretext, but for the Canadas in reality; and even whether these—much as I once desired such a contest—would be improved by the grip of our harpy financiers I very much doubt; while the only refuge of the flying African from real oppression, in its most odious form, would be cut off."

In the course of this year, Mr. Mackenzie became connected with the *New York Tribune*, of whose editor, Mr. Greeley, he continued to the day of his death to entertain the highest opinion. On the 1st May, he arrived in Albany, for the purpose of attending the convention to revise the State Constitution. He daily wrote to *The Tribune* a long letter on the proceedings of the convention. Commencing in the early part of June, the convention continued its sittings till the 9th of

October. Many suggestions made by Mr. Mackenzie were adopted and embodied in the amended constitution. I recollect him telling me that it was at his suggestion that the judges were made elective; and when I asked him if he did not hope to be forgiven for introducing so dangerous a principle, he defended its working, and contended that popular election was preferable to the Canadian mode of appointing judges. This could not have been over three years before his death. Almost immediately after arriving in Albany seven of the family took the smallpox; but they all recovered.

"I am more of a misanthrope than I once was," he wrote privately, Oct. 12, 1846; "I never attend or speak at public meetings, and creep as it were through the afternoon of life." But in some respects times with him had improved. He had plenty of offers of literary employment. He had found a real friend in Greeley; and he received from Mr. George Bruce, the great type founder of New York, a very tempting offer. The large printing establishment of Percy & Reid, New York, had been sold at sheriff's sale; and Mr. Bruce had become the purchaser at $10,000. He offered it to Mr. Mackenzie on a credit of ten years, with means to carry on the business. The offer was gratefully received, but was rejected, contrary to the advice of his family and friends, principally because the business would have required a partner, and Mr. Mackenzie disliked partnerships. He remained in Albany one year; in the latter part of which he performed the duties of correspondent in the Legislative Assembly for *The Tribune.*

On the 5th March, he wrote to his son, from Albany, referring to past experience: "You never can, never will, know what I have borne and suffered, in many ways. Yet I am here, healthy and (somewhat) hopeful, though poor and within a week of fifty-two." And he adds: "After what I have seen here, I frankly confess to you that, had I passed nine years in the United States before, instead of after, the outbreak, I am very sure I would have been the last man in America to be engaged in it."

When he returned to New York, Mr. Mackenzie continued his connection with *The Tribune*, till Mr. McElrath, one of the partners in the establishment, expressed some dissatisfaction with his writings, and he left with the intention of never returning. This was early in April, 1848. He spent some time in the composition of a work on British America, which he never completed. He always continued on good terms with Mr. Greeley; and in October, 1848, he agreed to attend the next session of Congress as correspondent of *The Tribune*. But he did not leave New York till about the New Year.

By the end of the year 1843, an amnesty—not general but very comprehensive—had enabled numerous political exiles to return to Canada. But while Papineau, Rolph, Duncombe, and O'Callagan were pardoned, Mackenzie was still proscribed. Mr. Hume wrote him, stating that the exclusion arose from the belief entertained by the English Ministry that the origin of the rebellion was due to him. Three years after, Mr. Isaac Buchanan wrote to Sir Robert Peel and Lord Palmerston, begging that they would have

Mr. Mackenzie included in the amnesty. The reply was that, before this would be done, the Canadian Ministry must recommend the measure. But the latter were adverse to such a course, and to them alone his continued exclusion from Canada was owing. The remembrance of this circumstance probably infused some gall into his opposition to the men who composed this ministry after his return to Canada. In 1848, the Canadian Assembly unanimously addressed the Queen to grant a general amnesty of all political offences.

On the 17th of July of this year, his daughter Margaret died after a long and painful illness. Next year, February 3d, 1849, Mr. Mackenzie addressed a communication to Earl Grey, at the Colonial Office, containing some remarkable confessions; the good faith of which is sufficiently guaranteed by numerous statements in private letters, some examples of which have already been given. From this communication I quote the following remarkable extracts:

"A course of careful observation, during the last eleven years, has fully satisfied me, that, had the violent movements in which I and many others were engaged on both sides of the Niagara proved successful, that success would have deeply injured the people of Canada, whom I then believed I was serving at great risks; that it would have deprived millions, perhaps, of our own countrymen in Europe, of a home upon this continent, except upon conditions which, though many hundreds of thousands of immigrants have been constrained to accept them, are of an exceedingly onerous and degrading character. I have long been sensible of the errors committed during that period to which the intended amnesty applies. No punishment that power could inflict or nature sustain, would have equaled the regrets I have felt on account of much that I did, said, wrote, and published; but the past cannot be recalled." * * * "There is not a living man on this Continent who more sincerely desires that British Government in Canada may long continue, and give a home and a welcome to the old country-men than myself. Did I say so, or ask an amnesty, seven or eight years ago, till under the convictions of more recent experience? No; I studied earnestly the workings of the institutions before me, and the manners of the people, and looked at what had been done, until few men, even natives, had been better schooled. The result is—not a desire to attain power and influence here—but to help, if I can, and all I can, the country of my birth."

Pressed by Mr Hume and others, the Canadian Government, in 1849, originated a measure for a complete amnesty of all offences arising out of the events of 1837-8. Mackenzie had for some time been the last exile. It passed unanimously in both Houses, and in the name of the Queen, Lord Elgin, as Governor General, gave it the Royal assent, on the 1st of February, 1849. Immediately on receiving this intelligence, Mr. Mackenzie resolved to return to Canada permanently. But after so long an absence, he was in some doubts as to how he would be received there. In this state of uncertainty, he resolved to try the effect of a personal visit.

Before visiting Toronto, the scene of his former ex-

ertions and his future home, he called at Montreal,
then the seat of the Canadian Government. What
Sir George Arthur had ten years before denounced as ·
Mackenzie's scheme of Responsible Government was
now in full operation;* but it was administered by
persons, only one of whom, Mr. Hincks, paid the least
attention to the man who had been reviled as its
author so long as it was deemed odious or unpopular.
This member of the Government had paid him a
casual visit in the Rochester prison; while others
from Toronto, on whose friendship he had much
greater claims, had passed on without giving any
proof that they retained a consciousness of his existence. While in Montreal, he visited the Legislative
library, in his right as an ex-member, and on the
assurance of the deputy librarian as to the uniform
practice. He was consulting the catalogue when Col.
Prince, a member of the House, went up to him and
demanded to see the ticket of the member by whom
the ex-member was introduced; or, said he, with em-
phasis, " I will kick you down stairs if you don't leave
this moment." Mr. Mackenzie, thus assailed, left the
library. Col. Prince met him in the lobby and renewed his threats. The Post office messenger of the
House, named Webster, thought himself entitled to
imitate such distinguished ruffianism; for which he
was very severely reprimanded by M. Morin. Col.
Prince, who has the generous feelings which are often
allied to impulsiveness, soon expressed his regret for
this occurrence. In a letter to Dr. Barker, of Kingston, written only seven days after the occurrence, he

* Dispatch to the Marquis of Normanby, August 21st, 1839.

said: "I acted on the impulse of the moment; and I
tell you candidly that, had I known then what you and
Chisholm have since informed me of, he might have
enjoyed his studies in our library as long as he pleased,
without any interruption from me." Mr. Mackenzie
was afterwards introduced to the library by a volunteer
member, Hon. Sandfield Macdonald, with whom he
had no previous personal acquaintance. A story is
told that when Mr. Macdonald returned to Glengarry,
his Highland constituents complained of his suspicious
civilities to a pardoned rebel; and that Mr. Macdonald, who is entirely destitute of the objectionable
clannishness ascribed to some of his countrymen, replied: "Do you think I would see an Englishman
kick a Scotchman and not interfere?" This sufficed,
so the story goes, instantly to silence all complaint.
On his way westward, the returned exile was burnt in
effigy in Kingston.

His arrival in Toronto was the signal for a Tory
riot. On the evening of the 22d March, a mob collected in the streets, with flambeaux and effigies of
Attorney General Baldwin, Solicitor General Blake,
and Mackenzie. They marched defiantly past the
Police Office, burnt two of the effigies opposite the
residences of the Crown officers, and then proceeded
up Yonge Street, to the house of Mr. John McIntosh,
where Mr. Mackenzie was staying. Here, by the aid
of two or three blazing tar-barrels, the mob burnt the
remaining effigy and assailed the house, broke the
windows, and attempted to force their way through the
door. All the while, the Chief of Police and at least
one member of the City Council were quietly looking

on. Next day, the Mayor caused special constables to be sworn in with a view of preventing a repetition of these outrages; and an alderman, in his place in the Council, declared that he "would not hesitate an instant" to assassinate Mackenzie, were he not restrained by fear of the law! For many nights after the house was well guarded, and was not again attacked. *The Examiner* had condemned these outrages in fitting terms, and the premises of the proprietor were threatened with attack. A mob assembled in King Street for that purpose; but when it became known that there was a number of armed men in the building, they dispersed without attempting any violence. Two persons had been stationed on the ground floor with double-barrelled guns, and the first man who might have broken in would have been instantly shot.

On the 1st May, 1850, Mr. Mackenzie started with his family from New York for Toronto, where they arrived a few days after. So long as he remained in New York, his connection with *The Tribune* continued; and his regular salary gave him the means of supporting his family in comfort. Such was his confidence in his own popularity, that he resolved to stand for the first constituency that might become vacant. It happened to be Haldimand; for which county he was elected in April, 1851, his principal opponent being Mr. George Brown. This constituency he continued to represent till the summer of 1858, when he resigned his seat, partly, I believe, because he did not agree with his constituents on the merits of a particular railroad bill affecting their interests. While in the House, he never sought a leading position, and,

88

not allying himself closely with either party, he was free to criticize the doings of both. Considering all he had undergone, how many trials of temper he had had in twelve years of exile, it is surprising how free his speeches were of the gall which chronic opposition engenders. He would frequently draw upon his large fund of humor, and keep the house in roars of laughter by the hour. If any reference were made to the rebellion, he always treated the subject jocosely. "There's the Attorney General for Lower Canada," for instance, he would say; "when the British Government placed an estimate on our heads, they valued mine at four thousand dollars, and his at only two thousand." He generally voted in the minority, and sometimes, as in the case of the Municipal Loan Fund Bill, he stood alone. It is not long since, but a large majority of the people of Canada would now vote the same way.

Hope of brighter days always cheered him even in the darkest hour of adversity, and he was constantly trying to inspire others, with whom he was in intimate relations, with the same feeling. Here is an example, in a letter to his son James, October 3, 1850: "Cheer up—do not despond—there are moments of pain and anguish which time only can alleviate, and of these you are seemingly to have your share; but there are also green spots in the desert of life, and you and I may fall upon one or two of them yet: after the darkness comes light. The Bible tells us that they who have loved on earth shall meet in a land where pain and sorrow are no more: it is indeed a pleasing promise, a cheerful hope; and let us play our part here like men, fearless and faithful, trusting that 'in due time we shall reap if we faint not.'" Soon after this, political malice accused the man who thus wrote, in all the confidence of paternal affection, of Atheism or something of the kind. There never was a grosser libel. Two well-thumbed copies of the Bible, in which almost every passage bearing on liberty and oppression is underscored, show how carefully he read that book. There is scarcely a passage, such as the following, which is not marked round or underlined: "Behold, I cry out of wrong, but I am not heard: I cry aloud, but there is no judgment." He was very far from being contracted in his religious views; and, if he was not orthodox, he had the greatest respect for opinions sincerely held, no matter by what denomination, though he might not be able to share them.

Of a highly sensitive nature and somewhat secretive, he was never fully understood, perhaps, even by his most intimate friends. There was no sacrifice which he would not cheerfully make for his children; he could enter into all their childish feelings, and would at almost any time leave his studies to engage in their play; yet he was sometimes unapproachable. - The rude collision with the world, in which he received so many hard knocks, would temporally weaken the springs of his elastic temper, and till the fit was over the gloom that crowded upon his thoughts would cast its dark shade on all around. In his children he took the greatest pride; and the stern politician, who carried on so many relentless contests, wore the watch of his eldest daughter, around his neck, for twelve years

after her death, in almost superstitious veneration of
her who had passed away.

After his return to Canada, his stern independence
conciliated the respect of all parties. He was very far
from being rich; but he taught the world this moral,
that it is not necessary to be rich to be politically independent. Immediately after his return, Mr. Isaac
Buchanan, with that princely munificence for which he
is noted, offered to make him a gift of $1,000; but he
refused it, lest it should interfere with his independence of action. Twice he was offered office under
the government—once directly and once indirectly—
but he treated the offers as little short of insults; such
was his almost morbid jealousy of a covert attack on
his independence. The county of York paid him some
£300 due on account of previous Legislative services;
and the government paid for his services as Welland
Canal Director before the Union. In 1856, some
friends started a subscription for a " Mackenzie Homestead;" and after several years' exertions, some £1,250
was collected; £950 was invested in a house, in Toronto, and the rest was loaned by the committee to
himself. Owing to a difference of opinion between
himself and the committee, he inserted a notice in the
public journals, in 1859, refusing to allow any more
subscriptions—of which there were about $1,500 out-
standing—to be collected. From February 1853 to
the Autumn of 1860, he published a weekly paper,
Mackenzie's Message, but not with great regularity.

Pecuniary embarrassments threw a gloom over the
last days of Mr. Mackenzie's existence. His health
was failing; he was without income. He owed nearly

$3,000. Bills matured and he had not the means wherewith to pay. What could he do? He had tried his best—and failed. Hope, his constant companion in the darkest hours of his life, failed him at last. There remained nothing but for him to lay down and die! During his last illness, he would take no medicine, take no stimulant, obey no medical directions. As he sank gradually, intervals of unconsciousness would occur of sometimes over thirty hours.* On the 28th of August, 1861, his wearisome life came to a close, and the troubled spirit sank to rest. Four days after, a mournful *cortége*, extending half a mile in length, accompanied his mortal remains to the Toronto Necropolis.

> " Mute is the tongue that eloquently plead
>   Our country's right, our country's sacred cause,
> Whose burning words not seldom have availed
>   To gain for freemen, freemen's rights and laws.

> " Cold is the heart that never ceased to yearn
>   For Canada, her welfare and her weal,
> Consuming lavishly life's precious oil
>   In deep, unresting, and undying zeal.

> " And if the glowing zeal that fired his heart,
>   Crushed by injustice and oppression long,
> Burst into action, erring, rash, and wild,
>   Maddened by private and by public wrong—

* It is proper here to notice a gross fabrication which appeared in the Albany *Evening Journal*, stating that Mr. Mackenzie had written long letters to Mr. Weed, its editor, in depreciation of England, and taking a particular view of the war in the United States; and that he had continued to write up to within four days of his death. I deliberately charge Mr. Weed with inventing the whole story for some base purpose of his own. Medical testimony, as well as that of myself and every member of his family, can be adduced to show that Mr. Mackenzie was incapable of writing a single word, a full month before his death..

"Yet was the flashing of that rebel brand
  The herald of Canadian liberty;
A beacon light to guide our country's bark
  Safely into the harbor of the free.

"An alien and an outlaw from the land
  His darkest errors had conspired to bless,
Sinning—though sinned against—it was denied
  To give atonement, or to find redress.

"Blighted life's harvest years—their due reward
  Snatched from the ready pen and busy brain,
Exile, imprisonment, and penury,
  Stamped on his heart and brow deep lines of pain.

"Longing for, loving still, his chosen land,
  Finding no rest upon a foreign shore;
The ban removed, with gladly hastening feet,
  He trod the soil of Canada once more,—

"And stood within her legislative halls,
  Lifting his voice for truth and right again;
In his innate integrity of soul,
  Scorning the bribes of place and power and gain.

"But time and change had marked his exiled years,
  And suffering had quelled his spirit's fire;
Hopes, promises, and plans of better days
  Lay in the ashes of their funeral pyre.

"And so he sadly laid his armor down,
  Feeling, perchance, his course was almost run,
No worldly honors crowned his life of toil,
  No laurel, when the weary race was won.

"Peace to his burning, patriotic heart,
  Peace to his fearless and undaunted soul,
Peace to his spirit, tried and tempest-tossed—
  In some fair haven, some calm, quiet goal!

"Although among the great ones of the earth
  His humble name may never find a place,
Posterity, this rarest epitaph
  Upon the Patriot's tomb shall proudly place—

" ' Here lieth one who prized the public weal
    Far above earthly honors, wealth, or fame,
Whose life-long labors in his country's cause
    Were pure from sordid end or selfish aim.

" Oppressed, wronged, exiled, spurned from the land
    He would have given his life to bless and save,
His country, on whose shrine his all was laid,
    Bestowed upon the Patriot—a grave.' "*

    * Mrs. Somerville in Toronto *Globe.*

APPENDIX.

APPENDIX A.

ABBREVIATIONS—All the Countries named here are to be marked thus: If English authors, e; Scottish authors, s; Irish authors, i; French authors, f; German authors, g. The period when read is set down thus: 1806, 6; 1807, 7; 1808, 8; 1809, 9; 1810, 10; 1811, 11; 1812, 12; 1813, 13; 1814,14; 1815, 15; 1816, 16; 1817, 17; 1818, 18; 1819, 19. The size is noted as follows: Folio, (2); Quarto, 4to.; Octavo, 8vo.; Duodecimo, 12mo; Smaller sizes, p.; Pamphlets, pt.

DIVINITY, &c.

1. Brown's annotations on the Bible. s. 6 and 7. (2). (Also other of author's notes). 2. Fisher's explication of the Assembly's catechism, s. 6. 12mo. 3. My grandfather's copy of Oliphant's catechism. s. 6. p. 4. Biographia Scoticanicola. The Scotch worthies. s. 6. 7. 8. 8vo. 5. The cloud of witnesses. s. 6. 7. 12mo. 6. Dyer's sermons. p. 7. 7. Rowe's letters from the dead to the living. e. 8. 12mo. 8. Addison's evidences of the Christian religion. e. 15. 8vo. 9. John Newton's narrative. e. 5. pt. 10. Westminster confession of faith. e. s. 6 and 7. 8vo. 11. Dr. Blair's sermons; 5 vols. s. 12 and 13, 8vo. 16. Rutherford's letters. s. 7. 12mo. 17. Crookshank's history of the state and sufferings of the Church of Scotland. s. 8 and 10. 8vo. 19. The works of Thomas Boston of Ettrick, s., viz: The crook in the lot, Human nature in its fourfold state; Sermons, &c. s. 7. 8. 9. 8vo. 22. Ebenezer and Ralph Erskine's works, 3 vols., containing the Gospel Sonnets. 7. 8. 8vo.; Sermons, &c. 7. 8. 9. 10. 25. Mr. Barclay of Urie's defence of the Quakers, (addressed to Charles the Second). 26. The Rev. T. W. Willison's (of Dundee) works; containing his sermons, the catechism, the afflicted man's companion, &c. s. 6—8, (2). 27. Death of Abel, by Gessner. g. 8. 12mo. 28. Drellincourt on death. f. 11. 8vo. 29. Marshall on sanctification. e. 8. 9. 12mo. 30. MacEwen on the types. s. 14. 12mo. 31. A dictionary of the Bible. s. 8vo. 33. Select

remains of John Brown, minister of Haddington. s. read often. 12mo. 84. Beattie on the immutability of moral truth. s. 14. 12mo. 85. The Messiah, from the German of Klopstock, 2 vols. g. 15. 12mo. 37. Sturm's reflections; 2 vols. g. 15. 8vo. 39. Book of common prayer. e. 15. 40. Evidences of the Christian religion, by the Rev. Dr. Chalmers, of Glasgow. s. 16. 12mo. 41. Sermons, by Vicesimus Knox, D. D., i. 18. 8vo. Bunyan's pilgrim's progress. e. 7—17. 8vo. 43. Bunyan's holy war. e. 19. 44. Pike and Hayward's cases of conscience. 11. 8vo. 45. Secession act and testimony. s. 8. 46. Hervey's meditations. e. 10, 11. 8vo. 47. Hervey's Theron and Aspasia. 2 vols. e. s. 10. 12mo. 49. Doddridge's rise and progress of religion in the soul. e. 14. 12mo. 50. Baxter's saint's everlasting rest. e. 14. 8vo. 51. Guthrie's trial of a saving interest in Christ. s. 6. 12mo. 52. Reflections on incredulity, by Lord President Forbes, of Culloden. s. printed in 1752; read in December, 1819. 12mo. 53. Glass' testimony of the King of Martyrs. s. 1820. 53. Case of William Mills, executed at Edinburgh, in 1785. pt. pp. 80.

HISTORY AND BIOGRAPHY.

1. Rollin's ancient history. f. 7. 8. 12mo. 13. Raynal's history of the settlement and trade of the Europeans in the East and West Indies; 6 vols. f. 8. 12mo. 19. Raynal's account of the revolution in America. f. 8. pt. 20. New annual register from the commencement in 178- to ——; (Stockdale). 16 vols. e. 1—16. 8vo. 36. Banks' life of Oliver Cromwell. e. 7. 12mo. 37. Life of John Churchill, Duke of Marlboro. e. 8. 12mo. 48. Life of Stanislaus Leczinsky, King of Poland, father-in-law of Louis XV. 8. 12mo. 39. Morrison of Perth's edition of the British Plutarch; 8 vols. s. 8. 9. 12mo. 47. Buchanan's history of Scotland; 2 vols. s. 8. 8vo. 49. The history of England, by David Hume, with a continuation, by Dr. Smollett; 16 vols. s. 15. 12mo. 65. Life of Petrarch; 2 vols. Italian. 9. 12mo. 67. Memoirs of the President Von Kotzebue, by himself; 3 vols. g. 18. 12mo. 70. Rapin's history of England; 2 vols. f. 9. (2). 72. Plutarch's lives, containing Dryden's life of Plutarch, Theseus, Romulus, Lycurgus, Numa Pompilius, Solon, Themistocles, Cimon and Pericles, Alcibiades, Coriolanus, Timoleon, Pelopidas, Cato, Philipœmen, Pyrrhus, Caius Marius, Lysander, Sylla, Eumenes, Agesilaus, Pompey, Alexander, Phocion, Julius Cæsar, Agis, Claudius, Demosthenes, Cicero; 8 vols. 80. The works of William Robertson, D.D., principal of the University of Edinburgh, &c., &c.; the history of Scotland; 3 vols. 10. 12mo. 83. History of Charles V; 5 vols. s. 14. 12mo. 88. History of America; 2 vols. s. 15. 8vo 90. Memoirs of Maximilian de Bethune, Duke of Sully; 5 vols. f. 11, 15. 12mo. 95. Life of Charles XII., by Voltaire. f. 12. 96. History of Egypt; 2 vols. e. s. 12. 8vo. 98. History of England, by Oliver Goldsmith. i. 12. 12mo. 99. History of Rome, by Oliver Goldsmith, i. 12. 12mo. 100. History of Scotland, by Robert Heron; 6 vols. s. 13. 14. 8vo. 106. Ascanius, or the young adventurer. 12mo. 107. Dr. Douglass' history of the rebellion in 1745—6. s. 12. 18.

12mo. 108. Livy's Rome, by Alexander Gordon. s. 14. 12mo. 109. Stark's Scottish biography. s. 14. 12mo. 110. Works of Frederick the Great, King of Prussia; seven years' war; correspondence with Voltaire, D'Alembert, &c.; 12 vols. g. 14. 15. 8vo. 122. Dr. Simson's history of Scotland, abridged; 1 vol. s. 15. 12mo. 123. Robertson's life of Bonaparte; 1 vol. s. 15. 8vo. 124. Life of Sir John Moore, K. B., by W. V. Moore. s. 15. 8vo. 125. The works of Flavius Josephus; 6 vols. Jewish. 11. 12. 12mo. 131. Account of the plague and fire in London, 1665—6 e. 12. 8vo. 132. Davis' life of Chatterton. e. 14. 12mo. 133. Life of Gustavus Vasa. 7. 12mo. 134. History of the war, by Ed. Baines, Leeds.; 2 vols. e. 17. 4to. 136. History of the war, by Hewson Clarke, Esq.; 3 vols. e. 17. 4to. 139. Life of Madame De Maintenon; 2 vols. f. 18. 12mo. 141. Newgate calendar, by Baldwin and Knapp; 4 vols. e. 18. 8vo. 145. Life of John Buncle; 2 vols. e. 19. 8vo. 147. Life of Arthur, Duke of Wellington, by F. L. Clarke, Esq.; 2 vols. e. 19. 8vo. 149. Knox's history of the Reformation in Scotland; 2 vols. s. 15. 8vo. 151. Dr. M'Crie's life of John Knox; 2 vols. s. 16. 8vo. 153. Life of Henry Home, Lord Kames, of Berwickshire; 2 vols. s. 19. 4to. (read the first volume only.) 155. Anecdotes of the life of Richard Watson, Lord Bishop of Llandaff, written by himself; 2 vols. e. 19. 8vo. 157. Lives of the British admirals; I vol. e. 15. 12mo. 158. Anecdotes of the life of William Pitt, Earl of Chatham, (7th edition,) Longman & Co.; 3 vols. e. 19. 8vo. 161. Life of William Hutton, of Birmingham, by himself and Catharine Hutton; 1 vol. e. 19. 8vo. 162. Historical memoirs of my own time, by Sir N. W. Wraxwall, Baronet; 2 vols. e. 19. 8vo. 164. Life of Frederick Baron Trenck; 1 vol. Prussian. 9. 8vo. 165. History of Catharine II, Empress of Russia, by J. Castera; translated by H. Hunter, D.D.; 1 vol. f. 19. 8vo. 166. Life of Abraham Newland, Esq., Cashier of the Bank of England, (Crosby, 1808). e. 19. 8vo. 167. J. B. Warden's history of the United States of America; Edin. 1819. 3 vols. 19. 8vo. 168. William Warden's (of the Northumberland) letters from St. Helena about Napoleon Bonaparte. London, 1816. e. 19. 8vo.

VOYAGES AND TRAVELS.

1. Travels in Arabia and Egypt, by M. Niebuhr, of Denmark; 2 vols. 7. 12mo. 3. Voyages of Columbus, Drake, Dampier, La Perouse; Buccaneers of America; To the Pelew Islands, &c. &c.; 3 vols. e. 8. 9. 8vo. 6. Commodore Anson's voyage around the world; 1 vol. e. 9. 8vo. 7. Commodore Byron's narrative; 1 vol. e. 7. 12mo. 9. Cook's voyages around the world; 2 vols. e. 9. (2). 11. Barrow's travels in Southern Africa; 1 vol. e. 6. 20. 8vo. 12. Sonnini's travels in Egypt; 1 vol. f. 10. 8vo. 13. Bruce's travels in Abyssinia; 7 vols. s. 11. 15. 8vo. 20. Park's travels in Africa; 1 vol. s. 4—8. 20. 21. Vaillant's travels in Africa; 2 vols. f. 11. 12mo. 23. Macdonald's travels in Denmark, Norway, &c.; 2 vols. s. 15. 25. New and select voyages and

travels, published by Sir Richard Phillips, London; 3 vols. e. 16. 8vo. 28. Simpson's (of Edinburgh) visit to the field of Waterloo; 1 vol. s. 17. 12mo. 29. The travels of Cyrus, by Ramsay; 2 small volumes. s. 10. 31. Dr. Moore's travels in France and Italy; 3 vols. s. 6. 12mo. N.B. This was one of the first books I ever read, and I afterwards purchased it. 34. A tour through Sicily and Malta, by Mr. Brydone; 2 vols. s. 12. 12mo. 36. Sketches of America, by Henry Bradshaw Fearon, and remarks on Birbeck's notes, by the same; [Longman & Co., second edition, 1818.] e. 19. 8vo. 37. The stranger in France, by Sir John Carr. s. 16. 8vo. 38. Travels of Anacharsis the younger in Greece, during the middle of the fourth century, before the Christian era; from the French of Barthelemy; 3 vols. f. 14. 8vo. 41. Ashe's travels in North America; 1 vol. 16. 8vo. 42. Letters from a gentleman in the north of Scotland to his friend in London [new edition]; first edition printed in 1754; 2 vols. e. 19. 12mo. 44. Paris re-visited in 1815, by John Scott, editor of the Champion [third edition, 1816]; 1 vol. s. 19. 8vo. 45. Letters from Illinois, by Morris Birbeck; [second edition, printed in 1818.] e. 19. 8vo. 46. Notes on a journey in America from Virginia to Illinois, by Morris Birbeck; [third edition, Ridgway, 1818]. e. 19. 8vo. 47. Paul's letters to his kinsfolk, being a series of letters from the continent; [second edition, Constable & Co.] s. 17. 8vo. 48. Travels in Greece, Palestine, Egypt, and Barbary, in 1806 and 1807, by F. A. De Chateaubriand; (translated by Shobert), [second edition, printed in London, March, 1820; first edition, in 1812.] 2 vols. f. 8vo. 50. Maria Graham's letters on India with etchings. s. 14. 8vo. 51. Travels in some parts of North America, in 1804, 1805, 1806, by Robert Sutcliff, (a Quaker), an entertaining and respectable writer, pp. 309; [second edition, York, 1815]. e. 20. 12mo. 52. The emigrant's guide to the Western States of North America, with an entertaining journal of the voyage outward, by Mr. Amphlett; [1818, by Longman & Co.]; e. 20. 12mo.

GEOGRAPHY AND TOPOGRAPHY.

1. Cooke's Geography; 3 vols. e. 8. 9. 4to. 4. Bloomfield's Geography; 2 vols. e. 8. (read the first volume only). 4to. 6. Ingram's introduction to geography. s. 8, (at school). 12mo. 7. Playfair's geography; (read volume first). s. 2—9. 8. Description of Scotland; [1809]. s. 10. 11. 8vo. 9. Pinkerton's modern geography, (abridged); 1 vol. e. 9. 10. Guthrie's geographical grammar; 1 vol. s. 14. 8vo. 11. Sir John Sinclair's statistical account of Scotland; 21 vols. s. (read a part of this work in 1810 and 1811.) 8vo. 82. A picture of Verdun; 2 vols. 14. 12mo. 34. Britton's beauties of Wiltshire; 1 vol. e. 19. 8vo. 35. Brooke's Gazetteer; 2 vols. e. (from time to time.) s. 8vo. 37. History of Edinburgh, by Hugo Arnot, Esq., advocate; 1 vol. s. 4to. 38. New picture of London for 1803. e. 1 thick 18mo.

1. Gentle Shepherd, by Allan Ramsay. s. 6. 2. Douglas, a tragedy, by the Rev. John Home. s. 6. 3. Life of Sir William Wallace; Life of Robert Bruce, by J. Barbour, Aberdeen. s. 6. 12mo. 4. Caledonian, English, and Irish musical repositories. s. e. i. 12mo. 7. Oliver and Boyd's comic songs; 2 vols. s. 15. 12mo. 9. Warblers, Olios, and other song books, ad infinitum. 10. The works of Wm. Shakespeare; 12 vols. e. 8. 12mo. 22. Gray's Poems. s. 7. pt. 23. Morrison's poems. s. 10. 12mo. 24. The Grave, a poem, by Robert Blair. s. 10. pt. 25. The works of James Thomson, Roxburghshire, containing the Seasons, plays, miscellaneous poetry, &c. ; 3 vols. s. 8. 9. 12mo. 28. The poems of Ossian, translated by J. MacPherson, M.P.; 2 vols. s. 13. 12mo. 30. Beattie's Minstrel and other poems. s. 10. 12mo. 81. Pope's works, containing Iliad, Oddysey, Dunciad, Essay on man, correspondence, poems, &c.; 4 vols. e. 10. 12mo. 35. Dryden's Virgil. e. 13. 36. Paradise lost and regained, and other poems, by John Milton; 2 vols. e. 8. 9. 12mo. 38. Provoked husband, by Cibber and Vanbrugh. e. 8. pt. 39. The dramatic works of Sir George Etheridge. e. 10. 12mo. 40. West Indian, by Cumberland. e. 9. Butler's Hudibras. e. 12. 12mo. 42. Scotland's skaith, or the waes of war, or Will and Jean, by Hector MacNeill, Esq. ; 1 vol. s. 9. 8vo. 43. The works of Robert Burns, Ayrshire, with the life of the author and his miscellaneous correspondence, edited by Dr. Currie, of Liverpool; 4 vols. s. e. 9. 8vo. (Read the Montrose edition of Burns; 4 vols. 19. 12mo.) 47. Allan Ramsay's poems and Scotch proverbs; 1 vol. s. 13. 8vo. 48. Goldsmith's plays and poems; 1 vol. i. often. 12mo. 49. Moliere's plays; 8 vols. f. 14. 12mo. 57. Watt's psalms and hymns. e. 18. 12mo. 58. Poems by Robert Ferguson, Aberdeenshire; 1 vol. s. 15. 12mo. 59. Dr. Young's works, containing Night thoughts, plays, correspondence, &c. ; 3 vols. e. 15. 12mo. 62. Poems by John Duff, Dunkeld; 1 vol. s. 16. 12mo. 63. The Shipwreck and other poems, by Wm. Falconer. s. 14. 18mo. 65. Lord Rochester's poems; (fine but obscene) ; 2 vols. e. 17. 12mo. Though not poetry, I add here: 67. The Bishop Burnet's account of the death of Lord Rochester. (I don't believe the bishop.) s. 68. Minstrelsy of the Scottish border ; 3 vols. s. 15. 8vo. 71. Marmion, a tale of Flodden field ; 1 vol. s. 15. 8vo. 72. Lord of the isles, by Walter Scott, Esq.; 1 vol. s. 19. 8vo. 73. The dramatic works of Wm. Congreve. 74. Johnson's poems. e. 9. pt. 75. School for scandal, by R. B. Sheridan, M.P. i. 10. pt. 76. Miss Baillie's tragedy of The family legend. e. 10. 77. The Hermit of Warkworth. e. 1807-8. 78. Rokeby, a poem by Walter Scott; 1 vol. s. 19. 8vo. 79. Sir Robert Howard's play of "The committee." e. 18. 80. Leonidas, by Glover. e. 9. 12mo. 81. Lady of the lake, by Walter Scott. s. 19. 8vo. 81. Beaux' stratagem, Beggars' opera, Belle's stratagem, Bold stroke for a wife, Busybody, Cato, Conscious lovers, Comus, Country girl, Cymon, Double dealer, Double gallant, Earl of Essex. 83. Fair penitent,

Gamester, Geo. Barnwell, Good natured man, Guardian, High life below stairs, Isabella, Jane Shore, Love for love, Love in a village, Mahomet. 84. Maid of the mill, Mock doctor, Mourning bride, Oroonoko, Rivals, Provoked husband, Rule a wife and have a wife, She stoops to conquer, Siege of Damascus, Tancred and Sigismunda, Venice preserved, Yara. N. B. Read most of these plays previous to 1812. 84. Careless husband, Castle spectre. 1808. 85. Childe Harold's pilgrimage, cantos 1st and 2d, and other poems, by Lord Byron; 1 vol. e. 10th ed. 19. 8vo. 86. Gertrude of Wyoming and other poems, by Thomas Campbell, author of Pleasures of hope; 1 vol. s. 19. thin 4to.

BOOKS OF EDUCATION, &c.

1. Gray's arithmetic. s. 6. 12mo. 2. Murray's introduction to English grammar. s. 8. 12mo. 3. Johnson's dictionary in miniature. e. 9. 4. Children's friend, by Charles Berquin; 4 vols. f. 7. 8. 12mo. 8. Youth's magazine, (several vols.) 12mo. 9. Swift's advice to servants. i. 7. 8. pt. 10. A present for an apprentice. e. 7. pt. 11. Chesterfield's letters to his son; 3 vols. e. 15. 12mo. 14. Morrison's book-keeping; 1 vol. s. 8. 4to. 15. Hamilton's merchandize; 1 vol. s. 8. 8vo. 16. Hamilton's arithmetic. s. 8. 9. 12mo. 17. Melrose's arithmetic, by Ingram; 1 vol. s. 16. p. 18. Morrison's (of Perth) modern precepts; 2 vols. s. 12. 13. 8vo. 20. Dr. Gregory's legacy to his daughters. s. pt. 21. Telemachus, by Fenelon. i. 13. 12mo. 22. Watts on the improvement of the mind; 2 vols. e. 15. 12mo. 24. Watts' logic; 1 vol. e. 14. 12mo. 25. Bonnycastle's geometry. e. 17. 12mo. 26. Crocker's land surveying. e. 15. 12mo. 27. Fordyce's sermons to young men; 1 vol. s. 16. 82. Fordyce's sermons to young women; 1 vol. e. 16. 29. Hutton's mensuration. c. 15. 12mo. 30. Hutton's mathematics; 2 vols. e. 17. 8vo. 32. Emerson's calculation, libration, and computation, &c.; 1 vol. e. 18. 19. 8vo. 33. Young man's companion. e. 17. 8vo. 34. Young woman's best companion. e. 17. 8vo. 35. Joyce's arithmetic; 1 vol. e. 19. 36. Misses' magazine; 2 vols. e. 8. 9. 12mo. 38. A description of three hundred animals. s. 8. 12mo. 39. Hannah More on female education; 2 vols. e. 10. 12mo. 41. Lennie's child's ladder. s. 20. 18mo.

ARTS, SCIENCES, AGRICULTURE, AND NATURAL HISTORY.

1. Several volumes of the Farmer's magazine. s. 2. Several vols. of the Repertory of arts. e. 3. Several vols. of Nicholson's philosophical journal. e. 4. Jamison's arts and sciences; 3 vols. e. 12mo. 7. Buchan's domestic medicine. s. 9. 8vo. 10. Buffon's natural history, with notes by Smellie; 2 vols. f. 9. thick 8vo. 12. Hill's herbal; 1 vol. 11. 8vo. 13. Culpepper's English herbal; 1 vol. e. 11. 8vo. 14. Sir John Sinclair's agricultural report for Scotland. s. 16. 8vo. 15. Willich's lectures on diet and regimen. e. 12. 8vo. 16. Duncan's Edinburgh dispensatory. e. 1805 ed. 15. 8vo. 17. Hooper's medical

dictionary. e. 15. 8vo. 18. The Practice of physic, by Dr. Thomas, of Salis-
bury. e. 15. 8vo. 19. Clater's Every man his own farrier, and Every man his
own cattle doctor; 2 vols. e. 15. 8vo. 21. MacDonald's cookery. s. 16. 12mo.
22. Frazer's cookery. s. 16. 12mo. 23. Rogers' agricultural report for Forfarshire. s. 16. 8vo. 24. The villa garden directory, by Walter Nicoll, Edinburgh. s. 16. 25. Seven numbers of Dr. Reese's Gazette of health for 1818, 19,
&c. e. 19. 8vo. 26. Spectacle de la nature; 8 vols. f. 18. 12mo. (read the first
six volumes.) 34. Cullen's practice of physic; 3 vols. s. 15. 8vo. 37. Circle
of the mechanical arts, by a civil engineer. e. 19. 4to. 38. Parkinson's chemical pocket-book. (printed 1807.) e. 20. 12mo. 39. A system of chemistry,
by J. Murray, lecturer on chemistry, and on materia medica, and on phar-
macy, Edin., ed. 1807; 4 vols. s. 20. 8vo. (read the last three volumes only.)
43. The Chemical catechism, with notes, illustrations, and experiments, by
Samuel Parkes, London. e. 7th ed. 16. 20. pp. 562. 8vo. 44. Haigh's Dyer's
assistant, printed 1800, read 1820. e. new ed. 12mo. (very old and useless directions.) 45. Langley's Builder's jewel, sq. plates. ed. 1805. 13. 12mo. 46.
The second volume of Conversations on chemistry, plates, Longman & Co. 20.
12mo. 47. Dr. Willich's domestic encyclopedia, London, 1802; 4 vols. 8vo.
51. Mather's Farmers' assistant. Dundee, 1819. 20. 4to.

MISCELLANEOUS.

1. Dundee repository; 2 vols. s. 7. 8. 12mo. 3. Dundee magazine, 1799,
1800, &c.; 3 vols. s. 12mo. 6. Dundee magazine. s. 15. 8vo. 7. History
of the Devil. e. 9. 12mo. 8. Athenian oracle, by Dean Swift; 2 vols. i. 8.
12mo. 10. Hocus pocus or Legerdemain. s. 7. pt. 11. I am uncertain how
many: Volumes of the Edinburgh review. s. 8vo. 12. Volumes of the Analy-
tical review. e. 8vo. 13. Volumes of the Monthly review. e. 8vo. 14. Volumes of the Quarterly review. e. 8vo. 15. Volumes of the Edinburgh magazine. s. 8vo. 16. Volumes of the Town and Country magazine. e. 8vo. 17.
Volumes of the Scots' magazine. s. 8vo. 18. Volumes of the Ladies' magazine.
e. 12mo. 19. Volumes of the Gentleman's magazine. e. 8vo. 20. Volumes of
the Monthly magazine. e. 8vo. 21. Volumes of the London magazine. e. 8vo.
22. Volumes of the European magazine. e. 8vo. 23. Universal museum,
1764, &c.; 2 vols. e. 19. 8vo. 25. Literary journal; 2 vols. e. 18. 19. 4to. 27.
Tegg's magazine of shipwrecks; 2 vols. e. 17. 12mo. 29. Spectator, by Addison and Steele; 8 vols. e. i. 9. 10. 12mo. 37. Sterne's works, containing
Tristram Shandy, sermons, Sentimental journey, &c.; 8 vols. 7. (pocket size.)
45. Dr. Blair's lectures; 2 vols. s. 10. 11. 4to. 47. Abelard and Heloise. f.
10. 12mo. 48. The life and essays of Dr. Benjamin Franklin, (etats unis.);
2 vols. 9. 12mo. (read very often since.) 50. Trial of Lord Melville, 1806. s.
10. 8vo. 51. Wonderful magazine; 6 vols. e. 8. 10. 8vo. 57. Lady Mary
Wortley Montague's letters; 2 vols. e. 10. 12mo. 59. Goldsmith's essays. i.
12. 12mo. 60. Montesquieu's Spirit of laws; 2 vols. f. 14. 12mo. 62. Zim-

merman on solitude. (Swiss.) 14. 8vo. 63. Memoirs of the Prince of Wales; ·
3 vols. e. 14. 12mo. 66. The rising sun; 3 vols. e. 14. 12mo. 69. Bell
on the bankrupt laws; 2 vols. s. 16. 4to. 71. The Persian letters, by
Lord Littleton; 2 vols. e. 9. 12mo. 73. Lord Lauderdale's enquiry into the
nature and origin of public wealth. s. 15. 8vo. 74. Letters from the mountains, by Mrs. Grant; 4 vols. s. 17. 12mo. 77. Volney's Ruins of empires. f.
10. 14. 12mo. 78. Mirabeau's works, vol. 3d., being a defence of atheism. f.
18. 12mo. 79. Acts of parliament for the Kennett and Avon canal. e. 19.
(2). 80. Regulations of the quarter sessions of Wiltshire. e. 19. pt. 81. Ta-
rantula or Dance of fools; 2 vols. e. 19. 12mo. 83. Miss—led General. e. 10.
12mo. 84. Miseries of human life, by Tim Testy and Sam Sensitive; 2 vols.
e. 19. 12mo. (read only the first volume.) 86. Economy of human life. e. pt.
(often.) 87. Ovid's metamorphosis. 8. 12mo. 88. The Lounger. s. 89. The
Bee, edited by Dr. Anderson, in volumes. s. 7. 8. 9. 12mo. 90. Harvest home,
by Mr. Pratt, containing Gleanings, "Hail fellow! well met!" poems, Love's
trials, Fire and frost, Sympathy, &c.; 3 vols. e. 19. 8vo. 93. The French con-
vert. 8. 12mo. 94. Anecdotes of eminent persons; 2 vols. e. 19. 8vo. 95.
Mrs. Chapone's letters. e. 10. 12mo. 96. Gay's fables. e. 10. 12mo. 97.
Æsop's fables. (Greek.) 8. 12mo. 98 Junius's letters. e. s. i. 12. 12mo. 99.
"Jokeby," a burlesque on Rokeby. 16. 12mo. 100. Court of requests, Birmingham described, by Wm. Hutton, F.A.S.S.; 1 vol. e. 19. 8vo. 101. Lava-
ter's physiognomy. (Swiss.); 1 vol. read in 1811 or 1812. 12mo. 102.
Arliss's pocket magazine for 1818, volume 2nd. e. 19. 12mo. 103. The Guar-
dian; 2 vols. 14. 12mo. 105. Anecdotes of the manners and customs of London from the Roman invasion to 1700, by James Peller Malcolm, F.A.S.,
Longman & Co.; 3 vols. 2nd ed. 11. 8vo. (read first and second volumes in
Oct. 1819.) 107. Literary recreations, by Henry Card, A.M.; 1 vol. e. 19.
8vo. 108. Encyclopedia of wit. (Phillips.); 1 vol. e. 19. 18mo. 109. Forbes
(President) on incredulity, 1757. s. 19. 18mo. 110. Abbot's Dundee directory.
s. 20. 12mo. 111. Cheap magazine, Haddington, 1813; 2 vols. s. 13. 14. 12mo.
113. Vicesimus Knox's essays; 3 vols. 16. 20. 12mo. 116. Blank-book, or
Corruption unmasked. (supposed by Wooler.) London, 1820. e. 20. 8vo.

NOVELS.

N. B. Novels are almost all 12mos. 1. Gil Blas, by Le Sage, translated
by Dr. Smollet; 4 vols. s. f. 7. 12mo. 5. Devil on two sticks, or Asmodeus,
by Le Sage; 2 vols. f. 8. 12mo. 7. The Fool of Quality, or history of Henry,
Earl of Moreland, by Wm. Brookes; 5 vols. 8. 12. Anna St. Ives, by Mrs.
Bennet; 5 vols. e. 8. 17. The Beggar girl, by Mrs. Bennet; 4 vols. e. 17.
21. Henrietta, a novel. 7. 22. Gulliver's voyages, by Dean Swift. i. 7. 23.
Tale of a tub and Battle of the books, by Dean Swift. i. 7. 8. 24. Captain
Singleton. e. 8. 25. Robinson Crusoe, by Daniel DeFoe. e. 6. 26. Philip
Quarll, or the English Hermit. e. 7. 8. 27. Tom Jones, by Henry Fielding;

3 vols. e. 8. 30. Amelia, by Henry Fielding; 3 vols. e. 9. 33. Joseph Andrews, by Henry Fielding; 2 vols. e. 11. 35. Castle of Otranto, by Horace Walpole. e. 8. 36. Belisarius, by Marmontel. f. 7. 8. 37. Numa Pompilius, by Florian. f. 16. 38. Heron's translation of the Arabian nights' entertainments; 4 vols. s. 7. 8. 9. 42. Continuation of Heron's translation of the Arabian nights' entertainments; 4 vols. s. 9. 10. 46. St. Clair of the Isles, or the Outlaws of Barra, by Elizabeth Helme; 4 vols. e. 9. 50. Thaddeus of Warsaw, by Miss Jane Porter of Edinburgh; 4 vols. s. 9. 54. Don Sebastian, by Miss Porter, of Edinburgh; 5 vols. s. 15. 59. Hungarian Brothers, by Miss Porter, of Edinburgh; 3 vols. s. 16. 62. Recluse of Norway, by Miss Porter, of Edinburgh; 3 vols. s. 16. 65. Scottish Chiefs, by Miss Jane Porter, of Edinburgh; 5 vols; s. 17. 70. Pastor's fireside; by Miss Porter, of Edinburgh; 4 vols. s. 17. 74. Peregrine Pickle, by Tobias Smollet, LL.D.; 4 vols. s. 8. 19. 78. Roderick Random, by Tobias Smollet; LL.D.; 2 vols. s. 9. 80. Sir Launcelot Greaves, by Tobias Smollet, LL.D.; 1 vol. s. 19. 81. Count Fathom, by Tobias Smollet, LL.D.; 2 vols. s. 8. 83. Humphrey Clinker, by Tobias Smollet, LL.D.; 2 vols. s. 10. 85. The Sorrows of Werter. g. 10. 86. Tales of the Castle, by Madame de Genlis; 4 vols. f. 8. 90. Paul and Virginia. f. 8. 91. Indian cottage, by Mons. Bernardin St. Pierre. f. 8. 92. Woman, or Ida of Athens, by Miss Owenson, now Lady Morgan; 4 vols. i. 9. 96. Novice of St. Dominick, by Miss Owenson, now Lady Morgan; 4 vols. i. 100. The wild Irish girl, by Miss Owenson, now Lady Morgan; 3 vols. i. 103. Memoirs of an Irish officer and his family, by Mr. Edgeworth. i. 14. 106. Tales of fashionable life, by Miss Edgeworth; 4 vols. i. 10. 110. Popular tales, by Miss Edgeworth; 4 vols. i. 10. 114. Patronage, by Miss Edgeworth; 4 vols. i. 17. 19. 118. Harrington and Ormond, by Miss Edgeworth; 3 vols. i. 19. 121. Travels of St. Leon, by Wm. Godwin; 4 vols. e. 9. 125. Caleb Williams, by Wm. Godwin; 3 vols. e. 9. 128. Rasselas, by Dr. Johnson. e. 9. 129. Henry, by Cumberland; 4 vols. e. 9. 133. Clarissa Harlowe, by Samuel Richardson. e. 139. Pamela, by Samuel Richardson; 2 vols. e. 12. 17. 8vo. 141. Sir Charles Grandison, by Samuel Richardson; 8 vols. 11. 15. 149. Temper, by Mrs. Opie; 3 vols. e. 17. 152. Simple tales, by Mrs. Opie; 4 vols. e. 11. 156. Adeline Mowbray, by Mrs. Opie; 2 vols. e. 17. 158. Valentine's Eve, by Mrs. Opie; 3 vols. e. 17. 19. 161. The Scottish adventurers, by Hector M'Neil, Esq. s. 17. 163. India voyage, by Mrs. Lefanu; 2 vols. e. 12. 165. Strathallan, by Mrs. Lefanu; 4 vols. e. 17. 169. Vicar of Wakefield, by Oliver Goldsmith. i. 13. 18. 170. Almoran and Hamet, by Dr. Hawksworth. e. 12. 171. Man of feeling, by Henry Mackenzie, Esq., Edinburgh. s. 9. 10. 11. &c. Man of the world, by Henry Mackenzie, Esq., Edinburgh. s. 15. 173. Julia de Roubigne, by Henry Mackenzie, Esq., Edinburgh. s. 12. 174. Elizabeth, or the Exiles of Siberia, by Madame Cottin. f. 15. 175. Adventures of Captain Robert Boyle. 7. 176. A winter in Edinburgh, by Honoria Scott; 3 vols. s. 14.

179. Evelina, by Miss Burney; 2 vols. e. 10. 14. 18. 181. Cicely Fitzowen; 2 vols. e. 14. 183. Ferney Castle; 4 vols. e. 14. 187. Cicely and Raby; 4 vols. e. 14. 191. Bryan Perdue, by Thos. Holcroft; 3 vols. e. 14. 194. Emily Montague, by Mrs. Brookes; 4 vols. e. 14. 198. Profligate Prince. e. 14. 199. Celia suited, or the Rival heiresses; 2 vols. e. 14. 201. Cottagers of Glenburnie, by Elizabeth Hamilton. i. 7th ed. 14. 202. Queen Hoo Hall and ancient times, by Joseph Strutt; 4 vols. e. 14. 206. A Tale of the times, by Mrs. West; 3 vols. e. 15. 209. The Loyalists, by Mrs. West; 3 vols. e. 17. 212. Five volumes by J. Horsely Curties. e. 14. 217. The Swiss emigrants; 2 vols. e. 15. 219. Moral tales, by Mrs. Fleury. e. 15. 220. Offspring of Mortimer; 4 vols. e. 15. 224. Fashionable infidelity; 3 vols. e. 15. 227. School for widows, by Clara Reeve; 3 vols. e. 15. 230. The young philosopher, by Charlotte Smith; 4 vols. e. 15. 234. Mysteries of Udolpho, by Anne Radcliffe; 4 vols. s. 15. 238. Castles of Athlin and Dunbayne, by Anne Radcliffe. s. 15. 239. The mysterious freebooter; 3 vols. 16. 242. Tales of the Genii; 2 vols. 8. 244. Discipline; 2 vols. s. 16. 246. Self-control; 2 vols. s. 16. 248. Smollet's translation of Don Quixote, by M. Cervantes, (Spain); 4 vols. s. 16. 252. Farmer of Inglewood forest, by Elizabeth Helme; 4 vols. e. 16. 256. The Wanderers, by Miss Burney; 5 vols. e. 15. 261. Cælebs in search of a mistress; 3 vols. e. 18. 264. Cælebs in search of a wife; 2 vols. e. 16. 266. Cælebs married; 1 vol. e. 17. 8vo. 267. The white cottage. (Blackwood.) s. 17. 268. The Widow's lodgings; 2 vols. s. 17. 270. Clan Albin; 4 vols. s. 17. 274. Marian, (Manners & Miller.); 3 vols. s. 17. 277. The Saxon and the Gael; 3 vols. s. 17. 280. Guelette's Tartarian tales; 2 vols. f. 19. 282. Orphan of Tintern Abbey; 4 vols. e. 18. 286. Good men of modern date, by S. Green; 3 vols. e. 18. 289. Waverly, by Walter Scott, Esq., Edinburgh; 3 vols. s. 16. 12mo. 292. Antiquary, by Walter Scott, Esq., Edinburgh; 3 vols. s. 17. 295. Guy Mannering, by Walter Scott, Esq., Edinburgh; 3 vols. s. 17. 298. Rob Roy, by Walter Scott, Esq., Edinburgh; 3 vols. s. 19. 301. Tales of my landlord, containing Black Dwarf, and Old Mortality, by Walter Scott, Esq., Edinburgh; 4 vols. s. 1st. ser. 17. 305. Tales of my landlord, or the Heart of Mid Lothian, by Walter Scott, Esq., Edinburgh; 4 vols. s. 14. 309. Telltale Sophas; 3 vols. e. 19, 312. Miss Greville; 3 vols. e. 19. 315. Chrysal, or the adventures of Alguinea; 4 vols. e. 10. 12. 319. Antar, by Terrich Hamilton, Esq.; 1 vol. 19. 320. A Sicilian romance, by Anna Radcliffe; 2 vols. e. (printed 1792.) 19. 12mo. 322. Cælebs deceived; 2 vols. e. 19. 12mo. 324. Tales of real life, by Mrs. Opie; 3 vols. e. 19. 12mo. 327. Father and daughter, by Mrs. Opie. e. 19. 12mo. 328. Jeannette, by the author of Melbourne, &c.; 4 vols. (printed 1800.) 19. 332. Tales of my landlord, containing Bride of Lammermoor, a Legend of Montrose, &c., by Walter Scott; 4 vols. s. 3d ser. 19. 12mo. 336. "I says, says I," written by the author of "Thinks I to myself," a clergyman of Litchfield and nephew of the Bishop; 2 vols. e. 19. 338. Donald; 3 vols. e. 15. 12mo. 341. De Valcourt; 2 vols.

e. 14. 12mo.   343. Faro table, or Gambling mothers; 2 vols. e. 16. 12mo.
345. Ned Evans; 4 vols. e. 13. 14. 12mo.   349. Women, or Pour et Contre,
by the Rev. R. C. Maturin, Dublin; 3 vols. 20. 12mo. (Highly praised by the
Edinburgh review.)   352. Campbell, or the Scots probationer, a novel, by a
native of Forfarshire.   York, 1820; 2 vols. 20.

APPENDIX B.

WHEN charged with publishing libels on the House, and a motion
had been made to expel the author and publisher, Mr. Mackenzie
made a long defence, of which the following are the material por-
tions :—

"The articles complained of," he said, "contain opinions unfavorable to the political character of members who compose the
majority of this House, also opinions unfavorable to those persons
who compose the Executive Council of the Colony. The former
are changed with sycophancy, the latter with being as mean and
mercenary as any other Colonial administration. It is alleged
that to propagate such opinions is criminal and deserves punishment. Undoubtedly, if there is a rule or law, it is wrong to
transgress it. But I know no law that is transgressed by propa-
gating these opinions. Let it even be supposed, for the sake of
argument, that the opinions complained of are false, though I
firmly believe that they are perfectly true. If all false quota-
tions and false opinions are improper, then all discussion either in
this House or through the press must be also improper, for one
set of opinions must be wrong. And if none but true opinions
can be given or quoted by either party, then there can be no
argument. The newspaper press of this Colony takes different
sides on political questions. Four-fifths of the twenty-five journals published in this Colony are in raptures with the Lieutenant
Governor, the Councils, and House of Assembly; they continually laud and extol them to the skies for the wonderful benefits
they are conferring, and (as they say) about to confer upon the

Province. The remaining journals, comparatively few in number, but of very extensive circulation, disapprove generally of
the manner in which public affairs are conducted. Shall they not
possess the power to blame, if they think fit, that which the
others praise? May not they who find fault be in the right, and
the others who praise in the wrong? How are the people to
know when to approve or to disapprove of the conduct of their
rulers, if the freedom of expressing all opinions concerning public men be checked? In English Law, it is said that though discussion should be free it should be 'decent,' and that all inde-
cency should be punished as libelous. The law of libel leaves
the terms 'indecent discussion' undefined, and in old English
practice, as Bentham justly remarks, what is 'decent' and 'what
the judge likes' have been pretty generally synonymous. Inde-
cency of discussion cannot mean the delivery either of true or
false opinions, because discussion implies both; there is presumed
to be two parties, one who denies, and another who affirms; as
with us, where twenty journals are in favor of the majority in
this House and only five generally opposed to them. Would you
wish all check from the press put a stop to? Assuredly there is
no medium between allowing all opinions to be published, and of
prohibiting all. Where would you draw the line? Those among
us who may wish to conceal the abuses of our defective government will denounce the paragraphs complained of as libelous,
because it is a point of great importance with them to keep the people in ignorance, that they may neither know nor think they have
any just cause of complaint, but allow the few to riot undisturbed
in the pleasures of misrule at their expense. They say, West India
negro law is admirable. The Solicitor and Attorney General
have already gratuitously denounced the paragraphs before the
House, as tending to bring the government into contempt, and
impede its operation. If the government is acting wrongly, it
ought to be checked. Censure of a government causes inquiry,
and produces discontent among the people, and this discontent is
the only means known to me of removing the defects of a vicious

government, and inducing the rulers to remedy abuses. Thus the press, by its power of censure, is the best safeguard of the interests of mankind; and unless the practical freedom of the press were guaranteed by the spirit and determination of the people of Upper Canada, it is doubtful to me whether this House itself, as an elective body, would be an advantage to the community. I rather think it would not. It is by no means an improbability that the electors of this House should sometimes make a bad choice. That I think they have done so now is evident from my votes upon most questions. It is by the liberty of the press, and the freedom of expressing opinions, that a remedy can be had for an unfortunate choice; the more the country know of your acts, the more severely editors on whom they depend animadvert on your public conduct, the more will that conduct become a matter of inquiry and discussion, and the country will look into your actions and weigh your character thereby. If the people support a press and expect independent opinions from the editor, would you have that editor deceive them by praising the most notorious selfishness and sycophancy, and dressing these vices in the garb of virtue?

"If one man in a legislative assembly saw that he might promote misrule for his own advantage, so would another; so would they all; and thus bad government be reared and upheld. Unless there be a check in the people upon governors and legislators, founded on a knowledge of their character, governments will inevitably become vicious. If the legislature shall (as these proceedings indicate in my case) assume the power of judging censures on their own public conduct, and also assume the power to punish, they will be striking a blow at the interests of the people and the wholesome liberty of the press. Where bad judges, hypocritical governors, wicked magistrates, sycophantic representatives, can, by the doctrine of contempts, exercise at will a censorship over the press, and punish the journalist who strives to promote the public interest by a fearless discharge of an unpleasant duty, misrule and injustice will be the inevitable consequence. It is

our duty to watch the judges; but were they to assume the power
of punishing editors summarily for animadversions on their conduct on the bench, how would the people know what that conduct had been, or learn whether we did or did not do our duty in
striving to secure for them a perfect judicature? There is assuredly no security for good government, unless both favorable
and unfavorable opinions of public men are freely allowed to be
circulated. To have the greater benefit in the one case, you must
submit to the lesser evil in the other. But it will perhaps be said
that the language of these paragraphs is passionate, and that to ·
censure you in passionate language is libelous. Who shall define what is and what is not violent and passionate language? Is
not strong and powerful emotion excited in one man's mind by
expressions which in another man produces no such effect? Will
you affirm that opinions ought to be put down if conveyed in
strong language, or what you may be pleased to consider strong
terms? This doctrine would leave to the judges the power of in-
terpreting the law favorably or unfavorably in all cases. Libel
might thus mean one thing in York and another thing in Sandwich. The freedom of the press has been for many years practically recognized by all factions, sects, and parties in these Colonies; and each, in its turn, has had resort to that powerful lever
in attempting to direct public opinion. Opinions both favorable
and unfavorable, both true and false, have been safely promulgated, and truth and error advocated by opposite sides, of which
I will now refer to some examples. It cannot even be alleged by
my judges, the public agents for the Gore *Mercury*, (Messrs.
Mount, Burwell, Shade, Ingersoll, and Robinson,) owned by the
learned member opposite (Mr. McNab), that that newspaper has
changed and become more violent than at the onset. Mr. McNab
told us in his first number that 'Believing decency and good
manners to compose some part of virtue, we shall endeavor to
exclude from our columns all selections or communications having in the least a contrary tendency. All personal reflections,
private scandal, and vituperative attacks upon individual charac-

ter, we openly declare we wish never to have even sent to us.'
And in the very same number, he gave several delectable verses
as his own definition of this 'virtue,' 'decency,' and 'good manners.' I may as well give the House a specimen from his opening number, where he speaks of the majority of the last House
of Assembly :—

> " 'Each post of profit in the House
>   To greedy sharks assigned,
> And public records of the state
>   Clandestinely purloined.

> " 'The Attorney from the Senate House
>   Endeavored to expel,
> Whose Hall they made look like a room
>   Where raving drunkards dwell.

> " 'For months this ribald conclave
>   Retailed their vulgar prate,
> And charged two dollars each per day
>   For spouting billingsgate.

> " 'Two years their saintships governed us
>   With lawless, despot rule,
> At length the sudden change broke up
>   The league of knave and fool.'

" After apportioning to your predecessor in that chair a due
share of this decent poetry, the learned gentleman opposite informed the people of Wentworth that their late representatives,
of whom I was one, were so many 'juggling, illiterate boobies—
a tippling band—a mountebank riff-raff—a saintly clan—a sad-
dle-bag divan—hacknied knaves;' and that they possessed other
equally pleasant and agreeable qualities, which it appears his fine
sense of virtue, decency, and good manners did not allow him to
forget in his future productions, which my judges, his agents
(Messrs. Shade, Robinson, &c.), have taken such unequaled pains
to circulate among our worthy constituents. I declare I think it
a severe punishment to be obliged to seek for specimens of 'the
liberty of the press' as practiced by the majority of this House,

in such a vehicle as the *Mercury*, but it nevertheless appears to me the best and most effectual way of exhibiting to the country the gross and shameful partiality of this proceeding. I will now call the attention of the House to Mr. McNab's *Mercury* of the 9th June and 15th September last. Courtiers are seldom slow in perceiving what pleases a government, and are always ready to use the means, however improper. It has been found no difficult road to the favor of His Excellency and his Council to cast opprobrium on Mr. Ryerson, the Methodists, Mr. Bidwell, and others whom His Excellency had no friendship for; accordingly we find Mr. McNab and the agents of his *Mercury* stating that Mr. Ryerson is 'a man of profound hypocrisy and unblushing effrontery, who sits blinking on his perch, like Satan when he perched on the tree of life, in the shape of a cormorant to meditate the ruin of our first parents in the garden of Eden,' and the ally of 'shameless reprobates.' My brother members go on, and civilly publish in the *Mercury*, that my soul was going with a certain potentate of darkness to his abode; that I, 'the rascal,' had been guilty of 'dark calumnies and falsehoods—false oaths, false acts—with many other sins of blackest hue.' I will not read the production; it is too gross; but those who wish to refer to the proofs of 'good manners' afforded by those of my judges who circulate the *Mercury* may have the perusal of the paper itself. In the *Mercury* printed on the day this Session was convened, I find that Mr. McNab and his agents circulated (from the Kingston *Chronicle*) an opinion that I had been 'wickedly employed in exciting' the people of Upper Canada 'to discord, dissension, and rebellion.' I presume this was published as a fair specimen of the degree of politeness due from one member to another; for the two honorable members for Wentworth used precisely similar language at the great public meeting held last summer at Hamilton. This brings me to notice the meeting of the inhabitants of York last July, and the petitions to the King and this House, of which Messrs. McNab and Gurnett, and their agents, give an account in their journals as follows:—

"'The whole proceeding, however, is so superlatively ridiculous, and so palpably fraudulent and deceptive, that we find the utmost difficulty in taking the subject up at all as a serious matter, or in alluding to it with any other language than that of ridicule and contempt. And as these are also the feelings and the sentiments with which every man of common sense, of every sect and party in the Province, look at, and laugh at, those extravagant proceedings—always excepting the little knot of half a dozen disappointed and revengeful political aspirants who constitute the nucleus of the old central junto party, and of every other disaffected body which has been organized under different appellations in this country within the last seven years; always, we say, excepting this knot of worthies, and those ever ready tools of their dishonest purposes—the illiterate and mentally enslaved adherents of Ryersonian Episcopal Methodism—with these exceptions we repeat, every man in Upper Canada thoroughly penetrates the fraudulent proceedings by which the party in question, through the agency of their hired tool, Mr. Mackenzie, are now attempting to attain their selfish and dishonest object.

"'But the question naturally presents itself, how, in defiance of these incontrovertible facts, can so large a number of the people of the Province be induced to give the sanction of their signatures to the complaints contained in Mr. Mackenzie's addresses? This is a question, however, to which every intelligent man in the country is prepared to answer. "First; through the influence, direct and insidious, which the crafty Methodist Episcopal priesthood exercise over their illiterate, but well organized and numerous adherents; and secondly, through the fraud, falsehood, or sheer humbug, which is resorted to by Mr. Mackenzie at his pretended Township Meetings."'

"There is language for us, Mr. Speaker, language calculated to please the heads of the Government, and intended doubtless as illustrative of the benefits we of the minority might derive from the liberty of the press. Let us now examine who are the accredited partners, public supporters, or rather, as they are called,

91

agents of the *Courier*.   Col. Ingersoll, M. P., Mr. Mount, M. P.,
Col. Burwell, M. P., your Hon. colleague, the York Bank agent
at Dundas, the Hon. Counsellor Crooks, at Flambro', Mr. Jones
at Prescott, Mr. Berczy at Amherstburg, and a long list of officials.   Will those gentlemen named who have places on this floor,
and who are all pressing forward this prosecution, be able to per-
suade the country that they are not parties to one of the most
partial and shameful schemes ever hatched against a fellow mor-
tal?   Well and truly does Mr. McNab tell his readers in one of
his numbers, that 'HATRED can survive all change, all time, all
circumstance, all other emotions; nay, it can survive the accom-
plishment of revenge, and, like the vampire, prey on its dead
victim.'   The majority of this House, whatever may be their
practice in regard to sycophancy, profess to dread and abhor the
very name of sycophants; yet are they willing to use the freedom of the press to bestow remarkable titles on others.   The
Mercury and the *Courier*, and their agents, my brother members
here present, in their account of the Hamilton Meeting, jointly
honor me with the appellations of a 'politico-religious juggler
—mock patriot—contemptible being—groveling slanderer—wandering impostor,' whose 'censure is praise,' and whose 'shameless
falsehoods,' 'foul deeds,' 'envious malignity,' and 'impotent slanders' point me out as 'the lowest of the vile.'   All this it is expected I should quietly submit to, and so I do.   Next, it appears
to be expected that I should patiently endure the most insulting
abuse on this floor from persons in authority under the Government; and that too I have been found equal to.   Thirdly, I must
not call things by their right name in the newspaper called the
Advocate; but either praise the most undeserving of public men,
be silent as death, or go back to the freeholders of the country
with the brand of a 'false, atrocious, and malicious libeler' on
my forehead.   If such shall be your measure of justice, I will not
shrink from the appeal to the country.   Not one word, not one
syllable do I retract; I offer no apology; for what you call libel
I believe to be solemn truth, fit to be published from one end of

the Province to the other. I certainly should not have availed myself of my privilege or made use of the language complained of on this floor; but since I am called to avow or disavow that language, as an independent public journalist, I declare I think it mild and gentle; for, be it remembered, Mr. Speaker, I see for myself how matters are carried on here; your proceedings are not retailed out to me at second hand. When the petitions of the people, numerous beyond all precedent since the days of Chief Justice Robinson, Jonas Jones, and the Alien question were brought into this House, praying for economy and retrenchment, for the regulation of wild lands sales by law, for the abolition of crown and clergy reserves, and all reservations except for education, for the means of education, for an abolition of banking monopolies, for a reduction of law fees and a simplification of law practice, for the equal distribution of intestate estates, for the establishment of the mode of trying impeachments, for assuring the control of the whole public revenue, for a revision of the corrupt jury packing system, for the repeal of the everlasting salary bill, for disqualifying priests and bishops from holding seats in the two councils, for taking the freeholders' votes at convenient places, for allowing the people the control over their local taxes, for inquiring into the trade law of last April, for the abolition of the tea monopoly, and for an equal representation of the people in this House, how was I treated by those who press on this infamous proceeding? Contrary to all parliamentary usage, the petitions were consigned to a select committee chiefly composed of the bitter enemies of the improvements prayed for, and myself and the other members who introduced them excluded by your vote. My motions for referring these petitions to their known friends, in order that through them bills agreeable to the wishes of the country might be brought before you, were negatived at the request of a member who has openly abandoned the principles which procured him a seat on this floor and a silver cup elsewhere, and adopted a course which has elevated him to the rank of a deputy crown clerk, a justice of the quorum, and a favorite in the circle of officials, at the west end of this city; in more vulgar language, 'he has turned his coat,' and I might add, 'his waistcoat also.' [Cries of order.] The hon. member for Frontenac (Mr. Thomson), who has made these several somersaults for his convenience, is a public journalist, and consequently like me a dealer in opinions. In his Kingston *Herald* of the 26th October last, he calls the petitions of the country, with the consideration of which this House has since entrusted him, a 'humbug,' and tells his brother member (Mr. Buell) that he 'must plead guilty, if it be "illiberal and unjust" to expose the unprincipled conduct of an individual (meaning myself) whom we (meaning himself) conceive to be an enemy to our country, and a promoter of discord and disaffection.' What a generous, just, unbiased, and impartial judge he will make in his own cause, Mr. Speaker, on the present occasion!

"Again, speaking of the Address to His Majesty which has already been signed by ten thousand freeholders and inhabitants he uses the following terms in the *Herald* of July last:—

"'We need not inform our readers that the uncalled-for, and, as the *Patriot* justly designates it, "impertinent" address, is the production of Mr. Mackenzie of *The Colonial Advocate*, whose object is to excite discontent in the minds of the farmers within the sphere of his influence, and at the same time to offer a deliberate insult to the Legislature of which he happens to be a member.' The honorable gentleman assumes to himself the right of denouncing at will his brother representative as a traitor to his country, a promoter of rebellion, and for no other reason than that that member (myself) had originated an address to our present most excellent Sovereign King William, which ten thousand of our fellow subjects have since sanctioned by their signatures! He declares by his votes on this question that he, as one of the majority in this House, may brand me with every infamous epithet which ill will may see fit to embody in a resolution, but that I, as a public journalist, must be expelled and perhaps disqualified if I once venture to hint at the glaring political subserviency of public men. Our late Colonial minister, Sir George Murray, in a speech addressed to the Electors of Perthshire, is reported to have said, that 'It would be well if the people would at all times bear in mind that crowds have their courtiers as well as monarchs. Wherever there is power there will be flatterers, and the people do not always sufficiently recollect that they are liable to be flattered and misled as well as princes, and by flatterers not less mean, cringing, and servile, and above all, not less false or less selfish than the filthiest flatterer who ever frequented a palace, to serve his own private ends by betraying the interests of his master.'

"Mr. Speaker, I never was so well convinced that crowds have their sycophants in Upper Canada as well as courts, as since I had the honor of a seat in this Assembly. In another of Mr. Thompson's journals, published before he fell from a state of political grace, when he was an adherent to the party who bestowed on him the cup, I find he quotes from the late *York Observer* the following curious passage, without passing an opinion concerning its noxious or innoxious qualities:—'Mr. Fothergill has com- menced replying to Mr. Macaulay's letter; we regret to perceive that he is advancing doctrines so much tinged with arrogance and tyranny, and so opposite to that glorious constitution which is the boast of Englishmen, and the admiration of every lover of freedom, that no man, except a slavish dependent upon a "jackanapes," lawless, disgusting, and slanderous Commons would maintain or countenance.—*Observer*, March 13.' It hence appears that this honorable body, in its earlier stages, was not so tender of its privileges and so fond of encroaching on the freedom of the press as the legislators of the present day; if it had, the *Observer's* unfavorable opinion, thus plainly expressed, would have left room for the exercise of its powers. But the flatterers of that day, if any there were, seem to have been wise in their generation. In another number of the Kingston *Herald*, published before its editor had received the new light of official patronage, he complains that 'a grand jury consisting of his political oppo-

nents' (now his dear friends) had indicted him for libel, because
he had made a 'fair, justifiable animadversion upon a public official act of the late administration.'   And then Mr. Thomson in
his journal proceeded to show that his brother justice, Mr. Mac-
Farlane, had scolded the House of Assembly as hard as he pleased,
and that while he (Mr. Thomson) was persecuted, his then opponent, now partner in the statute job, was pensioned, and paid, and
recompensed.   As Mr. Thomson's paper shows the usages of the
administration presses in a very clear light, I will trouble the
House to listen to his description of the state and condition of
the liberty of the press, A. D., 1829.   'It (meaning the Kingston
Chronicle) stigmatized Messrs. John Rolph, W. W. Baldwin, Paul
Peterson, James Wilson, Lockwood, Mackenzie, Malcolm, Dalton,
Blacklock, Randal, Hornor, and Mathews' by name, and called
them 'besotted fools,' and added, 'It is evident they are actuated
by no other feeling than malice, to gratify which they pay no regard to truth or decency.   For instance, the report of the Committee on Collins' case contains absolute falsehoods, known to be
such to both Rolph and Baldwin, and yet they join in the report.'
'Let me here ask a candid public what there is in the character
of John B. Robinson, acting in his capacity of Attorney General,
more sacred than in the character of John Rolph or W. W. Baldwin, acting in their capacity of Members of the Provincial Assembly? or upon what principle of law or justice Francis Collins
is prosecuted for libel, and James McFarlane exempted from prosecution for similar but more aggravated libels?   In a communication published in the *Chronicle*, addressed to Louis J. Papineau,
Esq., Speaker of the House of Assembly of Lower Canada, there
are these among many other libelous expressions: 'Sir, my charge
against you is threefold—falsehood, defamation, and scurrility.'
'I then convicted you, in the face of your country, of having gone
officially into the presence of the Representative of our most gracious Sovereign, with a base and designing falsehood on your
lips.'   'I ought to have been assured that a career like yours,
commenced in iniquity, must inevitably terminate in crime and

confusion.' 'There are no bounds to your malevolence.' 'No character, however pure, is safe from your envy and falsehoods.' 'The very air is tainted with the poison of your malignant disposition.' 'You seem to traffic in defamation; you move in an orbit of public slander, and have rallied round you, as satellites, all the baser feelings of a rancorous and diabolical heart.' 'If you have any other titles but those of a cowardly heart and a malevolent disposition, produce them, I entreat of you, but conscience whispers to you that you cannot. I declare, in the face of my country, that the House of Assembly, as at present constituted, is corrupt, and an intolerable nuisance.' These disgusting extracts from the *Chronicle* are not made to prejudice the editor of that paper, but to show, in the light of a fair contrast, the true character and bearing of the one-sided system of libel prosecutions commenced under the late Administration.

"One more extract from Mr. Thomson's *Herald*, and I have done. It is where he speaks of the libel bill you tomahawked last winter: 'We perceive that the attempt to get rid of one of the relics of barbarous and oppressive times has failed in our Assembly. "The greater the truth the greater the libel," is an excellent doctrine to prevent deeds done in darkness coming to the light, and an excellent instrument in the hands of the rich and influential to exercise a spirit of revenge upon such as offend them, providing they can disguise the matter so far as to induce a jury to give a verdict in accordance to their feelings.' Surely, Mr. Speaker, the scriptural advice offered to him that standeth, that he take heed lest he fall, is deserving of deep consideration, when we see the editor of the Kingston *Herald* ranged among the prosecutors of the press; (order, order;) the parable, too, of the servant who after being forgiven a heavy debt was ungrateful enough to send his fellow servant to prison because the latter was unable to pay an hundred pence, might be applied practically to the present proceeding; (order, order;) but since the House desires it I will forbear."

After referring at some length to the case of Queen Caroline, Mr. Mackenzie concluded, as follows: "As we have English law

here, I am determined to have English usage, and be assured, Mr.
Speaker, that were every representative on this floor to join the
movers of these resolves in denouncing and condemning the articles you have selected as libelous, I would republish them *verba-
tim* the following Thursday, and test how far the people of Canada are disposed to protect the free discussion of the public
conduct and characters of public bodies and public men.   Once
more, however, I would recommend to you to quash these proceedings, for you may depend upon it that although your dungeon
were ready, and your tipstaff at my elbow, I would not yield an
inch."

APPENDIX C.

THE SECOND RIDING OF YORK ELECTION IN 1836.

TO THE HONORABLE THE COMMONS OF UPPER CANADA IN PROVINCIAL PAR-
LIAMENT ASSEMBLED:

*The humble Petition of William Lyon Mackenzie, of the City of
Toronto, Printer,*

SHEWETH,—That at the last election for a member to represent the Second Riding of the County of York in the Legislature, William Hepburn, Esquire, acting Trustee to the Six
Nations Indians, was the Returning Officer; and the candidates
proposed, and for whom a poll was demanded, and opened, were
Edward William Thomson, Esquire, the sitting member, and your
petitioner.

That His Excellency the Lieutenant-Governor, Sir F. B.
Head, unduly interfered with the election, and tampered with
the rights of the freeholders.

1st. By putting forth a variety of threatening, inflammatory
harangues, in violent language, under the form of replies to certain addresses, which were circulated in the shape of hand-bills,
evidently with the intention of biasing the minds of the yeomanry
previous to the then approaching election.

2d. By issuing new deeds after the prorogation and dissolution, and even after polling had commenced, with a view to prevent the election of your petitioner, who had been six times successively returned for the County, and once for the Riding, for which he was, for the eighth time, a candidate.

3d. By allowing Magistrates, persons dependent on his will, and others, who were to receive Crown deeds, on condition of performing settlement duties, to obtain their deeds, such duties not having been performed, and this to influence the election.

4th. By inducing persons, with expectation of offices of honor and emolument, to violate the law, in order to prevent your petitioner's election—as, for instance, in the matter of Andrew Shore and wife, committed to jail, on a charge of grand larceny, by Alderman Denison; and by him and Alderman Gurnett (the latter a most indefatigable agent in spreading the Lieutenant Governor's political replies through the Riding) admitting Shore to bail, insufficient bail, contrary to the statute, which requires all such cases to be brought before one of the Judges of the Court of King's Bench, and allowing Mrs. Shore to go free. Shore was instantly hurried off, by Mr. Gurnett, and his constitutional society connections, to Streetsville to vote for the government candidate. For several months after he was at liberty. He was convicted at the last assizes of the crime of stealing in a dwelling-house, and is now an inmate of the penitentiary. Mr. Gurnett, the agent in this dishonorable affair, has, since the election, been promoted to a Commissionership in the Court of Requests in this city, in the place of Mr. Small, removed.

5th. By issuing Crown deeds without a description of boundaries, under improper advice, in order to affect the election.

6th. By declining, or refusing, to discountenance Orange Lodges and party proceedings, although in possession of the Royal pleasure and the decision of the Legislature respecting them.

7th. By issuing Crown deeds for lands at Port Credit, although the conditions of the sale had not been fulfilled, and by issuing such deeds, in some cases, to other persons than the original.

nominees or purchasers, although the practice has been not to sanction transfers by those who had no titles, except under the Heir and Devisee Act.

8th. And, as your petitioner is advised, by contributing, with his officers, to funds intended to affect the election; by issuing Crown deeds to individuals, upon the condition, express or implied, that they would vote for Mr. Thomson, and this, in some cases, without payment of the purchase money, or upon unusual terms.

That the Returning Officer, William Hepburn, Esquire, in the performance of the duties of his office at the said election, acted, in many respects, partially, illegally, and ignorantly. Amongst others—

He administered the oath required to be taken by freeholders, under the Statute 4th William IV., chap. 14, for several days after the commencement of the polling, invariably omitting the description of the estate on which the elector voted, and substituting only the words "a freehold," notwithstand the remonstrances of your petitioner against his doing so; and your petitioner often endeavored to convince him that any person who had a freehold any where, even if it were in England, could take such an oath as he had substituted. After several days, he began to swear the voters to the freehold they voted on, as by law required.

He rejected the votes of many electors who offered their votes for your petitioner, and refused to record their names or votes; and discouraged others from coming to the hustings, by deciding, on an objection to a vote raised by Mr. Thomson, that freeholders born in the United States, or in any foreign country, should not vote, although they might have been resident in Canada half a century, and duly taken the oath of allegiance, and although they publicly offered to take the oaths prescribed by the statutes; unless each voter, on presenting himself, could produce a paper, purporting to be a Commissioner's certificate, that he had taken the oath of allegiance; such paper not being evidence even when shown.

Early in the election he permitted this class to go home, fetch the paper, and return and vote; but afterwards he laid down a rule, that if they had it not with them when asked they could not return and vote.

There are many cases to be cited—your petitioner will refer only to two at this time, by way of illustration.

Andrew Cook, father of Jacob Cook, of Cooksville, one of the oldest freeholders in the Province, and who had voted at many elections, was turned from the hustings, because he had not a certificate with him, although he offered to take the oaths required by the statute.

Wait Sweet, an old freeholder, who has been half a century in Upper Canada, and voted five times for your petitioner, who took the oath of allegiance, before Colonel Joel Stone, in 1801, and served in the late war, offered to vote, and asked to have the oaths required or prescribed by statute to be administered to him. He was turned from the hustings, because his certificate was not in his pocket, his right to vote denied, and he was further told not to come back. But he soon returned with the Colonel's certificate of 1801, and a certificate of his war services, and he was turned from the hustings, and his vote rejected by the Returning Officer, who even refused to enter your petitioner's objections on the poll-book.

These and similar illegal decisions discouraged many voters, who considered that to be turned away from the poll in presence of their neighbors, as aliens, was an insult they could not well brook.

The Returning Officer did not act uniformly on any rule—he turned away many who offered to take the oaths—he admitted others.

Your petitioner had reason to believe that several brothers— Messrs. M'Grath—sons to the church of England Clergyman in Toronto, one of them a Postmaster, another a Court of Requests Commissioner, captain of a troop of horse, had no title to the property they voted on, the title being in the Crown, (of which the Returning Officer had previously been apprized by them,) and a mortgage also intervening. Two of them would not answer any questions put to them, either by candidates or Returning Officer, and the latter decided they might vote on taking the oaths, which they did and voted for Mr. Thomson; while those of Messrs. Sweet, Cook, and many more, were refused, although tendered by old and undoubted freeholders, who were also ready to be sworn.

After the Returning Officer had acted for days on his rule, that no person born in a foreign country should vote without a certificate, a violent partisan of the Executive, Jacob D. Hagerman, came forward, admitted he was born in Germany, produced no certificate, and although it is understood that he and his brother, who voted upon the same lot, came in after 1827, and have not been naturalized, his vote for Mr. Thomson was recorded.

One Henry Miller, a drunken, disorderly character, who had been disturbing the poll for some time, and who has been often in the House of Correction here, was persuaded to tender his vote for Mr. Thomson; but although it was very doubtful whether he was aware of the nature of the oaths he took, and there was little reason to believe him a freeholder, his vote was at once recorded.

Postmasters and other dependent persons, excluded by the laws of England (adopted here) from interfering at elections, openly busied themselves, electioneered, and voted, although your petitioner objected to these proceedings.

Other officers of the Government subscribed money, and actively busied themselves at the election. Funds were collected from persons connected with the Executive and others, and employed in collecting, bringing up, treating, and intoxicating voters against your petitioner—in keeping taverns and pot-houses, the resort of worthless and disorderly persons, open, free of cost to them—and in collecting bullies and men of bad repute about the hustings, to the terror of peaceable farmers.

Priests, pensioned and hired by money, paid them by His Excellency and his Government, busied themselves to prevent the freedom of election, and to bias the minds of the electors.

William B. Jarvis, Esq., Sheriff of this District, interfered openly at the election, stood at the hustings with a whip in his hand, and harangued those present, reminding them that the Reformers were their enemies, and must be put down. He then came forward as a voter, and made use of most violent and intemperate language, calculated to promote disturbance. This conduct the Returning Officer did not check.

And your petitioner is advised, that the said Edward William Thomson was a party, in several instances, to the treating, bribery, threats, promises, and other illegal steps, of which complaint is herein made; and he contends that the return of the said Edward William Thomson, as a Member to serve in this present Parliament, is illegal, void, and unconstitutional, because he was not elected by the greatest number of qualified votes of the said Riding, as there is a majority of the said votes in favor of your petitioner; because the election was not lawfully conducted, but interfered with by the Lieutenant Governor and his officers, by the Orange Lodges, by the treating, force, and violence, and by the partiality and injustice of the Returning Officer.

Bribery, intimidation, and violence, as well as the unconstitutional exercise of the Royal prerogative and the Executive influence, were means made use of to induce electors to vote against your petitioner, or to prevent their voting for him—means utterly subversive of the freedom and purity of election.

Your petitioner further represents that the freedom and purity of the election and the rights of the electors were violated by combinations of persons in illegal societies, known by the name of Orange Lodges, formed for political purposes, secretly, if not openly, countenanced by His Excellency, the Lieutenant Governor, and usually headed and aided by magistrates and other officeholders, and exercising, by means of these illegal associations, an unconstitutional power and influence in the said election.

Your petitioner humbly prays that the election and return of the said Edward William Thomson may be declared null and void, by reason of the matters hereinbefore contained; that a new election may take place, so that the people may be truly and fairly represented; that the conduct of the Lieutenant Governor, his officers, the Returning Officer, and others, as above referred to, may be carefully inquired into, the result made known, and such proceedings had, if found necessary, as shall secure to the electors, in all time to come, a free and faithful representation in the Legislature.

And your petitioner will ever pray.

WM. L. MACKENZIE.

Toronto, 20th December, 1836.

I append the following extract from Dr. Duncombe's letter to Lord Glenelg, dated London, September 20, 1836 :—

" The following are some of the many instances of the unconstitutional interference by Sir F. B. Head and his dependents with the elective franchise.

" William Higgins, Bailiff to the Sheriff and Court of Requests, Toronto city, voted against the Reform candidate upon a deed signed by Sir F. B. Head, 27th June, 1836.

" George Walton, Bailiff, and Sub-Sheriff, after electioneering for the Tory candidate, took the oaths and voted upon about half an acre without buildings on it—patent dated the Monday previous.

" John Powell, Attorney, and grandson of the late Chief Justice, voted against the Reform candidate upon a quarter acre of land upon which there were no buildings—grant by Sir F. B. Head, 28th of June, 1836, during the progress of the election.

" Finlay Cameron voted against the Reform candidate—patent signed by Sir F. B. Head, during the election, 20th June, 1836.

" John Crighton and Hugh McLellan voted against the Reform candidate under a grant of Sir F. B. Head—patents dated 25th June, 1836.

" Alderman Doctor John King, of the city of Toronto, voted

against the Reform candidate in the Second Riding of York, under a grant of Sir F. B. Head of about one quarter of an acre of land without a house, dated during the election, 28th June, 1836.

" Robert Ruston and Thomas Johnson voted against the Reform candidate upon free grants from the Crown for one hundred acres each—patents dated 25th June, 1836. Most of the above persons resided out of the Second Riding of York where they voted.

" It is further alleged that many votes were created by giving patents to persons who had commuted their pensions, and who, without having any special claim for land, had been allowed to occupy small parcels under a license of occupation, without the power to dispose of it, contrary to the original intent of the location.

" That patents have been issued for parts of lots without a description of the part, when only a part of the original purchase money had been paid, contrary to the original order under which the same was located.

" That in other instances patents have been issued to individuals for the whole of the lots they had contracted for, without the payment of the whole of the purchase money originally demanded, contrary to the uniform practice which requires that the whole of the money shall be paid before the patent shall be issued; in all these cases the persons thus favored voted for the Tory candidate, and in no one instance did any of those persons vote for the Reform candidate.

" These examples serve to show some of the many ways by which votes were created by Sir F. B. Head, to support the Tory candidates and overwhelm the Reformers in different parts of the Province."

APPENDIX D.

THE FOLLOWING DECLARATION WAS ADOPTED ON THE 31ST JULY,
AND PUBLISHED IN THE "CONSTITUTION" AUGUST 2, 1837.

*The Declaration of the Reformers of the City of Toronto to their
Fellow Reformers in Upper Canada.*

THE time has arrived, after nearly half a century's forbearance under increasing and aggravated misrule, when the duty we owe our country and posterity requires from us the assertion of our rights and the redress of our wrongs.

Government is founded on the authority, and is instituted for the benefit, of a people; when, therefore, any Government long and systematically ceases to answer the great ends of its foundation, the people have a natural right given them by their Creator to seek after and establish such institutions as will yield the greatest quantity of happiness to the greatest number.

Our forbearance heretofore has only been rewarded with an aggravation of our grievances; and our past inattention to our rights has been ungenerously and unjustly urged as evidence of the surrender of them. We have now to choose on the one hand between submission to the same blighting policy as has desolated Ireland, and, on the other hand, the patriotic achievement of cheap, honest, and responsible government.

The right was conceded to the present United States, at the close of a successful revolution, to form a constitution for themselves; and the loyalists with their descendants and others, now peopling this portion of America, are entitled to the same liberty without the shedding of blood—more they do not ask; less they ought not to have. But, while the revolution of the former has been rewarded with a consecutive prosperity unexampled in the history of the world, the loyal valor of the latter alone remains amidst the blight of misgovernment to tell them what they might have been as the not less valiant sons of American independence. Sir Francis Head has too truly portrayed our country "as standing in the flourishing continent of North America like a girdled tree with its drooping branches." But the laws of nature do not, and those of men ought not, longer to doom this remnant of the new world to exhibit this invidious and humiliating comparison.

The affairs of this country have been ever against the spirit of the Constitutional Act, subjected in the most injurious manner to the interferences and interdictions of a succession of Colonial Ministers in England who have never visited the country, and can never possibly become acquainted with the state of parties, or the conduct of public functionaries, except through official channels in the Province, which are illy calculated to convey the information necessary to disclose official delinquencies and correct public abuses. A painful experience has proved how impracticable it is for such a succession of strangers beneficially to direct and control the affairs of the people four thousand miles off; and being an impracticable system, felt to be intolerable by those for whose good it was professedly intended, it ought to be abolished, and the domestic institutions of the Province so improved and administered by the local authorities as to render the people happy and contented. This system of baneful domination has been uniformly furthered by a Lieutenant Governor sent amongst us as an uninformed, unsympathising stranger, who, like Sir Francis, has not a single feeling in common with the people, and whose hopes and responsibilities begin and end in Downing Street. And this baneful domination is further cherished by a Legislative Council not elected and therefore responsible to people for whom they legislate, but appointed by the ever changing Colonial Minister for life, from pensioners on the bounty of the Crown, official dependents and needy expectants.

Under this mockery of human government we have been insulted, injured, and reduced to the brink of ruin. The due influence and purity of all our institutions have been utterly destroyed. Our Governors are mere instruments for effecting domination from Downing Street; Legislative Councillors have been intimidated into executive compliance, as in the case of the late Chief Justice Powell, Mr. Baby, and others; the Executive Council has been

93

stript of every shadow of responsibility, and of every shade of
duty; the freedom and purity of elections have lately received,
under Sir Francis Head, a final and irretrievable blow; our revenue has been and still is decreasing to such an extent as to render
heavy additional taxation indispensable for the payment of the
interest of our public debt, incurred by a system of improvident
and profligate expenditure; our public lands, although a chief
source of wealth to a new country, have been sold at a low valua-
tion to speculating companies in London, and resold to the settlers at very advanced rates, the excess being remitted to England to the serious impoverishment of the country; the ministers
of religion have been corrupted by the prostitution of the casual
and territorial revenue to salary and influence them; our Clergy
Reserves, instead of being devoted to the purpose of general education, though so much needed and loudly demanded, have been
in part sold to the amount of upwards of 300,000 dollars, paid
into the military chest and sent to England; numerous rectories
have been established, against the almost unanimous wishes of
the people, with certain exclusive, ecclesiastical, and spiritual
rights and privileges, according to the Established Church of
England, to the destruction of equal religious rights; public
salaries, pensions, and sinecures, have been augmented in number and amount, notwithstanding the impoverishment of our
revenue and country; and this parliament have, under the name
of arrearages, paid the retrenchments made in past years by
Reform parliaments; our Judges have, in spite of our condition,
been doubled, and wholly selected from the most violent political
partisans against our equal civil and religious liberties, and a
Court of Chancery suddenly adopted by a subservient parliament,
against the long cherished expectations of the people against it,
and its operation fearfully extended into the past so as to jeop-
ardize every title and transaction from the beginning of the
Province to the present time. A law has been passed enabling
Magistrates, appointed during pleasure, at the representation
of a Grand Jury selected by a Sheriff holding office during plea-

sure, to tax the people at pleasure, without their previous knowledge or consent, upon all their rateable property to build and
support work-houses for the refuge of the paupers invited by
Sir Francis from the parishes in Great Britain; thus unjustly
and wickedly laying the foundation of a system which must result in taxation, pestilence, and famine. Public loans have been
authorized by improvident legislation to nearly eight millions of
dollars, the surest way to make the people both poor and dependent; the parliament, subservient to Sir Francis Head's
blighting administration, have by an unconstitutional act sanctioned by him, prolonged their duration after the demise of the
Crown, thereby evading their present responsibility to the people,
depriving them of the exercise of their elective franchise on the
present occasion, and extending the period of their unjust, unconstitutional, and ruinous legislation with Sir Francis Head;
our best and most worthy citizens have been dismissed from the
bench of justice, from the militia, and other stations of honor
and usefulness, for exercising their rights as freemen in attending
public meetings for the regeneration of our condition, as in-
stanced in the case of Dr. Baldwin, Messrs. Scatchard, Johnson,
Small, Ridout, and others; those of our fellow subjects who go
to England to represent our deplorable condition are denied a
hearing, by a partial, unjust, and oppressive government, while
the authors and promoters of our wrongs are cordially and gra-
ciously received, and enlisted in the cause of our further wrongs
and misgovernment; our public revenues are plundered and mis-
applied without redress, and unavailable securities make up the
late defalcation of Mr. P. Robinson, the Commissioner of Public
Lands, to the amount of 80,000 dollars. Interdicts are continually sent by the Colonial Minister to the Governor, and by the
Governor to the Provincial Parliament, to restrain and render
futile their legislation, which ought to be free and unshackled;
these instructions, if favorable to the views and policy of the
enemies of our country, are rigidly observed; if favorable to
public liberty, they are, as in the case of Earl Ripon's despatch,

utterly contemned, even to the passing of the ever to be remembered and detestable Everlasting Salary Bill; Lord Glenelg has sanctioned, in the King's name, all the violations of truth and of the constitution by Sir Francis Head, and both thanked and titled him for conduct, which, under any civilized government, would be the ground of impeachment.

The British Government, by themselves and through the Legislative Council of their appointment, have refused their assent to laws the most wholesome and necessary for the public good, among which we may enumerate the Intestate Estate equal distribution bill; the bill to sell the Clergy Reserves for educational purposes; the bill to remove the corrupt influence of the Executive in the choosing of juries, and to secure a fair and free trial by jury; the several bills to encourage emigration from foreign parts; the bills to secure the independence of the Assembly; the bill to amend the law of libel; the bills to appoint commissioners to meet others appointed by Lower Canada, to treat on matters of trade and other matters of deep interest; the bills to extend the blessings of education to the humbler classes in every township, and to appropriate annually a sum of money for that purpose; the bill to dispose of the school lands in aid of education; several bills for the improvement of the highways; the bill to secure independence to voters by establishing the vote by ballot; the bill for the better regulation of the elections of members of the Assembly, and to provide that they be held at places convenient for the people; the bills for the relief of Quakers, Mennonists, and Tunkers; the bill to amend the present obnoxious courts of requests laws, by allowing the people to choose the commissioners, and to have a trial by jury if desired; with other bills to improve the administration of justice and diminish unnecessary costs; the bills to amend the charter of King's College University so as to remove its partial and arbitrary system of government and education; and the bill to allow free competition in banking.

The King of England has forbidden his governors to pass laws of immediate and pressing importance, unless suspended in their operation till his assent should be obtained; and when so suspended, he has utterly neglected to attend to them. He has interfered with the freedom of elections, and appointed elections to be held at places dangerous, inconvenient, and unsafe for the people to assemble at, for the purpose of fatiguing them into his measures, through the agency of pretended representatives; and has, through his Legislative Council, prevented provision from being made for quiet and peaceable elections, as in the case of the late returns at Beverley.

He has dissolved the late House of Assembly for opposing with manly firmness Sir Francis Head's invasion of the right of the people to a wholesome control over the revenue, and for insisting that the persons conducting the government should be responsible for their official conduct to the country through its representatives.

He has endeavored to prevent the peopling of this Province and its advancement in wealth; for that purpose obstructing the laws for the naturalization of foreigners, refusing to pass others to encourage their migration hither, and raising the conditions of new appropriations of the public lands, large tracts of which he has bestowed upon unworthy persons his favorites, while deserving settlers from Germany and other countries have been used cruelly.

He has rendered the administration of justice liable to suspicion and distrust, by obstructing laws for establishing a fair trial by jury, by refusing to exclude the chief criminal Judge from interfering in political business, and by selecting as the judiciary, violent and notorious partisans of his arbitrary power.

He has sent a standing army into the sister Province to coerce them to his unlawful and unconstitutional measures, in open violation of their rights and liberties, and has received with marks of high approbation military officers who interfered with the citizens of Montreal, in the midst of an election of their representatives, and brought the troops to coerce them, who shot several persons dead wantonly in the public streets.

Considering the great number of lucrative appointments held

by strangers to the country, whose chief merit appears to be their
subservience to any and every administration, we may say with
our brother colonists of old—" He has sent hither swarms of
new officers to harass our people and eat out their substance."

The English Parliament have interfered with our internal affairs and regulations, by the passage of grievous and tyrannical
enactments, for taxing us heavily without our consent, for prohibiting us to purchase many articles of the first importance at
the cheapest European or American markets, and compelling us
to buy such goods and merchandise at an exorbitant price in markets of which England has a monopoly.

They have passed resolutions for our coercion, of a character
so cruel and arbitrary, that Lord Chancellor Brougham has recorded on the journals of the House of Peers, that " they set all
considerations of sound policy, of generosity, and of justice, at
defiance," are wholly subversive of " the fundamental principle
of the British constitution, that no part of the taxes levied on
the people shall be applied to any purpose whatever, without the
consent of the representatives in Parliament," and that the Canadian " precedent of 1837 will ever after be cited in the support
of such oppressive proceedings, as often as the Commons of any
colony may withhold supplies, how justifiable soever their refusal
may be ;" and (adds his lordship) " those proceedings, so closely
resembling the fatal measures that severed the United States
from Great Britain, have their origin in principles, and derive
their support from reasonings, which form a prodigious contrast
to the whole grounds, and the only defence, of the policy during
latter years, and so justly and so wisely sanctioned by the Imperial Parliament, in administering the affairs of the mother
country.   Nor is it easy to imagine that the inhabitants of either
the American or the European branches of the empire should
contemplate so strange a contrast, without drawing inferences
therefrom discreditable to the character of the Legislature, and
injurious to the future safety of the state, when they mark with
what different measures we mete to six hundred thousand inhabitants of a remote province, unrepresented in Parliament, and

to six millions of our fellow citizens nearer home, and making themselves heard by their representatives. The reflection will assuredly arise in Canada, and may possibly find its way into Ireland, that the sacred rules of justice, the most worthy feelings of national generosity, and the soundest principles of enlightened policy, may be appealed to in vain, if the demands of the suitor be not also supported by personal interests, and party views, and political fears, among those whose aid he seeks; while all men perceiving that many persons have found themselves at liberty to hold a course towards an important but remote province, which their constituents never would suffer to be pursued towards the most inconsiderable burgh of the United Kingdom, an impression will inevitably be propagated most dangerous to the maintenance of colonial dominion, that the people can never safely intrust the powers of government to any supreme authority not residing among themselves."

In every stage of these proceedings we have petitioned for redress in the most humble terms; our repeated petitions have been answered only by repeated injuries.

Nor have we been wanting in attention to our British brethren. We have warned them from time to time of attempts by their Legislature to extend an unwarrantable jurisdiction over us. We have reminded them of the circumstances of our emigration and settlement here. We have appealed to their native justice and magnanimity, and we have conjured them by the ties of our common kindred to disavow these usurpations which would inevitably interrupt our connection and correspondence. They too have been deaf to the voice of justice and consanguinity.

We, therefore, the Reformers of the City of Toronto, sympathizing with our fellow citizens here and throughout the North American Colonies, who desire to obtain cheap, honest, and responsible government, the want of which has been the source of all their past grievances, as its continuance would lead them to their utter ruin and desolation, are of opinion, 1. That the warmest thanks and admiration are due from the Reformers of Upper Canada to the Honorable Louis Joseph Papineau, Esq., Speaker of the House of Assembly of Lower Canada, and his compatriots in and out of the Legislature, for their past uniform, manly, and noble independence, in favor of civil and religious liberty; and for their present devoted, honorable, and patriotic opposition to the attempt of the British Government to violate their constitution without their consent, subvert the powers and privileges of their local parliament, and overawe them by coercive measures into a disgraceful abandonment of their just and reasonable wishes.

2. And that the Reformers of Upper Canada are called upon by every tie of feeling, interest, and duty, to make common cause with their fellow citizens of Lower Canada, whose successful coercion would doubtless be in time visited upon us, and the redress of whose grievances would be the best guarantee for the redress of our own.

To render this co-operation the more effectual, we earnestly recommend to our fellow citizens that they exert themselves to organize political associations; that public meetings be held throughout the Province; and that a convention of delegates be elected, and assembled at Toronto, to take into consideration the political condition of Upper Canada, with authority to its members to appoint commissioners to meet others to be named on behalf of Lower Canada and any of the other colonies, armed with suitable powers as a Congress, to seek an effectual remedy for the grievances of the colonists.

T. D. MORRISON, *Chairman of Com.*   JOHN ELLIOT, *Secretary.*

COMMITTEE.

David Gibson.	Edward Wright.
John Mackintosh.	Robert McKay.
Wm. J. O'Grady.	Thomas Elliott.
E. B. Gilbert.	James Armstrong.
John Montgomery.	James Hunter.
John Edward Tims.	John Armstrong.
James H. Price.	William Ketchum.
John Doel.	Wm. L. Mackenzie.
M. Reynolds.	

Dr. Morrison addressed the meeting at great length, and was enthusiastically cheered. He then moved, seconded by Mr. E. B. Gilbert, that the report of the special committee, just read as above, be adopted as the sense of this meeting, and that the declaration of the Reformers of this city be countersigned by the Secretary on behalf of this meeting. Which was agreed to by acclamation.

Edward Wright, Esq., seconded by Mr. James Armstrong, moves that it be

Resolved, That, reposing the greatest confidence in our fellow citizens, John Rolph, M. P. P., Marshal S. Bidwell, T. D. Morrison, M. P. P., James Lesslie, James H. Price, John Edward Tims, and Robert McKay, Esquires, we do hereby nominate and appoint them members of the Provincial Convention for the City of Toronto.—Carried unanimously and by acclamation.

Moved by John Edward Tims, Esq., seconded by Mr. Robert McKay,

Resolved, That the members of the Committee who have reported the draft of a declaration of the Reformers of Toronto, be a permanent Committee of Vigilance, for this city and liberties, and to carry into immediate and practical effect the resolutions of this meeting for the effectual organization of the Reformers of Upper Canada—that Mr. John Elliot be requested to continue to officiate as the Secretary in ordinary—*that W. L. Mackenzie, Esq., be invited to perform the important duties of Agent and Corresponding Secretary*—and that when this meeting adjourns it stand adjourned to the call of the said committee through its chairman.—Carried unanimously.

Mr. John Doel, seconded by Mr. M. Reynolds, moves that it be

Resolved, That we will, in the pursuit of the objects of this meeting, as far as possible, rigidly abstain, so long as our duty to our country requires it, from the consumption of articles coming from beyond sea, or paying duties, in order that no revenues raised from the people shall be made instrumental in the continuance of their bad government, which will assuredly be perpetu-

94

ated as long as our folly supplies the means.—Carried—ten to one.

Mr. Mackenzie, seconded by Mr. James Hunter, moves—*Resolved*, That the right of obtaining articles of luxury, or necessity; in the cheapest market, is inherent in the people, who only consent to the imposition of duties for the creation of revenues with the express understanding that the revenues so raised from them shall be devoted to the necessary expenses of government, and apportioned by the people's representatives; and therefore when the contract is broken by an Executive or any foreign authority, the people are released from their engagement, and are no longer under any moral obligation to contribute to, or aid in the collection of, such revenues. Mr. M. briefly addressed the meeting in favor of the resolution, which was put and carried without opposition.

(Signed) JOHN MACKINTOSH, *Chairman.*
JOHN ELLIOT, *Secretary.*

After which, D. Gibson, Esq., M. P. P., took the chair, the meeting returned thanks to its officers, for their services, and adjourned to the call of the Chairman of the Committee of Vigilance.

APPENDIX E.

THE following draft of Constitution was prepared by Mr. Mackenzie, to be submitted to the proposed convention for adoption, after a Provisional Government should have been established in Upper Canada. It was actually published by Mr. Mackenzie in *The Constitution,* on the 15th of November, 1837, a few days before the 7th of December was fixed upon for a descent upon Toronto. When he left Toronto for the country, thirteen days before the intended outbreak, he took a small press and a printer with him, for the purpose of striking off copies of this document.

The Constitution of the United States was the model on which
this was formed; the variations being chiefly the result of different circumstances:—

WHEREAS the solemn covenant made with the people of Upper
and Lower Canada, and recorded in the statute book of the
United Kingdom of Great Britain and Ireland, as the thirty-first
chapter of the Acts passed in the thirty-first year of the reign
of King George III., hath been continually violated by the
British Government, and our rights usurped; *And Whereas* our
humble petitions, addresses, protests, and remonstrances against
this injurious interference have been made in vain—We, the people of the State of Upper Canada, acknowledging with gratitude
the grace and beneficence of God, in permitting us to make choice
of our form of Government, and in order to establish justice,
ensure domestic tranquillity, provide for the common defence,
promote the general welfare, and secure the blessings of civil and
religious liberty to ourselves and our posterity, do establish this
Constitution.

1. Matters of religion and the ways of God's worship are not
at all intrusted by the people of this State to any human power,
because therein they cannot remit or exceed a tittle of what their
consciences dictate to be the mind of God, without willful sin.
Therefore the Legislature shall make no law respecting the establishment of religion, or for the encouragement or the prohibition
of any religious denomination.

2. It is ordained and declared that the free exercise and enjoyment of religious profession and worship, without discrimination or preference, shall forever hereafter be allowed within this
State to all mankind.

3. The whole of the public lands within the limits of this State,
including the lands attempted, by a pretended sale, to be vested
in certain adventurers called the Canada Company (except so
much of them as may have been disposed of to actual settlers
now resident in the State), and all the land called Crown Reserves, Clergy Reserves, and rectories and also the school lands,

and the lands pretended to be appropriated to the uses of the University of King's College, are declared to be the property of the State, and at the disposal of the Legislature, for the public service thereof.* The proceeds of one million of acres of the most valuable public lands shall be specially appropriated to the support of Common or Township schools.

4. No Minister of the Gospel, clergyman, ecclesiastic, bishop or priest of any religious denomination whatsoever, shall, at any time hereafter, under any pretence or description whatever, be eligible to, or capable of holding a seat in the Senate or House of Assembly, or any civil or military office within this State.

5. In all laws made, or to be made, every person shall be bound alike—neither shall any tenure, estate, charter, degree, birth, or place, confer any exemption from the ordinary course of legal proceedings and responsibilities whereunto others are subjected.

6. No hereditary emoluments, privileges, or honors, shall ever be granted by the people of this State.

7. There shall neither be slavery nor involuntary servitude in this State, otherwise than for the punishment of crimes whereof the party shall have been duly convicted. People of color, who have come into this State, with the design of becoming permanent inhabitants thereof, *and are now resident therein*, shall be entitled to all the rights of native Canadians, upon taking an oath or affirmation to support the constitution.

---

* Without explanation this would look like a proposal to confiscate the lands of the Canada Company; but the question of their reverting to the Crown had been raised by the company itself several years before. The company complained that, in continuing to dispose of Crown Lands, the government was forcing upon it an impossible competition, and they threatened to resign their charter. The Lieutenant Governor of the day, Sir John Colborne, gave as a reason for not acting upon the threat, and receiving the lands back, that it was impossible to do without the revenue. Mr. Mackenzie doubtless argued that if the company was at liberty to give up its charter, if it suited its own interest to do so, it might be forfeited, upon re-payment of the purchase money, in the interest of the public.

8. The people have a right to bear arms for the defence of themselves and the State.

9. No man shall be impressed or forcibly constrained to serve in time of war; because money, the sinews of war, being always at the disposal of the Legislature, they can never want numbers of men apt enough to engage in any just cause.

10. The military shall be kept under strict subordination to the civil power. No soldier shall, in time of peace, be quartered in any house without the consent of the owner, nor in time of war but in a manner to be prescribed by law.

11. The Governor, with the advice and consent of the Senate, shall choose all militia officers above the rank of Captain. The people shall elect their own officers of the rank of Captain, and under it.

12. The people have a right to assemble together in a peaceful manner, to consult for their common good, to instruct their representatives in the Legislature, and to apply to the Legislature for redress of grievances.

13. The printing presses shall be open and free to those who may wish to examine the proceedings of any branch of the government, or the conduct of any public officer; and no law shall ever restrain the right thereof.

14. The trial by jury shall remain for ever inviolate.

15. Treason against this State shall consist only in levying war against it, or adhering to its enemies, giving them aid and comfort. No person shall be convicted of treason unless on the testimony of two witnesses to the same overt act, or on confession in open court.

15A. No ex post facto law, nor any law impairing the validity of legal compacts, grants, or contracts, shall ever be made; and no conviction shall work corruption of blood or forfeiture of estate.

16. The real estate of persons dying without making a will shall not descend to the eldest son to the exclusion of his brethren, but be equally divided among the children, male and female.

17. The laws of Entail shall be forever abrogated.

17A. There shall be no lotteries in this State. Lottery tickets shall not be sold therein, whether foreign or domestic.

18. No power of suspending the operation of the laws shall be exercised except by the authority of the Legislature.

19. The people shall be secure in their persons, papers, and possessions, from all unwarrantable searches and seizures; general warrants, whereby an officer may be commanded to search suspected places, without probable evidence of the fact committed, or to seize any person or persons not named, whose offences are not particularly described, and without oath or affirmation, are dangerous to liberty, and shall not be granted.

20. Private property ought, and will ever be held inviolate, but always subservient to the public welfare, provided a compensation in money be first made to the owner. Such compensation shall never be less in amount than the actual value of the property.

21. *And Whereas* frauds have been often practiced towards the Indians within the limits of this State, it is hereby ordained, that no purchases or contracts for the sale of lands made since the —— day of —— in the year——, or which may hereafter be made with the Indians, within the limits of this State, shall be binding on the Indians and valid, unless made under the authority of the Legislature.

22. The Legislative authority of this State shall be vested in a General Assembly, which shall consist of a Senate and House of Assembly, both to be elected by the people.

23. The Legislative year shall begin on the —— day of ——, and the Legislature shall every year assemble on the second Tuesday in January, unless a different day be appointed by law.

24. The Senate shall consist of twenty-four members. The Senators shall be freeholders and be chosen for four years. The House of Assembly shall consist of seventy-two members, who shall be elected for two years.

25. The State shall be divided into six senate districts, each of which shall choose four Senators.

The first district shall consist of, &c.

The second district shall, &c.—(and so on, as a convention may decide.)

26. An enumeration of the inhabitants of the State shall be taken, under the direction of the Legislature, within one year after the first meeting of the General Assembly, and at the end of every four years thereafter; and the senate districts shall be so altered by the Legislature after the return of every convention, that each senate district shall contain, as nearly as may be, an equal number of inhabitants, and at all times consist of contiguous territory; and no county shall be divided in the formation of a senate district.

27. The Members of the House of Assembly shall be chosen by counties, and be apportioned among the several counties of the State, as nearly as may be, according to the numbers of their respective inhabitants. An apportionment of Members of Assembly shall be made by the Legislature, at its first session after the return of every enumeration.

28. In all elections of Senators and Members of the House of Assembly, the person or persons having the highest number of votes shall be elected. In cases in which two or more persons have an equal number of votes, where only one is required to be elected, there shall be a new election.

29. All elections shall be held at those places which may be considered by the electors to be the most central and convenient for them to assemble at. No county, district, or township election shall continue for a longer period than two days.

30. In order to promote the freedom, peace, and quiet of elections, and to secure, in the most ample manner possible, the independence of the poorer classes of the electors, it is declared that all elections by the people, which shall take place after the first session of the Legislature of this State, shall be by ballot, except for such town officers as may by law be directed to be otherwise chosen.

31. Electors shall in all cases, except treason, felony, or breach

of the peace, be privileged from arrest during their attendance at elections, and in going to and returning from them.

32. The next election for Governor, Senators, and Members of Assembly, shall commence on the first Monday of —— next; and all subsequent elections shall be held at such time in the month of —— or ——, as the Legislature shall by law provide.

33. The Governor, Senators, and Members of Assembly shall enter on the duties of their respective offices on the first day of —— next.

34. And as soon as the Senate shall meet, after the first election to be held in pursuance of this Constitution, they shall cause the Senators to be divided by lot, into four classes, of six in each, so that every district shall have one Senator of each class; the classes to be numbered 1, 2, 3, and 4. And the seats of the first class shall be vacated at the end of the first year; of the second class, at the end of the second year; of the third class, at the end of the third year; of the fourth class, at the end of the fourth year; in order that one Senator may be annually elected in each senate district.

35. A majority of each House shall constitute a quorum to do business, but a smaller number may adjourn from day to day and compel the attendance of absent members. Neither House shall, without the consent of the other, adjourn for more than two days.

36. Each House shall choose its Speaker, Clerk, and other officers.

37. In each House the votes shall, in all cases when taken, be taken openly, and not by ballot, so that the electors may be enabled to judge of the conduct of their representatives.

38. Each House shall keep a Journal of its proceedings, and publish the same except such parts as may require secrecy.

39. Each House may determine the rules of its own proceedings, judge of the qualifications of its members, punish its members for disorderly behavior, and with the concurrence of two-thirds expel a member, but not a second time for the same cause.

40. Any bill may originate in either House of the Legislature;

and all bills passed by one House may be amended or rejected by the other.

41. Every bill shall be read on three different days in each House—unless, in case of urgency, three-fourths of the whole members of the House where such bill is so depending shall deem it expedient to dispense with this rule; in which case the names of the majority or members present and consenting to dispense with this rule shall be entered on the Journals.

42. Every bill, which shall have passed the Senate and Assembly, shall, before it becomes a law, be presented to the Governor. If he approve, he shall sign it; but if not, he should return it with his objections to that House in which it shall have originated, which shall enter the objections on its Journal, and proceed to reconsider it. If, after such reconsideration, two-thirds of the members present shall agree to pass the bill, it shall be sent, together with the objections, to the other House, by which it shall likewise be reconsidered; and if approved by two-thirds of the members present it shall become a law. In all such cases, the votes of both Houses shall be determined by yeas and nays, and the names of the persons voting for and against the bill shall be entered on the Journals of each House respectively. If any bill shall not be returned by the Governor within ten days (Sundays excepted) after it shall have been presented to him, the same shall be a law, in like manner as if he had signed it, unless the Legislature shall, by its adjournment, prevent its return, in which case it shall not be a law.

43. No member of the Legislature, who has taken his seat as such, shall receive any civil appointment from the Governor and Senate, or from the Legislature, during the term for which he shall have been elected.

44. The assent of the Governor, and of three-fourths of the members elected to each branch of the Legislature, shall be requisite to authorize the passage of every bill appropriating the public moneys or property for local or private purposes, or for creating, continuing, altering, or renewing any body politic or

95

corporate; and the yeas and nays shall be entered on the Journals at the time of taking the vote on the final passage of any such bill.

45. The Members of the Legislature shall receive for their services a compensation to be ascertained by law and paid out of the public treasury.

46. Members of the General Assembly shall, in all cases, except treason, felony, and breach of the peace, be privileged from arrest during their continuance as such members; and for any speech or debate in either House, they shall not be questioned in any other place.

46A. No person shall be a Senator or Member of the House of Assembly who shall not have attained the age of —— years, and been —— years a citizen of the State, and who shall not, when elected, be an inhabitant of the State.

47. No Judge of any Court of Law or Equity, Secretary of State, Attorney General, Register of Deeds, Clerk of any Court of Record, Collector of Customs or Excise Revenue, Postmaster or Sheriff, shall be eligible as a candidate for, or have a seat in, the General Assembly.

48. No person who hereafter may be a collector or holder of the public moneys, shall have a seat in the General Assembly, until such person shall have accounted for and paid into the treasury all sums for which he may be accountable or liable.

49. All officers holding their offices during good behavior, or for a term of years, may be removed by joint resolution of the two Houses of the Legislature, if two-thirds of all the members elected to the Assembly, and a majority of all the members elected to the Senate, concur therein.

50. The House of Assembly shall have the sole power of impeaching, but a majority of all its members must concur in an impeachment.

51. All impeachments shall be tried by the Senate, and when sitting for that purpose, its members shall be on oath or affirmation to do justice according to law or evidence; no person shall

be convicted without the concurrence of two-thirds of all the Senators.

51. The Legislature shall have power to pass laws for the peace, welfare, and good government of this State, not inconsistent with the spirit of this Constitution—To coin money, regulate the value thereof, and provide for the punishment of those who may counterfeit the securities and coin of this State.

   I. To fix the standard of Weights and Measures.

   II. To establish a uniform rule of Naturalization.

   III. To establish uniform laws on the subject of Bankruptcies.

   IV. To regulate Commerce.

   V. To lay and collect Taxes.

   VI. To borrow money on the credit of the State, not, however, without providing at the same time the means, by additional taxation or otherwise, of paying the interest, and of liquidating the principal within twenty years.

   VII. To establish Post Offices and Post Roads.

52. Gold and Silver shall be the only lawful tender in payment of debts.

53. No new County shall be established by the General Assembly, which shall reduce the County or Counties, or either of them, from which it shall be taken, to less contents than four hundred square miles, nor shall any County be laid off of less contents.

54. There shall be no sinecure offices. Pensions shall be granted only by authority of the Legislature.

55. The whole public revenue of this State, that is, all money received from the public, shall be paid into the treasury, without any deduction whatever, and be accounted for without deduction to the Legislature, whose authority shall be necessary for the appropriation of the whole. A regular statement and account of the receipt and expenditures of all public money shall be published once a year or oftener. No fees of office shall be received in any department which are not sanctioned by Legislative authority.

56. There shall never be created within this State any incorporated trading companies, or incorporated companies with banking powers. Labor is the only means of creating wealth.

57. Bank Notes of a lesser nominal value than —— shall not be allowed to circulate as money, or in lieu thereof.

58. The Executive power shall be vested in a Governor. He shall hold his office for three years. No person shall be eligible to that office who shall not have attained the age of thirty years.

59. The Governor shall be elected by the people at the times and places of choosing Members of the Legislature. The person having the highest number of votes shall be elected; but in case two or more persons shall have an equal, and the highest number of votes, the two Houses of the Legislature shall, by joint vote, (not by ballot,) choose one of the said persons for Governor.

60. The Governor shall have power to convene the Legislature, or the Senate only, on extraordinary occasions. He shall communicate by message to the Legislature at every session, the condition of the State, and recommend such matters to them as he shall judge expedient. He shall transact all necessary business with the officers of government; expedite all such measures as may be resolved upon by the Legislature; and take care that the laws are faithfully executed. He shall, at stated times, receive a compensation for his services, which shall neither be increased nor diminished during the term for which he shall have been elected.

61. The Governor shall have power to grant reprieves and pardon, after conviction, for all offences, except in cases of impeachment. A notice of all such pardons or reprieves shall be published, at the time, in some newspaper published at the seat of government.

62. The Governor shall nominate by message, in writing, and, with the consent of the Senate, shall appoint the Secretary of State, Comptroller, Receiver General, Auditor General, Attorney General, Surveyor General, Postmaster General, and also all

Judicial Officers, except Justices of the Peace and Commissioners of the Courts of Request, or Local Courts.

63. In case of the death, impeachment, resignation, or removal of the Governor from office, the Speaker of the Senate shall perform all the duties of Governor, until another Governor shall be elected and qualified, or until the Governor so impeached shall be acquitted, as the case may be.

64. The Executive authority shall issue writs of election to fill up vacancies in the representation of any part of the Province in the General Assembly.

65. The Judicial power of the State, both as to matters of law and equity, shall be vested in a Supreme Court, the members of which shall hold office during good behavior, in District or County Courts, in Justices of the Peace, in Courts of Request, and in such other Courts as the Legislature may from time to time establish.

66. A competent number of Justices of the Peace and Commissioners of the Courts of Request shall be elected by the people, for a period of three years, within their respective cities and townships.

67. All courts shall be open, and every person for any injury done him in his lands, goods, person, or reputation, shall have remedy by the due course of law; and right and justice shall be administered without delay or denial.

68. Excessive bail shall not be required; excessive fines shall not be imposed, nor cruel and unusual punishments inflicted.

69. All persons shall be bailable by sufficient sureties, unless for capital offences, where the proof is evident or the presumption great; and the privilege of the writ of Habeas Corpus shall not be suspended by any act of the Legislature, unless, when in cases of actual rebellion or invasion, the public safety may require it.

70. In all criminal prosecutions, the accused hath a right to be heard by himself and his Counsel, to demand the nature and cause of the accusation against him, and to have a copy thereof;

to meet the witnesses face to face; to have compulsory process for obtaining witnesses in his favor; and in prosecutions by indictment or presentment a speedy public trial, by an impartial and fairly selected jury of the County, District, or Division in which the offence shall be stated to have been committed; and shall not be compelled to give evidence against himself—nor shall he be twice put in jeopardy for the same offence.

71. In prosecutions for any publication respecting the official conduct of men in a public capacity, or when the matter published is proper for public information, the truth thereof may always be given in evidence, and in all indictments for libel, the jury shall have a right to determine the law and the fact.

72. No person arrested or confined in jail shall be treated with unnecessary rigor, or be put to answer any criminal charge except by presentment, indictment, or impeachment.

73. It shall be the duty of the Legislature so to regulate the proceedings of Courts of Civil Jurisdiction, that unnecessary delays and extravagant costs in legal proceedings may not be a cause of complaint.

74. Sheriffs, Coroners, Clerks of the Peace, and Registers of Counties or Districts, shall be chosen by the electors of the respective Counties or Districts, once in four years, and as often as vacancies happen. Sheriffs shall hold no other office, and be ineligible for the office of Sheriff for the next two years after the termination of their offices.

75. The Governor and all other Civil Officers under this State, shall be liable to impeachment for any misdemeanor in office; but judgment in such cases shall not extend farther than removal from office, and disqualification to hold any office of honor, profit, or trust, under this State. The party, whether convicted or acquitted, shall nevertheless be liable to indictment, trial, judgment, and punishment according to law.

76. After this Constitution shall have gone into effect, no person shall be questioned for any thing said or done in reference to the public differences which have prevailed for some time past,

it being for the public welfare and the happiness and peace of families and individuals that no door should be left open for a continued visitation of the effects of past years of misgovernment after the causes shall have passed away.

76A. For the encouragement of emigration, the Legislature may enable aliens to hold and convey real estate, under such regulations as may be found advantageous to the people of this State.

77. The River St. Lawrence of right ought to be a free and common highway to and from the ocean; to be so used, on equal terms, by all the nations of the earth, and not monopolized to serve the interests of any one nation, to the injury of others.

78. All powers not delegated by this Constitution remain with the people.

79. Such parts of the common law, and of the acts of the Legislature of the Colony of Upper Canada, as together did form the law of the said colony on the ———— day of ———— shall be and continue the law of this State, subject to such alterations as the Legislature shall make concerning the same. But all laws, or part of laws, repugnant to this Constitution are hereby abrogated.

80. The Senators and Members of the House of Assembly, before mentioned, and all Executive and Judicial Officers within this State, shall, before entering upon the duties of their respective offices or functions be bound, by an oath or solemn affirmation, to support the Constitution; but no religious test shall ever be required as a qualification to any office or public trust under this State.

81. This Constitution, and the laws of this State, which shall be made in pursuance thereof, and all treaties, made, or which shall be made under the authority of this State, shall be the supreme law of the land, and the judges shall be bound thereby.

Several clauses for the carrying a Constitution like the above into practice are omitted, the whole being only given in illustration of, and for the benefit of a comparison in detail, with other systems.

We have not entered upon the questions, whether any, and if so, what restrictions ought to be laid upon the right of voting, or as to residence in the State, taxation, performance of militia duty, &c. These matters, however, might be advantageously discussed by the public press.

Committee Room, Nov. 13, 1837.

APPENDIX F.

THE following document was printed in handbill form, and distributed among Mackenzie's friends about ten days before the outbreak was to have taken place. Sir F. B. Head is in error in saying (*Emigrant*) that it was published in Mackenzie's newspaper ; and that the Attorney General advised His Excellency that this was the first time Mackenzie had overstepped the limits of the law. This is given as an excuse for the government not interfering sooner. The truth is, however, that this document was not printed in the newspaper at all; but secretly and anonymously, in the country ; and as to the power of interfering sooner with the preparations for revolt, there could have been no difficulty about it. As early as August Mr. Mackenzie had published in his newspaper an appeal to arms, which, along with the words "Liberty or death," had been paraded on a flag at Lloydtown.

INDEPENDENCE!

There have been Nineteen Strikes for Independence from European Tyranny, on the Continent of America. They were all successful! The Tories, therefore, by helping us will help themselves.

> The nations are fallen, and thou still art young,
> The sun is but rising when others have set ;
> And though Slavery's cloud o'er thy morning hath hung,
> The full tide of Freedom shall beam round thee yet.

BRAVE CANADIANS ! God has put into the bold and honest hearts óf our brethren in Lower Canada to revolt—not against "lawful" but against "unlawful authority." The law says we shall not be taxed without our consent by the voices of the men of our choice; but a wicked and tyrannical government has trampled upon that law, robbed the exchequer, divided the plunder, and declared, that, regardless of justice, they will continue to roll their splendid carriages, and riot in their palaces, at our expense; that we are poor, spiritless, ignorant peasants, who were born to toil for our betters. But the peasants are beginning to open their eyes and to feel their strength; too long have they been hoodwinked by Baal's priests—by hired and tampered-with preachers, wolves in sheep's clothing, who take the wages of sin, and do the work of iniquity, "each one looking to his gain in his quarter."

CANADIANS! Do you love freedom? I know you do. Do you hate oppression? Who dare deny it? Do you wish perpetual peace, and a government founded upon the eternal heaven-born principle of the Lord Jesus Christ—a government bound to enforce the law to do to each other as you wish to be done by? Then buckle on your armor, and put down the villains who oppress and enslave our country—put them down in the name of that God who goes forth with the armies of his people, and whose Bible shows that it is by the same human means whereby you put to death thieves and murderers, and imprison and banish wicked individuals, that you must put down, in the strength of the Almighty, those governments which, like these bad individuals, trample on the law, and destroy its usefulness. You give a bounty for wolves' scalps. Why? Because wolves harass you. The bounty you must pay for freedom (blessed word!) is to give the strength of your arms to put down tyranny at Toronto. One short hour will deliver our country from the oppressor; and freedom in religion, peace, and tranquillity, equal laws, and an improved country will be the prize. We contend, that in all laws made, or to be made, every person shall be bound alike—neither should any tenure, estate, charter, degree, birth, or place. confer any exemption from the ordinary course of legal proceedings and responsibilities whereunto others are subjected.

CANADIANS! God has shown that he is with our brethren, for he has given them the encouragement of success. Captains, Colonels, Volunteers, Artillerymen, Privates, the base, the vile hirelings of our unlawful oppressors, have already bit the dust in hundreds in Lower Canada; and although the Roman Catholic and Episcopal Bishops and Archdeacons are bribed by large sums of money to instruct their flocks that they should be obedient to a government which defies the law, and is therefore unlawful, and ought to be put down; yet God has opened the eyes of the people to the wickedness of these reverend sinners, so that they hold them in derision, just as God's prophet Elijah did the priests of Baal of old and their sacrifices. Is there any one afraid to go to fight for freedom, let him remember, that

> God sees with equal eye, as Lord of all,
> A hero perish, or a sparrow fall:

That the power that protected ourselves and our forefathers in the deserts of Canada—that preserved from the cholera those whom he would—that brought us safely to this continent through the dangers of the Atlantic waves—aye, and who has watched over us from infancy to manhood, will be in the midst of us in the day of our struggle for our liberties, and for governors of our free choice, who would not dare to trample on the laws they had sworn to maintain. In the present struggle, we may be sure, that if we do not rise and put down Head and his lawless myrmidons, they will gather all the rogues and villains in the country together—arm them—and then deliver our farms, our families, and our country to their brutality. To that it has come, we must put them down, or they will utterly destroy this country. If we move now, as one man, to crush the tyrant's power, to establish free institutions founded on God's law, we will prosper, for He who commands the winds and waves will be with us; but if we are cowardly and mean-spirited, a woeful and a dark day is surely before us.

CANADIANS ! The struggle will be of short duration in Lower Canada, for the people are united as one man. Out of Montreal and Quebec, they are as one hundred to one—here we Reformers are as ten to one; and if we rise with one consent to overthrow despotism, we will make quick work of it.

Mark all those who join our enemies, act as spies for them, fight for them, or aid them; these men's properties shall pay the expense of the struggle;* they are traitors to Canadian freedom, and as such we will deal with them. ✳

CANADIANS ! It is the design of the friends of liberty to give several hundred acres to every volunteer—to root up the unlawful Canada Company, and give *free deeds* to all settlers who live on their lands ; to give free gifts of the Clergy Reserve lots, to good citizens who have settled on them ; and the like to settlers on Church of England Glebe lots, so that the yeomanry may feel independent, and be able to improve the country, instead of sending the fruit of their labor to foreign lands. The fifty-seven Rectories will be at once given to the people, and all public lands used for education, internal improvements, and the public good. £100,000, drawn from us in payment of the salaries of bad men in office, will be reduced to one quarter, or much less, and the remainder will go to improve bad roads and to "make crooked paths straight;" law will be ten times more cheap and easy—the bickerings of priests will cease with the funds that keep them up —and men of wealth and property from other lands will soon raise our farms to four times their present value. We have given Head and his employers a trial of forty-five years—five years. longer than the Israelites were detained in the wilderness. The promised land is now before us—up then and take it—but set not the torch to one house in Toronto, unless we are fired at from the houses, in which case self-preservation will teach us to put down

* At the close of the Revolutionary War of the United States, the property of many of the United Empire Loyalists, who took refuge in the remaining British Colonies, had their property confiscated. There was therefore a precedent for the hard terms threatened in this manifesto.

those who would murder us when up in the defence of the laws. There are some rich men now, as there were in Christ's time, who would go with us in prosperity, but who will skulk in the rear, because of their large possessions—mark them! They are those who in after years will seek to corrupt our people, and change free institutions into an aristocracy of wealth, to grind the poor, and make laws to fetter their energies.

MARK MY WORDS, CANADIANS! The struggle is begun—it might end in freedom; but timidity, cowardice, or tampering on our part, will only delay its close. We cannot be reconciled to Britain—we have humbled ourselves to the Pharaoh of England, to the Ministers and great people, and they will neither rule us justly nor let us go; we are determined never to rest until independence is ours—the prize is a splendid one. A country larger than France or England, natural resources equal to our most boundless wishes; a government of equal laws; religion pure and undefiled; perpetual peace; education to all; millions of acres of lands for revenue; freedom from British tribute; free trade with all the world—but stop—I never could enumerate all the blessings attendant on independence!

Up then, brave Canadians! Get ready your rifles, and make short work of it; a connection with England would involve us in all her wars, undertaken for her own advantage, never for ours; with governors from England, we will have bribery at elections, corruption, villainy, and perpetual discord in every township, but independence would give us the means of enjoying many blessings. Our enemies in Toronto are in terror and dismay; they know their wickedness and dread our vengeance. Fourteen armed men were sent out at the dead hour of night, by the traitor Gurnett, to drag to a felon's cell the sons of our worthy and noble-minded brother departed, Joseph Sheppard, on a simple and frivolous charge of trespass, brought by a Tory fool; and though it ended in smoke, it showed too evidently Head's feelings. Is there to be an end of these things? Aye, and now's the day and the hour! Woe be to those who oppose us, for "In God is our trust."

APPENDIX G

Proclamation by William Lyon Mackenzie, Chairman pro. tem.
of the Provincial Government of the State of Upper Canada.

INHABITANTS OF UPPER CANADA!

FOR nearly fifty years has our country languished under the blighting influence of military despots, strangers from Europe, ruling us, not according to laws of our choice, but by the capricious dictates of their arbitrary power.

They have taxed us at their pleasure, robbed our exchequer, and carried off the proceeds to other lands—they have bribed and corrupted Ministers of the Gospel, with the wealth raised by our industry—they have, in place of religious liberty, given Rectories and Clergy Reserves to a foreign priesthood, with spiritual power dangerous to our peace as a people—they have bestowed millions of our lands on a company of Europeans for a nominal consideration, and left them to fleece and impoverish our country—they have spurned our petitions, involved us in their wars, excited feelings of national and sectional animosity in counties, townships, and neighborhoods, and ruled us, as Ireland has been ruled, to the advantage of persons in other lands, and to the prostration of our energies as a people.

We are wearied of these oppressions, and resolved to throw off the yoke. Rise, Canadians! Rise as one man, and the glorious object of our wishes is accomplished.

Our intentions have been clearly stated to the world in the Declaration of Independence, adopted at Toronto on the 31st of July last, printed in the *Constitution, Correspondent and Advocate*, and the *Liberal*, which important paper was drawn up by Dr. John Rolph and myself, signed by the Central Committee, received the sanction of a large majority of the people of the Province, west of Port Hope and Cobourg, and is well known to be in accordance with the feelings and sentiments of nine-tenths of the people of this State.

We have planted the Standard of Liberty in Canada, for the attainment of the following objects :

Perpetual Peace, founded on a government of equal rights to all, secured by a written constitution, sanctioned by yourselves in a convention to be called as early as circumstances will permit.

Civil and Religious Liberty, in its fullest extent, that in all laws made, or to be made, every person be bound alike—neither shall any tenure, estate, charter, birth, or place, confer any exemption from the ordinary course of legal proceedings and responsibilities whereunto others are subjected.

The Abolition of Hereditary Honors, of the laws of Entail and Primogeniture, and of hosts of pensioners who devour our substance.

A Legislature, composed of a Senate and Assembly chosen by the people.

An Executive, to be composed of a Governor and other officers elected by the public voice.

A Judiciary, to be chosen by the Governor and Senate, and composed of the most learned, honorable, and trustworthy, of our citizens. The laws to be rendered cheap and expeditious.

A Free Trial by Jury—Sheriffs chosen by you, and not to hold office, as now, at the pleasure of our tyrants. The freedom of the press. Alas for it, now! The free presses in the Canadas are trampled down by the hand of arbitrary power.

The Vote by Ballot—free and peaceful township elections.

The people to elect their Court of Request Commissioners and Justices of the Peace—and also their Militia Officers, in all cases whatsoever.

Freedom of Trade—every man to be allowed to buy at the cheapest market, and sell at the dearest.

No man to be compelled to give military service, unless it be his choice.

Ample funds to be reserved from the vast natural resources of our country to secure the blessings of education to every citizen.

A frugal and economical Government, in order that the people may be prosperous and free from difficulty.

An end forever to the wearisome prayers, supplications, and mockeries attendant upon our connection with the lordlings of the Colonial Office, Downing Street, London.

The opening of the St. Lawrence to the trade of the world, so that the largest ships might pass up to Lake Superior, and the distribution of the wild lands of the country to the industry, capital, skill, and enterprise of worthy men of all nations.

For the attainment of these important objects, the patriots now in arms under the Standard of Liberty, on NAVY ISLAND, U. C., have established a Provisional Government of which the members are as follows, (with two other distinguished gentlemen, whose names there are powerful reasons for withholding from public view,) viz:

WILLIAM L. MACKENZIE, *Chairman, pro. tem.*

Nelson Gorham,
Samuel Lount,
Silas Fletcher,
Jesse Lloyd,
Thomas Darling,*
Adam Graham,

John Hawk,
Jacob Rymall,
William H. Doyle,
A. G. W. G. Van Egmond,
Charles Duncombe.

We have procured the important aid of General Van Rensselaer of Albany, of Colonel Sutherland, Colonel Van Egmond, and other military men of experience; and the citizens of Buffalo, to their eternal honor be it ever remembered, have proved to us the enduring principles of the Revolution of 1776, by supplying us with provisions, money, arms, ammunition, artillery, and volunteers; and vast numbers are floating to the standard under which, heaven willing, emancipation will be speedily won for a new and gallant nation, hitherto held in Egyptian thraldom by the aristocracy of England.

* Mr. Darling refused to accept his appointment, and complained that his name had been published in the Proclamation.

BRAVE CANADIANS! Hasten to join that standard, and to make common cause with your fellow citizens now in arms in the Home, London, and Western Districts. The opportunity of the absence of the hired red coats of Europe is favorable to our emancipation. And short sighted is that man who does not now see that, although his apathy may protract the contest, it must end in *Independence*—freedom from European thraldom for ever!

Until Independence is won, trade and industry will be dormant, houses and lands will be unsaleable, merchants will be embarrassed, and farmers and mechanics harassed and troubled; that point once gained, the prospect is fair and cheering, a long day of prosperity may be ours.

The reverses in the Home District were owing, First, to accident, which revealed our design to our tyrants, and prevented a surprise; and Second, to the want of artillery. Three thousand five hundred men came and went, but we had no arms for one in twelve of them, nor could we procure them in the country.

Three hundred acres of the best of the public lands will be freely bestowed upon any volunteer, who shall assist personally in bringing to a conclusion the glorious struggle in which our youthful country is now engaged against the enemies of freedom all the world over.

Ten millions of these lands, fair and fertile, will, I trust, be speedily at our disposal, with the other vast resources of a country more extensive and rich in natural treasures than the United Kingdom or Old France.

Citizens! Soldiers of Liberty! Friends of Equal Rights! Let no man suffer in his property, person, or estate—let us pass through Canada, not to retaliate on others for our estates ravaged, our friends in dungeons, our homes burnt, our wheat and barns burnt, and our horses and cattle carried off; but let us show the praiseworthy example of protecting the houses, the homes, and the families of those who are in arms against their country and against the liberties of this continent. We will dis-claim and severely punish all aggressions upon private property, and consider those as our enemies who may burn or destroy the smallest hut in Canada, unless necessity compel any one to do so in any cause for self-defence.

Whereas, at a time when the King and Parliament of Great Britain had solemnly agreed to redress the grievances of the people, Sir Francis Bond Head was sent out to this country with promises of conciliation and justice—and *whereas*, the said Head hath violated his oath of office as a Governor, trampled upon every vestige of our rights and privileges, bribed and corrupted the local Legislature, interfered with the freedom of elections, intimidated the freeholders, declared our country not entitled to the blessings of British freedom, prostrated openly the right of trial by jury, placed in office the most obsequious, treacherous, and unworthy of our population—and sought to rule Upper Canada by the mere force of his arbitrary power; imprisoned Dr. Morrison, Mr. Parker, and many others of our most respected citizens; banishing in the most cruel manner the highly respected Speaker of our late House of Assembly, the Honorable Mr. Bidwell, and causing the expatriation of that universally beloved and well tried eminent patriot, Dr. John Rolph, because they had made common cause with our injured people, and setting a vast price on the heads of several, as if they were guilty persons—for which crimes and misdemeanors he is deserving of being put upon his trial before the country—I do therefore hereby offer a reward of £500 for his apprehension, so that he may be dealt with as may appertain to justice.

In Lower Canada, divine providence has blessed the arms of the Sons of Liberty—a whole people are there manfully struggling for that freedom without which property is but a phantom, and life scarce worth having a gift of. General Girard is at the head of fifteen thousand determined democrats.

The friends of freedom in Upper Canada have continued to act in strong and regular concert with Mr. Papineau and the Lower Canada Patriots—and it is a pleasing reflection that be-

tween us and the ocean a population of six hundred thousand
souls are now in arms, resolved to be free.

The tidings that worthy patriots are in arms is spreading
through the Union, and the men who were oppressed in England,
Ireland, Scotland, and the continent, are flocking to our standard.

We must be successful!

I had the honor to address nearly three thousand of the citizens of Buffalo, two days ago, in the theatre. The friendship
and sympathy they expressed is honorable to the great and flourishing Republic.

I am personally authorized to make known to you that from
the moment that Sir Francis Bond Head declined to state in
writing the objects he had in view, in sending a flag of truce to
our camp in Toronto, the message once declined, our esteemed
fellow citizen, Dr. John Rolph, openly announced his concurrence
in our measures, and now decidedly approves of the stand we are
taking in behalf of our beloved country, which will never more
be his until it be free and independent.

CANADIANS! My confidence in you is as strong and powerful,
in this our day of trial and difficulty, as when, many years ago,
in the zeal and ardor of youth, I appeared among you, the humble advocate of your rights and liberties. I need not remind
you of the sufferings and persecutions I have endured for your
sakes—the losses I have sustained—the risks I have run. Had
I ten lives I would cheerfully give them up to procure freedom
to the country of my children, of my early and disinterested
choice. Let us act together; and warmed by the hope of success in a patriotic course, be able to repeat in the language so
often happily quoted by Ireland's champion,

> The nations are fallen and thou still art young,
>   Thy sun is but rising when others have set;
> And though Slavery's cloud o'er thy morning hath hung,
>   The full tide of Freedom shall beam round thee yet.

Militia men of 1812! Will ye again rally round the standard
of our tyrants! I can scarce believe it possible. Upper Canada

Loyalists, what has been the recompense of your long tried and devoted attachment to England's Aristocracy? Obloquy and contempt.

Verily we have learnt in the school of experience, and are prepared to profit by the lessons of the past. Compare the great and flourishing nation of the United States with our divided and distracted land, and think what we also might have been, as brave, independent lords of the soil. Leave then Sir Francis Bond Head's defence to the miserable serfs dependent on his bounty, and to the last hour of your lives the proud remembrance will be yours—"We also were among the deliverers of our country."

Navy Island, December 13, 1837.

APPENDIX H.

THE following is Mr. John Montgomery's account of the escape of himself and several other political prisoners from Fort Henry, Kingston, C. W., to Watertown, State of New York:

"We were taken from town to Fort Henry in the Sir Robert Peel, in charge of Sheriff Jarvis and a guard of negroes. Seven of us were allowed to occupy the cabin, the rest were placed on deck under guard. Several of us proposed to seize the vessel, and Anderson and myself, being chained together, were deputed to go on deck and watch the signal when we were to seize the man at the helm. We watched until in sight of the harbor, when, no signal being given, we went below, and found that the idea had been abandoned. On landing, we were immediately sent to Fort Henry, where our irons were knocked off. Next morning Dr. Shellen, Mr. Hodge, and the American prisoners, were marched off to Quebec. Having managed to secrete my money, to the amount of $75 in bills, and my watch, in my boots, we were enabled to make up a purse of $30 for those about to leave us, as otherwise they would have been destitute.

"We had been but a small time in the fort, when, through information given by a person kindly affected towards me, we learned that there was a possibility of our being enabled to effect our escape. This information we did not at first pay much attention to; but after Lord Durham had, on his arrival from Quebec, twice visited the fort, each time refusing our prayer for an interview, and when we had been told that any complaint should be in the form of a petition, we sent one down to Quebec and received for answer a simple acknowledgment of its receipt, by Lord Durham, accompanied with an assurance that it would be forwarded to Sir George Arthur, in whom Lord Durham had the greatest confidence. We felt that it was useless to look for mercy, and that we might at least make a venture. Accordingly we organized a committee to investigate into the correctness of the information received, and, hearing the former account substantiated, we began to make our arrangements.

"We had learned that a portion of the wall in our room, although four and a half feet thick, had been completed only a short time, and the mortar was not yet dry. Behind this wall was an oak door, leading to a subterranean passage which opened into a gun room; and as the shutters which covered the port holes hung on chains, we could easily let ourselves down by means of ropes made of our sheets into the sally port of a depth of ten feet; and by the same means were enabled to get on level ground. Our sole implements of labor consisted of a piece of iron ten inches in length, and a disk nail. Having obtained half a cord of wood, we piled it up in the middle of the floor, as if for the purpose of airing our bed clothes, but in reality to hide the stone and mortar which we took from the hole. The jailer, mistrusting, caused the wood all to be pulled down; but finding nothing he allowed us to rearrange it. We had prayers daily by Mr. Parker previous to our airing in the yard of the fort. We, at length, went boldly to work; the unusual noise at first attracted the attention of the sentry, who came up to the window where I was reading the Bible, and asked the cause of it. I answered by pointing to two men who, apparently for their amusement, but in reality to deaden the strokes on the wall, were, with shovel and tongs, beating the stove with all their might, and eliciting thereby roars of laughter from their companions; while I earnestly requested them to stop such trifling, and think of their apparently serious position. We were not again interrupted. We commenced on Tuesday and it was Sunday ere we had made a hole sufficiently large to enable us to get through. As the keeper had been married the Thursday before, we begged him to take his wife to church, and allow us to refrain from our usual airing. This he was very glad to do. We then requested fourteen or fifteen pounds of biscuit, as we did not like the meat, and they kept better than bread; he sent four and a half pounds, all they had at the canteen. We had hung up blankets, by permission of the keeper, to keep out the musquitoes, and were thus enabled to complete our preparations without interruption.

"When the guard beat the evening tattoo and descended from the ramparts, we commenced our escape. We reached the sally port in safety; but here I had the misfortune to fall into the pit and break my leg. One of my companions descended and took my hand, and we were pulled up by the rest. We had decided to be called by numbers, and when we had succeeded in scaling the wall, which we did during a fearful storm, we found No. 10, J. G. Parker, missing. Thinking he had fallen into the pit, Brophy and Morden volunteered to put over the scaling ladder and search the sally port, which they did, but in vain. In fact, Parker had deserted us; and we afterwards learned that he had been retaken on Monday, and sent to England. This was a serious defection. Parker was the only man amongst us who knew anything of Kingston, and to his knowledge we had trusted for guidance after leaving the fort. It was a fearful night of storm and lightning, but we decided to take down towards the river, and when daylight came to take to the woods. We had resolved to divide into parties for greater safety. We therefore divided our biscuits equally among fourteen men, Brophy, Mor-

den, Chase, and myself decided to make for Cape Vincent,
agreeing to meet the others at Watertown, should we not be
retaken.

"We traveled a considerable distance on Monday, and in the
evening tried to get a boat. My leg having become greatly inflamed, and as I found it impossible to proceed, it was decided
that we should rest in the woods and try, by application of cold
water, to reduce the inflammation. This was done; we remained
for some time; at length, having got a boat, I was helped down
to it, and about midnight we started in the direction of Kingston,
and then crossed to Long Island, in order to escape a government vessel sent in search of us.

"We landed on Long Island, and pulled our boat up into the
woods, but finding ourselves near people known to be unfriendly,
we decided to cross the island and ascertain our chances of escape
from the other side. We were obliged to carry our boat; which
was very difficult to do with my broken leg, but I carried paddles
and other articles. With great pain, and in a state of exhaus-
tion, we at length succeeded in launching our boat and proceeded
to what we felt sure was the mainland. On arriving here we
knelt down and thanked God for our safety, and earnestly prayed
for that of our companions.

"We soon found, however, that we were again on an island.
Re-entering our boat almost famished, our slender provisions,
two biscuits a day since leaving the fort, exhausted, we started
for Vincent, but were obliged to put ashore, being unable to
manage the boat. We pulled her up and went to a house near
the shore, and there learned that we were on American ground.
We asked a woman whom we saw there to get us a carriage to
take us to Cape Vincent; but she refused, and sent to the field
for her husband, who consented for $1.50 to take us in the boat.
We asked him if he had heard of the escape from the fort; he
said 'Yes, that day at noon,' adding, 'I wish I knew where the
poor fellows are, I would tell Bill Johnson and have them safe off
before I sleep.' When we told who we were, he earnestly re-

quested us to take the money back; and on landing threw up his hat and gave three cheers for the Patriots.

"A crowd was soon collected, and I was relieved from the necessity of walking. Great sympathy and attention were shown us. A public dinner, largely attended, was given in our honor. On our arrival at Watertown, we were met by Anderson and his party, and at length all joined us, save Watson and Parker, who were retaken and put in heavy irons.

"Being demanded by the British authorities, we were secreted until the opinion of the Governor of New York could be known. He decided that we should not be given up. While still suffering severely from the pain of my leg, I, a short time after arriving in Rochester, was knocked down by a large team and my skull fractured. I was for weeks unconscious, and it was a long time ere I recovered my usual health."

APPENDIX I.

THE following are the names and persons arrested in Upper Canada, and placed in confinement in the prisons of Toronto, and other places in the Province, on a charge of insurrection or treason; the dates of their arrest and discharge; and, if tried, whether by court-martial or civil courts, with the result of such trials severally, from the 5th December, 1837, to the 1st November, 1838. At that time twenty-seven were still in custody.

EASTERN, OTTAWA, AND BATHURST DISTRICTS.—No prisoners confined in the above districts on a charge of insurrection or treason.

JOHNSTOWN DISTRICT:

Thos. Wilson, Methodist preacher, Dec. 13, 1837, Dec. 15, 1837, n. t., dis. by m.*

* EXPLANATIONS AND ABBREVIATIONS.—The first of the two data given indicates, in each case, the time of arrest; the second the time of discharge. Abbreviations—Dis by m, for discharged by magistrates; n. e, no evidence; n. t, for not tried; lib. on b. by Q C, for liberated on bail by Queen's Counsel; ad. to b. by A. G., admitted to bail by Attorney General; Lieut. Gov., for Lieutenant Governor; dis. by com. after ex., discharged by commission after examination; p. on s. pardoned on giving security to keep the peace; ban., banished from the Province; pet., for petitioned under 1 Vic. c. 10; dis. on s. for g. b., discharged on security for good behavior.

Wm. H. Sherman, shoemaker, Dec. 18, 1837, Feb. 16, 1838, n. t., dis. by m.
Wellesley Pike, yeoman, Dec. 18, 1837, Dec. 18, 1837, n. t., dis. by m., n. e.
Charles Swift, saddler, Dec. 27, 1837, Jan. 23, 1838, n. t., dis. by magistrate.
George R. Brian, baker, Jan. 2, 1838, Jan. 2, 1838, n. t., discharged by mag.
John Thomas, yeoman, Feb. 6, 1838, Feb. 10, 1838, n. t., dis. by mag., n. e.
James Malone, tailor, July 25, 1838, July 26, 1838. n. t., dis. by m., no ev.
William Parrot, laborer, Aug. 3, 1838, Aug. 3, 1838, n. t., dis. by mag., n. e.

PRINCE EDWARD DISTRICT.—No prisoner confined in this district on a
charge of insurrection or treason.

MIDLAND DISTRICT:

George R. Huffman, tanner, Dec. 12, 1837, Jan. 4, 1838, n. t., lib. on b. by Q. C.
Francis M. Weafer, teacher, Dec. 12, 1837, Jan. 10, 1838, n. t., lib. on b. by Q. C.
Augustus Thibodo, yeoman, Dec. 12, 1837, Dec. 13, 1837, n. t., dis. by mag.
John Burley, gentleman, Dec. 12, 1837, Dec. 13, 1837, n. t., dis. by magistrate.
William Cunningham, artist, Dec. 14, 1837, Dec. 16, 1837, n. t., dis. by mag.
Reuben White, yeoman, Dec. 17, 1837, Jan. 2, 1838, n. t., ad. to bail by At. G.
Joseph Canniff, miller, Dec. 17, 1837, Jan. 2, 1838, n. t., ad. to bail by A. G.
Joseph Lockwood, yeoman, Dec. 17, 1837, Jan. 2, 1838, n. t., ad. to b. by A. G.
Norr. H. Herns, yeoman, Dec. 17, 1837, Jan. 2, 1838, n. t., ad. to b. by A. G.
Joseph P. Cavalar, yeoman, Dec. 17, 1837, Jan. 2, 1838, n. t., ad. to b. by A. G.
Gideon Turner, township clerk, Dec. 17, 1837, Jan 2, 1838, n. t., ad. to b. by A.G.
Peter Davidson, yeoman, Dec. 17, 1837, Jan. 2, 1838, n. t., ad. to b. by A. G.
C. H. McCollum, merchant, Dec. 17, 1837, Dec. 20, 1837, n. t., lib. by L. Gov.
Thomas Anderson, yeoman, Dec. 19, 1837, May 2, 1838, n. t. ind. but bill ig.
Oliver Robinson, yeoman, Dec. 19, 1837, May 20, 1828, n. t., ind. but bill ig.
Richard Tucker, yeoman, Dec. 19, 1837, May 20, 1838, n. t., ind. but bill ig.
Anson M. Day, yeoman, Dec. 19, 1837, July 7, 1838, oyer and ter., acquitted.
Anson Hayden, doctor, Dec. 19, 1837, Jan. 2, 1838, n. t., ad. to bail by A. G.
Cornelius Parks, innkeeper, Dec. 19, 1837, Jan. 2, 1838, n. t., ad. to b. by A. G.
John Jacobs, shoemaker, Dec. 20, 1837, Jan. 29, 1888, n. t., ad. to b. by A. G.
James O. Hare, yeoman, Dec. 22, 1837, Jan. 5, 1838, n. t., ad. to b. by A. G.
James McCann, teacher, Dec. 22, 1837, Jan. 12, 1838, n. t., ad. to b. by A. G.
Hiram Banazar, yeoman, Dec. 20, 1837, Jan. 5, 1838, n. t., ad. to b. by A. G.
Nel. C. Reynolds, merchant, Dec. 26, 1837, July 6, 1838, oy. and ter., acquitted.
John Belby, butcher, Dec. 26, 1837, Jan. 2, 1838, n. t., dis. upon sec. for g. b.
John B. Wheeler, yeoman, Dec. 31, 1837, Jan. 12, 1838, n. t., dis. upon s. for g. b.
Charles N. Phillips, shoemaker, Jan. 1, 1838, Feb. 9, 1838, n. t., dis. up. s. g. b.
Thomas Mullins, yeoman, Jan. 2, 1838, Jan. 5, 1838, n. t., dis. upon s. for g. b.
Sam'l. Parkeymore, yeoman, Jan. 5, 1838, Jan. 9, 1838, n. t., dis. upon s. for g. b.
Christ. Lafontaine, yeoman, Feb. 22, 1838, July 8, 1838, oy. and ter., acquitted.
Samuel Marsh, yeoman, Feb. 22, 1838, July 8, 1838, oyer and ter., acquitted.
Asa Lewis, yeoman, Feb. 22, 1838, July 8, 1838, oyer and terminer acquitted.

Peter Orr, yeoman, Feb. 22, 1838, July 8, 1838, oyer and terminer, acquitted.
Charles Marsh, yeoman, Feb. 22, 1838, July 8, 1838, oyer and ter., acquitted.
Wm. A. Forward, attorney, Feb. 22, 1833, March 13, 1838, n.t., ad. to b. by Q.C.
Hiram Mott, yeoman, Feb. 23, 1838, May 11, 1838, n. t., ind., but b. ignored.
Stephen Mott, yeoman, Feb. 23, 1838, May 11, 1838, n. t., indicted, but bill ig.
Wm. Anderson, yeoman, Feb. 28, 1838, March 29, 1838, n. t., ind., but b. ig.
Abram Collard, yeoman, Feb. 28, 1838, April 22, 1838, n. t., admitted to bail.
Samuel Babcock, yeoman, Feb. 28, 1838, March 26, 1838, n. t., ad. to bail.
Robert Bird, miller, Feb. 27, 1838, March 8, 1838, n. t., dis. by m. on giv. b.
Peter Robertson, merchant, Feb. 27, 1838, May 16, 1838, n. t., bill ig. by g. j.
Joshua Smith, merchant, Feb. 27, 1838, May 9, 1838, n. t., bill ig. by g. jury.
Robert Robertson, merchant, Feb. 27, 1838, May 16, 1838, n. t., bill ig. by g j.
Amos Proctor, yeoman, Feb. 27, 1838, May 16, 1838, n. t., bill ig. by grand j.
Blecker W. Myers, yeoman, Feb. 27, 1838, May 16, 1838, n. t., bill ig. by g. j.
Peter Lott, yeoman, Feb. 27, 1838, May 16, 1888, n. t., bill ig. by g. jury.
John W. Stickles, yeoman, Feb. 27, 1838, May 16, 1888, n. t., bill ig. by g. j.
Nicholas O. Cave, yeoman, Feb. 27, 1838, May 16, 1838, n. t., bill ig. by g. j.
James Getty, yeoman, Feb. 27, 1838, May 16, 1838, n. t., bill ig. by g. jury.
Ivy R. Roblin, yeoman, Feb. 27, 1838, May 16, 1838, n. t., bill ig. by g. jury.
Samuel Stephen, yeoman, Feb. 27, 1838, March 23, 1838, n. t., ad. to bail.
Elijah Ockerman, yeoman, Feb. 27, 1838, May 13, 1838, n. t., bill ig. by g. j.
Edward Hickey, yeoman, Feb. 27, 1838, May 13, 1838, n. t., bill ig. by g. jury.
Tobias Myers, yeoman, Feb. 27, 1838, July 8, 1838, n. t., a true bill found, but
    counsel declined prosecuting, as others charged with same crime had been acq.
John C. Pennock, cooper, Feb. 27, 1838, May 14, 1838, n. t., bill ig. by g. j.
John Pockard, yeoman, Feb. 29, 1838, Aug. 16, 1838, n. t., lib. by Lieut G.
George Holsenburgh, yeoman, Feb. 29, 1838, Aug. 16, 1838, n. t., lib. by L. G.
John Martin, yeoman, Feb. 29, 1838, Aug. 16, 1838, n. t., lib. by Lieut. Gov.
Ebenezer B. Stores, yeoman, Feb. 29, 1838, Aug. 16, 1838, n. t., lib. by L. G.
John Herman, yeoman, Feb. 29, 1838, Aug. 16, 1838, n. t., lib. by Lieut. G.
Daniel Davidson, yeoman, March 2, 1838, May 12, 1838, n. t., bill ig. by g. j.
Nelson Long, carpenter, March 2, 1838, May 12, 1838, n. t., bill ig. by g. j.
Jacob Lott, yeoman, March 2, 1838, May 16, 1838, n. t., bill ig. by g. jury.
William Leslie, merchant, March 2, 1838, May 14, 1838, n. t., dis. by mag.
James L. Chatsey, yeoman, March 3, 1838, March 7, 1838, n. t., dis. by mag.
Absalom Day, yeoman, March 3, 1838, April 22, 1838, n. t., charged with aid-
    ing the escape of a traitor. Case not proceeded with, the principal being acq.
Christopher Greniser, yeoman, March 3, 1838, April 2, 1838, n. t., ditto. ditto.
Harvey Stratton, yeoman, March 3, 1838, April 18, 1838, n. t., ad. to bail.
James Ketchipaw, yeoman, March 3, 1838, March 7, 1838, n. t., ad. to bail.
Vanranslaer Robins, laborer, March 12, 1838, March 13, 1838, n. t., dis. by m.
Philo Smith, laborer, March 14, 1838, May 15, 1838, n. t., bill ig. by g. jury.
Samuel Star, shoemaker, March 14, 1838, May 11, 1838, n. t., bill ig. by g. jury

Benjamin Proctor, tinsmith, April 24, 1838, May 12, 1838, n. t., bill ig. by g. j.
Pierre Lassage, carter, May 9, 1838, July 7, 1838, n. t., true bill found. Case
not proceeded with, the witnesses having absconded.

NEWCASTLE DISTRICT:

William Purdy, miller, Dec. 13, 1837, Jan. 8, 1838, n. t., dis. by magistrates.
William Richardson, farmer, Dec. 16, 1837, Jan. 3, 1838, n. t., dis. by mag.
Joseph Pearson, farmer, Dec. 16, 1837, Jan. 3, 1838, n. t., dis. by magistrates.
Jacob Kellar, laborer, Dec. 31, 1837, Feb. 17, 1838, n. t., dis. by magistrates.
John Davis, laborer, Jan. 27, 1838, Feb. 22, 1838, n. t., dis. by magistrates.
S. V. Wicklin, blacksmith, Feb. 6, 1838, March 19, 1838, n. t., dis. by mag.
Francis Ferguson, laborer, Feb. 24, 1838, March 10, 1838, n. t., dis. by mag.
Peter Nix, farmer, Jan. 11, 1838, April 16, 1838, n. t., dis. at the assizes.
Charles Powers, iron founder, Dec., 1817, n. t., arrested on suspicion of sedi-
tious practices, but discharged by the magistrates, without imprisonment.
John Gilchrist, physician, Dec., 1837, n. t.   ditto.   ditto.   ditto.
Munro Merriman, laborer, Dec., 1837, n. t.   ditto.   ditto.   ditto.
Robert Waller, merchant, Dec., 1837, n. t.   ditto.   ditto.   ditto.

HOME DISTRICT:

James Foster, laborer, Dec. 4, 1837, Dec. 23, 1837, n. t., dis. by com. after ex.
Jay Cody, farmer, Dec. 4, 1837, Oct., 1838, pet. under 1 Vict. c. 10, pardoned,
on giving security to keep the peace, and be of good behavior for three years.
Daniel Winstow, laborer, Dec. 6, 1837, Dec. 11, 1837, n. t., dis. by com. after ex.
Louis Brine, laborer, Dec. 6, 1837, Dec. 21, 1837, n. t., dis. by com. after ex.
James Raggat, laborer, Dec. 6, 1837, Dec. 11, 1837, n. t., dis. by com. after ex.
Patrick Casey, laborer, Dec. 7, 1837, Dec. 11, 1837, n. t., dis. by com. after ex.
H. Carlton, laborer, Dec. 7, 1837, Dec. 21, 1837, n. t., dis. by com. after ex.
Arthur Laidlaw, laborer, Dec. 7, 1837, Dec. 9, 1837, n. t., dis. by com. after ex.
J. McGilles, laborer, Dec. 6, 1837, Dec. 21, 1837, n. t., dis. by com. after ex.
W. Young, laborer, Dec. 7, 1838, Dec. 9, 1837, n. t., dis. by com. after ex.
John Anderson, innkeeper, Dec. 11, 1857, special oy. and ter., guilty, sentenced
to death; commuted to transportation. Escaped from Fort Henry, Kingston.
Ira Anderson, innkeeper, Dec. 11, 1837.   ditto.   ditto.   ditto.
James Smith, laborer, Dec. 6, 1837, Dec. 21, 1837, n. t., dis. by com. after ex.
Peter Deguire, laborer, Dec. 7, 1837, Dec. 21, 1837, n. t., dis. by com. after ex.
Cornelius Duncan, laborer, Dec. 7, 1837, Dec. 21, 1837, n. t., dis. by com. af. ex.
Wm. Kendrick, laborer, Dec. 7, 1837, Dec. 21, 1837, n. t., dis. by com. after. ex.
George Ireland, laborer, Dec. 7, 1837, Dec. 19, 1837, n. t., dis. by com. after ex.
Joseph Horne, laborer, Dec. 7, 1837, Dec. 17, 1837, n. t., dis. by com. after ex.
Maurice Fitzgerald, laborer, Dec. 7, 1837, Dec. 9, 1837, n. t., dis. by com. af. ex.
George Carrol, laborer, Dec. 6, 1837, Dec. 21, 1837, n. t., dis. by com. after ex.
Samuel Carpenter, laborer, Dec. 7, 1837, Dec. 21, 1837, n. t., dis. by com. af. ex.

X Thomas Burrill, laborer, Dec. 5, 1837, December 8, 1837, n. t., dis. com. af. ex.

X Thomas Rerdon, tinsmith, Dec. 5, 1837, Dec. 9, 1837, n. t., dis. by com. af. ex.

x John Kennedy, laborer, Dec. 7, 1837, Dec. 9, 1837, n. t., dis. by com. after ex.

x John Kennedy (2), carpenter, Dec. 8, 1837, Dec. 9, 1837, n. t., dis. by com. af. ex.

X Pat. McChrystal, laborer, Dec. 8, 1837, Dec. 11, 1837, n. t., dis. by com. af. ex.

X W. T. Kennedy, clerk, Dec. 6, 1837, Dec. 21, 1837, n. t., dis. by com. after ex.

X W. Milney, yeoman, Dec. 4, 1837, Dec. 19, 1837, n. t., dis. by com. after ex.

X F. Wardrope, yeoman, Dec. 4, 1837, Dec. 9, 1837, n. t., dis. by com. after ex.

X George Farley, yeoman, Dec. 4, 1837, Dec. 9, 1837, n. t., dis. by com. after ex.

X Henry Hall, yeoman, Dec. 4, 1837, Dec. 13, 1837, n. t., dis. by com. after ex.

X John Dunn, laborer, Dec. 7, 1837, Dec. 19, 1837, n. t., dis. by com after ex.

X William Pearson, yeoman, Dec. 7, 1837, Dec. 21, 1837, n. t., dis. by com. af. ex.

X Andrew Dragoon, laborer, Dec. 7, 1837, Dec. 21, 1837, n. t. dis. by com. af. ex.

X Fred. Anderson, laborer, Dec. 7, 1837, Dec. 19, 1837, n. t., dis. by com. after ex.

X James Bergin, laborer, Dec. 7, 1837, Dec. 15, 1837, n. t., dis. by com. after ex.

Henry Cowen, blacksmith, Dec. 7, 1837, Dec. 21, 1837, n. t., dis. by com. af. ex.

X Cristin Ninny, laborer, Dec. 7, 1837, Dec. 23, 1837, n. t., dis. by com. after ex.

A Wm. Alderney, laborer, Dec. 7, 1837, Dec. 9, 1837, n. t., dis. by com. after ex.

Francis Lyons, laborer, Dec. 7, 1837, Dec. 9, 1837, n. t., dis. by com. after ex.

X Daniel Gamble, laborer, Dec. 8, 1837, Dec. 23, 1837, n. t., dis. by com. after ex.

Wm. Robertson, laborer, Dec. 8, 1837, Dec. 21, 1837, n. t., dis. by com. af. ex.

X Robert Stibbert, laborer, Dec. 8, 1837, April 10, 1838, special oy. and ter., acq.

X James Johnson, laborer, Dec. 9, 1837, Dec. 21, 1837, n. t., dis. by com. af. ex.

· Gordon Burgess, laborer, Dec. 9, 1837, Dec. 17, 1837, n. t., dis. by com. af. ex.

John Burgess, laborer Dec. 9, 1837, Dec. 17, 1837, n. t., dis. by com. after ex.

· John Pearson, laborer, Dec. 9, 1837, Dec. 11, 1837, n. t., dis. by com. after ex.

Jas. Hutchinson, laborer, Dec. 9, 1837, Dec. 26, 1837, n. t., dis. by com. after ex.

Richard Taylor, laborer, Dec. 9, 1837, Dec. 26, 1837, n. t., dis. by com. after ex.

Robert Baillie, laborer, Dec. 9, 1837, Dec. 23, 1837, n. t., dis. by com. after ex.

Seymour H. W. Stogdill, laborer, Dec. 9, 1837, Oct., 1838, pet. under 1 Vict.
    c. 10, pardoned, on giv. security to keep the peace and be of g. b. for 3 years.

Col. Van Egmond, yeoman, Dec. 7, 1837, Dec. 30, 1837, n. t., died in hospital.

X James Hunter, physician, Dec. 10, 1837, Dec. 21, 1837, n. t., dis. by com. af. ex.

Wm. Watson, laborer, Dec. 10, 1837, Dec. 21, 1837, n. t., dis. by com. af. ex.

Leonard Watson, laborer, Dec. 10, 1837, petitioned under 1 Vict. c. 10, trans-
    portation to Van Diemen's Land for life.

Eli Bateman, laborer, Dec. 10, 1837, Dec. 19, 1837, n. t., dis. by com. after ex.

Joseph Sheppard, yeoman, Dec. 11, 1837, May 12, 1838, pet. under 1 Vic. c. 10,
    pardoned, on giving security to keep the peace, and be of good b. for 3 years.

Jacob Sheppard, yeoman, Dec. 11, 1837, May 12, 1838, ditto. ditto. ditto.

A John Brown, yeoman, Dec. 10, 1837, Dec. 11, 1837, n. t., dis. by com. after ex.

X James Latimer, printer, Dec. 11, 1837, Dec. 14, 1837, n. t., dis. by com. af. ex.

Wm. Alves, laborer, Dec. 11, 1837, pet. under 1 Vict. c. 10, trans. for 14 years.

✗ Edward Hilton, laborer, Dec 11, 1837, Dec. 23, 1837, n. t., dis. by com. af. ex.

George Nelson, laborer, Dec. 11, 1837, Dec. 14, 1837, n. t., dis. by com. af. ex.

John Montgomery, innkeeper, Dec. 11, 1837, spe. oy. and ter., guilty, sentenced
to death; commuted to transportation. Escaped from Fort Henry, Kingston.

✗ Henry Brock, laborer, Dec. 11, 1837, Dec. 21, 1837, n. t., dis. by com. after ex.

✗ Edward Brock, laborer, Dec. 11, 1837, Dec. 21, 1837, n. t., dis. by com. af. ex.

— ✗ Robert Brock, laborer, Dec. 11, 1837, July 13, 1838, pet. under 1 Vict. c. 10,
pardoned, on giving security to keep the peace, and be of good b. for 3 years.

✗ Michael Vincent, laborer, Dec. 11, 1837, Dec. 19, 1837, n. t., dis. by com. af. ex.

✓ John Whiting, laborer, Dec. 11, 1837, Dec. 20, 1837, n. t., dis. by com. af. ex.

✗ William Clay, laborer, Dec. 11, 1837, Dec. 30, 1837, n. t., dis. by com. af. ex.

✗ James Egar, laborer, Dec. 11, 1837, Dec. 17, 1837, n. t., dis. by com. after ex.

✗ Robt. Middleton, laborer, Dec. 11, 1837, Dec. 26, 1837, n. t., dis. by com. af. ex.

✗ Wm. Ballard, laborer, Dec. 11, 1837, Dec. 27, 1837, n. t., dis. by com. af. ex.

✗ Samuel Read, laborer, Dec. 11, 1837, Dec. 17, 1837, n. t., dis. by com. af. ex.

✗ John Russel, laborer, Dec. 11, 1837, Dec. 17, 1837, n. t., dis. by com. after ex.

✗ Wm. M. Plasted, laborer, Dec. 11, 1837, Dec. 13, 1837, n. t., dis. by com. af. ex.

Godlip Eickart, yeoman, Dec. 11, 1837, May 12, 1837, pet. under 1 Vict. c. 10,
pardoned, on giving security to keep the peace, and be of good b. for 3 years.

✗ Gregory Innis, laborer, Dec. 11, 1837, Dec. 26, 1837, n. t., dis. by com. af. ex.

✗ George Eickart, laborer, Dec. 11, 1837, Dec. 21, 1837, n. t., dis. by com. af. ex.

✗ George Chewett, laborer, Dec. 11, 1837, Dec. 23, 1837, n. t., dis. by com. af. ex.

John Steeple, laborer, Dec. 11, 1837, Dec. 26, 1837, n. t., dis. by com. after ex.

Wm. Jackson, laborer, Dec. 11, 1837, Dec. 21, 1837, n. t., dis. by com. af. ex.

Andrew Eickart, laborer, Dec. 11, 1837, Dec. 21, 1837, n. t., dis. by com. af. ex.

David Cash, laborer, Dec. 11, 1837, Dec. 20, 1837, n. t., dis. by com. after ex.

Robert Stiver, laborer, Dec. 11, 1838, Dec. 14, 1837, n. t., dis. by com af. ex.

Daniel Hibner, laborer, Dec. 11, 1837, Dec. 21, 1837, n. t., dis. by com. af. ex.

Daniel Sheppard, laborer, Dec. 11, 1837, Dec. 31, 1837, n. t., dis. by com. af. ex. —

✗ Fred. Eickart, laborer, Dec. 11, 1837, Dec. 21, 1837, n. t., dis. by com. af. ex.

William Pool, laborer, Dec. 11, 1837, July 13, 1838, pet. under 1 Vict. c. 10,
pardoned, on giving security to keep the peace, and be of good b. for 3 years.

John Brett, laborer, Dec. 11, 1837, Dec. 21, 1837, n. t., dis. by com. after ex.

. Francis Way, laborer, Dec. 11, 1837, Dec. 19, 1837, n. t., dis. by com. after ex.

Peter Storey, laborer, Dec. 11, 1837, Dec. 19, 1837, n. t., dis. by com. after ex.

John McMillan, laborer, Dec. 11, 1837, Dec. 26, 1837, n. t., dis. by com. af. ex.

Henry Earl, laborer, Dec. 11, 1837, Dec. 26, 1837, n. t., dis. by com. after ex.

Edward Snider, laborer, Dec. 11, 1837, Dec. 15, 1837, n. t., dis. by com. af. ex.

Henry Shaver, laborer, Dec. 11, 1837, Dec. 15, 1837, n. t., dis. by com. af. ex.

Eman. Tomlinson, laborer, Dec. 11, 1837, Dec. 23, 1837, n. t., dis. by com. af. ex.

Wm. Rogers, laborer, Dec. 11, 1837, Dec. 23, 1837, n. t., dis. by com. after ex.

Samuel Brock, laborer, Dec. 11, 1837, Dec. 23, 1837, n. t., dis. by com. af. ex.

✓ Philip Bussom, laborer, Dec. 12, 1837, Dec. 23, 1837, n. t., dis. by com. af. ex.

George Garbut, laborer, Dec. 12, 1837, Dec. 21, 1837, n. t., dis. by com. af. ex.

John Brammer, laborer, Dec. 12, 1837, May 12, 1838, pet. under 1 Vict. c. 10, pardoned, on giving security to keep the peace, and be of good b. for 3 years.

Philo Belfry, yeoman, Dec. 12, 1837, May 11, 1838, ditto ditto ditto.

Alex. Read, yeoman, Dec. 12, 1837, Jan. 11, 1838, ditto ditto ditto.

Wm. Nelson, yeoman, Dec. 12, 1837, July 13, 1838, ditto ditto ditto.

John Cuyler, laborer, Dec. 12, 1837, March 23, 1838, n. t., escaped from hospital.

Joshua Stevens, laborer, Dec. 12, 1837, Dec. 23, 1837, n. t., dis. by com. af. ex.

W. R. Lount, laborer, Dec. 12, 1837, Dec. 21, 1837, n. t., dis. by com. after ex.

Philip Wideman, yeoman, Dec. 12, 1837, May 10, 1838, pet. under 1 Vict. c. 10, pardoned on giving security to keep the peace, and be of good b. for 3 years.

Charles Burling, yeoman, Dec. 12, 1837, Dec. 23, 1837, n. t., dis. by com. af. ex.

Richard Watson, yeoman, Dec. 13, 1837, May 12, 1838, pet. under 1 Vict. c. 10, pardoned, on giving security to keep the peace, and be of good b. for 3 years.

Peter Rogers, yeoman, Dec. 13, 1837, July 13, 1838, ditto ditto ditto.

William King, yeoman, Dec. 13, 1837, Dec. 23, 1837, n. t., dis. by com. af. ex.

Wm. Rogers, yeoman, Dec. 13, 1837, April 18, 1838, spe. oy. and ter., acquitted.

J. W. Kendrick, laborer, Dec. 13, 1837, Dec. 23, 1837, n. t., dis. by com. af. ex.

George Hill, laborer, Dec. 13, 1837, Dec. 16, 1837, n. t., dis. by com. af. ex.

Joseph Gould, yeoman, Dec. 13, 1837, Oct., 1838, pet. under 1 Vict. c. pardoned, on giving security to keep the peace, and be of good b. for 3 years.

Abraham Haling, laborer, Dec. 13, 1837, pet. under 1 Vict. c. 10, ban. from Pro.

Joseph Newlove, laborer, Dec. 13, 1837, Dec. 15, 1837, n. t., dis. by com. af. ex.

George Wilson, laborer, Dec. 13, 1837, Dec. 15, 1837, n. t., dis. by com. af. ex.

William Asher, laborer, Dec. 13, 1837, Dec. 15, 1837, n. t., dis. by com. af. ex.

John Beilby, laborer, Dec. 13, 1837, Dec. 15, 1837, n. t., dis. by com. after ex.

Joseph Wilson, laborer, Dec. 13, 1837, Dec. 15, 1837, n. t., dis. by com. af. ex.

Periphen Hawke, laborer, Dec. 13, 1837, May 12, 1838, pet. under 1 Vict. c. 10, admitted to bail and pardoned, on giving security to keep the peace, &c.

Gideon Vernon, laborer, Dec. 13, 1837, Feb. 23, 1838, ditto ditto ditto.

Isaac Masterson, laborer, Dec. 13, 1837, May 18, 1838, ditto ditto ditto.

Weldon Hughes, laborer, Dec. 13, 1837, May 12, 1838, ditto ditto ditto.

Abraham Musselman, yeoman, Dec. 13, 1837, Feb. 27, 1838, ditto ditto.

Peter Pence, yeoman, Dec. 13, 1837, Jan. 8, 1838, ditto ditto ditto.

Henry Johnson, yeoman, Dec. 14, 1837, May 12, 1838, ditto ditto ditto.

James Johnson, yeoman, Dec. 14, 1837, May 12, 1838, ditto ditto ditto.

Joseph Johnson, yeoman, Dec. 14, 1837, April 20, 1838, ditto ditto ditto.

John Clarke, yeoman, Dec. 14, 1837, Dec. 21, 1837, n. t., dis. by com. after ex.

John Browne, yeoman, Dec. 14, 1837, pet. under 1 Vict. c. 10, ban. from Prov.

Hugh D. Wilson, yeoman, Dec. 14, 1837, Oct., 1838, pet. under 1 Vict. c. 10, pardoned, on giving security to keep the peace, and be of good b. for 3 years.

John D. Wilson, yeoman, Dec. 14, 1837, May 12, 1838, pet. under 1 Vict. c. 10, discharged by commission after examination.

✝ Wm. Brougham, yeoman, Dec. 14, 1837, Dec. 21, 1837, n. t., dis. by com. af. ex.

⊰ Peter Grant, yeoman, Dec. 14, 1837, Dec. 19, 1837, n. t., dis. by com. after ex.

Joseph Millburn, yeoman, Dec. 14, 1837, Oct., 1838, pet. under 1 Vict. c. 10, pardoned, on finding security to keep the peace, and be of good b. for 3 years.

⋋ David Dean, yeoman, Dec. 14, 1837, Dec. 23, 1837, n. t., dis. by com. after ex.

⤬ Peter Munro, yeoman, Dec. 14, 1837, Dec. 23, 1837, n. t., dis. by com. after ex.

⊰ Samuel Munro, yeoman, Dec. 14, 1837, Dec. 27, 1837, n. t., dis. by com. after ex.

✦ John McKay, yeoman, Dec. 14, 1837, Dec. 26, 1837, n. t., dis. by com. after ex.

Peter Matthews, yeoman, Dec. 14, 1837, s. oy. and ter., guilty, exe. April 12, 1838.

John Stewart, yeoman, Dec. 14, 1837, pet. under 1 Vict. c. 10, sentenced to transportation, but escaped from Fort Henry, Kingston.

John Wilkie, laborer, Dec. 14, 1837, Oct. 1838, pet. under 1 Vict. c. 10, pardoned, on finding security to keep the peace, and be of good b. for 3 years.

Reuben Lundy, laborer, Dec. 14, 1837, May 12, 1838, ditto. ditto. ditto.

Emanuel Doner, laborer, Dec. 15, 1837, Dec. 21, 1837, n. t., dis. by com. af. ex.

Joseph Doner, laborer, Dec. 15, 1837, Dec. 21, 1837, n. t., dis. by com. af. ex.

John Sheppard, laborer, Dec. 15, 1837, Dec. 21, 1837, n. t., dis. by com. af. ex.

⤬ Jacob Troyer, laborer, Dec. 15, 1837, Dec. 21, 1837, n. t., dis. by com. after ex

David Blair, laborer, Dec. 15, 1837, Dec. 21, 1837, n. t. dis. by com. after ex. ′

⏐ L. S. W. Richardson, laborer, Dec. 15, 1837, Jan. 21, 1838, n. t., dis. by c. af. ex.

Geo. Robinson, laborer, Dec. 15, 1837, Dec. 19, 1837, n. t., dis. by com af. ex.

Benj. Winhup, laborer, Dec. 15, 1837, Dec. 21, 1837, n. t., dis. by com. af. ex.

Thomas Wilson, laborer, Dec. 15, 1837, Oct., 1838, pet. under 1 Vict. c. 10, pardoned, on finding security to keep the peace, and be of good b. for 3 years.

David Porter, yeoman, Dec. 15, 1837,   ditto   ditto   ditto.

W. G. Edmonstone, teacher, Dec. 15, 1837, July 12, 1838,   ditto   ditto.

⸰ George Holborn, laborer, Dec. 15, 1837, Dec. 21, 1837, n. t., dis. by com. af. ex.

Geo. Lamb, laborer, Dec. 15, 1837, pet. under 1 Vict. c. 10, sent to penitentiary, at Kingston, for three years, and then to be banished from the Prov. for life.

Townsend Wixon, laborer, Dec. 15, 1837, May 20, 1838, pet. under 1 Vict. c. 10, pardoned, on finding security to keep the peace and be of good b. for 3 years.

Silas Bardwell, laborer, Dec. 15, 1837, pet. under 1 Vict. c. 10, ban. from Prov.

Colin Scott, laborer, Dec. 15, 1837, pet. under 1 Vict. c. 10, sent to penitentiary, at Kingston, for three years, and then banished from the Province for life.

John Gibson, laborer, Dec. 15, 1837, July 31, 1838, pet. under 1 Vict. c. 10, pardoned, on finding security to keep the peace, and be of good b. for 3 years.

Hasel H. Scott, laborer, Dec. 15, 1837, July 13, 1838,   ditto   ditto   ditto.

Hiram Matthews, Dec. 15, 1837, May 16, 1838,   ditto   ditto   ditto.

Russel Baker, laborer, Dec. 15, 1837, May 22, 1838,   ditto   ditto   ditto.

John Prout, laborer, Dec. 15, 1837, May 12, 1838,   ditto   ditto   ditto.

Charles Crocker, laborer, Dec. 15, 1837, May 12, 1838, ditto   ditto   ditto.

Gilbert F. Morden, shoemaker, Dec. 15, 1837, special oy. and ter., guilty, sentenced to transportation, but escaped from Fort Henry, Kingston.

✗James McQueen, laborer, Dec. 15, 1837, Dec. 17, 1837, n. t., dis. by com. af. ex.

Michael Sheppard, yeoman, Dec. 15, 1837, pet. under 1 Vict. c. 10, sentenced to transportation, but escaped from Fort Henry, Kingston.

Thomas Sheppard, Dec. 15, 1837,   ditto   ditto   ditto.

Robert Walker, blacksmith, Dec. 15, 1837, pet. under 1 Vict c. 10, transportation for life to Van Diemen's Land.

✓ Joseph Clarkson, laborer, Dec. 15, 1837, Dec. 23, 1837, n. t., dis. by com. af. ex.

✗ Arthur Squires, laborer, Dec. 15, 1837, Dec. 23, 1837, n. t., dis. by com. after ex.

John McDougall, laborer, Dec. 15, 1837, Apr. 17, 1838, sp. oyer and term. (ac.)

✓ Peter Rush, laborer, Dec. 16, 1837, Dec. 21, 1837, n. t., dis. by com. after ex.

Wm. Wilson, laborer, Dec. 16, 1837, Dec. 23, 1837, n. t., dis. by com. af ex.

Jacob Kirty, laborer, Dec. 16, 1837, Dec. 19, 1837, n. t., dis. by com. af. ex.

Adam Rupert, laborer, Dec. 16, 1837, Dec. 21, 1837, n. t., dis. by com. af. ex.

Adam Scott, laborer, Dec. 15, 1837, Jan. 10, 1838, n. t., dis. by com. after ex.

William Stockdale, laborer, Dec. 16, 1837, pet. under 1 Vict. c. 10. sentenced to transportation; escaped from Fort Henry, Kingston, but retaken, and not yet removed out of the country.

∠George Bolton, laborer, Dec. 16, 1837, Dec. 23, 1837, n. t., dis. by com. af. ex.

✗ John Mitchell, laborer, Dec. 16, 1837, Dec. 23, 1837, n. t., dis. by com. af. ex.

✗ James Harman, laborer, Dec. 16, 1837, Dec. 23, 1837, n. t., dis. by com. af. ex.

John G. Parker, laborer, Dec. 5, 1837, pet. under 1 Vict. c. 10. transportation for life to Van Diemen's Land.

∠ Samuel Waford, laborer, Dec. 13, 1837, Dec. 17, 1837, n. t., dis. by com. af. ex.

Adam Baird, laborer, Dec. 17, 1837, Dec. 21, 1837, n. t., dis. by com. after ex.

Asa Wixon, laborer, Dec. 17, 1837, pet. under 1 Vict. c. 10, banished from the Province.

Charles Low, laborer, Dec. 17, 1837, July 13, 1838, pet. under 1 Vict. c. 10. pardoned, on finding security to keep the peace, and be of good b. for 3 years.

Solomon Sly, laborer, Dec. 17, 1837,   ditto   ditto   ditto.

Joel Wixon, laborer, Dec. 17, 1837, pet. under 1 Vict. c. 10, ban. from the Prov.

John Hill, laborer, Dec. 17, 1837,   ditto   ditto   ditto.

Andrew Hill, laborer, Dec. 17, 1837, May 12, 1838, pet. under 1 Vict. c. 10. pardoned on finding security to keep the peace, and be of good b. for 3 years.

William Wilson, laborer, Dec. 17, 1837, April 12, 1838, pet. under 1 Vict. c. 10., pardoned on security to keep the peace and be of good behavior for 3 years. William Wilson died in the hospital.

Abraham Wilson, laborer, Dec. 17, 1837, May 16, 1838, pet., under 1 Vict. c. 10, pardoned, on finding security to keep the peace, and be of good b. for 3, years.

✗ Sampson Harris, laborer, Dec. 17, 1837, July 27, 1838, n. t., ad. to b. on his rec.

✗ Patrick Garry, laborer, Dec. 17, 1837, Dec. 19, 1837, n. t., dis. by com. af. ex.

John Marr, laborer, Dec. 17, 1837, pet. under 1 Vict. c. 10. ordered for transportation, but escaped from Fort Henry, Kingston.

✗ Thos. Wilson, laborer, Dec. 17, 1837, Dec. 17, 1837, n. t., dis. by com. af. ex.

Robert Berrie, laborer, Dec. 17, 1837, May 12, 1838, pet. under 1 Vict. c. 10, pardoned, on finding security to keep the peace, and be of good b. for 3 years.

Joseph Elthorp, yeoman, Dec. 17, 1837, Dec. 26, 1837, n. t., dis. by com. af. ex.

John Graham, yeoman, Dec. 17, 1838, May 12, 1838, pet. under 1 Vict. c. 10. pardoned, on finding security to keep the peace, and be of good b. for 3 years.

William Bently, yeoman, Dec. 17, 1837, Dec. 26, 1837, n. t., dis. by com. af. ex.

Geo. S. Yeomens, yeoman, Dec. 17, 1837, Dec. 26, 1837, n. t., dis. by com. af. ex.

Wm. Graham, laborer, Dec. 17, 1837, Dec. 26, 1837, n. t., dis. by com. af. ex.

Nelson Flanagan, laborer, Dec. 17, 1837, Dec. 26, 1837, n. t., dis. by com. af. ex,

J. Matthews, laborer, Dec. 27, 1837, May 16, 1838, pet. under 1 Vict. c. 10., pardoned on finding security to keep the peace, and be of good b. for 3 years.

Henry Weaver, laborer, Dec. 17, 1837, May 20, 1838,   ditto   ditto   ditto.

George Barclay, yeoman, Dec. 17, 1837, pet. under 1 Vict. c. 10., to be confined in penitentiary, Kingston, for three years, and then banished from the Province for life.

Thomas Gray, yeoman, Dec. 17, 1837, Dec. 21, 1837, n. t., dis by com. af. ex.

Wilson Read, tanner, Dec. 17, 1837, pet. under 1 Vict. c. 10, ordered for transportation, but escaped from Fort Henry, Kingston.

John Read, tanner, Dec. 17, 1837, pet. under 1 Vict. c. 10, pardoned, on finding security to keep the peace, and be of good behaviour for 3 years.

Wesley Duncan, laborer, Dec. 17, 1837, Dec 21, 1837, n. t,, dis. by com. af. ex.

John McLafferty, artist, Dec. 17, 1837, May 22, 1838, n. t. ad. to b. on his rec.

John Devins, yeoman, Dec. 17, 1837, pet. under 1 Vict. c. 10., pardoned on finding security to keep the peace, and be of good b. for 3 years.

Thomas Watts, yeoman, Dec. 17, 1837,   ditto   ditto   ditto.

Wm. Read, Jr., yeoman, Dec. 16, 1837, May 12, 1838,   ditto   ditto   ditto.

Thomas Wilson, yeoman, Dec. 16, 1837, May 12, 1838,   ditto   ditto   ditto.

George Fletcher, yeoman, Dec. 18, 1837, May 12, 1838,   ditto   ditto   ditto.

William Carney, laborer, Dec. 18, 1837, Dec. 23, 1837, n. t., dis. by com. af. ex.

Nelson Carver, laborer, Dec. 18, 1837, May 18, 1838, pet. under 1 Vict. c. 10. pardoned, on finding security to keep the peace, and be of good b. for 3 years.

Joseph Noble, laborer, Dec. 18, 1837. Dec. 26, 1737, n. t., dis. by com. af. ex.

Charles Doan, laborer, Dec. 18, 1837, May 10, 1838, pet. under 1 Vict. c. 10. pardoned, on finding security to keep the peace, and be of good b. for 3 years.

Randal Wixon, yeoman, Dec. 18, 1837, pet. under 1 Vict. c. 10., transportation to Van Diemen's Land for fourteen years.

William Hill, tanner, Dec. 19, 1837, May 12, 1838, pet. under 1 Vict. c. 10, pardoned, on finding security to keep the peace, and be of good b. for 3 years.

Eli Irwin, yeoman, Dec. 19, 1837, May 12, 1838,   ditto   ditto   ditto.

Francis Robbins, yeoman, Dec. 19, 1837, pet. under 1 Vict. c. 10. to be confined in the penitentiary for three years, and then banished from the Prov. for life.

Jesse Doan, yeoman, Dec. 19, 1837, pet. under 1 Vict. c. 10, pardoned, on finding security to keep the peace, and be of good b. for 3 years.

✓ Dougal Campbell, yeoman, Dec. 17, 1837, Dec. 21, 1837, n. t., dis. by com. af. ex.

✗ Donald Campbell, yeoman, Dec. 17, 1837, Dec. 21, 1837, n. t., dis. by com. af. ex.

/John Campbell, yeoman, Dec. 17, 1837, Dec. 21, 1837, n. t., dis. by com. af. ex.

Adam Graham, yeoman, Dec. 20, 1837, May 12, 1838, pet. under 1 Vict. c 10, pardoned, on finding security to keep the peace, and be of good b. for 3 years.

Luther Elton, tailor, Dec. 20, 1837, pet. under 1 Vict. c. 10, sent to the peni-¹ tentiary for three years, and then banished from the Province for life.

Joseph Watson, carpenter, Dec. 20, 1837,   ditto   ditto   ditto.

✗ Andrew Rowand, laborer, Dec. 20, 1837, July 13, 1838, pet. under 1 Vict. c. 10, pardoned, on finding security to keep the peace, and be of good b. for 3 years.

Joseph Brammer, laborer, Dec. 20, 1837, May 12, 1838,   ditto ditto ditto.

✓ Frs. McDonald, laborer, Dec. 21, 1837, Dec. 24, 1837, n. t., dis. by com. af. ex.

—✗—W. J. Comfort, yeoman, Dec. 21, 1837, April 4, 1838, pet. under 1 Vict. c. 10. discharged on his own recognizances.

✓ Jacob Lane, yeoman, Dec. 21, 1837, Dec. 27, 1837, n. t., dis by com. af. ex.

— M. P. Empey, merchant. Dec. 22, 1837, Feb. 17, 1838, pet. under 1 Vict. c. 10, discharged on his own recognizances.

Gerard Irwin, shoemaker, Dec. 22, 1837, May 12, 1838, pet. under 1 Vict. c. 10, par. on finding security to keep the peace, and be of good b. for 3 years.

William Doan, laborer, Dec. 22, 1837, May 11, 1838,   ditto ditto ditto.

· Thos. Thompson, laborer, Dec. 22, 1837, Dec. 27, 1837, n. t., dis. by com. af. ex.

Henry Styles, laborer, Dec. 22, 1837, Dec. 29, 1837, n. t., dis. by com. after ex.

✓ Elisha Mitchell, laborer, Dec. 22, 1837, Dec. 27, 1837,   ditto   ditto.

— Ebenezer Moore, laborer, Dec. 22, 1837, Dec. 27, 1837,   ditto   ditto.

✓ Webster Stevens, laborer, Dec. 23, 1837, Dec. 29, 1838,   ditto   ditto.

John Gillingham, laborer, Dec. 23, 1837, Aug. 1838, pet., under 1 Vict. c. 10, pardoned, on finding security to keep the peace, and be of good b. for 3 years.

John McCormack, physician, Dec. 23, 1837,   ditto ditto ditto.

Ira Anderson, blacksmith, Dec. 6, 1837, pet. under 1 Vict. c. 10, transportation to Van Diemen's Land for seven years.

Jacob Lamoureaux, laborer, Dec. 21, 1837, May 12, 1838, pet. under 1 Vict. c. 10, par. on finding security to keep the peace, and be of good b. for 3 years.

✗ G. G. Parker, laborer, Dec. 16, 1837, Dec. 21, 1837, n, t., dis. by com. after ex. Parker again arrested on Dec. 20, and discharged on the 14th of April, 1838, and the bill ignored by grand jury.

James Long, laborer, Dec. 23, 1837, Dec. 27, 1837,   ditto   ditto   ditto.

William Curtis, laborer, Dec. 23, 1837, July 29, 1838, n. t., dis. on his own rec.

✗ Arch. Molloy, laborer, Dec. 24, 1837, Dec. 29, 1837, n. t., dis. by com. af. ex.

Arthur Kelly, laborer, Dec. 25, 1837, May 12, 1838, pet. under 1 Vict. c. 10, pardoned, on finding security to keep the peace, and be of good b. for 3 years.

James Keene, laborer, Dec. 25, 1837, July 13, 1838,   ditto   ditto   ditto.

Joseph McGrath, laborer, Dec. 25, 1837, May 12, 1838, ditto   ditto   ditto.

Thomas Sly, laborer, Dec. 25, 1837, May 16, 1838,   ditto   ditto   ditto.

99

Thos. D. Morrison, physician, Dec. 16, 1837, June, 1838, spe. oy. and ter., acq.

Charles Durand, attorney, Dec. 19, 1837, special oy. and ter., guilty, sentence of death commuted to banishment from the Province.

James Lesslie, bookseller, Dec. 19, 1837, Dec. 19, 1837, n. t., dis. by com. af. ex.

—— Lesslie, bookseller, Dec. 19, 1837, Dec. 19, 1837, n. t., dis. by com. af. ex.

John Doel, brewer, Dec. 19, 1837, Dec. 19, 1837, n. t., dis. by com. after ex.

Robert Johnson, laborer, Dec. 26, 1837, Feb. 9, 1838, n. t., dis. by com. af. ex.

James Brown, laborer, Dec. 26, 1837, pet. under 1 Vict. c. 10, transportation for seven years to Van Diemen's Land.

Asher Wilson, laborer, Dec. 26, 1837, April 20, 1838, n. t., discharged by special commission of oyer and terminer.

Louis Terry, laborer, Dec. 27, 1837, Dec. 31, 1837, n. t., dis. by com. after ex.

Robert Taylor, laborer, Dec. 27, 1837, May, 12. 1838, pet. under 1 Vict. c. 10, pardoned, on finding security to keep the peace, and be of good b. for 3 years.

Thos. Hill, laborer, Dec. 27, 1837, Feb. 27, 1838, n. t., sent to hospital and died.

John Rummerfeldt, laborer, Dec. 28, 1837, pet. under 1 Vict. c. 10, sent to penitentiary, at Kingston, for 3 years, and then to be ban. from the Prov. for life.

John P. Plank, laborer, Dec. 23, 1837, Dec. 29, 1837, n. t., dis. by com. after ex.

William Kilburn, laborer, Dec. 29, 1837, May 12, 1838, pet. under 1 Vict. c. 10, pardoned, on finding security to keep the peace, and be of good b. for 3 years.

George Wright, laborer, Dec. 30, 1837, Jan. 2, 1838, n. t., dis. by com. after ex.

C C Scott, laborer, Dec. 30, 1837, pet. under 1 Vict. c. 10, sent to penitentiary, at Kingston, for three years, and then banished from the Province for life.

Abraham Faulkner, laborer, Dec. 30, 1837, Jan. 2, 1838, n. t., dis. by c. af. ex.

Thos. Sherrard, laborer, Dec. 30, 1837, Jan. 2, 1838, n. t., dis. by com. after ex.

Joshua Haskill, laborer, Dec. 30, 1837, July 28, 1838, n. t. dis. by on his recog.

Joseph Martin, laborer, Dec. 30, 1837, Jan. 25, 1838, n. t., dis. by com. af. ex.

Charles Rayner, laborer, Dec. 30, 1837, Jan. 3, 1838, n. t., dis. by com af. ex.

Abraham Anderson, laborer, Dec. 30, 1837, Jan. 2, 1838, n. t., dis. by c. af. ex.

Joshua Wixon, laborer, Dec. 30, 1837, Jan. 2, 1838, n. t., dis. by com. after ex.

James Kane, laborer, Dec. 30, 1837, May 12, 1838, pet. under 1 Vict. c. 10, pardoned, on finding security to keep the peace, and be of good b. for 3 years.

James Barry, laborer, Dec. 30, 1837, Jan. 2, 1838, n. t., dis. by com. after ex.

John Wilkie, (2d), blacksmith, Dec. 30, 1837, May 12, 1838, pet. under 1 Vict. c. 10, par., on finding security to keep the peace, and be of good b. for 3 years.

Peter Grant, (2d), laborer, Dec. 30, 1837, Jan. 30, 1838, n. t., sent to hos. and died.

Burton Attwell, laborer, Dec. 30, 1837, Jan. 4, 1838, n. t., dis. by com af. ex.

John P. Cherry teacher, Dec. 30, 1837, April 14, 1838, bill ig., dis. by court.

John Plank, laborer, Dec. 29, 1837, Jan. 2, 1838, n. t., dis. by com. after ex.

R. S. Smith, laborer, Dec. 10, 1837, Jan. 2, 1838, n. t., dis. by com. after ex.

Lazarus Ellis, laborer, Dec. 13, 1837, Jan. 2, 1838, n. t., dis. by com. after. ex.

Jonathan Doan, laborer, Dec. 22, 1837, Jan. 28, 1838, n. t., dis. on his recog.

Lucius C. Thomas, laborer, Jan. 2, 1838, Jan. 4, 1838, n. t., dis. by com. af. ex.

Eber Thomas, laborer, Jan. 2, 1838, Jan. 4, 1838, n. t., dis. by com. after. ex.

Elias Crery, laborer, Jan. 2, 1838, Jan. 4, 1838, n. t., dis. by com. after ex.

Royal Hopkins, laborer, Jan. 2, 1838, Jan. 4, 1838, n. t., dis. by com. after ex.

Timothy Doyle, laborer, Jan. 5, 1838, Jan. 11, 1838, n. t., dis. by com. after ex.

Alex. Cluny, laborer, Jan. 5, 1838, Jan. 7, 1838, n. t., dis. by com. after ex.

D. Hutchinson, laborer, Jan. 6, 1838, Feb. 3, 1838, n. t., dis. by com. after ex.

Michael Corrigan, laborer, Jan. 6, 1838, May 12, 1838, pet. under 1 Vict. c. 10, pardoned, on finding security to keep the peace, and be of good b. for 3 years.

John Haling, laborer, Jan. 6, 1838, pet. under 1 Vict. c. 10, ban. from the Prov.

John Doyle, laborer, Jan. 6, 1838, Jan. 11, 1838, n. t., dis. by com. after ex.

John McAnany, laborer, Jan. 6, 1838, Jan. 11, 1838, n. t., dis. by com. af. ex.

James McGuire, laborer, Jan. 6, 1838, May 12, 1838, pet. under 1 Vict. c. 10, pardoned, on finding security to keep the peace, and be of good b. for 3 years.

James Parker, laborer, Jan. 6, 1838, Feb. 25, 1838, n. t., dis. by com. after ex.

Donald Cameron, laborer, Jan. 11, 1838, May 10, 1838, spe. oy. and ter., acq.

Ewen Cameron, laborer, Jan. 11, 1838, Jan. 12, 1838, n. t., dis. by com. af. ex.

John Cameron, laborer, Jan. 11, 1838, Jan. 12, 1838, n. t., dis. by com. af. ex.

Dnncan McNab, laborer, Jan. 11, 1838, Jan. 14, 1838, n. t., dis. by com. af. ex.

Charles Axtell, laborer, Jan. 11, 1838, Jan. 14, 1838, n. t., dis. by com. af. ex.

J. F. Farley, laborer, Jan. 13, 1838, Jan. 16, 1838, n. t., dis. by com. af. ex.

Gilbert Decker, laborer, Jan. 13, 1838, Jan. 30, 1838, n. t., admitted to bail.

Thomas Elliott, innkeeper, Jan. 7, 1838, Jan. 15, 1838, n. t., admitted to bail; first confined in Hamilton, Gore District, December 23, 1837.

William Carroll, yeoman, Jan. 7, 1838, Jan. 15, 1838, ditto ditto ditto.

Jas. McDonald, laborer, Jan. 13, 1838, Jan. 16, 1838, n. t , dis. by com. af. ex.

Isaac Moins, laborer, Jan. 13, 1838, Jan. 16, 1838, n. t., dis. by com. af. ex.

John Houck, laborer, Jan. 13, 1838, Jan. 16, 1838, n. t., dis. by com. after ex.

Matthew Hayes, laborer, Jan. 18, 1838, July 25, 1838, n. t., dis. on his recog.

Samuel Lount, blacksmith, Jan. 18, 1838, spe. oy. and ter., guilty, executed April 12, 1838.

James Murray, laborer, Jan. 15, 1838, May 18, 1838, n. t., dis. by com. af. ex.

Martin Smith, laborer, Jan. 16, 1838, Feb. 27, 1838, n. t., dis. by com. af. ex.

Henry McGarry, laborer, Jan. 18, 1838, April 20, 1838, spe. oy. and ter., acq.

Jas. Edmonstone, laborer, Jan. 21, 1838, Jan. 24, 1838, n. t., dis. on his recog.

W. Brewer, laborer, Jan. 21, 1838, Jan. 22, 1838, n. t., dis. by Mayor of Toronto.

Terence Fergusson, laborer, Jan. 21, 1838, Jan. 22, 1838, n. t., ditto ditto.

Peter McConville, laborer, Jan. 23, 1838, Jan. 26, 1838, n. t., ditto ditto.

John Hawkes, laborer, Jan. 23, 1838, Jan. 26, 1838, n. t., ditto ditto.

John Kline, laborer, Jan. 24, 1838, March 29, 1838, n. t., dis. by com. af. ex.

Michael Flood, laborer, Jan. 24, 1838, Jan. 27, 1838, n. t., dis. by com. af. ex.

Wm. Irwin, laborer, Jan. 24, 1838, Jan. 27, 1838, n. t., dis. by com. after ex.

James McIsaac, laborer, Jan. 24, 1838, Jan. 30, 1838, n. t.. dis. by com. af. ex.

Dennis Leahy, laborer, Jan. 24, 1838, Jan. 30, 1838, n. t., dis. by com. af. ex.

Dennis O'Connor, laborer, Jan. 24, 1838, Jan. 28, 1838, n. t., dis. by com. af. ex.

John Condon, laborer, Jan. 24, 1838, Jan. 30, 1838, n. t., dis. by com. after ex.

John Keane, laborer, Jan. 24, 1838, Jan. 30, 1838, n. t., dis. by com. after ex.

Patrick Condon, laborer, Jan. 24, 1838, Jan. 27, 1838, n. t., dis. by com. af. ex.

John O'Brien, laborer, Jan. 24, 1838, Jan. 30, 1838, n. t., dis. by com. after ex.

James Keane, laborer, Jan. 24, 1838, Jan. 30, 1830, n. t., dis. by com. after ex.

Jeremiah C. Chapin, laborer, Jan. 25, 1838, April 20, 1838, no b., dis. by court.

William Shaw, laborer, Jan. 26, 1838, Jan. 30, 1838, n. t., dis. by com. af. ex.

Ewen Cameron, laborer, Jan. 29, 1838, May 10, 1838, n. t., dis. by com. af. ex.

Edward A. Theller, surgeon, taken in the schooner Anne, in Jan. 1838, at Amherstburgh, spe. oy. and ter., guilty, sentenced to death. Commuted to transportation for life. Escaped from Cape Diamond, Quebec.

Stephen P. Brophy, civil engineer, taken in the schooner Anne, in Jan., 1838, at Amherstburgh., pet. under 1 Vict. c. 10, ordered for transportation, but escaped from Fort Henry, Kingston.

Claude Campeau, yeoman, taken in the schooner Anne, in Jan., 1838, at Amherstburgh, May 30, 1838, pet. under 1 Vict. c. 10, pardoned by Lieutenant Governor, and sent back to the United States.

Augustus D. Berdeneau, mariner, taken in the schooner Anne, in Jan., 1838, at Amherstburgh, May 30, 1838, pet. under 1 Vict. c. 10, pardoned by the Lieutenant Governor, and sent back to the United States.

Francis St. Augustin, laborer, taken in the schooner Anne, in Jan., 1838, at Amherstburgh, May 30, 1838, pet. under 1 Vict. c. 10, pardoned by the Lieutenant Governor, and sent back to the United States.

Henry Johnston, laborer, taken in the schooner Anne, in Jan., 1838, at Amherstburgh, May 30, 1838, pet. under 1 Vict. c. 10, pardoned by the Lieutenant Governor, and sent back to the United States.

Abram W. Partridge, laborer, taken in the schooner Anne, in Jan., 1838, at Amherstburgh, pet. under 1 Vict. c. 10, sent to Kingston, and still in custody.

Theron Culver, painter, taken in the schooner Anne, in Jan., 1838, at Amherstburgh, pet. under 1 Vict. c. 10, sent to Kingston, and still in custody.

Louis Lenoux, laborer, taken in the schooner Anne, in Jan., 1838, at Amherstburgh, May 30, 1838, n. t., par. by Leut. Gov. and sent back to U. S.

Francis Clutier, laborer, taken in the schooner Anne, in Jan., 1838, at Amherstburgh, May 30, 1838, n. t., par. by Lieut. Gov., and sent back to U. S.

Benjamin F. Pew, laborer, taken in the schooner Anne, in Jan., 1838, at Amherstburgh, May 30, 1838, n. t., sent to Quebec, and still in custody.

Henry L. Hull, laborer, taken in the schooner Anne, in Jan., 1838, at Amherstburgh. n. t., par. Lieut. Gov., and sent back to the United States.

George Davis, laborer, taken in the schooner Anne, in Jan., 1838, at Amherstburgh, May 30, 1838, n. t., par. by Lieut. Gov., and sent back to the U. S.

Walter Chase, laborer, taken in the sch. Anne, in Jan. 1838, at Amherstburgh, pet. under 1 Vict. c. 10. ord. for transp., but es. from Ft. Henry, Kingston.

Squire Thayer, aborer, taken in the schooner Anne, in Jan. 1838, at Amherstburgh, n. t., sent to Quebec, and still in custody.

Nathaniel Smith, laborer,   ditto   ditto   ditto.

W. W. Dodge, merchant, taken in the schooner Anne, Jan., 1838, at Amherstburgh, pet. under 1 Vict. c. 10, sent to Quebec, and escaped from thence.

Chancey Parker, laborer, Jan. 30, 1838, pet. under 1 Vict. c. 10, sent to Quebec, and still in custody.

William Ketchum, tanner, Feb. 7, 1838, Feb. 8, 1838, n. t., admitted to bail.
Absconded, but subsequently pardoned.

Aaron Freele, laborer, Feb. 2, 1838, May 16, 1838, pet. under 1 Vict. c. 10.
discharged on finding security to keep the peace, and be of good b. for 3 years.

Thos. Tracy, laborer, Feb. 4, 1838, pet. under 1 Vict. c. 10, ordered for transportation, but escaped from Fort Henry, Kingston.

Chancey Hawley, laborer, Feb. 10, 1838, Feb. 15, 1838, n. t., dis. on bail.

John Robinson, laborer, Feb. 21, 1838, pet. under 1 Vict. c. 10. to be confined
in the penitentiary, Kingston, for three years, and then banished from the
Province for life.

Edward Keays, laborer, Jan. 24, 1838, May 22, 1838, n. t., discharged on bail.

Simon Servos, laborer, Jan. 24, 1838, July 27, 1838, n. t., dis. on his own rec.

Joseph Wixon, laborer, Feb. 27, 1838, May 12, 1838, n. t., bill ignored by the
grand jury.

R. A. Parker, merchant, Feb. 24, 1830, April 24, 1838, n. t., dis. on bail.

Joseph Earl, laborer, Feb. 28, 1838, Apr. 5, 1838, pet. under 1 Vict. c. 10, discharged on bail.

Francis Clarkson, laborer, March 1, 1838, May 14, 1838, pet. under 1 Vict. c. 10.
discharged on bail.

Hugh Carmichael, merchant, Mar. 4, 1838, April 24, 1838, n. t., dis. by com.
on bail after examination.

Jesse Cleaver, laborer, Mar. 5, 1838, pet. under 1 Vict. c. 10, ban. from Prov.

Wm. Delaney, laborer, Mar. 5, 1838, Mar. 5, 1838, pet. under 1 Vict. c. 10,
pardoned, on finding security to keep the peace, and be of good b. for 3 years

Titus Root, laborer, March 8, 1838, May 3, 1838,   ditto   ditto   ditto

Daniel Schell, laborer, Mar. 8, 1838, Oct., 1838,   ditto   ditto   ditto.

John D. Staples, laborer, Mar. 12, 1838, pet. under 1 Vict. c. 10, to be confined in penitentiary, for three years, and then ban from the Prov. for life.

John Cane, laborer, Mar. 15, 1838, Mar. 25, 1838, n. t., dis. by com. af. ex.

Jas. Cane, laborer, Mar. 15, 1838, Mar. 25, 1838, n. t., dis. by com. after ex.

Robt. Wilson, laborer, Mar. 15, 1838, Mar. 25, 1838, n. t., dis. by com. af. ex.

Jas. Squires, laborer, Mar. 15, 1838, Mar. 25, 1838, n. t., dis. by com. af. ex.

Timothy Munro, laborer, Mar. 15, 1838, May 12, 1838, pet. under 1 Vict. c.
10, pardoned on finding security to keep the peace, and be of good behavior
for three years.

Wm. Heron, laborer, Mar. 17, 1838, April 20, 1838, n. t., dis. by court, bill ig.

Wm Carney, laborer, Mar. 19, 1838, May 12, 1838, pet. under 1 Vict. c. 10,
pardoned, on finding security to keep the peace, and be of good b. for 3 years
Peter Milne, yeoman, March 21, 1838, Oct. 1838,   ditto   ditto   ditto.
Edward Kennedy, laborer, Mar. 23, 1838, pet. under 1 Vict. c. 10, ordered
for transportation, but escaped from Fort Henry, Kingston; first confined
in Gore District, January 25.

x Jno. Hill, (2) laborer, Mar. 23, 1838, April 20, 1838, n. t., dis. by court, bill ig.
Barthol. Plank, laborer, Mar. 24, 1838, May 12, 1838, pet. under 1 Vict. c. 10.
pardoned, on finding security to keep the peace, and be of good b. for 3 years.

X William Wilson, laborer, Feb. 24, 1838, May 12, 1838, n. t., pardoned on finding security to keep the peace, and be of good behavior for three years.
James Yule, laborer, Feb. 25, 1838, May 18, 1838,   ditto   ditto   ditto.

✓ Ira White, laborer, April 2, 1838, May 3, 1838, n. t., dis. by com. aftei ex.
Zachariah Dent, tailor, Dec. 20, 1837, May 16, 1838, pet. under 1 Vict. c. 10,
pardoned, on finding security to keep the peace, and be of good b. for 3 years.

ɹ James Leland, laborer, April 14, 1838, May 18, 1838, n. t., discharged on bail.
John Randal, laborer, April 14, 1838, May 4, 1838, n. t., dis. by com. af. ex.

.. Michael McFarlane, laborer, April 14, 1838, May 17, 1838, n. t., dis. on bail.
James Howie, laborer, April 14, 1838. May 18, 1838, n. t., dis. on bail.

Sylvanus Spencer, laborer, taken by Colonel Price on the ice, in the Western
District, in Feb., 1838, May 30, 1838, n. t., pardoned by Lieut. Governor,
and sent back to the United States.

Thos. J. Sutherland, (Gen'l) attorney, taken by Colonel Price on the ice, in the
Western District, in Feb. 1838; court-martial, guilty; transportation for life,
free pardon afterwards granted, on condition of finding security, &c., which
not being forthcoming, he is in custody at Quebec.

Edward Carmon, yeoman, first arrested in Dec., 1837, in the London District,
and sent down to the Home District gaol for trial, in June, 1838, pet. under
1 Vict. c. 10, to be confined in the penitentiary for three years, and then
banished from the Province for life.

Horatio Fowler, yeoman, first arrested in Dec., 1837, in the London District,
and sent down to the Home District gaol for trial, in June 1838, Oct., 1838,
pet. under 1 Vict. c. 10., pardoned on security to keep the peace and be of
good behavior for three years.

Finlay Malcolm, yeoman, first arrested in Dec., 1837, in the London District
and sent down to the Home District gaol for trial, in June, 1838, pet. under
1 Vict. c. 10., transportation to Van Diemen's Land for fourteen years.

Joseph Hart, yeoman, first arrested in Dec., 1837, in the London District, and
sent down to the Home District gaol for trial, in June, 1838, Oct, 1838, pet.
under 1 Vict. c. 10, pardoned, on finding security to keep the peace, and be
of good behavior for three years.

James Bell, yeoman,   __ __. ditto__   ditto   ditto   ditto.
John Arthur Tidy, yeoman,   ditto   ditto   ditto   ditto.

John Kelly, yeoman, first arrested in Dec., 1837, in the London District, and sent to the Home District gaol for trial, in June, 1838, July 25, 1838, pet. under 1 Vict. c. 10, pardoned, on finding security to keep the peace, and be of good behavior for three years.

Paul Bedford, yeoman, first arrested in Dec., 1837, in the London District, and sent down to the Home District gaol for trial, in June, 1838, pet. under 1 Vict c. 10, transportation for life to Van Diemen's Land.

Harvey Bryant, yeoman, first arrested in Dec., 1837, in the London District, and sent down to the Home District jail for trial, in June, 1838, Oct., 1838, special oyer and terminer, guilty, sentenced to death, but pardoned, on finding security to keep the peace, and be of good behavior for three years.

Enoch Moore, yeoman,   ditto   . ditto   ditto   ditto   ditto.

Philip Jackson, laborer, taken prisoners at Point au Pelèe, in the Western District, in Feb, 1838, still in custody.

Diogenes McKenzie, laborer, not tried,	dittto	ditto	ditto.
Benjamin Warner, laborer,	ditto	ditto	ditto.
Philip Brady, laborer,	ditto	ditto	ditto.
Isaac Myers, laborer,	ditto	ditto	ditto.
William McCarrick, laborer,	ditto	ditto	ditto.
Samuel Woods, laborer,	ditto	ditto	ditto.
James Mace, laborer,	ditto	ditto	ditto.
John McIntyre, laborer,	ditto	ditto	ditto.

William Bell, laborer, June 28, 1838, July 10, 1838, n. t., dis. by com. af. ex.

Joan McLeod, laborer, June 28, 1838, Aug. 7, 1838, n. t., dis. by com. af. ex.

Ebenezer Wilcox, laborer, first arrested in London District, in 1837, Oct. 1838, special oyer and terminer, guilty, pardoned, on finding security to keep the peace, and be of good behavior for three years.

Robert Cook, yeoman,   ditto   ditto   ditto   ditto   ditto.

Alvaro Ladd, yeoman,   ditto   ditto   ditto   ditto   ditto.

NIAGARA DISTRICT.

Ira Smith, gunsmith, Dec. 18, 1837, Jan. 1, 1838, n. t., dis. on bail for good b.

Thos. Higgins, wheelwright, Dec. 18, 1837, Jan. 10, 1838,   ditto   ditto.

Fisher Hanagan, laborer, Dec. 19, 1837, Jan. 10, 1838,   ditto   ditto.

William Law, printer, Dec. 26, 1837, Feb. 2, 1838,   ditto   ditto.

Samuel Chandler, wagon maker, June 25, 1838, civil court, guilty, prisoners taken at the Short Hills, having invaded the Province from the United States; sentence of death commuted to transportation for life.

Norman Mallory, laborer, June 25, 1838,   ditto   ditto   ditto.

James Waggoner, farmer, June 25, 1838,   ditto   ditto   ditto.

Benjamin Waite, clerk, June 25, 1838,   ditto   ditto   ditto.

Solomon Camp, shoemaker, June 25, 1838, Aug., 1838, civil court, acquitted.

John Grant, wheelwright, June 25, 1838, civil court, guilty, Short Hill prisoner; sentence of death commuted to transportation for life.

Edward Seymour, laborer, June 25, 1838, Aug., 1838, civil court, acquitted.

John J. McNulty, carpenter, June 25, 1838, civil court, guilty, Short Hill prisoner; sentence of death commuted to transportation for life.

Garret Van Camp, laborer, June 25, 1838,   ditto   ditto   ditto.

James Gammell, laborer, June 26, 1838,   ditto   ditto   ditto.

Murdoch McFadden, laborer, June 26, 1838, civil court, guilty, Short Hill prisoner; to be confined in the penitentiary, Kingston, for three years.

Robert Kelly, blacksmith, June 26, 1838, July 23, 1838, n. t., bill ignored by the grand jury, discharged on bail.

Freeman Brady, farmer, June 26, 1838, Aug., 1838, civil court, acquitted.

Loran Hedger, blacksmith, June 26, 1838, July 23, 1838, n. t., bill ignored by the grand jury; discharged on bail.

Street Chase, wagon maker, June 26, 1838, Aug., 1838, civil court, acquitted.

Abraham Clarke, blacksmith, June 27, 1838, July 23, 1838, n. t., bill ignored by grand jury; discharged on bail.

Eber Rice, innkeeper, June 27, 1838, Aug., 1838, civil court, acquitted.

James Morrow, tanner, June 27, 1838, civil court, guilty, executed, July 30, 1838.

David Taylor, farmer, June 27, 1838, civil court, guilty, prisoners taken at the Short Hills, having invaded the Province from the United States. Sentence of death commuted to transportation for life. (Taylor dead.)

George Cooley, farmer, June 27, 1838,   ditto   ditto   ditto.

William Reynolds, saddler, June 27, 1838,   ditto   ditto   ditto.

George Buck, farmer, June, 1838, civil court, guilty, Short Hill prisoner, as above. Sentence of death commuted to confinement in the penitentiary for three years.

Louis Wilson Miller, law student, June 27, 1838, civil court, guilty, Short Hill prisoner, as above. Sentence commuted to transportation for life.

Alexander McLeod, farmer, June 28, 1838,   ditto.   ditto   ditto.

Alexander Brady, farmer, June 30, 1838, Aug., 1838, civil court, acquitted

Erastus Warner, farmer, July 7, 1838, civil court, guilty, transportation to Van Diemen's Land for fourteen years.

Stephen Hart, laborer, July 7, 1838, Aug. 1838, n. t., bill ig. by grand jury.

James Doan, miller, July 17, 1838, n. t., bill ignored by grand jury.

William Whitson, tailor, July 17, 1838, Aug. 4, 1838, civil court, acquitted.

John W. Brown, laborer, July 17, 1838, civil court, guilty, to be confined in the penitentiary, at Kingston, for three years.

John Vernon, carpenter, July 17, 1838, civil court, guilty, Short Hill prisoner. Sentence of death commuted to transportation for life.

William Yerks, carpenter, July 17, 1838, Aug. 3, 1838, civil court, acquitted.

Samuel D. Haslip, shoemaker, July 17, 1838, Aug. 3, 1838, civil court, acquitted.

APPENDIX. 391·

Chas. Malcolm, laborer, July 17, 1838, July 21, 1838, n. t., dis. on bail for g. b.

Geo. Malcolm, laborer, July 17, 1838, July 21, 1838, n. t., dis. on bail for g. b.

Neal Brown, laborer, July 17, 1838, July 21, 1838, n. t., dis. on bail for good b.

Clarke Bowers, blacksmith, July 17, 1838, Aug., 1838, civil court, acquitted.

Duncan Willson, laborer, July 20, 1838, n. t., dis. on bail for good behavior.

Jacob R. Beamer, carpenter, July 28, 1838, civil court, guilty, Short Hill prisoner. Sentence of death commuted to transportation for life.

GORE DISTRICT:

Robt. Armstrong, blacksmith, Dec. 12, 1837, March, 1838, n. t., bill ig. by g. j.

Philip Henry, yeoman, Dec. 13, 1837, Oct. 1838, pet. under 1 Vict. c. 10, pardoned, on finding security to keep the peace, and be of good b. for 3 years.

Henry Winegarden, yeoman, Dec. 15, 1837, June 6, 1838, ditto ditto.

Robert Elliott, tanner, Dec. 15, 1837, March 15, 1838, ditto ditto.

William Stants, yeoman, Dec. 15, 1837, March 15, 1838, n. t., no bill found.

Abra. Vanduzen, medical quack, Dec. 15, 1837, March 20, 1838, n. t., no bill f.

John Tulford, yeoman, Dec. 15, 1837, Oct., 1838, civil court, guilty, sentenced to death; pardoned on finding security to keep the peace, &c., for 3 years.

Joseph Smith, yeoman, Dec. 15, 1837, March 21, 1838, n. t., no bill found.

Peter Coon, blacksmith, Dec. 15, 1837, March 21, 1838, n. t., no bill found.

John Whalen, laborer, Dec. 15, 1837, March 20, 1838, n. t., no bill found.

Alonzo Foster, laborer, Dec. 15, 1837, March 20, 1838, n. t., no bill found.

John Heap, laborer, Dec. 15, 1837, March 20, 1838, n. t., no bill found.

John L. Uline, tanner, Dec. 15, 1837, March 21, 1838, civil court, acquitted.

Charles P. Walrath, laborer, Dec. 15, 1837, civil court, guilty, sentence of death commuted to transportation for life. Escaped from jail.

Isaac Edmunds, miner, Dec. 16, 1837, March 15, 1838, n. t., no bill found.

Peter Ladon, laborer, Dec. 16, 1837, March 15, 1838, n. t., no bill found.

John Jacklin, cordwainer, Dec. 16, 1837, March 15, 1838, n. t., no bill found.

James Johnson, laborer, Dec. 16, 1837, March 15, 1838, n. t., no bill found.

John Johnson, cordwainer, Dec. 16, 1837, April 2, 1838, n. t., no bill found.

Albus Connor, laborer, Dec. 16, 1837, March 15, 1838, n. t., no bill found.

Charles McIntosh, laborer, Dec. 16, 1837, March 15, 1838, n. t., no bill found.

Oliver Edmonds, yeoman, Dec. 16, 1837, March 15, 1838, n. t., no bill found.

Joseph Beemer, yeoman, Dec. 16, 1837, March 20, 1838, n. t., admitted to bail to keep the peace for one year.

Henry Goff, teacher, Dec. 16, 1837, March 20, 1838, n. t., no bill found.

Jonathan Bishop, laborer, Dec. 16, 1837, Feb. 17, 1838, n. t., no bill found.

James Benham, yeoman, Dec. 16, 1837, March 28, 1838, civil court, acquitted.

James Peters, yeoman, Dec. 16, 1837, March 28, 1838, civil court, acquitted.

James Butchart, yeoman, Dec. 16, 1837, March 28, 1838, civil court, acquitted.

Lyman Chapin, yeoman, Dec. 16, 1837, June 6, 1838, pet. under 1 Vict. c. 10, pardoned, on finding security to keep the peace, and be of good b. for 3 years.

100

Dudley Newton, yeoman, Dec. 17, 1837, March 15, 1838, n. t., no bill found.

Malcolm Brown, yeoman, Dec. 17, 1837, June 6, 1838, pet. under 1 Vict. c. 10, pardoned, on finding security to keep the peace, and be of good b. for 3 years.

Thomas Balls, laborer, Dec. 17, 1837, March 15, 1838, n. t., no bill found.

Adam Winegarden, yeoman, Dec. 17, 1837, June 6, 1838, pet. under 1 Vict. c. 10, par. on finding security to keep the peace, and be of good b. for 3 years.

Horatio A. Hills, laborer, Dec. 17, 1837, civil court, guilty, sentence of death, commuted to transportation for life, but died in jail.

William Webb, yeoman, Dec. 17, 1837, Oct., 1838, civil court, guilty, pardoned, on finding security to keep the peace, and be of good b. for 3 years.

Willard Sherman, yeoman, Dec. 17, 1837, March 28, 1838, civil court, acquitted.

John Sherman, yeoman, Dec. 17, 1837, Dec. 18, 1838, n. t., dis. by magistrate.

Asahel Davis, yeoman, Dec. 17, 1837, Dec. 24, 1838, n. t., dis. by magistrate.

Gilbert Davis, yeoman, Dec. 17, 1837, Dec. 24, 1838, n. t., dis. by magistrate.

William Lyons,* yeoman, Dec. 21, 1837, March 30, 1838, civil court, acquitted.

William Winegarden, yeoman, Dec. 21, 1837, June 6, 1838, n. t., pardoned, on finding security to keep the peace, and be of good behavior for 3 years.

Lord Wellington Winegarden, yeoman, Dec. 21, 1837, June 6, 1838, n. t., pardoned, on finding security to keep the peace, and be of good b. for 3 years.

Wm. Thompson,* blacksmith, Dec. 21, 1837, Oct., 1838, pet. under 1 Vict. c. 10, pardoned, on finding security to keep the peace, and be of good b. for 3 years.

Charles Chapin,* yeoman, Dec. 21, 1837,   ditto   ditto   ditto.

John Austin,* yeoman, Dec. 23, 1837, Jan. 21, 1838, n. t., discharged on bail.

Oliver Smith, medical quack, Dec. 23, 1837, March 30, 1838, civil court, acq.

John Van Norman, innkeeper, Dec. 23, 1837, Feb. 20, 1838, n. t., discharged on bail, and absconded.

John Malcolm,* yeoman, Dec. 23, 1837, March 10, 1838, n. t., bill ignored.

Isaac B. Malcolm, yeoman, Dec. 23, 1837, June 6, 1838, pet. under 1 Vict. c. 10, pardoned, on finding security to keep the peace, and be of good b. for 3 years.

Finlay Malcolm,* late member of the Provincial Parliament, Dec. 23, 1837, March 31, 1838, civil court, acquitted.

Norman Malcolm,* son to above, Dec. 23, 1837, March 31, 1838, civil court, acq.

Solomon Lossing, magistrate, Dec. 23, 1837, April 3, 1838, civil court, acquitted.

Ephraim Cook, physician, Dec. 23, 1837, civil court, guilty, banished from the Province for life.

Elias Snider,* yeoman, Dec. 23, 1837, Oct., 1838, civil court, guilty, pardoned, on finding security to keep the peace, and be of good behavior for 3 years.

Garry V. Delong, yeoman, Dec. 23, 1837, Feb. 4, 1838, n. t., dis. on bail, and ab.

Adam Yeigh,* yeoman, Jan. 23, 1837, March 31, 1838, civil court, acquitted.

Nathan Town, unlicensed doctor, Dec. 24, 1837, Oct., 1838, civil court, acq., pardoned, on finding security to keep the peace, and be of good b. for 3 years.

Robert Alway, M. P. P., Dec. 25, 1837, March 28, 1838, n. t., dis. on bail.

Michael Showers,* yeoman, Jan. 2, 1838, March 17, 1838, n. t., bill ignored.

* Marked thus are respectable.

George Rouse, laborer, Jan. 2, 1838, March 31, 1838, civil court, acquitted.

Samuel Marlatt, yeoman, Jan. 2, 1838, March 31, 1838, civil court, acquitted.

David Ghent,* yeoman, Jan. 3, 1838, Jan. 3, 1838, n. t., discharged on bail.

John Tyler, hatter, Jan. 3, 1838, Jan. 5, 1838, n. t., dis. by the magistrate.

Thomas Sirpell, laborer, Jan. 3, 1838, Feb. 6, 1838, n. t., dis. by magistrate.

George Roberts, laborer, Jan. 3, 1838, Feb. 6, 1838, pet. under 1 Vict. c. 10, pardoned, on finding security to keep the peace, and be of good b. for 3 years.

Andrew Millet, land surveyor, Jan. 3, 1838, March 8, 1838, n. t., bill ignored.

Joshua Lind, land surveyor, Jan. 3, 1838, March 8, 1838, n. t., bill ignored.

Jacob Emery, laborer, Jan. 3, 1838, March 15, 1838, n. t., bill ignored.

Charles Hammond, laborer, Jan. 3, 1838, March 15, 1838, n. t., bill ignored.

Silvanus F. Wrigley, laborer, Jan. 25, 1838, March 31, 1838, n. t., dis. on bail.

James Dace, laborer, Jan. 25, 1838, Feb. 15, 1838, n. t., discharged on bail.

Aaron Glover,* yeoman, Jan. 25, 1838, Feb. 3, 1838, n. t., discharged on bail.

John Hammill, carpenter, March 9, 1838, Oct., 1838, civil court, guilty, pardoned, on finding security to keep the peace, and be of good b. for 3 years.

Duncan McPhederain, yeoman, March 9, 1838, June 6, 1838, pet. under 1 Vict. c. 10, par. on finding security to keep the peace, and be of g. b. for 3 years.

Robert Laing, yeoman, March 9, 1838, June 6, 1838,   ditto   ditto.

Collins Skelly, yeoman, March 14, 1838, March 19, 1838, n. t., dis. by mag.

Wm. Armstrong, yeoman, Mar. 16, 1838, March 27, 1838, civil court, ac.

Calvin Lyman, yeoman. Mar. 16, 1838, March 27, 1838, civil court, acquitted.

James Parkinson, yeoman, Mar. 16, 1838, March 27, 1838, civil court, acquitted.

Hiram Dowling, yeoman, Mar. 16, 1838, March 27, 1838, civil court, acquitted.

Nathaniel Deo, yeoman, June 11, 1838, Oct., 1838, pet. under 1 Vict. c. 10, pardoned, on finding security to keep the peace and be of good b. for 3 years.

Peter Malcolm,* yeoman, Jan. 3, 1838, Oct., 1838, civil court, guilty, pardoned on finding security to keep the peace, and be of good b. for 3 years.

John Moore,* yeoman, June 11, 1838, Oct., 1838, civil court, guilty, pardoned, on finding security to keep the peace, and be of good b. for 3 years; first arrested in London District, Dec. 22, 1837.

William Sheppard, yeoman, June 25, 1838, July 17, 1838, n. t., dis. by mag.

Horace Lossing, magistrate's son, July 8, 1838, n. t., imprisoned subsequent to special assizes, and still in custody awaiting trial.

Calvin Austin, watchmaker, July 8, 1838, n. t.,   ditto   ditto.

John Fish, yeoman, July 8, 1838,   ditto   ditto   ditto.

Jesse Matthews, milwright, July 8, 1838,   ditto   ditto   ditto.

Edy Malcolm, laborer, July 23, 1838, July 31, 1838, n. t., dis. by the mag.

Stephen Smith, yeoman, Dec. 23, 1837, Oct., 1838, civil court, guilty, pardoned on finding security to keep the peace, and be of good b. for three years.

TALBOT DISTRICT.

No prisoner confined in this district on a charge of insurrection or treason.

* Marked thus are respectable

LONDON DISTRICT.

Cyrus McCartney, yeoman, Dec. 15,1837, Feb. 6, 1838, n. t., dis. by the mag.

James Canfield yeoman, Dec. 15, 1837, Jan. 4, 1838, n. t., dis. by the mag.

Andrew Martin, yeoman, Dec. 15, 1837, Jan. 4, 1838, n. t., dis. by the mag.

James Woods, Yeoman, Dec. 15, 1837, Oct., 1838, n. t., discharged on bail.

Alexander Sumner, yeoman, Dec., 15, 1837, Feb. 20, 1838, n, t., dis. by the m.

Thomas Hewman, yeoman, Dec. 15, 1837, Feb. 20, 1838, n. t., dis. by the m.

Judson Sweat, yeoman, Dec. 15, 1837, Feb. 20, 1838, n. t., dis by the mag.

John O'Gorman, yeomon, Dec. 16, 1837, Dec. 30, 1837, n. t., dis. by the mag.

Joseph Alway, yeoman, Dec. 16, 1837, Jan. 13, 1838, n. t., dis by the mag.

Robert Cavanaugh, yeoman, Dec. 16, 1837, Oct., 1838, pet. under 1 Vict. c. 10, pardoned, on finding security to keep the peace, and be of good b. for 3 years

Cornelius McCarty, yeoman, Dec. 16, 1837, Oct. 14, 1838, n. t., dis. by the m.

Levi Heaton, yeoman, Dec. 16, 1837, Oct. 12, 1838, n. t., dis. by the mag

James Waterman, yeoman, Dec. 16, 1837, Oct. 16, 1838, n. t., dis. by the m

James Coleman, yeoman, Dec. 16, 1837, June 7, 1838, pet. under 1 Vict. c. 10. pardoned, on finding security to keep the peace, and be of good b. for 3 years.

Benjamin Page, yeoman, Dec. 16, 1837, June 9, 1838,   ditto   ditto.

George Lester, yeoman, Dec. 16, 1837, Jan. 30, 1838, n. t., dis. by the mag.

Charles Reeves, yeoman, Dec. 17, 1837, Jan 2, 1838, n. t., dis. by the mag.

Jacob Esmond, yeoman, Dec. 17, 1837, Jan. 2, 1838, n. t., dis. by the mag.

James McClees, yeoman, Dec. 17, 1837, Jan. 26, 1838, n. t., dis. by the mag.

Simon B. Moses, yeoman, Dec. 17, 1837, Jan. 26, 1838, n. t., dis. by the mag.

John B. Nichols, yeoman, Dec. 17, 1837, Jan. 2, 1838, n. t, dis. by the mag.

Peter Philip, yeoman, Dec. 17, 1837, Jan. 4, 1838, n. t., dis. by the mag.

James Defields, yeoman, Dec. 17, 1837, Jan. 25, 1838, n. t., dis. by the mag.

William Loup, yeoman, Dec. 17, 1837, Jan. 23, 1838, n. t., dis. by the mag.

Robert Larraway, yeoman, Dec. 17, 1837, Jan. 16, 1838, n. t , dis. by the m.

Tracey Congdon, yeoman, Dec. 17, 1837, Dec. 29, 1837, n. t., dis. by the mag

Thomas Pool, yeoman, Dec. 17, 1837, Jan. 12, 1838, n. t., dis. by the mag.

Isaac Moore, yeoman, Dec. 17, 1837, May 1, 1838, civil court, acquitted!

Caleb Kipp, yeoman, Dec. 17, 1837, pet. under 1 Vict. c. 10, banished from the Province for life.

George Ribble, yeoman, Dec. 17, 1837, Jan. 11, 1838, n. t., dis. by the mag.

Robert Traney, yeoman, Dec. 17, 1837, June 7, 1838, pet. under 1 Vict. c. 10, pardoned on finding security to keep the peace, and be of good b. for 3 years.

Henry Emigh, yeoman, Dec. 16, 1837, Dec. 29, 1837, n. t , dis. by the mag.

Truman Sinclair, yeoman, Dec. 17, 1837, Jan. 26, 1838, n. t., dis. by the mag.

Robert Farr, yeoman, Dec. 17. 1837, Dec. 19, 1837, n. t., dis. by the magistrate.

Dennis Cavanaugh, yeoman, Dec. 17, 1837, June 7, 1838, pet. under 1 Vict. c. 10, pardoned on finding security to keep the peace, and be of good behavior for three years.

John H. Carr, yeoman, Jan. 1, 1838, Jan. 17, 1838, n. t., dis. by the mag.

Sheldon Sweet, yeoman, Dec. 17, 1837, Jan. 18, 1838, n. t. dis. by the mag.

Mark Hogle, yeoman, Dec. 17, 1837, Jan. 18, 1838, n. t., dis. by the mag.

Charles Christie, yeoman, Dec. 17, 1837, Jan. 18, 1838, n. t., dis. by the mag.

James Oswould, yeoman, Dec. 17, 1837, Jan. 18, 1838, n. t., dis. by the mag.

Thomas Headman, yeoman, Dec. 17, 1837, Jan. 18, 1838, n. t., dis by the m.

Charles Coonrod, yeoman, Dec. 17, 1837, Jan. 18, 1838, n. t., dis. by the mag.

John James Jolly, yeoman, Dec. 17, 1837, Jan. 12, 1838, n. t., dis. by the m.

John McCarren, yeoman, Dec. 17, 1837, Jan. 17, 1838, n. t., dis. by the mag.

Egbert Hellaker, yeoman, Dec. 17, 1837, Jan. 18, 1838, n. t., dis. by the mag.

Luke Hogle, yeoman, Dec. 17, 1837, Jan. 13, 1838, n. t., dis. by the mag.

Moses Cook, yeoman, Dec. 17, 1837, June 7, 1838, pet. under 1 Vict. c. 10,
  par., on finding security to keep the peace, and be of good behavior for 3 yrs.

William Norton, yeoman, Dec. 17, 1837, Jan. 26, 1838, n. t., dis. by the mag.

John Medcalf, yeoman, Dec. 18, 1837, June 9, 1838, pet. under 1 Vict. c. 10,
  pardoned, on finding security to keep the peace, and be of good b. for 3 yrs.

Josiah Woodhull, yeoman, Dec. 18, 1837, Dec. 25, 1837, n. t., dis. by the mag.

Matthew Berry, yeoman, Dec. 18, 1837, Jan. 6, 1838, n. t., dis. by the mag.

William Cheeseman, yeoman, Dec. 18, 1837, June 9, 1838, pet. under 1 Vict.
  c. 10, par on finding security to keep the peace, and be of good b. for 3 yrs.

John Legg, yeoman, Dec. 18, 1837, Jan. 24, 1838, n. t., discharged on bail.

Moore Stephens, yeoman, Dec. 19, 1837, May 7, 1838, civil court, acquitted.

William Lymburner, yeoman, Dec. 20, 1837, Feb. 14, 1838, n. t., dis. by mag.

Wm. Watterworth, yeoman, Dec. 20, 1837, Jan 22, 1838, n. t., dis. by the mag.

Joseph J. Lancaster, yeoman, Dec. 20, 1837, Jan. 6, 1838, n. t., dis. on bail to
  appear as a witness.

David Curtis, yeoman, Dec. 20, 1837, Jan. 26, 1838, n. t., dis. by the mag.

Andrew McLean, yeoman, Dec. 20, 1837, Jan. 1, 1838, n. t., dis. by the mag.

Alfred Adkins, yeoman, Dec. 20, 1837, Jan. 15, 1838, n. t, dis. on bail.

Lyman Davis, yeoman, Dec. 20, 1837, Jan. 15, 1838, n. t., absconded.

Solomon Sherrick, yeoman, Dec. 20, 1837, Jan. 18, 1838, n. t., dis. on bail.

Nelson Leach, yeoman, Dec. 20, 1837, Jan. 17, 1838, pet. under 1 Vict. c. 10,
  par. on finding security to keep the peace, and be of good behavior for 3 years.

Sobeisca Brown, yeoman, Dec. 20, 1837, Jan. 5, 1838, n. t., dis. on bail.

William Storey, yeoman, Dec. 20, 1837, Jan. 2, 1838, n. t., dis. by the mag.

Jonathan Steel, yeoman, Dec. 20, 1837, Oct., 1838, pet. under 1 Vict. c. 10. pardoned on finding security to keep the peace and be of good b. for 3 years.

Losee Denton, yeoman, Dec. 20, 1837, June. 9, 1838, ditto ditto ditto.

Joseph Moore, yeoman, Dec. 20, 1837, Jan. 20, 1838, n. t., dis. by the mag.

Isaac Phillips, yeoman, Dec. 20, 1837, Jan. 4, 1838, n. t., dis. by the mag.

Andrew Connors, yeoman, Dec. 20, 1837, June 12, 1838, pet. under 1 Vict. c. 10,
  pardoned, on finding security to keep the peace, and be of good b. for 3 years.

Lymanteus Chapel, yeoman, Dec. 20, 1837, Jan. 9, 1838, n. t., dis. by the mag.

Thomas Hall, yeoman, Dec. 20, 1837, Jan. 12, 1838, n. t., dis. by the mag.

John Kenny, yeoman, Dec. 20, 1837, Dec. 23, 1838, n. t., dis. by the mag.

Enoch D. Doxie, yeoman, Dec. 20, 1837, Oct., 1838, n. t., discharged on bail to keep the peace, and be of good behavior for three years.

John Parker, yeoman, Dec. 21, 1837, Feb. 6, 1838, n. t., dis. by the magistrate.

Josiah Wood, yeoman, Dec. 21, 1837, Jan. 3, 1838, n. t., dis by the mag.

S. Smith, yeoman, Dec., 21, 1837, Jan. 18, 1838, n, t., dis. by the magistrate.

Archibald Olds, yeoman, Dec. 21, 1837, Jan. 2, 1838, n. t., dis. by the mag.

George Phillips, yeoman, Dec. 21, 1837, Feb. 1, 1838, n. t., dis by the mag

James Nixon, yeomon, Dec. 21, 1837, Jan. 4, 1838, n. t., dis. by the mag.

Abel Cooper, yeoman, Dec. 21, 1837, Jan. 18, 1838, n. t., discharged on bail.

David Willson, yeoman, Dec. 26, 1837, Feb. 26, 1838, n. t., dis. by the m.

Duncan Willson, yeoman, Dec. 30, 1837, Apr. 7, 1838, n. t., discharged on bail.

Elias Moore, yeoman, Dec. 21, 1837, Apr. 9, 1838, n. t., discharged on bail.

Luther Hoskins, yeoman, Dec. 21, 1837, October, 1838, pet. under 1 Vict. c. 10, pardoned, on finding security to keep the peace, and be of good b. for 3 years.

Nathan Doan, yeoman, Feb. 17, 1838, Feb. 24, 1838, n. t., dis. by the mag.

Alonzo Hall, yeoman, Dec. 20, 1837, Jan. 12, 1838, n. t., dis. by the mag.

William Hall, yeoman, Dec. 15, 1837, May 2, 1838, civil court, acquitted.

Gideon Tiffany, yeoman, Dec. 15, 1837, May 7, 1838, civil court, acquitted.

William Putnam, yeoman, Dec. 15, 1837, May 2, 1838, civil court, acquitted.

John Stephens, yeoman, Dec. 15, 1837, May 7, 1838, civil court, acquitted.

James Nash, yeoman, Dec. 15, 1837, April 26, 1838, n. t. discharged on bail.

Thomas Arker, yeoman, Dec. 15, 1837, June 19, 1838, n. t., discharged by order of the Lieutenant Governor.

Morey Whithey, yeoman, Dec. 15, 1837, June 1, 1838,   ditto   ditto.

Charles Travers, yeoman, Dec. 16, 1837, June 1, 1838,   ditto   ditto.

John Grieve, yeoman, Dec. 20, 1837, April 10, 1838, n. t., discharged on bail.

Descom Simons, yeoman, Dec. 22, 1837, April 26, 1838, civil court, acquitted.

Chas. Lawrence, yeoman, Dec. 19, 1837, June 11, 1838, pet. under 1 Vict. c. 10, pardoned on finding security to keep the peace, and be of good b. for 3 years.

Anson Gould, yeoman, Dec. 24, 1837, April 26, 1838, civil court, acquitted.

Stephen Bronger, yeoman, Dec. 26, 1837, May 8, 1838, pet. under 1 Vict. c. 10, pardoned, on finding security to keep the peace and be of good b. for 3 years.

Joshua B. Moore, yeoman, Dec. 25, 1837, Apr. 18, 1838, n. t., discharged by proclamation ; no bill.

John Riley, yeoman, Dec. 30, 1837, May 9, 1838,   ditto   ditto.

William Watts, yeoman, Dec. 30, 1837, May 9, 1838, pet. under 1 Vict. c. 10, died May 5, 1838.

Lewis Norton, yeoman, Dec. 30, 1837, pet. under 1 Vict. c. 10, banished from the Province for life.

James Coville, yeoman, Dec. 30, 1837,   ditto   ditto   ditto.

Charles Latimer, yeoman, Dec. 17, 1837, May 2, 1838, civil court, acquitted.

David Hagerman, yeoman, Dec. 18, 1837, April 30, 1838, civil court, acquitted.

Daniel Bedford, yeoman, Dec. 18, 1837, June 9, 1838, pet. under 1 Vict. c. 10, pardoned, on finding security to keep the peace, and be of good b. for 3 years.

Alexander Neilly, yeoman, Dec. 19, 1837, June 11, 1838,   ditto   ditto.

Samuel Sands, yeoman, Dec. 21, 1837, June 11, 1838,   ditto   ditto.

Uriah Emmons, yeoman, Dec. 21, 1837, pet. under 1 Vict. c. 10, banished from the Province for life.

Ezekiel Manns, yeoman, Dec. 21, 1837, June 12, 1838, pet. under 1 Vict. c. 10, pardoned, on finding security to keep the peace, and be of good b. for 3 years.

William Childs, yeoman, Dec. 21, 1837, April 18, 1838, n. t., discharged by proclamation; no bill.

Abraham Sackrider, yeoman, Dec. 21, 1837, April 1, 1838, n. t., dis. by court.

John D. Brown, yeoman, Dec. 21, 1837, May 8, 1838, civil court, acquitted.

Stephen H. Secord, yeoman, Dec. 21, 1837, April 16, 1838, n. t., dis. on bail.

Orlando Inglis, yeoman, Jan. 1, 1838, April 16, 1838, n. t., dis. by pro.; no bill.

Patrick Malada, yeoman, Jan. 1, 1838, June 7, 1838, pet. under 1 Vict. c. 10, pardoned, on finding security to keep the peace, and be of good b. for 3 years.

George Blake, yeoman, Jan. 1, 1838, April 16, 1838, n. t., dis. by pro.; no bill.

Amos Bradshaw, yeoman, Jan. 1, 1838, pet. under 1 Vict. c. 10, banished from the Province for life.

George Hill, yeoman, Jan. 3, 1838,   ditto   ditto   ditto.

Joseph Bowes, yeomon, Feb. 2, 1838,   ditto   ditto   ditto.

Charles Tilden, yeoman, Feb. 15, 1838, May 10, 1838, n. t., dis. on his recog.

Andrew McLure, yeoman, April 12, 1838, June 6, 1838, pet. under 1 Vict. c. 10, par. on finding security to keep the peace, and be of good b. for 3 years.

Amos B. Thomas, yeoman, June 30, 1838, July 27, 1838, n. t., dis. by mag.

Jacob Lester, yeoman, July 1, 1838, July 15, 1838, n. t., dis. by magistrate

Samuel Forbes, yeoman, July 1, 1838, July 15, 1838, n. t., dis. by magistrate.

Amos Shaw, yeoman, July 1, 1838, July 25, 1838, n. t., dis. by magistrate.

Alex. Leadbeater, yeoman, July 1, 1838, July 25, 1838, n. t., dis. by mag.

Absalom Shaw, yeoman, July 1, 1838, July 25, 1838, n. t., dis. by magistrate.

Wm. A. Everitt, yeoman, July 1, 1838, July 25, 1838, n. t., dis. by magistrate.

Albert Stephens, yeoman, July 1, 1838, July 25, 1838, n. t., dis. by magistrate.

James G. Shaw, yeoman, July 1, 1838, July 20, 1838, n. t., dis. by magistrate.

Uriah Shaw, yeoman, July 1, 1838, July 20, 1838, n. t., dis. by magistrate.

Robert Taylor, yeoman, July 1, 1838, July 20, 1838, n. t., dis. by magistrate.

James Tucker, yeoman, July 1, 1837, July 20, 1838, n. t., dis. by magistrate.

Francis Jones, yeoman, July 1, 1838, July 20, 1838, n. t., dis. by magistrate.

Abraham Kilburn, yeoman, July 1, 1838, July 20, 1838, n. t., dis. by mag.

David Sherman, yeoman, July 1, 1838, July 20, 1838, n. t., dis. by magistrate.

William Day, yeoman, July 1, 1838, July 20, 1838, n. t., dis. by magistrate.

Wm. Jackman, yeoman, July 1, 1838, July 20, 1838, n. t., dis. by magistrate

Jacob B. Allen, yeoman, July 4, 1838, July 5, 1838, n. t., dis. by magistrate.

Abraham Graves, yeoman, July 5, 1838, July 28, 1838, n. t., dis. by mag.

Jacob Deo, yeoman, July 6, 1838, July 11, 1838, n. t., dis. by magistrate.

Sylvanus Shaw, yeoman, July 13, 1838, July 20, 1838, n. t., dis. by magistrate.

John Day, yeoman, July 13, 1838, July 20, 1838, n. t., dis. by magistrate.

Samuel Day, yeoman, July 13, 1838, July 20, 1838, n. t., dis. by magistrate.

John G. Wells, yeoman, July 13, 1838, July 20, 1838, n. t., dis. by magistrate.

Otis Inglis, yeoman, July 13, 1838, July 20, 1838, n. t., dis. by magistrate.

Jacob Aubery, yeoman, July 13, 1838, July 20, 1838, n. t., dis. by magistrate.

William Gibson, yeoman, July 5, 1838, n. t., still in custody.

Benjamin Hillaker, yeoman, July 7, 1838, n. t., still in custody..

William Hallaker, yeoman, July 7, 1838, n. t., still in custody.

John Dennis, yeoman, July 7, 1838, n. t., still in custody.

Benjamin Smith, yeoman, July 13, 1838, n. t., still in custody.

Pety Sullivan, yeoman, July 13, 1838, n. t., still in custody.

Benjamin West, yeoman, July 13, 1838, n. t., still in custody.

Henry Spencer, yeoman, July 13, 1838, July 20, 1838, n. t., dis. by magistrate.

Isaac L. Smith, yeoman, July 13, 1838, July 20, 1838, n. t., dis. by magistrate.

David Williams, yeoman, July 13, 1838, July 20, 1838, n. t., dis. by magistrate.

John Long, yeoman, July 13, 1838, July 20, 1838, n. t., dis. by magistrate.

James Lyons, yeoman, July 13, 1838, July 20, 1838, n, t., dis. by magistrate.

Christ. Hendershot, yeoman, July 13, 1838, July 20, 1838, n. t., dis. by mag.

WESTERN DISTRICT:

Horace Cooley, farmer, June 28, 1838, n. t., still in custody.

Charles Bourman, farmer, June 28, 1838, n. t., still in custody.

Louis Burnham, farmer, June 28, 1838, Sept., 1838, n. t., discharged on bail.

Orlando Boyington, farmer, June 28, 1838, Sept., 1838, n. t., dis. on bail.

Henry B. Nugent, farmer, June 30, 1838, Sept. 1838, n. t., discharged on bail.

Reuben Markham, farmer, Aug. 10, 1838, Sept., 1838, n. t., discharged on bail.

Lambert Beaubien, wheelwright, July 2, 1838, Sept., 1838, n. t., dis. on bail.

Malcolm Burnham, farmer, June 30, 1838, Sept., 1838, n. t., dis. on bail.

James Coll, farmer, July 10, 1838, Sept., 1838, n. t., discharged on bail.

Isaac Phillips, farmer, July 10, 1838, Sept., 1838, n. t., discharged on bail.

William Herrington tailor, July 10, 1838, n. t., still in custody.

Besides the above, there were sixty-one persons against whom indictments were found for High Treason, but who left the Province :—

1. John Rolph, physician, Home District, Member of Provincial Parliament.
2. William Lyon Mackenzie, printer, Home District.
3. Silas Fletcher, yeoman, Home District.
4. Jacob Rymal, yeoman, Home District.

. Richard Graham, yeoman, Home District.
. Jeremiah Graham, yeoman, Home District.
5. John Mantack, yeoman, Home District.
8. Joseph Borden, yeoman, Home District.
9. Joshua Winn, yeoman, Home District.
10. David Gibson, surveyor, Home District, Member of Provincial Parliament.
11. Landon Wurtz, laborer, Home District.
12. James Marshall, storekeeper, Home District.
13. Alem Marr, yeoman, Home District.
14. Joseph Clarkson, yeoman, Home District.
15. Dudley Wilcox, yeoman, Home District.
16. Edmond Quirk, yeoman, Home District.
17. Thomas Brown, yeoman, Home District.
18. Levi Parsons, yeoman, Home District.
19. Jesse Loyd, yeoman. Home District.
20. Aaron Munshaw, yeoman, Home District.
21. Henry Stiles, yeoman, Home District.
22. William Fletcher, yeoman, Home District.
23. Daniel Fletcher, yeoman, Home District.·
24. David McCarty, yeoman, Home District.
25. Seth McCarty, yoeman, Home District.
26. Nelson Gorham, yeoman, Home District.
27. Alexander McLeod, yeoman, Home District. Since taken at the Short
     Hills, sentenced to transportation for life. (See Niagara Dt., No. 28.)
28. Cornelius Willis, yeoman, Home District.
29. Erastus Clark, yeoman, Home District.
30. Charles Duncombe, M. P. P., London District, Mem. of Prov. Parliament.
31. James Dennis, yeoman, London District.
32. Eliakim Malcolm, yeoman, London District.
33. Peter Delong, yeoman, London District.
34. Orsimus B. Clark, merchant, London District.
35. Lyman Davis, Laborer, London District.
36. Henry Fisher, yeoman, London District.
37. James Malcolm, yeoman, London District.
38. Pelham C. Teeple, yeoman, London District.
39. Norris Humphrey, merchant, London District.
40. Jesse Paulding, innkeeper, London District.
41. Joel P. Doan, tanner, London District.
42. Joshua G. Doan, tanner, London District. Since taken, at Sandwich, in arms.
43. John Talbot, gentleman, London District.
44. Samuel Edison, jr., innkeeper, London District.
45. Abraham Sutton, yeoman, London District.
46. Moses Chapman Nickelson, yeoman, London District.

101

47. George Lawton, yeoman, London District.
48. John Massacre, yeoman, London District.
49. Elisha Hall, yeoman, London District.
50. Solomon Hawes, yeoman, London District.
51. George Alexander Clark, merchant, Gore District.
52. John Vanarnam, innkeeper, Gore District.
53. Michael Marcellus Mills, merchant, Gore District.
54. George Washington Case, gentleman, Gore District.
55. Joseph Fletcher, yeoman, Gore District.
56. Angus McKenzie, yeoman, Gore District.
57. Alonzo Merriman, merchant, Niagara District.
58. Aaron Winchester, yeoman, Niagara District.
59. David Jennings, laborer, Niagara District.
60. Chester Jillet, laborer, Niagara District.
61. Thomas Lambert, laborer, Niagara District.

NUMERICAL ABSTRACT OF THE FOREGOING TABLE.

Eastern District,	—
Ottawa District,	—
Johnstown District,	8
Bathurst District,	—
Prince Edward District,	—
Midland District,	75
Newcastle District,	12
Home District,	422
Niagara District,	43
Gore District,	90
Talbot District,	—
London District,	163
Western District,	11
Persons who have absconded	61
Grand Total,	885

Lightning Source UK Ltd.
Milton Keynes UK
UKHW020834281218
334534UK00004B/1215/P